THE ILLUSTRATED ENCYCLOPEDIA OF
HINDUISM

THE ILLUSTRATED ENCYCLOPEDIA OF
HINDUISM

A COMPREHENSIVE GUIDE TO HINDU HISTORY AND PHILOSOPHY, ITS TRADITIONS AND
PRACTICES, RITUALS AND BELIEFS, WITH MORE THAN 470 MAGNIFICENT PHOTOGRAPHS

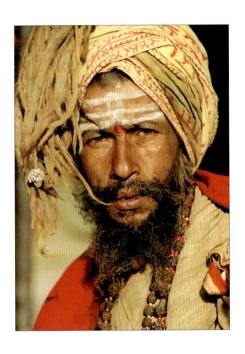

RASAMANDALA DAS
CONSULTANT: PROFESSOR M. NARASIMHACHARY

LORENZ BOOKS

CONTENTS

INTRODUCTION: ORIGINS OF HINDUISM

HINDUISM IS THE OLDEST LIVING RELIGION IN THE WORLD. ALTHOUGH IT CLEARLY GOES BACK AT LEAST 5,000 YEARS, IT IS DIFFICULT TO SAY PRECISELY HOW IT STARTED.

Hinduism reveres no singular founder, doctrine or scripture. It has no definite starting date. Throughout its long history, many founders and scholars have taught diverse philosophies through thousands of texts. To explain Hinduism's diversity, many authors describe it as 'a family of religions' and, for its lack of stress on belief or creed, as 'a way of life'.

Adherents often prefer alternative names to Hinduism, such as Sanatana Dharma (the eternal religion), Vaidika Dharma (the religion of the holy texts called the Vedas) or, more recently, Hindu Dharma (the Hindu religion). The alternative names indicate challenges in precisely defining Hinduism. Clearly, however, it is historically linked to geographic India: her tropical climate, her fertile river plains and her vulnerable north-west frontier.

Right A decorative 'Om', the sacred syllable used to represent the family of traditions now called Hinduism.

HISTORY

Trying to pinpoint Hinduism's origins is perplexing. Followers claim their tradition goes back indefinitely to previous 'glorious ages'. Standard texts date recent history to the onset of the present age, called the Kali-yuga (age of quarrel), coinciding with Lord Krishna's departure from the world 5,000 years ago. Modern scholars often cite more recent dates, believing that Hinduism emerged somewhere between 1900 and 1500BCE.

Accepting the Aryan invasion theory, early European intellectuals favoured the view that Hindu ideology came from beyond the subcontinent, from Europe or Central Asia. The hypothetical Aryans prevailed either by conquest or, it was later thought, by migration and cultural infiltration. Many Hindus argue that Hinduism has always been indigenous to India and often reverse the colonial interpretation by promoting India as 'the cradle of civilization'. These debates, fuelled by ethnic bias, may never be resolved. Nevertheless, the history of Hinduism is intimately linked to India's early civilizations, her domination by foreign powers and, more recently, national independence and global migration.

Left Shiva and the Ganges. Hinduism is also called the Sanatana Dharma (eternal religion). It teaches of an eternal reality and a repeatedly created material world, overseen by Lord Shiva and other deities.

SACRED TEXTS

Throughout history, most Hindus have located the core of their tradition within specific sacred texts, the Vedas and their corollaries. For this reason, Hindu orthodoxy has distanced itself from traditions that reject the Vedic authority, including Jainism and Buddhism. Orthodox texts are divided into two sectors, the Shruti ('that which is heard') and the Smriti ('that which is remembered'). The Shruti, consisting of the four Vedas, is the main canon, supported and explained by the Smriti, which includes moral codes, the Epics, the Puranas, and a wide range of supplementary literature.

In ancient Sanskrit, Veda means 'knowledge', implying acceptance of universal truth. This inclusive idea has allowed Hinduism to accommodate texts only indirectly connected to the Vedas, provided they support Vedic conclusions. These encompass many Tantric texts (Tantras) often shared with other religions such as Jainism, Buddhism and Tibetan Bon. The Tantric texts are specifically favoured by the Shramana, renouncer traditions, which have complemented the orthodox, brahmin-led religion called Brahminism.

Despite the current use of written texts, ancient Hindu wisdom was first passed down orally. Some Hindus believe oral transmission remains the only legitimate system, especially for the Shruti. Most scholars date the compilation of the first text, the Rig Veda, to around 1000BCE.

HINDU TEACHINGS

Belief in Veda as 'knowledge' does not confine truth to a single 'faith' or creed. Hinduism has largely managed to blend faith commitment with philosophical thought. None the less, most Hindus share distinctive core concepts, such as the notion of Brahman, the eternal reality. Brahman is first understood by apprehending the eternal self (atman), which trans-migrates through all species of life and attains ultimate salvation in union with God.

The Vedic teachings do not mention 'Hinduism' but refer instead to dharma, or 'religious duty'. The term implies preference for regulating practice rather than belief. More precisely, dharma means

Below This depicts the widely accepted Hindu worldview of an eternal self rein-carnating throughout numerous species.

'duties that sustain humans according to their intrinsic nature'. There are two main types. First, sanatana-dharma, duties that revive the eternal relationship between the soul and God. Second, varnashrama-dharma, or duties based on the eternal self's specific station in life, defined within four *varnas* (social classes) and four *ashramas* (stages of life). While

Above Hinduism has been nurtured largely in India. This map shows the main geographical features of 'the subcontinent'.

acknowledging spiritual and social inter-dependence, Hinduism also recognizes individual autonomy through its well-known doctrine of karma (moral accountability).

Based on the idea of Brahman, Hindu texts indicate an eternal, indestructible realm. They also describe the material world as ever-lasting, through a cyclical process of creation, destruction and re-creation.

Texts, while accepting the earth as but one planet, describe many populated worlds, stratified levels of reality, and vast stretches of time and space. Although India is just one region of a single planet, Hindus consider India to be sacred, a land sanctified by saints and avataras (divine incarnations). For nurturing spiritual awareness, it is central to the purposes of material creation. This creation is born of the sacred syllable Om, whose visual form is now often used to represent Hinduism.

SACRED PRACTICES

AS A PRACTICAL WAY OF LIFE, HINDUISM EMBRACES BOTH PERSONAL SPIRITUALITY AND ORGANIZED RELIGION. THE FOUR MAIN SPIRITUAL DISCIPLINES FOCUS ON SELF- AND GOD-REALIZATION.

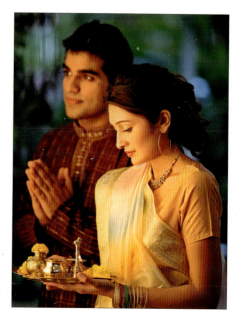

Hinduism teaches that human life is meant for liberation (moksha). There are three other auxiliary aims: righteous living (dharma), economic development (artha) and regulated sense pleasure (kama). They facilitate ultimate moksha by exhausting the self's material desires and re-establishing its affinity with the divine.

Below India abounds with sacred sites. Pilgrims enter a temple in Khajuraho, one of the 'seven wonders' of India.

LINKING WITH THE SUPREME
The aspiration to re-link with the Supreme is expressed by the word 'yoga', which literally means 'joining'. Although the term popularly refers to hatha-yoga, it actually embraces four main paths, correlating to action, knowledge, meditation and devotion.

Most paths embrace a concept of God and elements of worship. Hindu veneration therefore embraces a wide range of practices. The early

Above Worship, even if performed with others (as shown), aims at re-establishing the individual's link with the divine.

Vedic period was typified by the fire sacrifice, still widely used during rites of passage. During the classical age, it was superseded by ritual worship of the murti (sacred image), closely linked to emerging devotional traditions. Such worship (puja) entails bathing, dressing and offering food to the murti, and many other specific modes of worship such as the popular arati ceremony.

Puja has assimilated many practices intimately linked to non-devotional traditions. Meditation is a complete discipline in itself, favoured by the less-orthodox ascetic lineages. Scriptural study, central to the path of wisdom, is also a type of worship; so also is practical service to saints or society at large. Hence, acts of veneration draw from the four disciplines and encompass selfless or ritualistic action, philosophical study, meditational exercises and devotional adoration.

Worship usually focuses on a single divinity, but often through diverse representations. These will include not only the many gods and goddesses, but also the guru, family elders and various manifestations

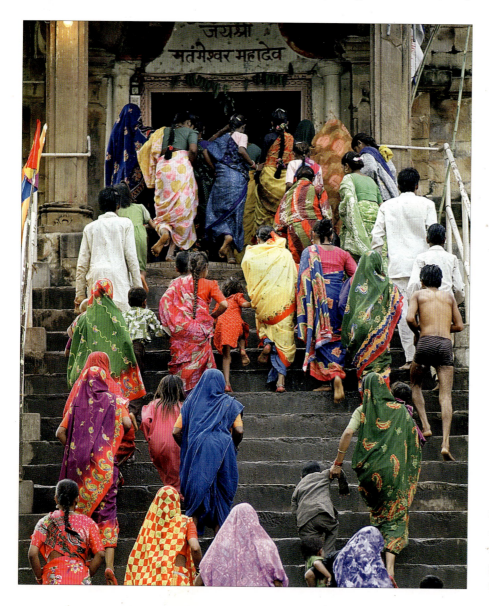

of nature, such as sacred plants, rivers and mountains. There is no specified day for worship, which is observed in three main places: outdoors, at home and in the temple.

THE HINDU DEITIES

Most Hindus share belief in karma, reincarnation and final liberation. Differences are most conspicuous in conceiving the nature and identity of God and explaining the many deities. Although some tribal or village practices are naively polytheistic, the high, scholarly strands propound a single God, whose unlimited forms and attributes are represented by a host of deities, often numbered at 330 million. Some view all deities as equal representatives of an impersonal Supreme; others consider them real, assigning them hierarchical positions beneath as single personal Deity.

Most important are the Trimurti, the three male deities named Brahma, Vishnu and Shiva. Brahma is rarely worshipped. Vishnu and Shiva are most widely regarded as Supreme. The third main object of worship is Shakti, meaning 'energy' or 'goddess'. Though broadly refer-

Below There are 16 standard samskaras (Hindu rites of passage), including the wedding ceremony, performed here in New York's Central Park.

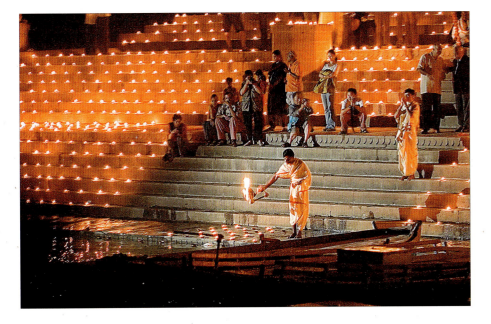

Above The festival of lights, Divali, here celebrated next to the Ganges, is the largest Hindu festival.

ring to the three wives of the Trimurti, Shakti specifically indicates Shiva's wife, Parvati, also called Durga or Kali. Hence, the three main traditions, respectively called Vaishnavas, Shaivas and Shaktas, are linked to the three 'divine couples'.

The list of six main deities – the Trimurti and their consorts – can be extended by adding six more. Ganesha and Skanda, the two sons of Shiva and Parvati, have their distinct followers. Vishnu is often worshipped through two incarnations, Rama and Krishna. Hanuman, servant of Rama, is also worshipped in his own right. And, finally, the sun god, Surya, is often connected to Vishnu. He is prominent among the many 'nature gods' popular during the Vedic period (1500–500 BCE)

SACRED PLACES

Hinduism is both other-worldly and closely allied to the earth. Heaven and earth intercede at holy places called tirthas or 'fords'. A tirtha is a place for crossing 'to the other side', a spot where deities descend as avataras and where humans are exalted to higher realms. Visiting such sites during pilgrimage is especially important for those retiring from family life, for it helps them to relinquish worldly attachment.

Holy places include temples, rivers, mountains, and places related to the lives of saints and deities. Pilgrimage sites now exist beyond India, often as replicas of their Indian prototypes.

SPECIAL OCCASIONS

For Hindus, life is a long journey, of which human life is but a single leg. Hindus mark various milestones with rites of passage, called samskaras. The literal meaning of samskara is 'mental impression', indicating aspiration to purify the consciousness throughout life in order to achieve final liberation, or at least a better birth. Texts list 16 standard samskaras. With belief in the eternal self and pre-existence, the first occurs before conception and the last after death.

Special occasions include many festivals. They usually celebrate birthdays or other major events in the lives of deities or saints. Others mark the revolving seasons and celebrate family relations, as between husband and wife, or sister and brother. The accompanying music, dance, decoration, fasting and feasting attest to the sensual and vibrant nature of Hinduism.

ACTING IN THE WORLD

SPIRITUAL PRACTICES NURTURE THE SOUL'S ETERNAL RELATIONSHIP WITH THE DIVINE. HINDUISM RECOGNIZES THE NEED TO ORGANIZE HUMAN SOCIETY, AND TO EXPRESS AND PERPETUATE RELIGIOUS WISDOM.

Religious duties include not just generic spiritual practices, for everyone, but also 'sva-dharma', personal responsibilities based on the individual's unique context and disposition. Traditionally, worldly duties were allocated according to the system of varnashrama-dharma, with its four varnas (classes) and four successive ashramas (phases of life).

THE HINDU SOCIAL SYSTEM

The varna system finds brief mention in the earliest scripture, the Rig Veda. Its outright identification with modern caste practice embarrasses many Hindus, who respond differently. Some distance themselves from caste's notoriety by dismissing it as a purely sociological phenomenon. It is true that caste extends beyond Hindu communities. However, most thinkers consider caste an aberration of varnashrama. The main difference is that caste is hereditary, whereas the early system was based on individual virtue and merit. Although both systems acknowledge a hierarchical reality, the earlier model permitted social mobility by recognizing the spiritual equality of all. Ideologically, the four varnas aimed at personal fulfilment and harmonious social intercourse.

The four ashramas explicitly promote spiritual progress. The word ashrama means 'place of spiritual nurture'. The first three ashramas, familiar to most human societies, correspond to student life, marriage and retirement. Hinduism stresses the spiritual aspects of these life-phases. Schooling should foster character and enlightenment, as well as career prospects. The householder ashrama, the economic base for society, stressed charity and ethical livelihood. Retirement called for penance and pilgrimage. Few men adopt the fourth stage, sannyasa, which entails relinquishing home to travel in preparation for the next life. The saffron-clad sannyasin is still shown respect. However, the notion

Above Hinduism enjoys a rich social, cultural and artistic heritage. This brahmin, a member of the highest varna (social class), rests on a brightly decorated chariot.

of duty based on a hierarchical universe often clashes with popular contemporary aspirations for personal freedom and a classless society.

HINDU CULTURE

For the high, brahmanical traditions, scholarship and Sanskrit have been crucial in transmitting philosophical and theological truths. The word Sanskrit means 'most refined', and the language is called deva-bhasha, 'the language of the gods'. The related term Sanskriti denotes 'culture', specifically as a means of spiritual refinement.

Until recently, the Hindu religion and its culture were inseparable. For example, practically all art, music and poetry bore religious themes derived from the Epics, Puranas or rich, southern 'Sangam' traditions. Even today, many Bollywood films feature religious themes, exploring the tensions between traditional and contemporary values. A recurring motif is the observance of social decorum, as when juniors offer obeisance to elders, who then reciprocate by giving blessings. Such practice implies a worldview that acknowledges the importance of grace as well as personal endeavour.

Left Three generations. Most Hindus aim to live dutifully in the world, often within the traditional extended family.

MOVEMENTS AND LEADERS

Hindu traditions have attempted to perpetuate themselves not just socially and culturally but through religious organizations. Most important is the spiritual lineage (sampradaya), an unbroken chain of teachers and disciples who pass on their heritage through both explicit teachings and personal example. Movements are often legitimized though links to such lineages and their previous acharyas (teacher-founders). The immediate guru-disciple relationship remains a vital institution, and many Hindus still take formal initiation. However, some contemporary traditions give less importance to faithfully following a guru, or to the guru's character and credentials.

As Hinduism has developed into a truly global religion, some organizations have become pivotal, not only in representing their own traditions but also in attempting to speak on behalf of the entire religion. Within Vaishnavism, the most successful have been the Swaminarayan Mission and the Hare Krishna movement. Among Shaivas, the Shaiva Siddhanta Church has widely distributed its colour magazine called *Hinduism Today*. In representing the Smarta tradition,

Below This Indian sadhu (holy man) has renounced home and family to concentrate solely on spiritual life.

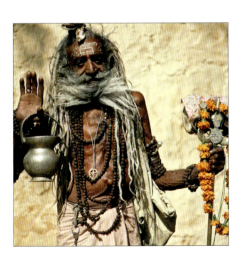

the Ramakrishna Mission has boldly assimilated elements of Shaktism. There are now many women gurus including Amma, the famous 'hugging saint'. Many contemporary groups are less overtly religious, catering to a broad interest in yoga and meditation.

THE MODERN AGE

Today, Hindus finds themselves trying to apply their apparently timeless and universal principles in a rapidly changing world; one that stresses rights over responsibilities (dharma), and self-determination over respect for authority. Although Hindu thought challenges many contemporary ideas, it is also relevant to many topical debates.

In meeting these challenges, two trends have emerged. First, there have been attempts to reinforce the relationship between Hinduism and India, not just as a geographical region but as a nation state. Hence, Hinduism

Above Hindu wisdom has been perpetuated by sacred lineages. Disciples surround famous guru, Pramukha Swami Maharaj, during his birthday celebrations.

has been defined, like some other world religions, with leaning towards exclusivity, credal conformity and an adversarial attitude. Other Hindus have tried to promote their tradition's universal, inclusive aspects, as the Santana Dharma. Hinduism is therefore gradually being redefined and redirected in various ways.

Hinduism has long shown an ability to live with the dynamics of tension, ambivalence and contradiction. It has rarely rejected its parental traditions, but has continuously assimilated new ideas and practices to make its timeless principle relevant to newer contexts. As a continuously evolving tradition, its wisdom, based on spiritual equality, is likely to make it relevant for many centuries to come.

TIMELINE

HINDUISM'S HISTORY IS COMPLEX AND HARD TO TRACE. IT CAN BE DIVIDED INTO SEVEN MAIN PERIODS, BEGINNING WITH ITS PRE-HISTORY AND THE SUBSEQUENT VEDIC PERIOD, STARTING AROUND 1500BCE.

c.3000BCE–1150BCE

- c.3000BCE According to Hindu tradition, Krishna appears on earth and speaks the Bhagavad-gita just before the start of the Kali-yuga (the age of quarrel).
- c.2500BCE The great cities of the Indus and Sarasvati valleys are at the height of their power.
- c.1500BCE According to Western scholars, the foundations of Hinduism are brought to India from outside by the Aryans.

c.500BCE–500BCE

- c.1500–500BCE During this 'Vedic period', the Vedas are composed in Sanskrit. Focus is on the sacred fire ceremony, reaching the ancestors in heaven, and deities representing the forces of nature.
- c.1200BCE Writing of the RigVeda.
- 500BCE Sixteen kingdoms extend across northern India.

Below According to tradition, Krishna spoke the Bhagavad-gita prior to the present age, called the Kali-yuga.

500BCE–500CE

- c.500BCE–500CE Buddhism spreads through India. Among Hindus, puja (worship of the murti) becomes popular. Vishnu, Shiva and Shakti as the main deities with their corresponding traditions. The Epics (the Ramayana and Mahabharata) and the Puranas are written.
- 327BCE Alexander the Great invades India, defeats King Porus and confronts the great Magadha Empire.
- 326BCE–184BCE The Mauryan Empire unites much of India. King Ashoka patronizes Buddhism.
- 320BCE–550CE The reign of the Gupta dynasty, a golden and classical age for Hindu arts.
- c.300BCE–300CE The Sangam literature, the earliest known Tamil literature, is compiled (though its oral roots may be much older).

Below An image of Shiva, one of the three main Hindu deities that emerged shortly after 500BCE.

Above This statue of the goddess Lalita dates from the 11th century when temple construction flourished in India.

500CE–c.1200CE

- 500–1000CE The poet-saints of South India compose devotional poems in the Tamil language.
- 535–700CE Rise of the Harsha Empire, uniting much of northern India.
- 550CE Collapse of the northern Gupta Empire.
- 800–1200CE Temple building flourishes, especially in southern India.
- 800CE Shankara teaches that God is everywhere. He re-establishes the importance of the Hindu holy books and formalizes the Smarta tradition. Subsequently, Buddhism declines further in India.
- 1000CE Abhinavagupta writes his Tantraloka, the basis for important Shaiva and Tantric traditions.
- 1000CE Muslim incursions into northern India escalate, with brutal raids by Mahmud of Gazni.
- 1010–1200CE The Chola Empire further extends Hinduism to Indo-China and Indonesia.
- c.1050CE Ramanuja extends Shankara's teachings, advocating that God is a person, living beyond this world.
- c.1140CE Construction of temple complex at Angkor Wat.

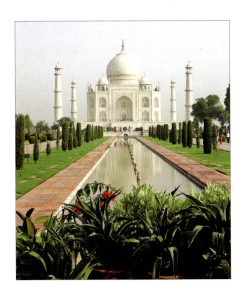

Above *The Taj Mahal in Agra, India, epitomises the significant social and cultural influence left by the Mughal empire.*

Above *The period of British domination of India was marred by the Indian Mutiny, as shown here by an English artist.*

Above *The modern BAPS Swaminarayan Temple, New Delhi, exemplifies the continuing popularity of Hinduism.*

1200–1750

- 1200–1500 Muslims become powerful in the north, but Hindu kingdoms flourish in the south, especially the Chola Empire.
- 1238 Birth of Madhva, founder of the Dvaita (dualism) Vedanta school.
- 1469 Birth of Guru Nanak, founder of the Sikh religion. Many devotional saints, such as Chaitanya, Mirabai and Tukarama, live during this period.
- 1469 Birth of Vallabha, who started the Pushti Marg ('path of nourishment').
- 1486 Birth of Chaitanya, charismatic saint and founder of the Bengali Vaishnava movement.
- 1526 The Mughal Empire is founded in India.
- 1556–1605 The liberal reign of Akbar.
- 1600s Many Europeans arrive in India to trade in cloth and spices.
- 1627–1680 The life of King Shivaji, who resisted the Mughals.
- 1632 The Mughal emperor Shah Jahan builds the Taj Mahal as a memorial to his wife.
- 1668–1707 The reign of Aurangzeb, the last great Mughal emperor, who destroyed many Hindu temples.

1750–1947

- 1757 Robert Clive wins the Battle of Plassey, bringing India under British domination.
- 1828 In response to European thought, the Brahmo Samaj is founded as one of many organizations seeking to reform Hinduism.
- 1830 onwards Many Hindus migrate to Fiji, Malaysia, Mauritius, the Caribbean, East Africa and South Africa.
- 1857 Army rebellion during the Indian Mutiny, which many Hindus now call 'the first war of independence'.
- 1858 India becomes part of the British Empire, as the Mughal Empire finally expires.
- 1869 Birth of Mahatma Gandhi, leader in the struggle for Indian independence.
- 1877 Queen Victoria proclaimed Empress of India.
- 1897 Ramakrishna Mission established in Calcutta by Swami Vivekananda.
- 1942 Gandhi starts the 'Quit India' movement.
- 1947 India gains independence, but loses territory to the newly created West and East Pakistan.

1947–PRESENT DAY

- 1947 Nehru is inaugurated as India's first prime minister.
- 1948 Assassination of Mahatma Gandhi at Birla Bhavan, New Delhi.
- 1950s–1970s Hindus migrate to North America, the UK and other countries, such as Holland and Australia.
- 1960s Indian thought and practice become popular in the West, through groups such as the Transcendental Meditation and Hare Krishna movements.
- 1966 Appointment of Indira Gandhi as first female prime minister of India.
- 1984 Assassination of Indira Gandhi causes rifts between Hindus and Sikhs.
- 1992 Destruction of the Babri Mosque precipitates violence between Muslims and Hindus.
- 2000 Continuing strife between Christians and Hindus over coerced religious conversions, especially in Orissa and Kerala.
- 2000 Hindus are socially, academically and economically well-established in the West. With the rise of the Indian middle class, vast temple complexes also flourish in India.

PART I

FOUNDATIONS AND ORIGINS

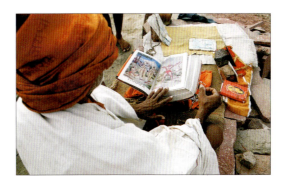

Many people identify Hinduism with its stereotypical images: its many deities, the revered cow and the saffron-clad ascetic; or with Indian poverty and the caste system. Some try to define it by identifying distinctive beliefs, such as karma and reincarnation. Others highlight its spiritual practices, such as yoga, worship and meditation.

The noun 'Hinduism', denoting a distinct, unified religion, was first coined by the British in the 19th century. Around the 8th century CE, Persians first used the adjective, 'Hindu', broadly indicating the people beyond the River Indus.

One alternative name, 'Vaidika Dharma', signifies adherence to specific holy texts, the Vedas and their supplements. For such belief in a universal, perennial wisdom, many Hindus call their tradition 'Sanatana Dharma', the eternal religion. Despite inclusive ideals, Hinduism features quite distinctive concepts, such as Dharma (religious duty) and Brahman (the absolute reality). Belief in reincarnation clearly differentiates Hinduism from materialistic philosophy or the Abrahamic view of a single human existence.

Opposite: Like this sacred banyan tree, Hinduism has old and deep roots, and has grown organically over several millennia.

Above A sadhu reads the Ramayana, one of two Hindu epics. This ancient wisdom, the Sanatana Dharma (eternal law), was first transmitted orally.

CHAPTER 1

HINDU HISTORY

In exploring any faith tradition, students usually ask 'when did it start?' and 'who founded it?' For the Hindu tradition, such questions yield no easy answers. Most historians consider Hinduism not a divergent expansion from one key event, but a convergence of many spiritual and cultural influences. Many Hindus themselves consider their wisdom eternal. In their view, time is boundless and cyclical, and space similarly extends beyond human perception.

Students of Hinduism often consider its scope and complexity problematic. Although the religion is hard to grasp, its multiformity has also been enriching. Indeed, its fluidity may have helped it prevail for more than five millennia, to become the world's oldest existing religion.

Hinduism is inextricably linked to the recorded history of India. Its vision has long transcended the particularities of a specific era and locale. In practice also, millions of Hindus now live beyond the sub-continent. People of other ethnic origins have adopted elements of Hindu thought and practice. The history of Hinduism, though running parallel to Indian history, is also different from it.

Opposite The Angkor Wat temple in Cambodia symbolizes an era of cultural expansion for Hinduism.

Above *A giant wheel of the sun-god at the Konark Temple, Orissa. Ancient Hindu deities acknowledged human dependence on God and nature.*

TRADITIONAL VIEWS ON ANCIENT HISTORY

HINDUISM IS THE WORLD'S OLDEST LIVING RELIGION, GOING BACK AT LEAST 5,000 YEARS. ACCORDING TO ITS OWN CYCLICAL WORLDVIEW, IT GOES BACK MUCH FURTHER, EVEN INDEFINITELY.

There are different accounts of Hinduism's early history, for three main reasons. First, Hinduism is not a single, unified religion, with a common founder, but embraces many distinctive branches. Second, there are differences of opinion, especially between Hindu practitioners and Western researchers, who hold variant views on what constitutes authentic research and evidence. Third, Hinduism is so old that its past recedes into uncertainty.

Some Hindus claim that their heritage regresses indefinitely. This distinctive view of time, and the allied idea of a hierarchical universe, clash with much contemporary

Below Lord Rama's triumphant return to Ayodhya illustrates Hindu belief in previous glorious ages.

opinion. However, if one is to study Hinduism thoroughly, to grasp the meaning behind its diverse practices, it is essential to explore Hinduism's own views on time, history and its own evolution.

ETERNAL, CYCLICAL TIME

Many Hindus call their tradition 'Sanatana Dharma' (the eternal religion'). Derived from the core concept of Brahman, the absolute reality, the term implies the existence of an eternal realm. However, the concept of an ever-receding past and an indefinitely extending future also applies to the transient material world. Hindu texts teach of a continuous cycle of universal creation, destruction and re-creation. Time is eternal and cyclical rather than bounded and linear.

UNDERSTANDING HINDUISM

Hinduism's age and complexity, and its own view of time, befuddle attempts to describe its development. The lack of a founder, or single historical event, implies that it is not like dropping a stone on to water, creating successive waves of development. Some have proposed a longer-term analogy, of a tree growing out of the ground and dividing into branches and sub-branches. This still suggests a divergent growth, sprouting from a single base. Others view Hinduism to the contrary, as the convergence of diverse spiritual, social and political influences, citing the analogy of many tributaries feeding into a single river. Other scholars have likened Hinduism to a family of religions, with each distinctive lineage bearing some family resemblance. Clearly, Hinduism fails to resonate with rigid or simplistic notions of religion or with ideas of uni-directional human emergence from a tribal and primitive past.

Since the creation of this universe, time has moved through successive cycles of four ages. Similar to the four seasons, they continuously repeat themselves. They are named after four metals, suggesting the gradual debasement of human virtue. During the golden age, all people were noble. Good qualities decreased through the silver and copper ages until we reached the present materialistic age, called the Kali-yuga, the age of iron. It is also called the 'age of hypocrisy' or the 'age of quarrel'. Hindu texts elaborate on the materialistic qualities prevalent in this age, and the exalted virtues of previous 'yugas'.

There are two Hindu 'histories', taking the form of long poems and popularly called 'the Epics'.

Left Krishna and Arjuna sound their conch shells to start the cataclysmic Battle of Kurukshetra.

or to oppose them, kings from throughout the known world prepared for battle at Kurukshetra, just north of modern New Delhi.

Just prior to hostilities, Lord Krishna – a key Hindu deity – narrated the Bhagavad-gita to the third Pandava brother, called Arjuna. Though a bold warrior, Arjuna was depressed at the prospect of battle with his own kinsmen. Krishna instructed him on all the important Hindu teachings, starting with the idea that the true self (the atman) is different from the physical body. Hearing Krishna's instructions, Arjuna regained his composure and fought with determination. He and his brothers emerged victorious, regaining the throne of the Indian Empire. Krishna departed the world 36 years later, marking the start of the present age.

Some scholars consider them fictional or mythological. They are certainly not ordered chronologically, and it appears that early Indian authors had little concern for history as we know it, the systematic and chronological classification of facts. Despite this, the Epics may give a peep into Indian history, and the progression of Hindu thought, practice and culture. The first epic, the Ramayana, tells the famous story of Rama and Sita, which may have happened as far back as the silver age. The second, the Mahabharata, 'the history of greater India', is more clearly linked to known human history.

THE KALI-YUGA

According to tradition, the Mahabharata recalls the final centuries of the previous era, the copper age. It relates the saga of five princes called the Pandavas, 'the sons of Pandu'. King Pandu was a descendant of King Bharata, after whom India is still called 'Bharatavarsha' (the land of Bharata), or simply 'Bharata'.

The Pandava's avaricious cousins, the Kauravas, usurped the throne of the vast Indian empire. After much intrigue, and extended appeals for peace, the Kauravas refused to give up any of their illegally occupied territory. To support the pious Pandavas,

Below Map showing India's seven holy rivers, seven ancient cities and some sites mentioned in the two Hindu epics, the Ramayana and the Mahabharata.

ARYAN INVASION THEORY

IN THE MID-1800s, WESTERN SCHOLARS BEGAN TO EXPLAIN THE EMERGENCE OF HINDUISM THROUGH THE ARYAN INVASION THEORY. IT HAS LONG BEEN CONTESTED, ESPECIALLY BY HINDUS THEMSELVES.

At the core of the Aryan invasion theory was the view that key elements of Hinduism developed outside of India. Critics, on the other hand, have long claimed that the theory is based on conjecture, political agendas, and dubious interpretation of linguistic and archaeological evidence. More positively, construction of an Indian history has highlighted the subjective and political dimensions of research and scholarship. Accounts of Indian and Hindu history were constructed largely during the European colonial period, influenced by prevalent and emergent ideas on

Below Map of excavation sites in the Indus and Sarasvati valleys. The legendary Sarasvati may have followed the course of the current Ghaggar-Hakra river.

the nation state and the pre-eminence of Western and Christian civilization. From the late 20th century, religious scholarship changed, to promote the importance of not only gathering sound data, but also of recognizing factors that skew its interpretation. The broad consensus today is that the Aryan theory is questionable, although many books habitually present its claims as incontestable fact.

LINGUISTIC THEORIES

The first Europeans to arrive in India knew little of Hinduism's origins. They found few historical records, for Hindu writers seemed uninterested in mere chronological accounts. Serious scholarship began during the days of British domination of India, with the development

Above Max Müller, the German Indologist usually credited as the first to propound the Aryan invasion theory.

of the study of philology (the science of language) and Indology (Indian studies), especially in Great Britain and Germany. Early scholars studied religious accounts of history, such as the two Epics, but considered them largely mythological and thus unreliable. In the very earliest text, the Rig Veda, information about the lifestyle and habitat of their authors was largely incidental.

However, scholars observed that Hindu scripture denoted certain people as 'aryan'. Although this Sanskrit term means 'noble people', academics hypothesized that it referred to a distinct race. At the same time, early philologists identified clear links between Sanskrit and European words, and, based on linguistic evolution, tried to construct an historical framework. In 1853, the German linguist Max Müller proposed that the highly advanced Aryans came from outside India, from the West, bringing with them the ancient Indo-European language of Sanskrit and the seeds of Hinduism.

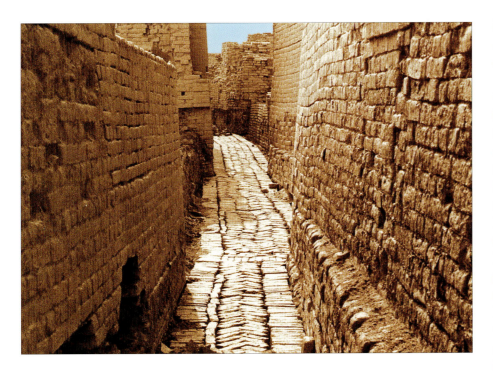

ARCHAEOLOGICAL EVIDENCE

At first, little was known of the proposed Aryan people. Then, in the 1920s, archaeologists unearthed the remains of two walled cities, Mohenjo-daro and Harappa, in present-day Pakistan. Evidence revealed detailed town planning, with kiln-fired bricks, orderly streets and sophisticated sewage and drainage systems. Clay seals unearthed from the sites revealed an elementary form of writing, although experts have yet to decipher the script. One seal carries a figure resembling Lord Shiva, a contemporary Hindu deity. Scholars were taken aback at the level of civilization shown and its sophistication. Even more surprisingly, the inhabitants seemed to have lived well before the Aryans, then considered the most advanced race of their time.

REVISED THEORIES

Rather than rejecting the original theory, scholars revised it. As an alternative theory to the conquest of an aboriginal people by the civilized, light-skinned Aryans, archaeologist Mortimer Wheeler advocated that the bellicose Aryans had plundered and destroyed the cities of the older, more advanced Indus civilization. What we called Hinduism, he claimed, was a fusion of Aryan belief with the sophisticated culture of the local, dark-skinned Dravidians. The term Dravidian still refers to the peoples of South India.

More recently found artifacts imply that the Indus valley civilization was more widespread than first imagined. Sites extend a thousand miles, making it unlikely that they were simultaneously abandoned with the intrusion of nomadic tribes. Ideas have been refined, so that migration and acculturation, and not military conquest, explain the Aryan infiltration of north-west India, probably around 1700BCE. Recent photographic evidence has enhanced the debate, by supporting the existence of the legendary River Sarasvati, frequently mentioned in the Rig Veda. This implies that the river was not entirely mythological, as earlier thought, and that Hindu accounts of history might be taken more seriously. Hindus texts, however, fail to mention an Aryan invasion. They conversely indicate a protracted westerly migration, carrying Hindu thought and culture to Greece and beyond.

ONGOING DEBATES

Many scholars now seriously consider the possibility that Hinduism developed entirely within the sub-continent. Some even refer to India as the 'cradle of civilization', an alternative to Central Asia or Europe. However, the debate remains politically charged, with Hindu nationalists mirroring their past colonial adversaries. They promote the supremacy of the ancient Indo-Hindu civilization, putatively well-versed in science, medicine and mathematics even as the West languished in fur-clad barbarism. Despite such possibly biased and over-stated claims, contemporary scholars are happier to reconsider previous theories. Many use the wider term 'the Indus-Sarasvati civilization' and entertain earlier dates, more consistent with Hinduism itself. Despite this convergence, conclusive establishment of the origins of Hinduism remains unlikely. Dates and events become relatively clear only as the first millennium CE approaches.

Below Found at Mohenjo-daro in the Indus Valley, this terracotta seal depicts a figure resembling Lord Shiva.

THE VEDIC PERIOD 1500BCE–500CE

THE VEDIC PERIOD IS THE ERA OF INDIAN HISTORY DURING WHICH THE VEDAS WERE COMPILED. IT IS MARKED BY SACRIFICIAL MODES OF WORSHIP DIRECTED TOWARD MANY 'NATURE' DEITIES.

Scholars suggest that these earliest Hindu texts represent the fusion of two cultures: the Aryan and Dravidian. Apparently, Aryan culture predominated, reaching the fertile Gangetic plain around 1000BCE and later infiltrating the southern peninsula. Some scholars claim that the disparity between the Aryan and Dravidian societies, particularly as defined along racial lines, has been over-emphasized. Whatever the precise history, the decline of the Indus-Sarasvati civilizations from around 1900BCE marks the beginning of the Vedic age, which roughly spanned the ten centuries from 1500 to 500BCE.

COMPOSING THE VEDAS

Although India's distant history is uncertain, its ancient wisdom was certainly passed down orally and later committed to writing. Some traditionalists still believe that the Vedas themselves should only be transmitted orally and never through written text. Scholars believe that these first books were composed around 1200BCE, starting with the Rig Veda.

Below An artist's impression of the ancient and grand fire sacrifice, often patronized by wealthy kings.

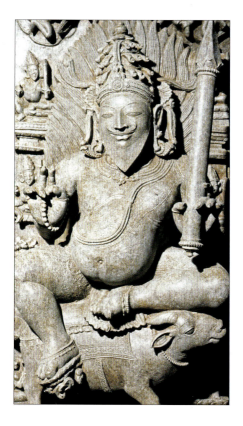

Above An 11th-century carving of Agni, god of fire, who was especially popular during the Vedic period.

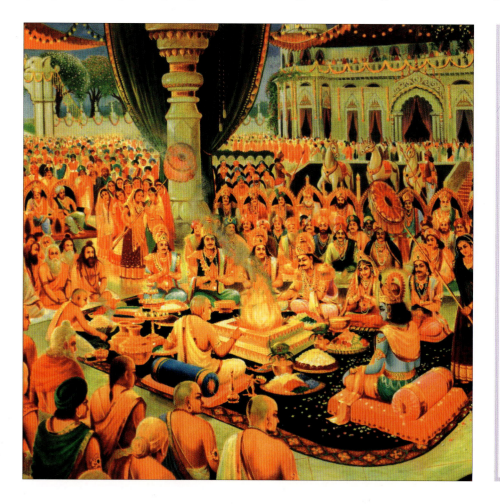

BRAHMIN-LED SOCIETY

The priestly class of the Vedic period were the brahmins, whose prime responsibility was to preserve tradition, originally through oral recitation and later through written texts. They formed the head of what is now known as Brahminical Hinduism, which valued social orthodoxy and family tradition. During the same period, there were early developments of the less orthodox and sometimes anarchical 'Shramana' traditions, whose members lived in forests and remote regions, practising meditation and asceticism and favouring alternative Tantric texts. Scholars suggest that Hinduism consists of these two competing but complementary strands, augmented by the simple folk traditions associated with village Hinduism.

Right The 16 'ancient kingdoms' stretched from modern Afghanistan in the west to the Ganges Delta in the east.

Veda literally means knowledge. Although it refers to a specific body of texts of largely India origin, it carries connotations of a universal wisdom, common to all people. This helped foster notions of an inclusive religion, which valued and assimilated diverse scholarly and cultural influences. The adjective 'Vedic' means 'related to the Vedas'. For this reason, this period is called 'the Vedic age', and the associated culture centred in northern India, 'the Vedic civilization'.

There are four main Vedas, classified as shruti, 'revealed knowledge'. They formed the basis for hundreds of later elaborations, alternatively designated as smriti, 'remembered knowledge'. Together, these two types of holy book are often called 'the Vedic literature'. The Vedas proper included hymns and chants for use in sacrificial rituals, and later philosophical sections called the Upanishads. Over the Vedic period, the importance of ritual gradually diminished as priority shifted to philosophical thought based on the Upanishads.

WORSHIP

The Vedas are primarily liturgical texts for use in ritual and worship. During the Vedic age, the performance of elaborate *yajnas* (sacrifices) aimed at worldly fulfilment and the

attainment of heaven. The sacrifices involved not only the immolation of animals but, more frequently, the offering into fire of clarified butter (ghee) and raw, whole grains such as rice and barley. There were two main types of sacrifice: public events, which included the sacred fire and the coronation ceremonies, and domestic rites, including sacraments for initiation, marriage and death.

Because the Vedas emphasized the need to live in harmony with natural and cosmological rhythms, called rita, the main deities were linked to nature. Most eminent were Indra, god of rain and 'king of heaven', and Agni, who presided over the sacrificial flames and first received the offerings. Soma, supervising the celestial moon planet, was associated with drinking a heady nectar distilled from the enigmatic Soma plant. Vishnu, and Shiva in his form as Rudra, were also venerated, but

Left A Hindu woman daubs sacred clay on her forehead by the banks of the River Yamuna. Most Vedic deities predominated over nature and the elements.

some claim they were relatively less popular deities. Other deities included Usha, goddess of the dawn, Varuna, god of the waters, and Goddess Sarasvati, associated with speech and the sacred river.

HINDU KINGDOMS

By the Vedic period, the noble Aryans had developed an aristocracy based on the varna system. They divided society into four occupational classes. The members of the highest varna, the brahmins, performed rituals and taught from the Vedic texts. They relied on patronage and protection from members of the second varna. These chivalrous kings were addressed as Maharaja (great king) or Mahajana (great man). During the late Vedic era, there emerged several powerful Hindu kingdoms, called 'mahajanapadas'. By 600BCE, 16 realms spanned the Indian plains, from modern-day Afghanistan in the west to beyond the Ganges delta in the east. They paved the way toward the great Mauryan Empire and the dawn of the classical age of Hinduism.

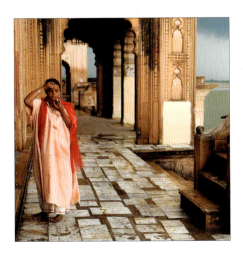

THE NORTH CLASSICAL AGE 500BCE–500CE

THE CLOSE OF THE VEDIC PERIOD USHERED IN A GOLDEN, CLASSICAL AGE IN THE NORTH. DURING THIS 1,000-YEAR PERIOD, MANY SECONDARY, SMRITI TEXTS WERE COMPILED.

Above A silver coin, minted around 300BCE, showing the head of the Greek ruler, Seleucus Nicator.

The close of the Vedic age heralded the ascendancy of Hindu culture and the rise of two great powers, the Mauryan and Gupta empires. The period also saw the writing of key scripts, significant changes in the mode of worship and the emergence of three main traditions based on specific focuses of worship.

THE MAURYAN EMPIRE
(*c.*321–185BCE)
The Magadha kingdom, mentioned in the Mahabharata, had risen to prominence toward the end of the Vedic period. From 350BCE, this eastern kingdom, corresponding to the modern states of Bihar and Bengal, was ruled by the Nanda Dynasty. In 326BCE, Alexander the Great of

Below A map depicting Alexander the Great's route towards India, and his subsequent retreat, which heralded the rise of the Mauryan Empire.

Macedonia alarmed them and other Hindu kings by conquering north-western India and defeating King Porus of the Punjab. However, upon nearing the formidable Magadha kingdom, Alexander's fatigued troops mutinied, turned south toward the coast and eventually moved westward away from the peninsula.

Seizing the opportunity, Chandragupta defeated the Nandas. After ascending the Magadha throne, he repulsed an incursion by remaining Greek forces and established a lasting friendship with their general, Seleucus. This alliance forged cultural ties between Greece and India, which later shared political power over kingdoms centred in Bactria, near the northern border of modern Afghanistan. Chandragupta extended his dominions to establish the mightiest empire of ancient India. His grandson, King Ashoka (r.273–232BCE), further extended

Mauryan territory, but later turned to Buddhism, ushering in an era of peace and non-violence. He propagated Buddhist ideals throughout India and beyond, even as far westward as Mediterranean Greece.

MORAL TEACHINGS
Chandragupta's personal advisor, Chanakya, had previously been a professor at Taxila University. He wrote two important texts: the Artha Shastra, a treatise on statecraft, economic policy and military strategy, and the Niti Shastra, a collection of proverbs still widely read. Many of his teachings were condensations of earlier, oral texts, such as the Manu Smriti (the laws of mankind), which were also committed to writing around this time. The Manu Smriti belongs to a key section of the Vedic canon called the Dharma shastras (moral codes).

The two Hindu epics, the Ramayana and the Mahabharata, were also composed at about this time. They explored the performance of dharma (religious duty), and especially the key roles played by noble kings and their learned advisers, the brahmin priests. By this time, these priests gave less attention to the elaborate Vedic sacrifices and engaged instead in puja, the scheduled worship

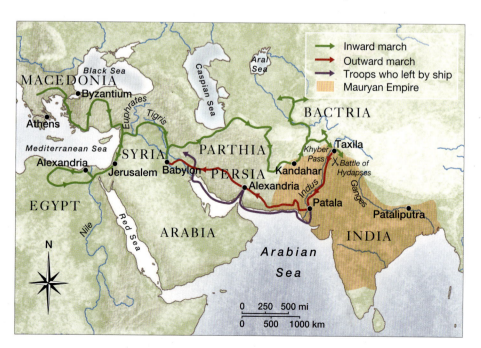

Legend:
- Inward march
- Outward march
- Troops who left by ship
- Mauryan Empire

Black Sea
MACEDONIA
Byzantium
Athens
Mediterranean Sea
Alexandria
EGYPT
Nile
Red Sea
ARABIA
N
Aral Sea
Caspian Sea
Euphrates
Tigris
SYRIA
Jerusalem Babylon
PERSIA
PARTHIA
Kandahar
Khyber Pass
Taxila
Battle of Hydaspes
Indus
Alexandria
Patala
Ganges
Pataliputra
INDIA
BACTRIA
Arabian Sea

0 250 500 mi
0 500 1000 km

of sacred images. Simultaneously, the focus of worship had moved from Indra, Agni and other nature gods, to three principal and all-powerful deities: Vishnu (previously a Vedic god), Shiva (earlier called Rudra) and Shakti (the goddess). This period also saw the emergence of renouncer traditions, possibly influenced by Jainism and Buddhism, and also the birth of northern devotional traditions focused on Vasudeva, an alternative name for Krishna, hero of the Mahabharata.

THE GUPTA DYNASTY

The reign of Ashoka was followed by a succession of weaker kings and the gradual erosion of the Mauryan Empire. Powerful nomadic tribes called the Kushans snatched power from the Greeks in Bactria and penetrated India's north-west frontier, extending the influence of Buddhist culture and establishing their eastern capital in Mathura on the Ganges.

The Kushans were expelled by the Gupta dynasty, based in Pataliputra, or present-day Patna in Bihar. For well over two centuries (280–450CE), they ruled all land north of the Vindhya Mountains. The Gupta Empire, though smaller

Right Contemporary classical dancers performing at the Chidambaram temple, Tamil Nadu. Temple construction and dance flourished during the Gupta period.

Left Top of the Ashoka pillar at Sarnath, India, erected by Ashoka. The wheel motif now features on the Indian national flag.

than the Mauryan before it, left a deep cultural impression on India. Historical evidence gleaned from coins, monuments, and travellers' journals indicates the presence of fine cities, well-equipped hospitals, thriving universities and a content and prosperous people.

GUPTA ARTS AND RELIGION

Gupta rule was based on Hindu teachings and divided society into four varnas (classes). Impressive achievements in art, music, literature, philosophy and architecture were also forms of religious expression. The first dances were performed in temples built to facilitate the increasing popularity of ritual worship (puja) and aligned to popular focuses of worship. Three major traditions evolved: two venerating the male deities, Vishnu and Shiva, and a third for the goddess called Shakti. Simultaneously, scholars crystallized the idea of three main deities, the Trimurti, each accompanied by his consort. Brahma, married to Sarasvati, was responsible for creation; Vishnu, married to Lakshmi, became 'the sustainer and protector'; and Shiva, the husband of Shakti, took charge of decay and destruction.

Stories of these deities, written down during this period, now constitute a collection of texts called the 'Puranas'. The most famous describe the activities of Krishna, a form of Vishnu, and the goddess Durga, a warlike form of Shakti. For Shaivas, the Linga Purana, Shiva Purana and Skanda Purana remain core texts glorifying their specific lord.

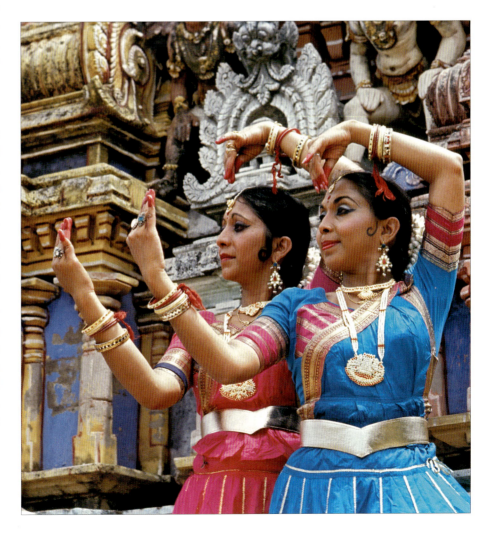

KINGS AND POETS OF THE SOUTH 500–1200CE

DURING THE NORTHERN CLASSICAL RENAISSANCE, THE TAMIL 'SANGAM' LITERATURE FLOURISHED IN THE SOUTH. AFTER 500CE, THE LONGEST STRIDES IN HINDUISM WERE TAKEN IN THE SOUTH.

The northern Gupta Empire collapsed around 550CE, largely due to military insurgency by the Hunas, the 'White Huns', based in Afghanistan. For a brief span between 535CE and 700CE, the Harsha Empire, centred at Kanauj on the River Ganges, united much of northern India and repulsed the marauding Hunas. King Harsha patronized Buddhism, established diplomatic links with China, and hosted Buddhist pilgrims, including the Chinese historian Hsuan Tsang. Toward the close of Harsha's reign, the Chalukya warrior dynasty assailed his kingdom and, after his death, expanded their empire to embrace central India.

THE CHOLA EMPIRE
(850–1279CE)
With the disintegration of the Harsha Empire around 700CE, and the brief rise of the Chalukyas, power in India shifted southward. The Chola dynasty, which had existed since the 1st century CE, gradually overcame the Chalukyas and other southern dynasties, such as the Pandhyas and Pallavas. At the height of their power, between the 9th and 13th centuries, the Cholas attacked the powerful Pala Dynasty, the Buddhist rulers of Bengal. Their most famous king was Rajaraja, whose great reign was commemorated by the magnificent Shiva temple in Thanjavur.

The Cholas were Shaivas (devotees of Shiva) but supported the other main traditions, Shaktism and Vaishnavism. Particularly in their capital city, Chidambaram, they built many impressive temples featuring *gopurams*, towering gateways decorated with ornate carvings of various gods and goddesses. Shiva remained

Below Map showing the extent of Chola influence in South-east Asia. The huge temples at Angkor Wat in modern Cambodia were built at the height of Chola power.

Above A 12th-century bronze of Lord Shiva as Nataraja, the 'king of dancers' revered by the southern Chola emperors.

the most popular deity, particularly in his form as Nataraja, the 'king of dancers'. The Cholas were perhaps the first Indian rulers to maintain a fleet to extend their territory beyond the peninsula.

SOUTH-EAST ASIA
Through trade and commerce, Hinduism may have reached Indo-China and Indonesia as early as the 1st century CE. Aided by their navy,

Below An 11th-century Shiva temple in Cholapuram, capital of the Chola dynasty.

INDIA

South China Sea

N

Bay of Bengal

SIAM

KHMER

Angkor Wat

SRI LANKA

Anuradhapura

MALAY

BORNEO

Extent of Chola Empire
Likely tributary states
Influence of predominately Buddhist Srivjaya Empire

SUMATRA

INDIAN OCEAN

JAVA

BALI

0   250   500 mi
0   500   1000 km

Above Traditional painting of Andal, the only woman among the 12 devotional saints called 'Alvars'.

the Chola Empire further colonized countries to the south and south-east, including the Maldive Islands, Sri Lanka and lands belonging to the largely Buddhist Srivijaya Empire in Indonesia, including Malaya, Java and Sumatra. On the Indo-China peninsula, Chola armies exacted tribute from the rulers of Siam (present-day Thailand) and the Khmer kingdom (modern-day Cambodia).

Around this time, Hinduism reached the island of Bali, where it remains the principal religion. Throughout South-east Asia, Hindu beliefs and practices intertwined with Buddhist and native traditions. This mixed culture still exists in many parts of Indo-China and Indonesia, as evident in the continuing use of long Sanskrit names and the cultural popularity of the Mahabharata and the Ramayana.

SOUTHERN POET-SAINTS

Between the 6th and 10th centuries CE, poet-saints in southern India helped Hinduism move away from the strict, brahmin-controlled ritual of the Vedic times. Focus on a personal God, rather than an impersonal absolute, laid early foundations for modern Hinduism. Writing in the Tamil tongue, the poet-saints established its importance as a sacred language, much like Sanskrit in the north.

Among the poet-saints were the 63 Nayanmars, fervent devotees of Shiva. Largely unconcerned with scholarship, they immersed themselves in practical service, such as cleaning temple premises, lighting the lamps, stringing flower garlands, feeding the devotees and performing other menial tasks. They regarded worship of Lord Shiva's devotees to be paramount, even higher than the worship of God himself. The Nayanmars helped establish the important tradition now called Shaiva Siddhanta.

The Vaishnava (Vishnu-worshipping) equivalents of the Nayanmars were the 12 Alvars, including the celebrated female saint, Andal. The 9th-century scholar, Nathamuni, compiled the poems of the 12 Alvars into an anthology of 4,000 verses called the 'Divya Prabhandham'. Singing the praises of Vishnu in his form as the four-handed Narayana it remains a core text, recited daily, in the famous Shrirangam Temple. Nathamuni also initiated the important tradition called Shri Vaishnavism.

BHAKTI MOVEMENTS

The poet-saints came from all occupations and cared little for the Hindu social structure, which by then had become rigid and hereditary. By accepting disciples from all social classes, the saints challenged the authority of caste-conscious brahmins. The poet-saints gave rise to popular bhakti (devotional) movements that later swept north to embrace all of India. One of the first was founded in the 12th century by a scholar called Basavanna. Members were called Lingayats, named for always carrying a miniature lingam, the cylindrical black stone representing Lord Shiva. The Lingayats believed in one God and rejected the Vedas, considering them to be polytheistic. They championed the underdog, teaching about the equality of all beings and, unusually for the time, accepting women as gurus (religious teachers). However, this upsurge of devotion was more than mere sentiment, and was accompanied by seminal developments in scholarship and the foundation of key doctrinal lineages.

Below Hindu temples on the Indonesian island of Bali, colonized by the Cholas.

WHO FOUNDED HINDUISM?

HINDUISM FEATURES NO SINGLE FOUNDER. INSTEAD, SEVERAL KEY FIGURES STARTED THIER OWN SPECIFIC TRADITIONS AND SACRED LINEAGES, AND TAUGHT DISTINCTIVE BRANCHES OF PHILOSOPHY.

Above The Plough contains the seven brightest stars in the constellation Ursa Major. They are often associated with the seven sages and seers known as the rishis.

Almost universally, God is considered the ultimate source of religion, and many sacred lineages (*sampradayas*) still consider their founder to be an avatara, a descent of God. The broad denominations are defined by their chosen deity, and sub-groups usually by their following a specific saint or scholar.

THE ANCIENT RISHIS

Tradition holds that in ancient times there lived seven great rishis, sages and seers who transmitted the universal wisdom later recorded in Vedic texts. The rishis, born from the mind of the creator Brahma, are often associated with the seven stars of the Plough. Hindu families claim to trace their dynasty (gotra) to one of the seven, whose names include Atri, Bhrigu, Angira, Gautama, Vashishta, Bharadvaja and Vishvamitra (though there are variant lists). These names appear repeatedly in the stories of the Epics, Puranas, and other texts. Although the rishis were born shortly after creation, some are reputed to be still alive. More recent rishis include the founders of the Six Darshanas (philosophical schools), most notably Vyasa who inaugurated Vedanta philosophy.

SHANKARA

After the fall of the northern Gupta dynasty, and while the poet-saints expounded devotion in the Tamil-speaking south, key thinkers (acharyas) started laying foundations for modern Hindu thought. Each acharya founded a branch of theology, transmitted through a specific sampradaya, a lineage of teachers and students. These founding acharyas reinforced the importance of the guru-disciple relationship.

The first prominent acharya was Shankara, also called Shankaracharya (780–812CE). Born in today's southern state of Kerala, he was instructed by his guru, Govinda Bhagavatapada – disciple of the renowned author Gaudapada – to write commentaries on Vedanta philosophy. By Shankara's time, Hinduism had lost momentum due to the competing influence of the non-Vedic religions, Jainism and Buddhism. By travelling throughout India and defeating contesting scholars, Shankara re-established the authority of the Vedic literature. He founded the Advaita school of Vedanta by equating the individual self with God. He also augmented the three main denominations – Vaishnavism, Shaivism and Shaktism – by revitalizing and formalizing a fourth, the Smarta tradition.

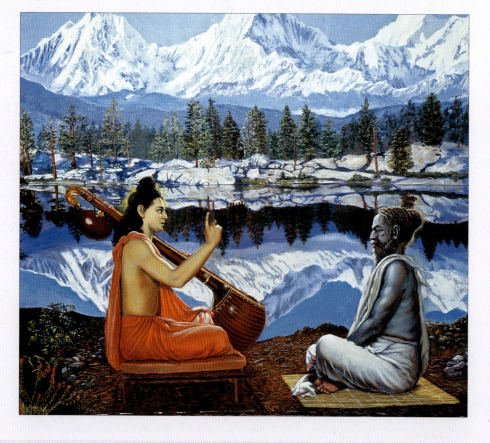

Left Modern painting of the ancient rishi (sage) Narada instructing Vyasa, who subsequently founded the philosophical system called Vedanta.

EARLY SHAIVA FOUNDERS

Some consider Shankara an incarnation of Lord Shiva, who is thought to have previously descended as Lakulisha (*c*.200CE). Considered the founder of Shaivism, or at least its first formal guru, Lakulisha is credited with compiling the Pashupati Sutra texts, central to the oldest Shaiva sect, the Pashupatis. The other five main Shaiva groups have their own founders.

One of the greatest was Vasugupta (*c*.860–925CE) who revealed the Shiva Sutras and founded the system called Kashmir Shaivism. Its greatest scholar was Abhinavagupta (*c*.950CE) who, unlike Shankara, favoured non-Vedic texts called Tantras. Of his 35 works, the largest is Tantraloka, an extensive treatise central to modern Kashmiri Shaivism and to many Shakti traditions. Since Abhinavagupta's time, there have been several other great Shaiva scholars, including Gorakshanatha (the Natha tradition), Basavanna (the Lingayats) and Rishi Tirumular

Below Madhva (1238–1317), depicted here with previous incarnations, lived after two other key scholars of Vedanta, namely Shankara and Ramanuja.

(Shaiva Siddhanta). Srikantha is notable for founding a branch of Vedanta and the corresponding Shaiva Advaita School.

RAMANUJA AND MADHVA

The four main Vaishnava lineages also subscribe to Vedanta. Ramanuja (1017–1137) is the acharya for the south-Indian Shri Vaishnava sampradaya, founded by Nathamuni (*c*.824–900CE). Ramanuja qualified Shankara's doctrine by proposing that God is not only the formless, but also a person with spiritual form. Ramanuja's theology of 'qualified monism' laid solid foundations for other monotheistic doctrines contesting Shankara's monism.

More strongly than Ramanuja before him, Madhva (1238–1317) stressed the personal form of God (as Krishna) and his eternal distinction from the soul. Madhva's philosophy, called 'pure dualism', is unique in Hinduism in advocating an eternal hell for sinners. The headquarters of the Madhva tradition are in Udupi in Karnataka.

The acharyas for the two other Vaishnava lineages are Nimbarka, whose dates are uncertain, and Vallabha (1481–1543), who followed the footsteps of Vishnuswami (dates

Above Rocky Island, Kanyakumari, is an important pilgrimage site for the followers of Swami Vivekananda.

unknown). Vallabha started the Pushti Marg ('path of nourishment') still popular in Gujarat and Rajasthan.

LATER FOUNDERS

After the main acharyas, many others founded subsequent groups, often as branches of previous lineages. The Ramakrishna Mission, founded by Vivekananda, pursued Shankara's Advaita doctrine. The Swaminarayan Movement, founded by Sahajananda Swami (1781–1830), modified and extended Ramanuja's teachings.

During that period of British rule in India, Hindu intellectuals founded more radical 'reform movements', attempting either to break from tradition or to revert to fundamental Vedic teachings. These movements still complement the main traditional lineages. Although some contemporary gurus derive authority solely from personal charisma, many still claim descent from previous founders and acharyas. The modern Hare Krishna movement, founded by Bhaktivedanta Swami, declares unbroken links to Madhva but also draws heavily on Ramanuja's thought.

ISLAM GAINS GROUND IN INDIA 1192–1526 CE

WHILST HINDU KINGDOMS PROSPERED IN THE SOUTH, RELIGIOUS LIFE IN THE NORTH WAS THREATENED, SPECIFICALLY BY THE ARRIVAL OF A RADICALLY DIFFERENT RELIGION AND CULTURE.

In the 7th century CE, the new religion of Islam had reached Indian shores via merchants plying the Arabian Sea. A hundred years later, Iraqi Arabs invaded and occupied the north-western state of Sind. Thereafter, Muslim warlords from Turkey and Central Asia superseded Persia as the major power to India's west, and began raiding through her vulnerable north-west frontier.

EARLY RAIDS

Particularly brutal were the incursions of Mahmud of Ghazni (971–1030), the Afghan emperor. As a zealous Sunni Muslim, he plundered the northern states 17 times, sacking Hindu temples and plundering their considerable wealth. In 1025, he razed the Shiva temple in Somnatha, slaughtered its residents and enchained thousands of slaves. Legend holds that, after personally hacking the sacred image to pieces, he sent the fragments back to Gazni for setting in the steps of a new mosque. Mahmud annexed much of north-western India, including modern Pakistan and Indian Punjab. However, his death in 1030 heralded the gradual erosion of his vast empire. Hindu kings reclaimed Punjab and, to the west of Gazni, Turks and Afghans from the city of Ghor seized power and continued the assault on northern India.

THE DELHI SULTANATE

To repulse these attacks, King Prithviraj consolidated the military might of the Rajputs, warriors

Above The 14th-century tomb of Tughluq, Sultan of Delhi, typifies the relatively stark, austere lines of Islamic architecture.

claiming ancestry from the glorious days of Lord Rama. However, in 1192, Muhammad of Ghor defeated Prithviraj at the second battle of Tarain and triumphantly entered Delhi. After Muhammad's assassination in 1206, Qutb ud-Din established the first Muslim kingdom in India.

The Delhi Sultanate refers to the Muslim dynasties and sultans who, from 1206 to 1526, subdued the entire sub-continent, with the exception

Left The 13th-century sun temple in Konark, Orissa, shows the fluid, sensual nature of Hindu architecture at that time.

THE BIRTH OF SIKHISM

Guru Nanak (1469–1539), the founder of the Sikh religion, was influenced by the mystical northern *sant* (saint) tradition. He taught the practice of chanting God's holy names, the equality of all people and the importance of *seva*, service to others. Nanak's new faith was at first closely connected to Hinduism, though conspicuous by its military flavour in first resisting the Mughals and later the British. Only much later on did Sikhism define itself as a religion quite distinct from Hinduism.

Right The saint Kabir, a lowly weaver, opposed social and religious discrimination. He drew inspiration from Sufism and the northern Sant tradition, which both favoured an impersonal Supreme.

of Kashmir in the far north and the southern Hindu kingdom of Vijayanagara. The fall of Delhi in 1192 heralded over five centuries of Muslim rule, which left a deep and enduring impression on India's religious landscape.

AREAS OF CONFLICT

Islam and Hinduism bore conflicting codes of social behaviour. Islam was inflexible, authoritarian and obligatory, and it stressed the equality of all within its community of 'believers'. Hinduism was flexible, discriminating and hierarchical, and it celebrated internal diversity. Religious beliefs were also different. Islam was austerely monotheistic, whereas Hinduism seemed richly polytheistic, though underpinned by inclusive forms of monotheism. For Muslims, image worship was an abomination; for Hindus it was an expression of divine love. For Muslims, the cow was a valuable source of meat; for Hindus, she was a gentle and revered mother who provided milk.

DEVOTIONAL POEMS

The bhakti saints opposed both caste practices and rigidly sectarian religion. They recognized the commonality of God, as sardonically expressed by Kabir:

'Rama, Rama!', chants the Hindu,
'Allah is one', proclaims the Muslim,
But my Lord pervades all.
The God of Hindus lives in
  the temple.
The God of Muslims resides in
  the mosque.
Who resides where there are
Neither temples nor mosques?

However, by the time Muslims arrived, Hinduism had developed its own brand of discrimination. The ancient Indian system of four varnas had become strictly hereditary. Birth in a high family ensured a prestigious livelihood. Those born in lower varnas, even if professionally talented, were condemned to poorly paid menial work. Many low-caste Hindus were either excluded from religious life or over-dependent on brahmins eager to monopolize their prestigious positions. Muslim rule exacerbated this marginalization by creating a governing elite, reinforcing class differences and largely excluding Hindus from civic life.

DEVOTION SWEEPS NORTH

From 1200CE onward, religious leaders arose from among the people, teaching personal piety and spiritual egalitarianism. The northern Sant (saint) tradition, which included Kabir, was highly eclectic, fusing

Hindu devotion with Sufism and ascetic yoga. Many bhakti traditions, such as the Ramanandi ascetic lineage, adopted forms of Vedanta philosophy and extended the teachings of Ramanuja and Madhva. Travelling saints also composed their own songs, poems and prayers, in local languages rather than Sanskrit, and popularized the glorification of God, ecstatic dancing, and the musical recitation of mantras.

Right The Vakari tradition of Maharashtra, shown here in procession, comes from the northern Sant tradition and from bhakti saints like Namdev, who preceded Kabir.

THE MUGHAL EMPIRE 1526–1858

THE DELHI SULTANATE GAVE WAY TO THE GREAT MUGHAL DYNASTY. THIS PERIOD SAW BOTH SOCIO-RELIGIOUS DISCORD AND SPIRITED ATTEMPTS TO TRANSCEND SOCIAL AND RELIGIOUS DIVISIONS.

Due to fierce rivalry between different factions, the Delhi Sultanate gradually descended into civil war. In 1398, Delhi was destroyed by Timur, a warlord claiming descent from the Mongol emperor, Genghis Khan. The Sultanate never fully recovered, and, in 1526, the capital eventually fell to Babur, a Muslim emperor from Central Asia. Babur established the Mughal dynasty, which ruled much of India for the next three centuries. His son, Humayun, spent much of his reign in exile and died during his resurgence and the consolidation of Mughal power.

AKBAR THE GREAT
The Mughal Empire reached the peak of its glory, though not its greatest territorial size, under Humayan's son, Akbar. Born and

Above Painted c.1590, this miniature depicts the court of Emperor Akbar, who welcomed scholars from many religions.

raised in India, Akbar displayed a tolerant attitude toward all religions, celebrating Hindu festivals such as Divali and inviting to religious debates not only Muslims, but also Hindus, Sikhs and Christians. He also encouraged members of other religions to enter his court, and founded a new philosophy called Din Ilahi which advocates the equality of all faith systems. During his long reign (1542–1605), Akbar extended the kingdom and left many fine buildings and works of art. He is remembered as the greatest of the Mughal emperors.

AURANGZEB
Akbar was succeeded by his son and then by his grandson, Shah Jahan (1592–1666), famed for building the Taj Mahal (in Agra) and the Red Fort (in Delhi). Shah Jahan's son, Aurangzeb, was tyrannical, slaying his brothers, imprisoning his father and proclaiming himself emperor. During his long reign (1668–1707), he discriminated against Hindus, imposing special taxes on them and defacing their temples and sacred images.

Aurangzeb's religious policies contributed to Muslim-Hindu conflict in India, creating resentment that endures to modern times. Where Aurangzeb did excel was in expanding Mughal territory, especially in the south. Upon his death, the Mughal Empire was at its largest, but rapidly fell into an irrecoverable

Left A modern statue of the 17th-century warrior king, Shivaji, who harassed the forces of Aurangzeb and the declining Mughal Empire.

decline. Later emperors witnessed the rise of British power, and concluded with Bahadur Shah II, the last Mughal emperor, who was exiled to Burma and died in 1857.

NEW HINDU KINGDOMS
During Muslim rule, two new Hindu kingdoms arose. In the south, the fabulously wealthy Vijayanagar (City of Victory) resisted the military might of both the Delhi Sultanate and the Mughals until its final collapse in 1565. This marked the end of the south as an autonomous political area. However, a more formidable foe of the Mughals emerged on the west coast of India, in the mountainous Maratha kingdom. The Maratha king Shivaji (1630–1680) and his successors relentlessly harassed Aurangzeb, hastening the end of Mughal dominion. Shivaji was a resistance fighter who exemplified the ancient Hindu ideal of a stern yet chivalrous warrior. For many modern Hindus, he remains a symbol of the righteous struggle against intolerance and oppression.

Above A plaster statue of Mirabai, a popular medieval bhakti saint.

HINDUISM UNDER THE MUGHALS

Under much Muslim rule, Hindus were required to pay the discriminatory jizya tax, inclining many, especially the poor, to convert to Islam. Some people were forcibly converted through intimidation or violence. By the end of the period of Mughal rule, almost a quarter of the Hindu population had embraced Islam, mainly in the north-western and eastern provinces.

At the same time, the bhakti movement were intent on developing personal devotion irrespective of social and political circumstance. The 'bhakti saints' drew on the earlier devotional sentiments of the southern poet-saints, but rather than worshipping Shiva and Vishnu, they focused more on Rama and Krishna, two of the principal incarnations of Vishnu.

The female poet Mirabai was apparently visited by Akbar who, disguised as a mendicant, was so moved by her singing that he draped her Krishna image with a diamond necklace. Mirabai is reported to have met the great scholar and renunciant Jiva Goswami (c.1515–1618), who wrote key theological texts for the Bengali Vaishnava movement started by the charismatic saint Chaitanya (1486–1534). At the same time, Vallabha's Pushti Marg, 'the past of nourishment', later popular in

Below An 18th-century, Mughal-style painting of Radha and Krishna, deities adored by many devotional movements.

A PERSONAL GOD
Unlike Kabir, many later bhakti saints propounded the notion of a personal God. Some criticized the doctrine of absolute monism, as Tukaram does in this poem.

This is why I abandoned home
  for the forest;
My love would be spoiled by
  the evil eye.
By listening to this doctrine
  of unity
I will lose my love for the Lord.
Tuka declares, 'This idea is false,
The notion that "God and I
  are one".
I will not let it divert me from
  his sacred service.'

Rajasthan and Gujarat, had just started. Legend holds that Vallabha was born as his parents fled Muslim atrocities in Varanasi prior to Mughal rule. In the West Indian state of Maharashtra, Tukaram (1606–50) appeared in the long 'Varkari' tradition, which worshipped Krishna, and is reputed to have instructed Shivaji, the great resistance fighter.

THE USE OF THE TERM HINDUISM
With the arrival of Islam, the ancient and inclusive tradition of Sanatana Dharma (as Hindus often call it) was forced to redefine itself. The ancient Persians had first coined the term 'Hindu' around the 8th century, referring to the people living on the far side of the River Indus. By the 1400s, the term had been adopted by practitioners, to distinguish themselves from members of other religions. Despite this, only later, during British domination of India, was the term 'Hinduism' first used.

BRITISH RULE AND HINDU REFORM 1757–1947

THE MUSLIM DOMINATION OF INDIA SAW THE EMERGENCE OF EGALITARIAN, DEVOTIONAL TRADITIONS. BRITISH RULE PROMOTED A MORE POLITICALLY AWARE RESPONSE TO ALIEN FAITH AND CULTURE.

In 1498, Vasco da Gama from Portugal became the first European to land in India, at the western port of Calicut. Subsequently, in 1510, the Portuguese ruthlessly conquered Goa. The wealth of India, especially her spices and textiles, also attracted the attention of many Dutch, French and British

Below Depiction of the capture of two Indian guns in 1858, during what the British termed 'the Indian Mutiny'.

explorers. In 1610 the British East India Company established a trading post in Surat and, within eight decades, further bases in Madras, Bombay and Calcutta. The company forged trade agreements with Mughal rulers and recruited local men into their private armies. As the East India Company expanded, tensions with local rulers led to armed conflict. Robert Clive's decisive victory at the Battle of Plassey (1757), in Bengal, heralded

Above Lord Robert Clive (1725–74), twice governor of Bengal, painted around 1764 by Thomas Gainsborough.

the end of the Mughal Empire. Within 12 years the East India Company had crushed its competitors, practically monopolizing European trade in India.

However, discontent at the expanding foreign presence was rife. In 1857, rumour spread among Indian troops that their rifle bullets were greased with the lard of cows and pigs, inconsistent with both Hindu and Muslim beliefs. The army rebelled during the Indian Mutiny, which many Hindus now call 'The First War of Independence'. The ensuing bloodshed prompted the British government to take direct control of India in 1857 and, 20 years later, Queen Victoria received the accolade, 'Empress of India'.

THE REFORM MOVEMENTS
The early colonialists gave Hindus free rein in their religious practice. Later, zealous missionaries, scholars and government officials deliberately attempted to convert Hindus to Christianity, and to 'civilize' them. Convinced of the moral supremacy of Christianity, Thomas Macaulay deliberately set about creating 'a class

The Indian Mutiny was sparked by apathy toward Hindu and Muslim belief. Hindu recruits objected that their bullets were greased with the lard of slaughtered cattle. For Hindus, the milk-providing cow was considered a mother-figure. The bull, extensively used in ploughing, was considered a father figure, the 'bread-winner' and an emblem of Dharma (religion). For these reasons, coupled with the ideal of ahimsa (non-violence), the cow and bull are still offered special respect. As many Hindus are vegetarian, milk products are considered essential for a balanced diet. Ghee (clarified butter) is used extensively: in cooking, for temple lamps and during such rituals as the ancient fire sacrifice.

The English idiom 'sacred cow' evolved in India to refer to irrational or superstitious belief. This derogatory term may reflect broad differences between Western and Hindu worldviews. Hindu scholarship widely

THE SACRED COW

Above Go-puja, veneration of the cow, during temple festivities in the sacred town of Vrindavana, north India.

accepts, without undue apprehension, the existence of paranormal phenomena. For example, human perception of ghosts is largely explained through reincarnation, by which the subtle body carries the soul to its next destination. Astrology is a science practised by respectable brahmins,

using Jyotisha, one of the six subsidiary Vedic texts. Mystical powers are widely accepted as credible, and not especially miraculous.

Some reform movements objected to what they also deemed superstition. To resist them, orthodox traditions collectively called themselves 'sanatanist', drawing on ideas of the Sanatana Dharma (eternal religion). These traditionalists argued that it is logical to accept life's spiritual dimensions, beyond direct perception. They considered the systematic abuse of cattle to be irrational and morally reprehensible. Just as colonial scholars constructed biased stereotypes of Hindus, so Hindus formed caricatures of Westerners; as unhygienic meat-eaters with a theology that propounded just one life and inadequately addressed the problem of evil and suffering. For many Hindus, cow slaughter begets human misfortune and remains a sign of incivility.

of persons Indian in blood and colour, but English in taste, in opinions, in morals and in intellect'. English became the official language for education. These policies, and the growing contact between Hinduism and the West, spawned various Hindu 'reform movements'. While they attempted to resist or influence change, they also assimilated many Christian and Western ideas.

One of the most influential groups was the Brahmo Sabha, founded in 1828 by Ram Mohan Roy and later renamed the Brahmo Samaj. Impressed by Christian theology, Ram Mohan Roy disagreed with caste practice, image worship and the idea of reincarnation. The

Right Portrait of Ram Mohan Roy (1774–1833), founder of one of the most influential 'reform movements'.

Arya Samaj, founded in 1875 by Swami Dayananda, took a different line. It wished to halt the Christian onslaught and return to the ancient, Vedic religion, purging its tradition of later Puranic impositions: pilgrimage, ritual bathing and veneration of sacred images. Its main form of worship remains the ancient, Vedic fire ceremony.

These reform movements had relatively little effect on popular Hindu practice, and the core traditions continued to predominate. However, reformers succeeded in making Hindus more reflective and aware of their own identity as a separate religion. They also spawned nationalist movements, which tried to rid India of foreign rule. British economic policy also resulted in the emigration of Hindus to other parts of the Empire.

MIGRATION TO THE COLONIES 1834–c.1900

BRITISH RULE IN INDIA HAD A HUGE IMPACT NOT ONLY ON HINDU THOUGHT, BUT ON MIGRATION AND THE SUBSEQUENT ESTABLISHMENT OF HINDU COMMUNITIES THROUGHOUT THE WORLD.

Emigration from India had been prevalent since the first millennium CE, mainly to South-east Asia for commercial reasons. However, during the colonial period, emigration occurred on an unprecedented scale, largely to provide inexpensive labour to the Dutch, French and British colonies. During the 19th century, the number of emigrants from India exceeded one-and-a-half million.

THE CARIBBEAN

In the British Caribbean, the abolition and phasing out of slavery, from 1834 onward, precipitated a manpower crisis. Western workers were hardly interested, largely due to the unhealthy and perilous tropical climate. Seeking alternative sources of cheap labour, the colonial governments turned their attention to densely populated India.

Below Map showing global Hindu migration from around 1840 until the early 1900s.

Beginning in the 1840s, indentured labourers, workers bound by contract, underwent the long and hazardous voyage to the Caribbean. For consenting to work for a specified number of years, they were promised fair wages and return tickets. However, due to prolonged debt, dishonest contracts and aspirations to build a new life, few returned home. The first Indians to arrive, mainly from Hindi-speaking north India, worked as labourers for the sugar industry in Trinidad. Others sailed to French Guyana and the Dutch island of Surinam to work on sugar and rubber plantations.

SOUTH-EAST ASIA AND AFRICA

In 1870 the British took formal control of the western states of Malay. Many Tamils, from what is now the southern state of Tamil Nadu, were subsequently shipped there to toil in the tin mines, railways, and rubber plantations. Others emigrated to Singapore and Burma

Above Indentured workers at a British tea plantation in Sri Lanka (formerly Ceylon) around 1900.

(present-day Myanmar). From 1879, thousands sailed east to the Fiji islands to labour on the sugar and cotton estates. Indians, many of them Hindus, also arrived on the Island of Mauritius, off the east coast of Africa, and on the adjacent French island of Reunion. Many Gujarati merchants and builders emigrated to East Africa, and other Indians to South

MIGRATION AND HINDU CULTURE

Emigration affected Hindu practice. As workers aspired for acceptance by their host communities, they often assimilated local lifestyle norms. The men, especially, began to wear Western clothes. They modified their eating habits, abandoning traditional, often vegetarian, diets. However, in some instances, Hindus living outside India became stricter, aware of the need to preserve their heritage, and bequeath it to their children and grandchildren. Emigration highlighted the struggle to maintain tradition, while at the same time adjusting appropriately to new situations.

Emigration routes
Raw cotton exports
Clothes imported to India

ARCTIC OCEAN

N

UNITED KINGDOM

ATLANTIC OCEAN

PACIFIC OCEAN

The CARIBBEAN

INDIA   BURMA

PACIFIC OCEAN

EAST AFRICA

MALAYSIA

SOUTH AFRICA

MAURITIUS and REUNION

FIJI

0   1500   3000 mi
0   3000   6000 km

INDIAN OCEAN

Africa, to lay railways or mine gold. It was in South Africa that Mohandas K. Gandhi, the most famous modern Hindu, practised law. He was alarmed at colonial abuse and, through personal experience, at the brutal treatment of Africans and Indians as second-class citizens.

THE COTTON TRADE

Shortly after his return to India in 1915, Gandhi stepped on to the political stage. He objected to the British economic policy of cultivating cash crops, such as indigo, despite a devastating famine. He also protested against the export of raw Indian cotton to Manchester and the subsequent import of clothes at inflated prices. His struggle for fair trade, and the preservation of India's village-based economy, became part of a burgeoning movement seeking to abolish colonial exploitation.

Frustration with British rule, and the influence of the intellectual reform movements, spawned various nationalist organizations. In 1909, leading members of the Arya Samaj founded the Hindu Mahasabha, 'the Great Hindu Assembly', to give Hindus a political voice. The Mahasabha declared India to be

Below The Triveni temple, built in Trinidad in 2002, testifies to the long-term influence of Hindu migration.

Hindustan, 'the land of the Hindus' and demanded government according to Hindu law. In 1932, their leader, Vir Savarkar, coined the term Hindutva. It literally means 'Hinduness', but the term is largely associated with organizations that promote Hindu nationalism. These movements included the Rashtriya Swayamsevak Sangh (RSS), established in 1925 to protect 'the interests of the people who treat India as their motherland'.

Gandhi led by example. Intent on undermining the British textile industry, his followers boycotted cloth milled in Western factories, and

Above Gandhi greeted jubilantly at the Greenfield Mill at Darwen, Lancashire, in 1931. He was trying to resolve trade tensions exacerbated by his boycott of milled cloth.

wore only home-spun cotton called 'khadi'. In 1939, he organized a 384-kilometre (238-mile) march to the sea, where demonstrators illegally manufactured their own salt, protesting against the British salt tax. In all these protests, Gandhi insisted on non-violence and 'passive resistance', even in responding to aggression. He also addressed mounting social ills, and upheld the rights of the socially excluded untouchables, whom he called 'harijans' (the children of God). However, Gandhi the reformer was in many ways a traditionalist, drawing strength and conviction from Hindu teachings, especially as found in the Ramayana and the Bhagavad-gita. Although he fought against the hereditary caste system, he believed in the original system of four varnas. He prayed daily, ate simple vegetarian food, and undertook long fasts as a means of both self-purification and social protest. In 1942, he started the 'Quit India' movement.

INDIAN PARTITION AND INDEPENDENCE 1947–

INDIAN INDEPENDENCE PROMISED NEW OPPORTUNITIES. IT ALSO SOWED THE SEEDS OF RELIGIOUS STRIFE, EXACERBATING TENSIONS BETWEEN HINDUISM AS A SPIRITUAL PATH AND AS A POLITICAL VEHICLE.

Gandhi led the initial negotiations for independence, which continued in earnest after the close of World War II (1939–45). Moves towards self-governance fuelled tensions between Hindus and Muslims. For the minority Islamic community, the imminent Hindu government promised no improvement on British rule. Gandhi pleaded for unity between the two groups. However, in 1946, Muhammed Jinnah, head of the Muslim League, conveyed the message that for his community an

Below Pandit Jawaharlal Nehru (1889–1964) conversing with Indian Independence leader Mahatma Gandhi in Bombay, 1946.

undivided India was no longer possible. Muslims were not prepared to live under a Hindu government.

PARTITION
On 15 August 1947, Indian independence coincided with the birth of a new nation, Pakistan. It consisted of two separate, predominantly Muslim states carved from the north-western and eastern parts of former Indian territory. Partition was marred by unprecedented horrors. Around half a million people perished as more than 11 million refugees – Hindus, Muslims, and Sikhs – criss-crossed the newly drawn borders. The following year, Gandhi, distraught by partition and the ensuing genocide, was

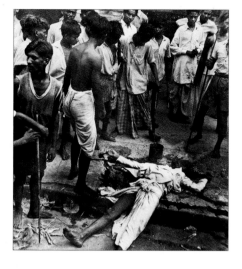

Above The corpse of a Calcutta resident killed in 1946 during communal riots between Hindus and Muslims.

assassinated, gunned down by a Hindu fanatic. His former ally, Jawaharlal Nehru, was sworn in as India's first prime minister.

BANGLADESH
East and West Pakistan constituted a single country divided by a thousand miles of Indian land, and by a gulf of cultural and linguistic differences. Feeling neglected by their government in West Pakistan, the eastern state declared independence in 1971, calling itself 'Bangladesh'. News reports exposed further mass slaughter, particularly of Bangladeshi students and intellectuals. In the ensuing war of independence, Bangladesh emerged victorious and the international community formally recognized her sovereignty in 1979. Her boundaries still embrace many Hindu pilgrimage sites, especially those connected to Bengali Vaishnavism.

KASHMIR
After partition, India forcibly assimilated smaller territories, including the independent Hyderabad, French India and later, in 1961, Portuguese Goa. Kashmir, a largely autonomous state, chose to join India, despite its Muslim majority. Pakistan objected, culminating in the

first Indo-Pakistan War (1948). A stalemate gave way to a ceasefire, and finally to the assimilation of Kashmir into India. Some boundaries remained unclear, and religious tensions continued into the 21st century, marring the prospects for a region once famed for its scenic landscapes and rich religious heritage. The cave at Amarnath, which is dedicated to Lord Shiva, remains an important Hindu pilgrimage site.

NEPAL

Although India and Pakistan divided on religious lines, the new secular India was neutral in matters of religion. After partition, the only remaining Hindu country in the world was Nepal, lying between India and China. It also became secular after the fall of the monarchy in 2008, with approximately three-quarters of its population still Hindus. Many Hindus of Nepalese origin also live in the Himalayan kingdom of Bhutan, and comprise a quarter of its population.

Right India after partition, showing countries and areas of specific contention. More recently, ideas of 'sacred land' have been used to promote Hindu nationalism.

Below A Hindu temple in a valley within the disputed territory of Kashmir.

INDIA AS A SACRED LAND

The relationship between Hinduism and India is contentious. The terms 'India' and 'Indian' are variously used, referring to the geographical land mass, the people living there, or the nation state. As a geographical area, India's natural features are associated with thousands of saints and avataras, and pilgrims often throng to its holy sites, walking barefoot out of respect for sacred ground. There has also developed a widespread belief that crossing the ocean rendered a Hindu impure, possibly because maintaining a vegetarian diet would be difficult. Some, mirroring the hereditary caste-system, suggest that a Hindu is identified exclusively by birth in a Hindu family.

Hindu ideas of sanctity don't generally derive from thinking their own religion 'special' (and thus sacred) but from the palpable presence of the divine in specific spots. Some Hindu texts condemn nationalism as a sign of misidentification with the external body. Such medieval bhakti saints as Kabir and Chaitanya also criticized any sectarian or nationalistic attitude, despite Indian occupation by Muslim rulers.

However, India's domination by foreign powers highlighted issues of protecting sacred land from aggressors, and from adversarial, proselytizing religions. The notion of sacred land has also been used for political purposes. Some have argued that Hinduism is an Indian religion, and that India should be a Hindu nation. Other Hindus claim the Indian peninsula to be special simply for its being conducive to spiritual development. For them, the strength and durability of Hinduism lies in its inclusivity, and its celebration of diversity. Overall, the precise relationship between India and Hinduism remains debatable, especially since increasing numbers of Hindus are born abroad, or come from non-Indian families.

A GLOBAL HINDUISM

INDIAN INDEPENDENCE MARKED THE IMMINENT DISSOLUTION OF THE BRITISH EMPIRE. IN PURSUIT OF INDIA'S EXAMPLE, MANY OTHER COLONIES SOUGHT INDEPENDENCE, ESPECIALLY IN THE 1960S.

In rapid succession, the East African colonies achieved self-rule: Uganda in 1962, Kenya in 1963 and the newly created Tanzania in 1964. Through policies known as 'Africanization', wealth and position were returned to Africans.

LEAVING EAST AFRICA

Many Indians opted to leave or were forcibly expelled, often relinquishing considerable wealth and business assets. As British citizens, many opted to settle within the United Kingdom, as factory workers or as self-employed grocers, newsagents and clothing manufacturers. Others filled emerging vacancies in the National Health Service. The first austere temples, often housed in disused school or church buildings, also served as community centres, and worship was highly eclectic, embracing many traditions and focuses. Although initially disadvantaged, the British Hindu community gradually integrated and

Below Map of Hindu migration patterns in the latter half of the 20th century following Indian independence.

established itself, and by the year 2000 had excelled in educational and professional fields. The many magnificent purpose-built temples, replacing the converted halls, testified to the growing wealth, prestige and influence of the Hindu community.

MIGRATION FROM INDIA

During the second half of the 20th century, many Hindus emigrated directly from India. Particularly popular was North America, especially the USA, where by 2000 the community numbered almost 1.5 million. Unlike their British counterparts, many were well-placed professionals, such as engineers and IT specialists. Other Indians moved to Europe, often from southern India and Sri Lanka, establishing the presence of the previously under-represented southern Hindu traditions. Since 1965, many Hindus have sought economic advantage in the oil-rich Arab States around the Persian Gulf. About one million now live there, mainly in Bahrain, Kuwait, Yemen, Saudi Arabia and the United Arab Emirates. They often support

Above A British mandir dedicated to the goddess Shakti. Hindu migrants from Africa established it around 1970 in a disused church hall.

relatives in India, where the money sent home is worth far more due to the comparatively low cost of living.

WORLDWIDE MOVEMENTS

During the post-independence era, many gurus travelled west to offer spiritual support to the fledgling communities in Europe and America. At the same time, westerners themselves were increasingly enamoured by Indian thought and culture, especially during the hippie movement of the 1960s, with its tendency to question and relinquish a materialistic way of life. Although the number of Western Hindus remained relatively small, practices such as yoga and meditation were gradually assimilated into society, although often stripped of all religious and ascetic trimmings. Such practices were often associated with a broad, inclusive and liberal spirituality. At the same time, on the opposite side of the spectrum, Hinduism was increasingly politicized.

Above Hare Krishna devotees chant and dance in Boston in 1969, when Hindu thought was popular among the youth counter-culture.

INDIAN POLITICS

India's first Prime Minister, Jawaharlal Nehru, was succeeded in 1964 by Lal Bahadur Shastri, and two years later by Nehru's daughter, Indira Gandhi. In 1984, during her second term of office, Sikhs lobbied for their own state in the Punjab and militants entrenched themselves within their most holy site, the Golden Temple in Amritsar. Government troops stormed the complex, killing many Sikhs and outraging their community. Shortly afterward, Gandhi was assassinated by Sikh members of her personal bodyguard. Bloody retaliation further strained the previously cordial relationship between Sikhs and Hindus. Tensions also continued between Hindus and Muslims – and, in 1992, Hindus demolished the Babri Mosque in Ayodhya, provocatively built over Rama's birthplace. In the south, especially Kerala, conflict has repeatedly erupted over attempts to convert Hindus to Christianity, and over counter-measures to bring converts back to the Hindu fold.

HINDU IDENTITY

For Hindus, global contact with other faiths and cultures raised fresh questions over their identity. The very notion of Hinduism as a single religion appears relatively recent. Hindu nationalists claim otherwise, advocating that Hinduism, as a unified and cohesive religion, has long been inseparable from India, her people and her governance. Whilst nationalism advertises India as a Hindu country, an alternative current of thought promotes the universality of Hinduism, transcending sectarian borders.

The Hindu community is faced with many trying questions. Are hierarchical worldviews relevant to life today? Are caste and varnashrama now outdated? Should Hindu women play identical roles to men? Can Hindus, in good conscience, embrace embryonic and genetic research? How do the Hindu ideals of chivalrous kingship relate to terrorism, contemporary warfare and democratic leadership?

For many Hindus, their beliefs and practices remain a source of personal inspiration. Hindu texts almost unanimously agree that without inner tranquillity, human society seldom finds peace, prosperity and fulfilment, despite social and scientific progress. In trying to adapt its ancient wisdom to a quickly changing world, Hinduism faces many hurdles, and yet remains a vibrant, evolving and enriching tradition. Its enduring values, based on service, sustainability and the spiritual equality of all beings, may positively contribute to the key issues and debates of the contemporary world.

Below Indian Prime Minister Indira Gandhi, just months before her assassination in 1984, which exacerbated discord between Sikhs and Hindus.

CHAPTER 2

HOLY TEXTS

Many people are familiar with the Hindu book called the Bhagavad-gita, which relates a battlefield dialogue between Lord Krishna and his friend, Prince Arjuna. All the teachings of Hinduism were originally disseminated orally, and only later written down. Some traditions maintain that oral recitation constitutes the only legitimate mode of transmission.

The original Hindu canon is therefore called Shruti, 'that which is heard'. It consists largely of the four Vedas and their philosophical sub-sections called the Upanishads. These core texts are supplemented by a second category, which make the core texts more accessible. This category is called Smriti, 'that which is remembered'. A third category of texts, called Tantra, has variously been assimilated into both sections of Vedic literature, though the status of some texts remains disputed.

Most texts were originally taught in Sanskrit, and some draw primarily from ancient Tamil literature. For practical purposes today, the Bhagavad-gita is most important for understanding Hinduism's main philosophical concepts. As with most Vedic texts, it has been translated into hundreds of vernacular languages and usually includes a distinctive commentary by the author.

Opposite Hindu teachings are traditionally transmitted orally. In this Mughal miniature, Shukadeva narrates the Bhagavat Purana to King Parikshit and a group of sadhus.

Above A priest reads holy texts in Mathura, an ancient city of learning in the north Indian state of Uttar Pradesh.

PHILOSOPHY AND THEOLOGY

FOR REGULATING PRACTICE RATHER THAN BELIEF, HINDUISM IS
CALLED 'A WAY OF LIFE'. DESPITE THIS, IT RIGOROUSLY ENGAGES WITH
THEORY THROUGH MANY BRANCHES OF PHILOSOPHY AND THEOLOGY.

Hinduism has little experience of the schism between faith and reason that has typified Western intellectual history. Its religious life has tended toward reflection, and its philosophy toward practical application, especially the pursuit of liberation. Leaders rarely exhort followers to declare allegiance to a particular faith or creed. Indeed, Hindu texts define religion distinctively, as a process of knowledge. They explore moral issues largely in terms of 'knowledge versus ignorance', indicating a particular slant on the causes of good and evil. Above superficial belief, or even a sound intellectual understanding, Hinduism stresses the importance of direct experience, through self- and God-realization.

Many Hindus call their tradition 'Sanatana Dharma', the eternal order. The truths regarding the universal law were divinely revealed to ancient sages and for many aeons were transmitted orally. They were first written down much later, apparently around the start of the Kali-yuga, when human memory began to deteriorate. A sage called Vyasa (Badarayana) is generally accredited with writing many core texts, such as the Upanishads, Vedanta Sutras and the Mahabharata. Such books are presented today with extensive commentaries to help the reader grasp their real meaning.

As Hinduism developed, it did not reject its parent traditions, but modified and assimilated them into newer schools of thought. For example, the ancient Vedic notion of sacrifice, and the later philosophies of Sankhya and Yoga, have all been assimilated into the more recent school of Vedanta. Even the more exclusive lineages do not entirely reject 'other doctrines', but claim

Above A brass murti of the great theologian called Ramanuja.

they demonstrate inferior understanding or are suitable for less spiritually mature practitioners.

THE SIX DARSHANAS
Despite a relatively inclusive approach, Hinduism has rejected doctrines that fail to acknowledge its scriptural authority. These include Jainism, Buddhism and the hedonistic philosophy of Charvaka. They are called 'nastika', differentiating them from the orthodox, 'astika' schools. However, 'Veda' literally means 'knowledge'. This generic meaning justifies the acceptance and assimilation of

Below A scene from the Mahabharata, with text written in Sanskrit. Story, rather than abstract philosophy, has helped transmit much popular Hinduism.

HIGH AND LOW TRADITIONS

Textual scholarship is largely the preserve of the 'high', brahmin-led traditions. Much popular, village Hinduism engages little with philosophy, but is transmitted largely through custom and ritual.

There is a similar disparity between Hindu ideals and reality. Abortion is formally disapproved of but widely practised. The ideal of spiritual equality is advertised, but discredited by caste practice. However, these dichotomies do not imply that popular Hinduism is simply a degenerate form of the higher textual traditions; degeneracy may occur at any level, as illustrated by those brahmins who have taught and exploited a rigid caste-consciousness.

There has long been significant interplay between popular Hinduism and its high, Sanskrit-based traditions. Minor gods and goddesses are often elevated by reinforcing links to major deities. Villagers and everyday, working Hindus have, in some places, long been conversant with Hindu texts. Although Hinduism is 'a way of life', the impact of its philosophy and theology is pervasive.

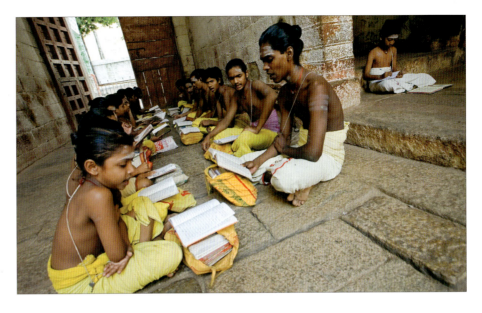

auxiliary texts, such as the Tantras, if they support the Vedic conclusions. Hinduism recognizes that no one tradition, including its own, has a monopoly on spiritual truth.

There are six main astika systems, called Darshanas ('ways of seeing'). Although they are distinctive 'schools of thought', they are also complementary, representing different perspectives on identical truths. The various groups and sub-groups within Hinduism usually subscribe to one or more of the Six Darshanas. They are grouped as three pairs, or 'sisters'. Within each pair,

one deals with theory and the other with the attendant practice and methodology. In this way, Sankhya forms the doctrinal basis for the discipline of Yoga; the atomic theory called Vaisheshika is grasped through Nyaya, logical debate; and Vedanta is the philosophy paired with the practice of ritual sacrifice. In reality though, the last pair have often locked horns, arguing for the supremacy of their respective practices and philosophies.

The precise age of the Six Darshanas is uncertain, though they date back at least to the Gupta period (240–550CE). Some groups consider them to be sequential, often with Vedanta as the culmination,

Above Students at a brahmin school, near Madurai in Tamil Nadu. The brahmin varna (class) was responsible for scriptural study and religious scholarship.

either chronologically or in terms of theological status. This is suggested by the fact that Vedanta means 'the end of the Vedas' or, less literally, 'the crown of knowledge'. Certainly, Vedanta today represents the more scholarly strands of Hinduism, and forms the doctrinal basis for most contemporary traditions.

Below Tree shrine dedicated to Kali in Andhra Pradesh, southern India. Much village practice shows little concern for Hindu scholarship.

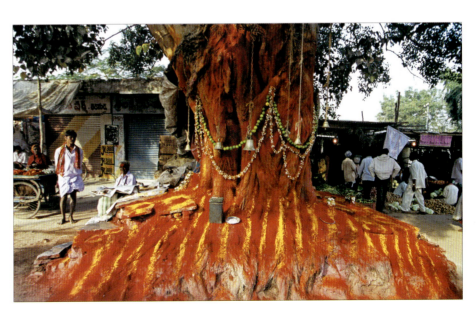

VAISHESHIKA AND NYAYA

HINDUISM'S RATIONAL APPROACH TO FAITH IS EXEMPLIFIED BY NYAYA – THE DISCIPLINE OF LOGICAL DEBATE. ITS 'SISTER' DARSHANA, VAISHESHIKA, RESEMBLES ONE SCHOOL OF GREEK PHILOSOPHY.

Vaisheshika falls within the broad philosophy called 'atomism' and was founded around 600BCE by a sage called Kanada. Legend states that he subsisted by collecting particles of grain (kana) scattered by the harvest, and earned the name Kanabhuk, 'atom-eater'. He compiled the treatise called Vaisheshika Sutra, on which several commentaries were later written. Around the 11th century, Vaisheshika was closely associated with its 'sister school', Nyaya or 'the school of logic', but by the 15th century their combined influence had waned. In modern Hinduism, Nyaya forms the epistemological basis for rationale and

Below Hindu scholars consulting texts. Although Hinduism values logic and human rationale, it also endorses scriptural authority.

philosophical thinking. Vaisheshika is relatively obscure, though modern Vedanta has adopted elements, such as its system for dividing and measuring time based on the movement of atomic particles.

VAISHESHIKA PHILOSOPHY

Similar to the Greeks, Kanada describes the elements, their characteristics and their interrelations. He classified all perceivable objects into six categories, to which a seventh category was later added. He propounded that all physical objects are reducible to a finite number of atoms and also postulated the existence of molecules. However, his philosophy is not a type of materialism, for he infers the existence of the eternal *atman*. To do this, however, he propounds a purely philosophical approach, accepting as

Above An 18th-century bust of the Greek philosopher Democritus, who taught a form of atomism.

valid only two sources of evidence, namely pratyaksha and anumana (empiricism and rationalism).

Despite a philosophical approach, Kanada endorses dharma as a means toward liberation, and prescribes traditional practices such as fasting, celibacy, and service to the guru. He further teaches that since all material objects are constructed from atoms, they are products, with the minute atoms themselves as causes. By introducing the principle of 'adrishta', a further, unknown and invisible cause, he opened the door for theistic doctrines, which proposed God as the remote and single cause of everything; he who orchestrates the innumerable atoms.

NYAYA

The school of logic known as Nyaya traces its origins to the disputations of Vedic scholars who cultivated debate as a sophisticated art, using the Upanishad as texts and developing notions of logical proof. The school of logic was more formally established by Akshapada Gautama. Born in the Himalayas around the

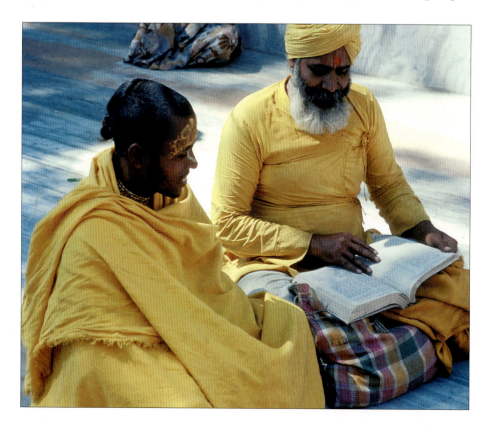

4th century BCE and systematized logic through books called the Nyaya Sutra. Thereafter, the school of Nyaya defined logic as a spiritual discipline aimed at apprehending truth and undermining the dishonest arguments that ensnare the soul.

The Navya-Nyaya (New School of Logic) developed from the 12th century and specialized in epistemology. As with Vaisheshika, it too accepted the need for sensory knowledge and inference, but added two further sources of evidence, namely *upamana* (analogy) and *shabda* ('sound' or scriptural testimony). Nyaya has also developed a sophisticated syllogism with five stages, rather like the three proposed by Aristotle. Distinctively, Nyaya texts philosophically argue for the existence of Ishvara (God), and many popular theistic schools still use its rationale arguments. Of the six Hindu systems, Nyaya enjoys the greatest respect from Western philosophers.

A FAMOUS DEBATE

One famous debate involved a young boy destined to become the great scholar called Yamunacharya. The contest took place between Yamuna and the king's proud chief advisor, Kolahala. The king and

queen were present and the queen favoured the young boy. The king confidently promised his wife that should Yamuna win, the boy would receive half the kingdom.

Yamuna put forward three statements and challenged his opponent to disprove them. He declared, 'First, your mother is not a barren woman: second, the king is supremely righteous: third, the queen is a model of chastity and faithfulness. Refute these if you can!'

Seeing the invitation to deny his own existence and to insult the king and queen, Kolahala squirmed in embarrassment and was stunned into silence. Visibly ruffled, he could only insist, as was formally required, that the boy refute his own propositions.

Yamuna calmly responded. 'The Manu Smriti states that one son is no son at all. You have no siblings and, therefore, in the eyes of scripture, your mother was barren.

Left Vaisheshika philosophy considers the atomic particle the absolute, indivisible truth.

Above Thousands of years ago, Sage Shukadeva instructed King Parikshit and a gathering of holy men. Discussion and debate are valued even outside the specific school of Nyaya (logic).

With regard for my second statement, the king accepts one sixth of his citizen's karma. In this materialistic age of Kali, people are more inclined to sin than piety. So the king, despite his own flawless character, is bearing a heavy burden of unrighteousness. As for the queen's chastity, holy texts applaud the monarch as the embodiment of all the demigods. Since the queen is also married to Indra, Agni, and Surya, how can she be called chaste?

As the court erupted in applause, Kolahala hung his head in shame. Yamuna won half the kingdom, but later renounced it for spiritual life, becoming the grand-guru of the famous theologian Ramanuja. The story teaches how logical thought is enhanced by humility and by knowledge derived from scriptural sources.

SANKHYA AND YOGA

THE OLDEST OF THE SIX DARSHANAS, SANKHYA, IS THE PHILOSOPHICAL FRAMEWORK UNDERPINNING THE PRACTICE OF YOGA, WHICH IS ESPECIALLY POPULAR AMONG THE ASCETIC, SHRAMANA TRADITIONS.

Sankhya is attributed to the sage Kapila who lived around 700 BCE. Some scholars claim that there were two Kapilas, teaching theistic and non-theistic versions of the same doctrine. Sankhya is a system of metaphysics based upon a subtle and sophisticated analysis of causation. To modern Hindu thought, Sankhya contributes the notion of individual agency, by which the soul creates its unique destiny by generating successive material bodies. By reversing this process, by sequentially peeling away layers of material coverings, the practice of Yoga aims to reveal the real, eternal self.

SANKHYA

The term Sankhya means 'number' or 'to count', and refers to a philosophical system of analysing matter. It aims to overcome suffering through discernment, thus releasing the soul, called the enjoyer (purusha), from its entanglement in matter (praktiti). It is highly dualistic,

based on apprehending the difference between spirit (Brahman) and matter (prakriti).

Sankhya was originally non-theistic, classifying 24 material 'truths' or elements. The soul became the 25th element. Theistic schools later added a 26th element called the parama-purusha, the 'supreme-enjoyer' (God). The later Tantric notion of Shiva-Shakti is similar to the purusha-prakriti model. Shiva is the male, the energetic, and Shakti the complementary female energy. The Vedanta schools, through texts such as the Bhagavad-gita, also assimilated many of the terms and concepts of Sankhya. A particularly important contribution is the idea of three gunas, the material qualities that permeate and regulate matter.

Significantly, Sakhya's framework applies to both the structure of the universe and the psycho-physical form of the living being. For both cosmos and creature, creation begins with the subtle and proceeds to the gross. This reveals the agency

Above A sadhu (Indian holy man) performing hatha-yoga outdoors in India. Sadhus followsa strict, regulated lifestyle, free of sensual distraction.

that spirit exhibits over matter. For the soul (atman), the first causal layer is false ego – 'identification with matter' – followed by intelligence, and thereafter mind. Mind generates ether, the first and finest of the five gross elements. The other four elements are generated in turn, culminating in earth. Each of the five gross elements has a corresponding perceptive sense and a sense-object; additionally, there are five 'working senses' or instruments of action.

Below A woman sits in a meditative pose at a yoga school in the USA, where the practice is adopted mainly for health and relaxation.

THE EIGHT STEPS OF YOGA

Astanga-yoga means the yoga of eight 'limbs' or steps, which are progressive and culminate in samadhi ('fixed-mind'), the final stage of yoga when the mind is focused on one point:

Yama – restraints and prohibitions
Niyama – positive observances
Asana – physical postures
Pranayama – regulation of breath
Pratyahara – sensory withdrawal
Dharana – concentration
Dhyana – meditation
Samadhi – complete absorption

Above Sage Kapila instructing his mother in Sankhya philosophy, which underpins traditional yoga practice.

THE 24 ELEMENTS OF SANKHYA PHILOSOPHY

1 Pradhana — The Pradhana is the unmanifest three gunas (goodness, passion and ignorance).

Three Subtle Elements The three subtle elements constitute the subtle (astral) body, and the five gross elements
2 False-ego — constitute the outward body. They are listed here in order from subtle to gross. The living
3 Intelligence — being has five knowledge-acquiring senses and five working senses, each of which
4 Mind — corresponds to one of the five elements and the corresponding sense-objects.

Five Gross Elements	Five Sense Objects	Five Perceptive Senses	Five Working Senses
5 Ether	10 Sound	15 Ear	20 Voice
6 Air	11 Touch	16 Skin	21 Legs
7 Fire	12 Sight	17 Eye	22 Arms
8 Water	13 Taste	18 Tongue	23 Reproductive organs
9 Earth	14 Smell	19 Nose	24 Evacuating organs

ASTANGA-YOGA

Yoga, the discipline of meditation, is intimately linked to Sankhya. It is also termed 'raja-yoga', indicating its perceived pre-eminence as 'the king of yogas', or 'Patanjali-yoga', after its founder. Sage Patanjali is considered an incarnation of Shesha, Vishnu's celestial serpent, and probably lived around the 2nd century BCE. His texts, the Patanjali Sutras, consist of 194 aphorisms divided into four padas (sections): samadhi (trance), sadhana (practice), vibhuti (mystic powers) and kaivalya (oneness), the ultimate aim.

The process itself is divided into eight limbs or 'angas'. Although popular hatha-yoga is related to astanga-yoga, the exercises in Patanjali's system are designed not for physical health, but to facilitate meditation and self-realization. Hatha-yoga enables the yogi to sit comfortably, without strain or slumber, and to exercise control over the breath. Patanjali warns the yogi not to be allured by the eight mystic siddhis (perfections), such as the ability to become 'smaller than the smallest' or to materialize objects from distant places. Rather, the yogi should remain fixed on the goal of directly discerning the eternal self, consistent with Sankhya philosophy.

Additionally, the yogi should purge himself of base qualities, such as lust, greed and anger, and develop complete mastery over mind and senses. Patanjali also recommends scriptural study and surrender to the Lord, which bestow peace, illumination and samadhi. *Kaivalya* refers to the realization that one is not the body but the soul within. It is achieved when the yogi is fixed in meditation on God within and no longer influenced by the prompting of the three gunas (material qualities). Many principles of Yoga and Sankhya have been integrated into popular theistic and devotional Hinduism.

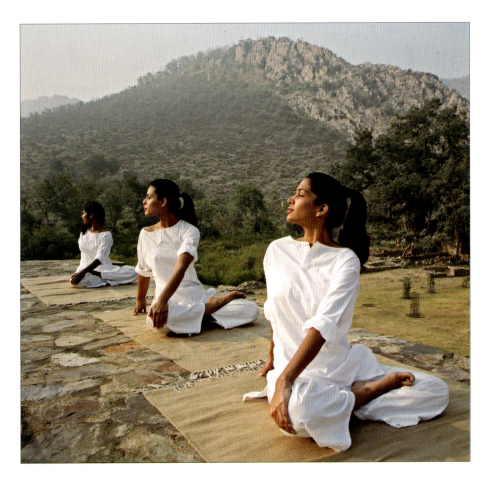

Right Women practising yoga in the ruins of Bhangarh, a city built by the Jaipur royal family in the 1500s.

MIMAMSA AND VEDANTA

THESE SISTER SCHOOLS ARE ALSO CALLED PURVA MIMAMSA (EARLY INQUIRY) AND UTTARA MIMAMSA (LATER INQUIRY). VEDANTA REPRESENTS MUCH CONTEMPORARY HINDU THOUGHT.

Above Mimamsa stresses adherence to duty (dharma) and the brahmin-led performance of ritual, especially the fire sacrifice, conducted here in Oxford, UK.

Mimamsa and Vedanta correspond to two main classifications within the Vedas, namely the karma-kanda (action section) and the jnana-kanda (knowledge section). They deal respectively with ritual and philosophy, and the corresponding concepts of dharma (duty) and Brahman (the absolute reality). Purva Mimamsa is largely associated with the early Vedic period and the brahmin-led, householder and sacrificial traditions intent on worldly and celestial enjoyment. Vedanta developed later, both as a complementary school and a counter-movement, stressing puja (worship), mysticism and liberation though renunciation. Vedanta had a pervasive influence on the intellectual and religious life of India, and remains the most prestigious school.

Below A boy studies the Upanishads, the section of the Vedas teaching Vedanta philosophy.

MIMAMSA

'Investigation' or Mimamsa is the earliest of the six darshanas, providing the ideas behind Vedic sacrifice and the first rules for textual interpretation. The inaugural text, the Mimamsa-sutra, is attributed to Rishi Jaimini, who lived around the 4th century BCE as the disciple of Vyasa, author of the Mahabharata. Jaimini's inaugural teachings were developed by a long line of commentators; first, Sabara (*c.*150CE), and then, around the 8th century, Kumarila Bhatta and Prabhakara Mishra. From 400 until 900CE, the school dominated Hindu thought.

Mimamsa explored the interpretation and explanation of scripture, it also fostered the study of philology, the philosophy of language. It also spawned theories of 'sacred sound', first consolidated by Bhartrihari, the 7th-century Sanskrit grammarian. Mimamsa is largely atheistic, or at least agnostic. It demanded diligent, almost mechanistic practice and the perfect intonation of mantras (incantations), with little emphasis on the underlying mood or attitude. To achieve happiness, it advocated the unfailing success of properly executed dharma (duty), rather than divine intervention by an independent, benevolent God.

From the turn of the first millennium, scholars such as Bopadeva developed theistic stands of Mimamsa, but the darshana was gradually eclipsed by the burgeoning school of Vedanta. Today two traditions survive; the Bhattas and the Prabhakaras, following Kumarila Bhatta and Prabhakara Mishra respectively. Much modern Hinduism has retained Mimamsa prayers, and rituals like the fire sacrifice, usually assimilating them within a theistic, Vedantic framework.

VEDANTA

The later Mimamsa school is usually called Vedanta, meaning either 'the end of knowledge', referring to its later development, or 'the crown of knowledge', indicating its perceived superiority. It expounds upon the Vedic notion of Brahman (the absolute) and derives philosophical impetus from the Upanishads and Vedanta Sutras. Vedanta philosophy is accredited to the sage and author Vyasa who traditionally goes back to the Mahabharata era. Vedanta came to the fore with Shankara (780–812CE), who revitalized interest in the Vedas and hastened the decline of Buddhism within southern Asia. For Shankara, spiritual liberation was achieved not by ritual action but by knowledge.

Vedantic schools revere scripture, or 'shabda', as the most authentic form of evidence (pramana). Sensory perception (pratyaksha) and logical inference (anumana) are also accepted but, being fallible, are accountable to scriptural standards. While recognizing limitations to the mind and senses, Vedanta asserts the eternal self's capacity, once enlightened, to perceive spirit. By controlling and purifying the mind and senses, the boundaries of perception can be extended to embrace the spiritual.

To be accepted as a genuine Vedantic school, a lineage must present commentaries on three scriptures: the Upanishads, the Vedanta Sutras and the Bhagavadgita, collectively called the 'prasthana trayi'. Some books list ten authentic

Below Vivekananda sitting in meditation. He pursued the advaita school of Vedanta, teaching about an impersonal Supreme.

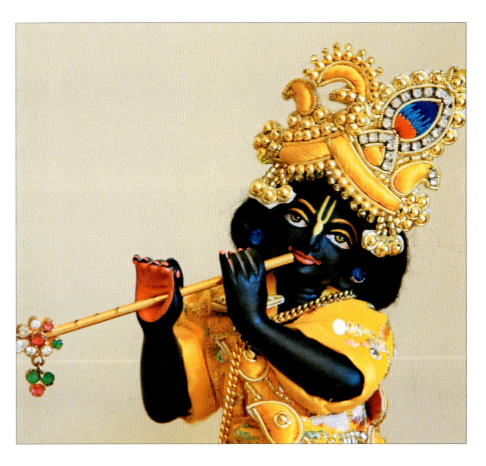

Above Some schools of Vedanta favour a personal God. Madhva (1197–1276) taught a dualistic philosophy and the worship of Krishna, who is shown here.

schools of Vedanta. After Shankara's 'monism', most important were the theologies of Ramanuja ('qualified monism') and Madhva ('pure dualism'). Ramanuja (1017–1137) qualified Shankara's monism, holding that salvation is attained neither though ritual nor knowledge, but devotion (bhakti) to a personal God. More firmly than Ramanuja before him, Madhva (1197–1276) contested Shakara's monism by asserting rigid and permanent distinctions between the self, God and matter.

MODERN VEDANTA

Well into the 20th century, many commentators saw Shankara's monistic doctrine as the epitome of Indian intellectual achievement. They thought Advaita synonymous with Vedanta. Recent awareness of devotional scholarship has promoted interest in alternative, theistic perspectives and recognition of those branches of Vedanta advocating a personal Supreme. Many of the large global movements, such as ISKCON

(the Hare Krishna Movement), the Swaminarayana lineages and the Ramakrishna Mission draw from Vedanta philosophy.

Vedanta is most favoured by two communities: Vaishnavism and Shankara's Advaita branch of the Smarta tradition. Amongs Shaivas, Vedanta is less central, though still intimately linked to the Shaiva Siddhanta traditions through a theologian called Shrikantha. For Shaktas, Vedanta is even less relevant, although Vivekananda attempted to establish links through his 'neo-Vedanta' adaptation of Shankara's Advaita. However, some forms of Advaita, such as Kashmiri Shaivism, are not forms of Vedanta but derive from Tantric texts. Even so, Vedanta dominates modern Hindu thought, and it has absorbed many ideas from the other Darshanas.

THE MAIN SACRED TEXTS

FOR MANY HINDUS, THE CORE OF THEIR TRADITION IS LOCATED WITHIN SPECIFIC HOLY TEXTS, THE VEDAS AND THEIR SUPPLEMENTS. DISTINCTIVE TO HINDUISM IS THE VAST NUMBER OF TEXTS.

The concept of Hinduism as a single monolithic religion is recent, dating back only to the 19th century. Hence, any definition of Hinduism remains somewhat arbitrary and provisional. Some followers prefer the alternative name, 'Vaidika Dharma', referring to those who follow the teachings outlined in the Vedas. These sacred books are certainly pivotal, and along with their corollary texts are collectively called 'the Vedic literature'.

SHRUTI AND SMRITI

The Vedic literature is divided into two main parts, called the Shruti ('that which has been heard') and the Smriti ('that which has been remembered'). Shruti, comprised of the four Vedas, connotes revealed, infallible and eternal truth. On the other hand, Smriti is supplementary, changes over time, and is authorized for conforming to the bedrock of truth found in Shruti. There are different opinions about the relative importance of each. Some Hindus stress the canonical importance of Shruti, whereas others consider Smriti equally important for making abstract truths more accessible.

The word Veda literally means 'knowledge'. The connotation of universal Truth, in contrast to exclusive belief, implies that any teaching consistent with the Veda may be accepted as 'Veda', legitimate knowledge. Hence, numerous writings have been assimilated into the Smriti, including vernacular works whose prominence is limited to a specific tradition or geographical region. A third block of literature,

Above The Shruti and Smriti were first transmitted orally and later also in writing, mainly in the Devanagari characters of Sanskrit, as in this late 19th-century scroll.

called Tantra, has its original source beyond Shruti and Smriti, but is accepted for its broad resonance with Vedic conclusions. Although many Tantras (also called Agamas) have been widely incorporated into the Vedic canon, the status and legitimacy of some remain contested.

DIVISIONS OF CONTENT

The content of texts, specifically the Shruti, is divided into two main divisions, namely karma-kanda, dealing with world-affirming ritual, and jnana-kanda, philosophical texts aimed at knowledge through world abnegation. Some traditions add a third category called upasana-kanda, denoting the worship section and, for some, a view that the world should be neither wholeheartedly embraced nor rigidly renounced.

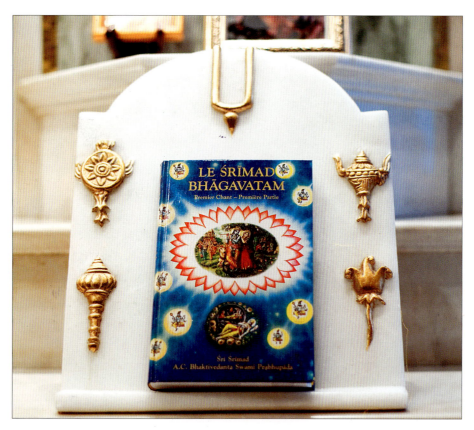

Left Late 20th-century French version of the Bhagavat Purana, part of the Smriti, venerated on a shrine at a Belgian theological college.

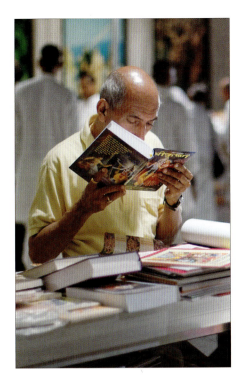

Above Texts are used for personal study. Here an Indian man inspects a volume at a temple bookshop.

The three sections correlate to the paths of karma (action), jnana (knowledge) and bhakti (devotion). Metaphorically, in relation to the human form, karma-kanda represents the limbs, jnana-kanda the head and upasana-kanda the heart. Philosophical debates most often revolve around the precise relationship between head and heart, and the relative roles of knowledge and devotion.

LANGUAGE

Early texts were written in classical Sanskrit, which translates as 'the most refined language'. The script itself is termed 'devanagari', signifying an exalted language spoken in 'the cities of the gods'. Sanskrit has often been the preserve of the learned, brahminical class, and ordinary folk spoke a variety of Prakrits, or 'natural languages', featuring Sanskrit roots but a simplified grammar. The non-Vedic, non-orthodox movements, such as Jainism and Buddhism, adopted Prakrits as their own sacred languages.

In parts of South India, Tamil has achieved a similar status to Sanskrit as a sacred language. Some lineages, particularly the Shri Vaishnavas, have amalgamated both linguistic traditions. Many subsidiary texts, particularly those by medieval bhakti writers, were written in local vernaculars, such as Avanti, Gujarati, Bengali, Telegu and Kannada. They are still used today. Many texts have been translated into non-Indian tongues, and there are continuing debates over how important a primary language is to the authentic transmission of Hindu teachings.

HOW TEXTS ARE USED

Ancient texts were transmitted orally and later written on leaves, such as palm. Today, printed and bound books are sturdier but still treated with great respect. They are never placed directly on the floor or touched with the feet or grubby hands, and may be wrapped in silk. Prayers are often recited before their use in public recitation, scholarly study and religious discourse (pravachana). They may be consulted on matters of spiritual and secular law. Today, the philosophically abstruse Vedas are studied mainly by scholars, whereas the Smriti texts are more widely used.

Below Scriptural verses identify a theme for religious lectures, as delivered by this sadhu at the BAPS Swaminarayana Temple in Neasden, London.

MAIN SHRUTI TEXTS	MAIN SMRITI TEXTS
The Four Vedas: 1 Rig Veda 2 Yajur Veda 3 Sama Vada 4 Atharva Veda	**The Vedanta Sutra** (codes of philosophy, the essence of Hindu theology) **The Two Epics** (or Itihasas, 'histories') (a) the Ramayana ('the journey of Rama', the shorter of the two epics) (b) the Mahabharata ('the history of Greater India', the longest known poem)
The 108 Upanishads (philosophical texts)	**The Bhagavad-gita** (philosophical part of the Mahabharata) **The Puranas** (literally 'very old', story and 'myth')
The Six Vedangas (skills to study/apply the Vedas)	**The Dharma Shastra** (law books and moral codes)

THE VEDAS AND UPANISHADS

THE FOUR VEDAS ARE PERHAPS THE OLDEST HINDU TEXTS. THE UPANISHADS ARE KEY SECTIONS DEALING WITH VEDANTA PHILOSOPHY BASED ON THE CORE NOTION OF AN ABSOLUTE REALITY.

The Vedas were compiled over an extended period beginning about 2,500 years ago, though the tradition often considers them older. Pinning down dates is problematic, for two main reasons.

First, the teachings were originally conveyed orally and only later written and re-written over extended periods, and by several authors. Second, there are different opinions, especially between Western academics and Hindus themselves. Adherents propound earlier dates and some teach that the Shruti should be heard only and never transmitted in written form. Tradition suggests that there was originally one Vedic lore, subse-

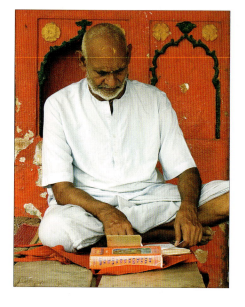

Above In front of his small shrine, a priest reads a modern translation of the four Vedas.

quently divided into the four Vedas. Western scholars consider the Rig Veda the oldest.

THE FOUR VEDAS

The Rig Veda is certainly the most important of the Vedas. Divided into ten books, or 'mandalas', it includes 1,028 hymns in praise of 'the Vedic' deities such as Indra, Agni, Rudra, Vishnu, and Varuna. It contains two central Hindu prayers: the famous Gayatri mantra, chanted thrice daily by brahmins, and the Purusha Shukta, narrating the story of creation from the purusha, the 'cosmic man' later associated with Vishnu.

The Yajur Veda is a handbook for priests in their performance of yajnas (sacrifices) and has two parts: the earlier 'black' section and the later 'white' section. The Sama Veda consists of chants and melodies for use during *yajna*. Unlike the former three Vedas, the Atharva Veda deals little with sacrifice, but contains hymns and incantations for protection from evil, achievement of life's various aims, and performance of rites of passage.

FOUR SECTIONS

Within each of the four books there are four types of composition. Some claim that only the first represents the 'true Vedas'. The first two divisions comprise the karma-kanda (ritual section) and relate to the performance of the sacrifices at the heart of the Mimamsa school. The second pair correspond to the jnana-kanda (the knowledge section), expounding the philosophy dear to the Vedanta schools. Some writers have suggested that the four sections, moving progressively toward detachment, correspond to the four ashramas, namely student life, household life, retirement and renunciation of the world.

UPANISHADS

The word Upanishad, 'sitting near', alludes to ancient tutorials in which students humbly sat at the guru's feet.

Below The Jagadambi Temple at Khadjuraho, built on architectural principles outlined in the Upavedas, specifically the Shilpa-veda.

FOUR SECTIONS

1 **The Samhitas** are literally 'collections', in this case of hymns and mantras.

2 **The Brahmanas** are manuals of ritual and prayer for priests, and they include early versions of traditional stories.

3 **The Aranyakas**, literally 'forest books', are philosophical treatises for hermits and saints.

4 **The Upanishads** are philosophical texts associated with Vedanta, 'the crown of the Vedas'.

Often considered the start of direct spiritual instruction, the Upanishads outline core teachings about the atman, reincarnation, karma and liberation. The traditional number is 108, though there are far more, including many of recent origin. However, 13 are considered principal. Of particular importance is the Svetashvatara Upanishad,

Below A painting used for the cover of a popular version of one of the main Upanishads, the Shri Ishopanishad, which alludes to a personal Supreme.

which, for Shaiva traditions, has attained a canonical status similar to the Bhagavad-gita. Although the Gita is technically part of the Smriti, for its eminence as a philosophical text it has been alternatively named the Gitopanishad.

VEDANTA SUTRAS

The word sutra literally means 'thread', referring to a code or aphorism that can be unwound indefinitely to reveal layer upon layer of truth. Using such codes, many voluminous texts on diverse topics were condensed into smaller books, also called sutras. They include the Dharma Sutras, summarizing religious and secular law, the Shrauta Sutras dealing with public sacrifice, and the Grihya Sutras, providing a summary of domestic rites. Most important, though, are the philosophical 'Vedanta Sutras'.

Sage Vyasa wrote the Vedanta Sutras, or the Brahma Sutras, to systematize the diverse teachings strewn throughout the Upanishads. Unlike the Upanishads, they belong to the Smriti. However, within Vedanta, they are attributed to a unique, third section called Nyaya (logic), thus creating the prashthan trayi (three canonical texts). The Upanishads are Shruti, the Bhagavad-gita is Smriti, and the

Above Students at a Gujarat school listen to their guru, Rameshbai Oza, who sits on the traditional and honorific raised seat. Upanishad literally means 'sitting near'.

Brahma Sutras are Nyaya. Various scholars wrote lengthy commentaries on these three to establish the different schools of Vedanta. However, because people are less philosophically adept in the modern age, the Upanishads and Vedanta Sutra are often inaccessible without the guidance of the Smriti literature, which includes history, story and myth, and moral guidelines.

BOOKS CLOSELY CONNECTED TO THE VEDAS

There are two important bodies of supplementary literature closely related to the Vedas, but considered Smriti. The Vedangas teach the sciences and skills required to understand and apply the Vedas. The Upavedas deal with traditional arts and sciences.

The six Vedangas
('limbs of the Vedas')
1 Kalpa (ritual detail)
2 Siksha (pronunciation)
3 Vyakarana (grammar)
4 Nirukti (etymology)
5 Chandas (metre)
6 Jyotisha (astronomy/astrology)

The four Upavedas
('following the Vedas')
1 Ayur-veda (medicine)
2 Gandharva-veda (music and dance)
3 Dhanur-veda (warfare)
4 Shilpa-veda (architecture)

SOUTH INDIAN LITERARY TRADITIONS

IN INDIA, THE NORTHERN AND SOUTHERN CULTURES AND TRADITIONS ARE SOMEWHAT DIFFERENT. SOUTH INDIANS ARE CALLED DRAVIDIANS, DIFFERENTIATING THEM FROM THE NORTHERN ARYANS.

Southern India has been less prone to invasion, occupation and assimilation of foreign influence. Differences with the north extend to linguistic, textual and scholarly heritages. As Sanskrit is widely considered a sacred language, Tamil has acquired a similar status in the south. Tamil texts can wield authority equal to the Vedas. Other southern languages, widely used for translating standard texts, have been less influential.

THE SANGAM LITERATURE

Tamil literature goes back to the remote past and three ancient assemblies (Sangams) of poets and scholars. Legend suggests that the earliest conventions were attended by deities such as Shiva and Murugan, and were based at Madurai or, according to some accounts, a fabled continent later swallowed by the sea. The earliest surviving Sangam literature dates from between 300BCE and 200CE. Its themes are largely secular and world-affirming, comparing the various human emotions to lush forest, towering mountains and other features of the luxuriant South Indian landscape.

DEVOTIONAL TEXTS

The rich aesthetic themes continued in the copious outpourings of the Alvars and Nayanmars, the devotional poets of the first millennium CE. The Nayanmar hymns dedicated to Shiva comprise a 12-book anthology called the Thirumurai. It includes a treatise on yoga by Rishi Thirumular. The hymns of the first seven books, collectively called the Thevaram, were set to music and remain part of contemporary temple liturgy. Legend holds that the abandoned Thirumurai texts were discovered by

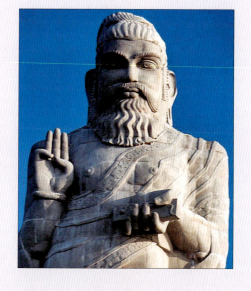

Above The giant statue of Saint Valluvar. His three raised fingers symbolize the key texts he wrote.

the Chola king, Rajaraja the First (r. 985–1014CE) and subsequently classified by a scholar named Nampi.

A further core text is the Thirukural, three books written in couplets (kurals) by St Thiruvalluvar. The books correspond to the first three of the four aims of human life outlined in Sanskrit texts. The first book explores *aram*, similar to the Sanskrit 'dharma', meaning 'duty'; the second is on *porul* or in Sanskrit 'artha', meaning prosperity; and the third on *inbam*, in Sanskrit 'kama', indicating sensual pleasure. At the southern tip of India a 133-feet (40.5m) tall statue of Thiruvalluvar has been carved out of rock. His height symbolizes the 133 chapters in his text, and his three straight fingers denote the themes of aram, porul and inbam.

SYNTHESIZING TRADITIONS

Tradition credits Nathamuni with recovering the lost hymns of the Vaishnava saints, the 12 Alvars. Nathamuni arranged these songs in canonical form and revived the practice of reciting them before the temple deity. In South India, the 4,000 verses are called the Valayiram

Below Women carry water from the Tungabhadra River, Hampi. South Indian literature drew rich, sensual metaphor from the lush southern landscape.

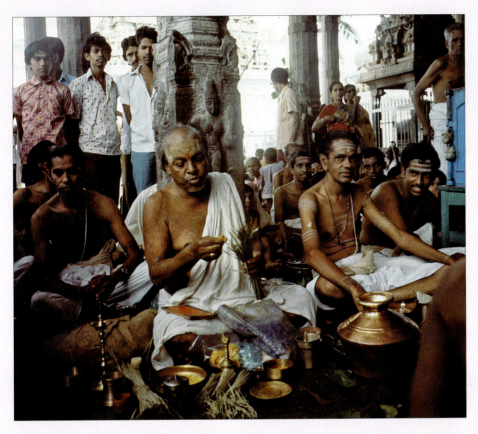

Above Brahmin priests, largely responsible for scholarship, officiate at a wedding in Kanchipuram.

('Four Thousand') in Tamil and the Divya Prabhandham ('Divine Composition') in Sanskrit. They are considered equal to the Vedas, and hence called 'the Dravidian Veda' or 'the Tamil Veda'. In many temples, the chanting of the Divya Prabhandham forms a major part of the daily service and the Shri Vaishnava tradition continues the recitation of both Tamil and Sanskrit texts.

After the collapse of the northern Gupta dynasty around 400CE, Hinduism's greatest strides were made in South India, hastening the decline of Jainism and Buddhism. The great theologian Shankara, who was born around 780CE, started the first important lineage of Vedanta philosophy, preaching Advaita or 'non-dualism'. Ramanuja (1017–1137CE) modified Shankara's doctrine to propose that God is ultimately a person. Ramanuja's

theology, infused with the sentiment of the Alvars, helped to fire the Vaishnava devotional traditions that engulfed India between 1200 and 1700CE. His theology may have significantly influenced southern Shaiva devotion, particularly the Shaiva Advaita school. Many of Hinduism's greatest theologians came from south India, contesting the ideas of Aryan, northern supremacy and of a rigid divide between the two cultures.

MEDIEVAL LITERATURE

Basavanna (1134–1196), born in what is now Karnataka state, rejected the brahmin hierarchy and started the first devotional movement, the Lingayats. During the same period, many 'sthala purana's (temple histories) were written, tracing the history of each religious building and its deity. There emerged several Tamil works in honour of specific deities, such as Murugan. However, not all texts honoured such deities. Kambhan wrote a Tamil version of the Ramayana, in which – some

claim – he reverses the values, glorifying the Dravidian hero Ravana pitted against the evil, invading Aryans led by Rama.

HINDUISM IN SRI LANKA

The Ramayana contains perhaps the earliest reference to Sri Lanka, off the south-eastern corner of India. It recounts the invasion of Ravana's kingdom by Rama's army of monkeys, setting a precedent for a history punctuated by coups, conquests and ethnic tension. Today, a declining 15 per cent of the populace are Hindu, mainly following folk customs such as fire-walking, animal sacrifice and possession by local gods, with minimal reference to scholarly traditions. Worship of minor deities, such as Kannaki, is often based on ancient and unique Tamil epics. Upper-class Tamils largely adhere to the Shaiva Siddhanta lineage. Their temples observe rituals based on the Sanskritized Agama (Tantric) texts, along with the recitation of Tamil hymns by specialized singers called Oduvar, representing further synthesis of southern and Sanskritic traditions.

Below A figure on the tower of a temple in Colombo. In Sri Lanka, Hinduism is represented mainly by South Indian folk tradition and the scholarly Shaiva Siddhanta lineage.

THE RAMAYANA

'THE JOURNEY OF RAMA', OR THE RAMAYANA, IS A SANSKRIT EPIC OF 24,000 VERSES. IT IS THE EARLIER AND SHORTER OF THE TWO HINDU EPIC POEMS: THE OTHER IS THE MAHABHARATA.

The Ramayana was compiled by the poet-sage Valmiki, who may have lived around the 4th century BCE. Tradition dates him far earlier. Scholars believe that the Valmiki Ramayana received its present shape as late as the 2nd century CE, though it contains much older material.

The text survives in many partial and complete manuscripts, the oldest dating from the 11th century CE. Though academics consider the Ramayana a mythical account, many Hindus consider Rama an historical figure, and date him back to the silver age, the Treta-yuga.

Above A modern painting of Rama, Sita and Lakshmana after Rama's banishment to the Dandakaranya forest.

SUMMARY OF THE STORY

Prince Rama was the eldest of four sons begotten by Dasharatha, King of Koshala. Just prior to Dasharatha's retirement and Rama's coronation, the prince was unfairly banished to the forest. His wife Sita and brother Lakshmana joined him. Despite the hardships, Rama relished forest life, for it allowed him to keep company with the saints and sages living there.

However, Ravana, king of the race of Rakshasas (man-eaters), heard of Sita's exquisite beauty and resolved to kidnap her. He conspired with the magician Maricha, who adopted the form of a delicate deer. As planned, it captivated Sita's mind and Rama set out to catch the playful yet elusive creature. Maricha also lured away Lakshmana. Ravana seized the unprotected Sita. Whisking her off on his aerial chariot to his capital, Lanka, he held her captive in his famed Ashoka garden.

Finding Sita gone, Rama was grief-stricken. Pacified by Lakshmana, he resolved to rescue his wife. Journeying south with determination,

Left This carving in a Balinese temple depicts how Maricha took the form of a deer to lure Rama away from Sita.

Above A modern rendition of the triumphant return to Ayodhya of Rama and Sita after their army defeated Ravana.

the brothers allied themselves with Sugriva, king of a race of monkey-like people. Sugriva's general, Hanuman, eventually found Sita on the isle of Lanka, but was detected by Ravana's son, Indrajit, and rewarded with a lighted tail. Hanuman escaped and, waving his famous tail, burned down most of the splendid city before bounding back to the Indian mainland.

Hearing of Sita's whereabouts, Rama ordered his army to toss giant boulders into the sea. Miraculously they floated, and the monkey warriors constructed a pontoon bridge extending to Lanka. The two armies clashed outside the city. Rama's troops gained the upper hand, and eventually Rama killed Ravana. Reunited, Rama and Sita returned to Ayodhya, where they reigned happily for many years.

However, due to a malicious rumour, Rama banished Sita to the ashrama of sage Valmiki, where she bore twin sons, Lava and Kusha. Years later, Sita and her two teenage princes briefly met Rama, though

Right A performance of the Ramayana in Java, Indonesia, where the story remains extremely popular.

the couple never reunited. In separation from Rama, Sita ended her life by entering the earth and, when Rama also departed, their two sons inherited the kingdom.

MEANING OF THE STORY

The story is interpreted from different perspectives. In the worldly sense, it describes Indian society at the time and the Hindu ideal of chivalrous kingship. It extols the virtues of worldly dharma (duty), of loyalty to family members, and of a powerful leadership that transcends personal ambition. It also shows the karmic consequences of lust and avarice, as embodied by Ravana. For some renouncer traditions, it illustrates the difficulties encountered when getting married.

On a higher lever, the story describes the eternal lila (spiritual pastimes) of the seventh avatara of Vishnu. Especially through the examples of Sita's chastity and Hanuman's service, it illustrates the virtues of devotion, surrender to God, and his saving grace. A much-quoted couplet, spoken by Rama, translates: 'If a person just once surrenders to me, sincerely saying, "My Lord, from this day I am yours", then from that point on I always give him protection. That is my vow.'

THE RAMAYANA IN ART

Over time, the message of the Valmiki Ramayana has been transmitted mainly through its vernacular versions, notably a Tamil version and the much-loved Hindi 'Ramcharit-manas' by Tulsidas. The Ramayana, with its elements of hero-worship, has been expressed and transmitted through such art forms as poetry, dance and drama; and, more recently, film and television. Its cultural transmission has allowed it to blend with other faith traditions. A Jain version exalts Rama not as an avatara of Vishnu but as a liberated soul.

The popularity of the Ramayana is most conspicuous in South-east Asia, with its numerous versions, such as the Thai 'Ramakien' and the Javanese 'Kakawin Ramayana', popularly performed through ballet. Scenes for the story also feature in bas-relief and sculpture, as in the Cambodian temple at Angkor Wat, or in Thailand, where huge statues of Sugriva and other characters decorate the courtyard of the royal palace. Ramayana sculptures also adorn the walls and balustrades of Buddhist temples, where some regard Rama as an avatara of the Buddha. Through its various artistic expressions, the story of Rama and Sita is also increasingly well-known to the Western world.

THE MAHABHARATA

THIS SECOND HINDU EPIC CONSISTS OF 100,000 COUPLETS, MAKING IT ONE OF THE LONGEST POEMS IN THE WORLD. MAHABHARATA MEANS 'THE HISTORY OF GREATER INDIA'.

According to tradition, the Mahabharata was originally narrated by sage Vyasa and written down by the elephant-headed Ganesha. Its composition may have undergone various stages. The intricate and multi-layered plot focuses on the political tensions between the five Pandavas and their 100 cousins, the Kauravas. Its climax is a detailed description of the fratricidal battle of Kurukshetra. Woven within the epic are many other historical tales, and several philosophical discourses, including the Bhagavad-gita. The text particularly explores the intricacies and ambiguities of dharma, especially for the priestly and warrior classes, and the decline in virtue that marked the end of an era.

Below Krishna supplies endless cloth to Draupadi as a Kaurava prince tries to disrobe her.

SUMMARY OF THE STORY

Pandu was the second of three princes but ascended the throne due to the blindness of his elder brother, Dhritarashtra. Pandu died prematurely, leaving a wife and five young sons. His younger brother, Vidura,

Above Arjuna successfully takes aim during the marriage contest, thus winning the hand of Princess Draupadi.

was the son of a maid-servant and disqualified from taking the throne. Subsequently, the court elders decided that Dhritarashtra should act as regent until rule rightfully passed to Pandu's sons, headed by Yudhisthira. However, as all the princes grew up, Dhritarashtra's 100 sons, headed by Duryodhana, were increasingly resentful that fate had deprived their family of the vast Indian empire.

They conspired to assassinate their cousins, the teenage Pandavas and their widowed mother, Kunti. However, the princes were warned, and escaped a burning wax palace via a pre-prepared tunnel. Now fully aware of their cousins' treachery, they chose to remain in the forest and to be considered dead. During this time, the third brother, Arjuna, won Draupadi as his bride during an archery contest. Due to a benediction from Lord Shiva, awarded in a previous life, Draupadi became the wife of all five brothers.

News eventually reached the blind Dhritarashtra that his nephews were still alive. Relieved of his guilt, and feeling repentant, he arranged to return half the kingdom to the Pandavas, though by far the worst

Above Troops prepare for the Battle of Kurukshetra, in a 12th-century bas-relief at the Cambodian Angkor Wat temple.

half. With the divine help of Krishna, the barren lands flourished and the kingdom became fabulously wealthy. Hearing news of Yudhisthira's fame, opulence and popularity, Duryodhana seethed with envy. He threatened and cajoled his blind and affectionate father to schedule a gambling match between the two groups of cousins.

Duryodhana devised that the dice be loaded. Yudhisthira lost everything, including his wife and brothers. At Duryodhana's behest, his brother Dussasana tried to disrobe Draupadi before the royal court, but Krishna protected her dignity by supplying an endless length of saree. None of the nobles intervened, and according to the law of karma, sowed the seeds of their inevitable destruction. There and then, the five brothers took terrible and irrevocable oaths to destroy the offenders. None the less, according to the terms of a gambling match, they were exiled to the forest for a further 13 years. As a condition, if they were

Right A scene from the 18-day battle. Krishna, impelled by affection for Arjuna, lifts a chariot wheel and almost breaks his vow to abstain from fighting.

discovered during the final and 13th year, they were to remain in exile for a further 12 years.

Thus the princes and their wife again entered the forest. After many adventures, they adopted disguises for the final year, marginally avoiding detection by the spies dispatched by their cousins. When they returned to reclaim their kingdom, the Kauravas bluntly refused. Duryodhana repeatedly thwarted Krishna's peace proposals, and so the two parties arrayed their troops on the plains of Kurukshetra. After 18 days of carnage, the Pandavas emerged victorious due to the presence and guidance of Lord Krishna.

Yudhisthira was crowned emperor, and his kingdom prospered for 36 years. With Lord Krishna's demise, the five Pandavas retired to the Himalayas, leaving Arjuna's grandson on the throne.

THE POPULARITY OF THE MAHABHARATA

The Mahabharata is a favourite subject of art and drama, and it is still tremendously popular in India and beyond, particularly in Indonesia. One specific version survives on the island of Java, and the relief work at the temple at Angkor Wat in Cambodia depicts many scenes from the story. One TV version, screened in the early 1990s, was so popular that it practically brought the whole of India to a halt. The story has also won the attention of Western directors such as Peter Brook, who staged a six-hour version in the 1980s. Tradition holds that the intrigue, romance and chivalry are especially meant to capture the attention of people in Kali-yuga, who prefer entertainment to philosophy. None the less, the message of the Mahabharata is ultimately spiritual, and at the heart of the epic is the Bhagavad-gita, narrated as the two armies stood poised for battle.

THE BHAGAVAD-GITA: SONG OF GOD

THE BEST-KNOWN HINDU SCRIPTURE WORLDWIDE, THE BHAGAVAD-GITA OR 'SONG OF GOD', PRESENTS A BROAD OUTLINE OF HINDU PHILOSOPHY, INCLUDING ALL THE MAIN CONCEPTS AND VALUES.

Above Hindus in Auckland, New Zealand, recite the Bhagavad-gita during the Gita Jayanti festival, which falls in December.

The Bhagavad-gita consists of 700 verses within 18 chapters. According to tradition, it was spoken around 3,000BCE, though scholars consider it more recent, dating its present form to *c.* 200CE. As part of the Mahabharata, it is technically a Smriti literature, but some have attempted to raise its status to Shruti by calling it the 'Gita-Upanishad'. There are now thousands of editions, translated into all major languages and usually published with extensive commentary illuminating and variously interpreting the text.

THE CONTEXT OF THE GITA

The Bhagavad-gita was spoken by Lord Krishna to his dear friend, Prince Arjuna, as they sat on a chariot between two armies eager for conflict. As the troops were making their final preparations, the blind Dhritarashtra was sitting in his palace in the capital, Hastinapura, worried as to how the proposed battle-site might favor his son's adversaries, the pious Pandavas. Even then, Kurukshetra was a famous pilgrimage site. Perturbed by these omens, Dhritarashtra confided in Sanjay, his personal secretary. Possessed of rare mystic vision, Sanjay saw within his heart events unfolding at Kurukshetra. In real time, he narrated to the blind monarch the entire Bhagavad-gita.

The Gita opens with Dhritarashtra's covert enquiry about the outcome of the battle. The king was subsequently encouraged to hear of Arjuna's hesitancy to fight, having seen friends, relatives and teachers on the opposite side. Dhritarashtra was positively elated when Arjuna, letting slip his fabled bow, refused to fight.

Overcome with despondency, Arjuna implored Krishna to become his mentor. Lord Krishna gladly explained how Arjuna's affection for his kinsmen was based on false compassion due to identification with the body. So illusioned, Arjuna viewed those connected with his physical body to be his kinsmen. In the first six chapters, Krishna explains how the real self (atman) is different from matter and can be elevated to self-realization through various types of yoga. During the second six chapters, he explores the Supreme, his service and his devotees. In the third and final six chapters, Krishna explains about the soul's entanglement with matter and how it achieves final liberation.

Inspired by these instructions, Arjuna lifted his bow, determined to fight. In the book's final verse, Sanjaya dashed Dhritarashtra's hopes by concluding, 'Wherever there is Krishna, the Supreme Lord, and wherever there is Arjuna, the greatest archer, there will certainly be morality, extraordinary power, opulence and victory. That is my opinion.'

THE CONTENT OF THE GITA

The late-medieval commentator Madhusudana Sarsvati divided the Gita into three sections, each of six chapters. By his classification, the first six chapters deal with karma-yoga (the path of action), the middle six with bhakti-yoga (the path of devotion)

Left This statue at the holy site of Kurukshetra depicts Krishna instructing Arjuna on the chariot.

Above A 20th-century painting of Krishna's universal form, as revealed to Arjuna in the 11th chapter of the Gita.

and the last six with jnana-yoga (the path of knowledge). Some commentators claim this progression indicates the supremacy of knowledge. To counter this, devotional scholars have compared the Gita to a sandwich, with the all-important conclusion spread in the middle. The Gita appears less amenable to the ritualistic karma-yoga, though it supports action tempered with knowledge and devotion.

The Gita has five subjects; the first three, typical of all Vedanta, are the self, God and matter. To these are added two others, namely karma (activity) and kala (time). Although the sacred dialogue is essentially a Vedantic text, it has assimilated elements of the other Darshanas, especially Yoga and Sankhya. Though not totally dismissive of the venera-

tion of lesser deities, it is critical of pragmatic polytheism, the worship of specific deities for corresponding personal gains. It is less clear as to whether its proposed Supreme Deity is ultimately personal or impersonal.

The final six chapters provide many references to the Sankhya notion of three gunas (material qualities), providing a theological basis for evaluating ethical issues, as an alternative to texts dealing exclusively with dharma and morality, such as the more dated Manu Smriti. Though a few traditions grant the Gita scant authority, many accept it as a comprehensive guide to Hindu philosophy.

Below Krishna and Arjuna prepare for battle in this illuminated Bhagavad-gita produced in India over 200 years ago.

ARJUNA'S MORAL DILEMMA

Just before the battle, Arjuna faced a moral dilemma. He could regain his rightful kingdom only through fighting, and most likely killing, his friends and relatives. However, he anticipated that without his kinsmen's company, his kingdom would prove a hollow and fruitless victory.

His confusion epitomizes the ambivalence experienced by humans, who desire enjoyment but also foresee suffering for themselves and others. They resolve such tensions in two main ways: by subjugation of selfish desire or by indulgent abandonment. The former leads to upliftment and liberation, the latter to degradation and, in animal life, a temporary respite from the weight of moral responsibility. The unique human dilemma is expressed succinctly in the proverb, 'Two living beings are happy; the pig and the paramahamsa ('swan-like saint')'.

THE PURANAS AND OTHER TEXTS

ALTHOUGH HINDU TEXTS DISCUSS PHILOSOPHY, THEY ALSO REGULATE CONDUCT. THEY EXPLORE SOCIAL AND PERSONAL MORALITY AND PRESCRIBE VARIOUS MODES OF SADHANA (SPIRITUAL PRACTICE).

Narrative is important in providing examples of how Hindu ideals are expressed in everyday life and in making moral choices. Besides the two epics, most stories are found within the Puranas, which remain an important source of popular Hinduism.

THE PURANAS

Purana means 'ancient', and the books themselves claim greater antiquity than the Vedas. Scholars consider them more recent, going back to the time of the Gupta Empire between the 3rd and 5th centuries CE. Attributed to sage Vyasa, they describe the later deities, especially the Trimurti and their

Above Tales of the child Krishna, such as his stealing butter – as shown here – are perhaps the most popular Puranic stories.

respective consorts. There are 18 *maha* ('great') Puranas; three clusters of six, dedicated respectively to Brahma, Vishnu and Shiva. They extol the virtues of their favoured deity and theological concepts relevant to the corresponding community. There are also 18 'upa' or subsidiary Puranas. In South India, four Tamil Puranas glorify Lord Shiva who incarnated to teach the four boy-saints called the Kumaras.

The Puranas include accounts of creation, descriptions of stratified worlds, genealogies of deities and patriarchs, practical rules for living, and many popular myths and stories. They have been retold many times, taking the form of 'stories within a story'. Today, some of them are recited publicly at events called 'kathas'. Widely retold are the Bhagavata and Devi-Bhagavata Puranas, which include the famous

story of the goddess Durga killing the buffalo demon. Perhaps most popular is the Bhagavata Purana, which glorifies Lord Vishnu and 22 of his incarnations. It includes the much-loved stories of Lord Krishna.

THE DHARMA SHASTRAS

The Dharma Shastras include the law codes of Hinduism, which deal with three main subjects; codes of conduct, civil and criminal law, and punishment and atonement. Most important is the Manu Smriti, which is still consulted by the Indian legislature. It was written by Manu, the 'ruler of mankind' and the first lawgiver. The word 'man' is said to derive from the title 'Manu', and there are 14 Manus during each universal creation. The Manu Smriti, containing 2,700 verses divided into 12 chapters, was probably written between 300 and 600BCE.

Other important dharma texts were written by the sages Narada, Parashara and Yajnavalkya. Some Hindus now consider these texts dated, for they seem relevant only within the ancient Indian social context. In exploring contemporary ethical issues, modern Hindus often refer to texts like the Bhagavad-gita,

Below Many stories tell of the conflict between the gods and demons. Here, in a rare moment of co-operation, they churn the ocean of milk.

attempting to grasp the essence of moral principles rather than their literal application.

Another set of moral texts is the Artha Shastra, which explores the acquisition of wealth and power. One such popular work is by Chanakya, also known as Kautilya. As the prime-minister of King Chandragupta, he apparently helped the king defeat the Nandas, repulse Alexander the Great and establish the Mauryan Empire. Chanakya meticulously studied scripture to compile an anthology of popular wisdom (Niti-shastra) in the form of proverbs. The broad category of Niti-shastra also includes the famous fables of the Panchatantra and the Hitopadesha. Rather like Aesop's fables, they attribute specific characteristics to animals, such as nobility, foolishness or cunning. It is largely up to the reader to identify the moral of each story.

THE AGAMAS AND SECTARIAN LITERATURE
The Agamas do not derive their authority directly from the Vedas, but have been assimilated into the Vedic canon. They are also found within Jain and Buddhist traditions.

Left A modern painting of a tale called The Blue Jackal, *from the Panchatantra.*

Above A Mandi school painting, dated 1775, depicts the Puranic story of Durga slaying the buffalo demon.

In Hinduism, they form an enormous collection of Sanskrit scripture, often going by other names, such as Tantras and Samhitas. The Vaishnava Agamas feature two main sections, the Pancharatra Samhita and Vaikhanasas Samhita, which regulate all aspects of temple puja (worship). The Shaiva Agamas are more explicitly canonical texts and often considered Shruti by the Shaiva Siddhanta and Kashmiri Shaiva lineages. For Shaktas, there are 27 main Agamas, often called 'Tantras', usually taking the form of dialogue between Parvati and Shiva. All these texts expand on central theological teachings, usually in manner relevant to, or biased toward, the associated denomination.

Besides the Agamas, there are many other sectarian texts, central to one lineage but largely unknown to others. They usually derive legitimacy from the Vedic canon, taking the form of commentaries or summaries, often in vernacular languages. They also include hagiographies, the biographies of key saints and founders. Most sectarian texts are accommodated under Smriti, but may be considered revealed Shruti, equal in authority to the Vedas. While these two classifications are widely accepted, the precise status of any text and the dating of the work are often controversial. Hindus themselves have generally been uninterested in precise dating, considering the spirit and purpose of the books more important.

CHAPTER 3

HINDU TEACHINGS

Much Western intellectual history has been marked by tensions between the Church and the academic. In contrast, Hinduism has largely managed to reconcile faith and reason. Its philosophy is pragmatic, aimed at human liberation. Its religious commitment is philosophical, granting little credibility to mere conformity of belief. It strives to balance ambivalent views, and has little rejected its parent traditions, but instead adapted and assimilated them into progressively refined modes of understanding.

Hindu wisdom has been specifically perpetuated through lineages of gurus and their disciplines. In addition to its scholarly 'high' traditions, Hinduism features popular and village practices, based largely on meeting everyday needs. In all spheres, there are differences between the ideals of 'textual' Hinduism and the realities of daily practice.

Despite diversity of thought, Hinduism displays recurring themes, such as belief in a transmigrating self. Exploring the core notion of dharma (duty), texts list many human virtues, and examine morality through story and in relation to the Supreme. In discussing the nature and identity of God, Hinduism displays both bewildering diversity and great sophistication.

Opposite A contemporary painting depicting transmigration of the eternal self, a widely accepted concept that underpins much Hindu thought.

Above On the banks of the River Ganges, a Hindu guru delivers a Pravachan, a religious and philosophical talk on scriptures.

THE ETERNAL SELF

MODERN HINDU TEACHINGS USUALLY BEGIN WITH EXPLORING NOT GOD BUT THE INDIVIDUAL SELF. THE SANSKRIT WORD FOR SELF IS ATMAN, WHICH ULTIMATELY REFERS TO THE ETERNAL SOUL.

Hindu theology largely revolves around three main 'truths', namely the self, God and matter. Exploration of the relationships between these three generates further distinctive concepts. These notions lend some unity to Hinduism's diverse branches. However, in discussing the nature and identity of God, there is considerable diversity of opinion, with key debates focusing on the precise relationship between the self and the Supreme.

BRAHMAN

In Vedic times, the Supreme was called Brahman, the absolute and eternal reality. The Upanishads

Below Swami Tanmayananda Sarasvati performs meditation in his simple dwelling near Hampi, northern India. Traditionally, yoga, meditation and other spiritual practices aimed at realization of the practitioner's true, eternal identity.

and Vedanta philosophy describe Brahman as the all-pervading spirit. It is the source of the material creation, its support and its final resting place. Brahman has been identified with the individual self and with God, differentiating these two 'truths' from matter. However, it is imprecise to translate Brahman as 'God'. More accurately, Brahman refers to spirit, the eternal, conscious absolute standing in contrast to the relative and transient world of matter.

THE ATMAN

Hindu knowledge is largely intuitive and experiential, rather than theoretical or credal. Insight into Brahman (spirit) begins with contemplation on the nature of the self, as implied by the Upanishads, which declare 'That you are!' Similarly, Krishna begins his instructions in the Bhagavad-gita by discerning the self from the body. He states, 'Never was there a time I did not exist, nor

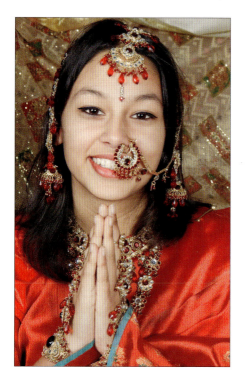

Above A Hindu bride gives the namaste greeting, which acknowledges the presence of the eternal in all others.

you, nor all these kings; nor in the future, shall any of us cease to be.' Krishna then explains that humans experience the self as unchanging throughout life, despite a constantly transmuting body. Consistent with Vedanta philosophy, he refutes the idea that consciousness emerges from matter, or that transient combinations produce an enduring self. Although material objects appear to

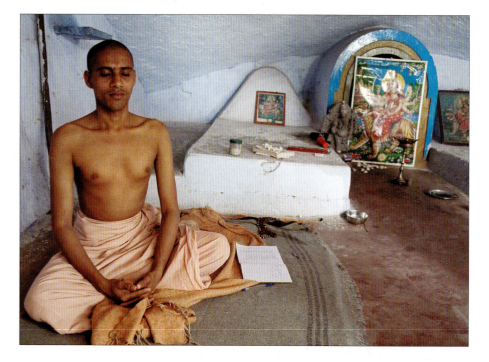

MATTER AND SPIRIT

Although the Vedas assert that 'everything is Brahman' (spirit), Brahman is initially differentiated from matter by its different characteristics, as shown below:

The self (spirit)	The body (matter)
Never-changing	Ever-changing
Eternal	Temporary
Conscious	Unconscious
Active	Inert
Alive	Dead

HINDU PHILOSOPHY

The notion of the eternal self is one of a number of concepts shared by most Hindu groups, and it greatly informs its various rituals and practices. Below is a concise overview of Hindu thought:

Almost all Hindus believe that the real self (*atman*) is eternal, made of spirit (*brahman*). The soul may take on a temporary material covering (physical body) and, by identifying with matter (*prakriti*), is entrapped by illusion (*maya*). Impelled by lust, greed and anger, he endures the cycle of repeated birth and death (*samsara*). Each soul creates its unique destiny determined by the universal law of karma (action and reaction). Under the influence of eternal time and the three material *gunas* (qualities), he moves throughout the creation, sometimes reaching higher planets, sometimes moving in human society, and at other times descending into lower species. Human life gives the opportunity to achieve *moksha*, liberation from this perpetual cycle, through re-identifying with the eternal Supreme (Brahman). Hinduism accepts different paths toward this common goal (liberation though union with God). At the same time, it stresses adherence to universal principles through performance of one's specified duty (*dharma*), as revealed through authorized holy books and the authentic *guru* (spiritual mentor).

endure for some time, factually they are constantly changing. Krishna therefore explains, 'Those who are seers of the truth have concluded that of the nonexistent (the material body) there is no endurance and of the eternal (the soul) there is no change.' Whereas Western dualistic philosophy discerns mind from matter, Hindu thought holds that spirit, Brahman, is different from both gross matter (the physical body) and subtler forms (such as the mind).

VARIOUS ANALOGIES

Hindu texts present not only arguments but also many analogies to explain the self. For example, the atman is compared to the driver of a vehicle. As a chariot or car cannot run without a driver, similarly, the body will not work without the presence of the soul. The driver may tend to identify with his vehicle and feel kinship with drivers of a similar make and model. Similarly, feelings of friendship or enmity arise from identification with the body. By such identification, the driver also feels happiness or distress on account of the condition of the vehicle. In the event of an accident he may even cry out, 'You hit me!'

Hindu texts list further analogies. The mind and body are compared to layers of clothes worn by the self. To explain how the self becomes conditioned by matter, and yet does not change, they compare it to a diamond obscured by mud.

Above A modern artist attempts to show how the changeless soul inhabits successive bodies, even within a single lifetime.

THE CYCLE OF BIRTH AND DEATH

ACCORDING TO HINDU THOUGHT, BECAUSE THE REAL SELF (ATMAN) IS UNCHANGING, IT SURVIVES DEATH. IN THIS WORLD, IT CONTINUOUSLY REINCARNATES, PASSING FROM ONE BODY TO THE NEXT.

The Bhagavad-gita explains: 'As the embodied soul continually passes in this body from boyhood to youth to old age, the soul similarly passes into a new body at death.' Through this process, called reincarnation, the self is carried within the subtle, astral body to its next destination. The precise nature of the new body is determined by the state of mind at death, and the mental impressions accumulated throughout life. The soul's destination is specifically influenced by two factors: the soul's desires and its accumulated merit (karma).

THE WORLD OF SAMSARA
Samsara broadly refers to this transient world and specifically to the cycle of repeated birth and death. Hindus consider consciousness to be present in all forms of life. Its potential is smothered, or conversely exhibited, to different degrees. Aquatics and plants are most covered, almost unconscious. Humans are most alert and spiritually awake. Souls, with their various levels of awareness, are accommodated within six hierarchical categories of life. They are, in order: aquatics; plants; insects and reptiles; birds; animals; and humans, including the residents of heaven. Most Hindus consider embodied life a painful cycle of four recurring problems: birth, disease, old age and death.

HEAVEN AND HELL
Explicit teachings on reincarnation date back to the Upanishads, and more rudimentary ideas informed the Vedic sacrifices, which elevated the performer to Indra's heaven.

Above In Kolkata, a mother protects her sleeping baby. For Hindu parents, the person within the new, infant body has arrived from elsewhere.

Today, dutiful sons still observe post-funeral rights, helping parents attain pitri-loka, 'the world of the ancestors' or other desirable destinations. The rites also prevent the departed soul from loitering as a ghost, or otherwise experiencing grief. The Sanskrit word for son, putra, means 'one who delivers from hell'. Although hell is largely associated with the lower species, the Puranas describe specific hellish worlds, overseen by the Lord of Death, Yama. However, residence in such 'hells' is usually considered temporary; so also the sojourn within Indra's heaven. Later teachings promoted an eternal paradise from which the self never returns. Contrary to traditional teachings, some contemporary gurus refute the idea of falling from human life into animal species.

A REINCARNATION STORY
King Bharata was such a pious and powerful king that India and Bharat are equally official short names for the Republic of India. As was then customary, he finally renounced the world, leaving the throne to the eldest of his 100 sons. After retiring to the

Left The Hindu funeral, like this one in Kanchipuram, marks the close of only one chapter of life.

OLD CLOTHES

The Bhagavad-gita compares the body to a set of clothes, which are replaced once they become old. As a person buys clothes on the basis of personal taste and available funds, the soul similarly obtains its next body according to its desires and its karmic credits. As a person wears layers of clothes, the soul is sheathed with layers of material coverings. They are primarily two: the subtle or astral body (lingam sharira), which continuously changes and accompanies the self at death, and the physical body, which is relinquished.

forest for austerity and meditation, he developed all saintly qualities, becoming gentle, soft-hearted and compassionate. One day, he rescued a baby deer from a raging river, and took it to his hermitage. There he fed the doe daily with fresh green grass and made sure it was comfortable. He lay down with it, bathed with it and even ate with it. When Bharata went to the forest to collect fruits and roots he would take the deer with him for fear that dogs, jackals or tigers might attack it. He enjoyed watching the deer leap, gambol and frolic like a child, and with great affection would carry it on his shoulders. However, as Bharata's heart filled with love for his pet, his inclination for spiritual practice drained away. Distracted from the path of self-realization and his meditation upon the Supreme, he thought of nothing but the delicate and innocent deer.

He was therefore mortified when, one morning, he found it absent from his side. In desperation, he searched everywhere. Wandering far from his ashram, he eventually

Right King Bharata died thinking of his pet fawn, and so entered a deer's body in his next life.

slipped from a cliff to his premature death. Thinking of the deer, he took a similar body in his next life. Because of his spiritual merit, his memory remained intact and, as a deer, he kept company with the saints in the forest. In the subsequent life, he was born as a great sage called Jada Bharata ('Stone-like Bharata'). To avoid further distraction from his spiritual quest, he ignored the world

Above A contemporary Hindu diorama depicts the self's transmigration through all stages of life.

and looked like a madman, unmindful of heat and cold, hunger and thirst or honour and dishonour. Internally, however, he always remembered God and, at death, finally attained release from the cycle of birth and death.

THE LAW OF KARMA

HINDU IDEAS ON REINCARNATION ARE CLOSELY LINKED TO NOTIONS OF KARMA, A TERM THAT HAS NOW ENTERED THE ENGLISH LANGUAGE. IT REFERS TO THE LAW OF UNIVERSAL ACCOUNTABILITY.

The Sanskrit term karma literally means 'action', but often refers to the corresponding reactions, or to the accumulated stock of such reactions. Thus, Hindus talk of 'good karma' and 'bad karma', the stored reactions that gradually fructify to reveal the soul's unique destiny.

Below Hindu children pet a young cow at the Pashupati temple on Kathmandu. Non-violence is based on empathy and an understanding of karma.

The accountability of the individual soul rests on its capacity for free will. Choice is exercised only in human form, for in passing through lower species the atman is bound by instinct and takes no moral decisions. Karma takes two main forms, namely punya (pious activities) and papa (impious activities). The Bhagavad-gita talks about a third type of action, akarma, which bestows neither good nor bad results, but grants liberation.

Above A modern, graphic depiction of the law of karma, from a tradition teaching strict vegetarianism.

GOOD AND BAD KARMA

Attaining a heavenly destination is compared to going on holiday. By pious conduct, the atman wins a celestial birth to enjoy without the toil of human existence. However, when the soul's pious credits are exhausted, he falls again to earth, just as the spent holidaymaker must return to the drudgery of work. With great facility for pleasure, the residents of heaven do not generally perform sinful actions, though texts abound with tales of celestials cursed to fall to earth for some indiscretion.

A lower birth is compared to confinement in prison. For transgressing universal laws, the self is degraded to the animal species. While there, the soul loses its exercise of free will and is condemned to a particular 'sentence'. Thereafter, through suffering, the atman is gradually purified and rises again to the human platform. Once more, the individual can choose to comply with nature's way or try to circumvent the law. The idea of karma is closely connected to the Vedic notion of rita (the natural order) and the later idea of dharma (prescribed duty). Karma is considered a natural and universal law, rather like the law of gravity.

THE SADHU'S BLESSINGS

A guru and his disciple were strolling through the city. By chance, they passed the crown prince of the kingdom mounting his fine white stallion. 'Greetings, holy man,' the prince called out. 'Please grant me your blessings.' Raising his palm, the sadhu replied, 'May you live forever.' As the prince gleefully cantered off, the sadhu explained, 'He now enjoys a life of unrestricted sense pleasure. However, when he dies he may suffer for his greed and licentiousness. It's best he lives forever.'

Later, they passed a celibate student collecting alms for his teacher. Seeing the sadhu, he placed his palms together and offered respect. The sadhu responded, 'May you die immediately.' The disciple queried, 'Master, why did you curse him to die?' The sadhu chuckled. 'That was a blessing. If he continues to live, his future is uncertain. At present, he is pure and sinless,

Left A guru teaches his disciples about karma and personal accountability.

having performed many austerities. If he dies right now, he will attain the higher worlds.'

As they approached the market place, a ruddy-faced butcher called out to the sadhu, 'Morning! Any blessings for me today?' Raising his palm, the guru replied, 'May you neither live nor die.' The butcher scratched his head, muttering, 'What a strange blessing!' Turning to his equally perplexed disciple, the guru explained, 'The butcher's life is now hellish. And, for killing whimsically, without regulation, he will be born as an animal for thousands of lives. Whether he lives or dies, he will suffer.'

Next, they passed a temple where a devotee was praying to God. She did not even notice the sadhu approaching, but he called out, 'May you live or may you die.' 'Let me guess,' ventured the disciple, 'by remembering God, a devotee is always happy and free from karma. It makes no difference whether she lives or dies, for she will continue serving God in this life and in the next.' Smiling, the sadhu replied, 'My disciple, you are learning well.'

FREE WILL AND DESTINY

Karma suggests that each individual creates a unique destiny: therefore, fate can be changed. Most generally, this means that the individual may not necessarily avoid what is destined, but can choose a suitable response. Through the exercise of free will and choice, destiny for humans is in a constant state of flux. However, should the self fall from human form, free will is suspended and he must pass mechanically through the animal species.

There is wide debate about how karma can be nullified, as through penance, astrological remedy and surrender to God. Some schools of thought have developed sophisticated

theologies, listing four types of karmic reaction which include the impetus to repeat the action, potentially initiating a chain of habitual behaviour. Particularly within village Hinduism, notions of karma are linked to belief in the power of curses, blessings and

the evil eye. There are also debates about transference of karma, though most schools teach that the individual is ultimately responsible for his or her actions. The self cannot legitimately lay blame at the feet of others, including God.

Right Devotees immerse deities in the Yamuna River alongside foam from chemicals. In the modern world, karma is relevant to environmental issues.

MATTER

MATTER REFERS TO NON-CONSCIOUS ELEMENTS OF CREATION, WHICH CONSTITUTE INERT OBJECTS AS WELL AS THE MIND AND BODY. MATTER OPERATES ACCORDING TO THREE GUNAS (QUALITIES).

Most Hindu thought discerns spirit (Brahman) from matter (prakriti). Sankhya philosophy analyses prakriti and calls spirit the purusha (the enjoyer). In tantra, this dualism is represented as Shiva, the supreme male, and Shakti, representing matter. Modern Vedanta philosophy has assimilated the twin concepts of spirit and matter.

THE THREE GUNAS
Unlike spirit, matter is transient and undergoes the three stages of creation, maintenance and destruction. According to the Sankhya view, these phases correspond to three material qualities. The Sanskrit term is 'guna'. The three gunas are: goodness (sattva), which sustains; passion

Below Coloured powders sold during Holi festivities. As three primary colours can produce innumerable hues, so the three gunas, mixed in different proportions, fashion all species of life.

(rajas), which creates; and ignorance (tamas), which destroys. The gunas and their respective functions correspond to the three main deities; Brahma the creator, Vishnu the maintainer and Shiva the destroyer. The Bhagavad-gita explains how all material phenomena, including human conduct, can be analysed in terms of the gunas.

THE GUNAS AND COLOURS
The three gunas are represented as three colours. The purity of sattva is represented by yellow. The fiery nature of passion is symbolized by red. The darkness of ignorance is denoted by dark blue. The metaphor of three colours further explains the gunas. As from just the three primary colours a whole palette can be created, so combinations of the three gunas generate the entire range of life forms. They fall into three main categories. Human society, living in the middle planetary systems, is

Above Each guna is identified with one of the Trimurti (three main deities). The Trimurti once descended as a single avatar called Dattatreya, shown here.

propelled mainly by passion. The residents of the celestial realms are guided by goodness. The animal species submit to the tight grip of ignorance. Therefore, by developing the virtues of sattva, humans may be elevated; conversely, contamination with tamas binds the self and propels it into the lower species. Even within human society, predominated by passion, mixtures of the gunas create diversity and various psychophysical characteristics.

RELATED PRACTICES
The guna-model is used to classify human conduct. In modern Hinduism, it is useful in determining moral responses and lifestyle choices. Sattva represents desirable conduct; passion is acceptable; and ignorance is to be avoided. At the same time, all three are important, since even the functions of ignorance, such as sleep, are essential to life. The Bhagavad-gita also teaches that the original system of four

varnas was based not on birth, but on guna and karma: the person's qualities and disposition toward a particular type of work. Although the quality of goodness, and related social functions such as education, are deemed most desirable, all elements of society are essential.

Similarly, although animals are under the sway of ignorance, they should be treated kindly. Their exhibition of consciousness, however faint, suggests the presence of the atman. In Hindu texts, knowledge is defined not as facts or information but as values. Most important is human empathy. A lack of sensitivity toward other people and all living creatures is a primary symptom of ignorance. Many Hindus therefore regard the process of transmigration as a means by which the eternal self learns by experience; for example, a person unkind to animals may be awarded such a body. Some traditions list three specific bodies the self takes immediately before ascending again to human life; they are the contented cow, which symbolizes goodness; the lion, which represents the royal quality of passion; and the mischievous monkey, which represents ignorance.

Below Each of the gunas is represented by an animal that reflects its characteristics.

SATTVA (GOODNESS)	RAJAS (PASSION)	TAMAS (IGNORANCE)
Sustainability (Vishnu)	Creativity (Brahma)	Destruction (Shiva)
Serenity, contentment, knowledge, purity, seeing things clearly, honesty, self-control and magnanimity	Desire, ambition, action, attachment, intense endeavour and the desire to enjoy and control	Inertia, hopelessness, darkness, intoxication, madness, excessive sleep and refusal to consider consequences
Results in wisdom	Results in greed	Results in illusion/madness
Qualities of a qualified Brahmin according to system of four varnas	Qualities of the Kshatriya (mixed with sattva) and Vaishya (mixed with tamas)	Qualities strong in the Shudra class, those employed by others
At death, elevated to higher, heavenly planets	Reincarnates again as a human on earth	Enters lower species or lower planets at death
Knowledgeable, seeing all living beings as equal, with concern for their wellbeing	Discriminates between different people and various creatures	Unaware of, or ignores, the feelings and suffering of other living beings
Food is balanced, healthy and tasty; promotes longevity	Food is too rich, sweet, hot etc., and taken just for pleasure	Food is old, unhealthy or unhygienic, made by violence or fermentation
Acting like this is painful at first but gives long-term joy	Gives immediate pleasure, but regret in the long-tern	Acting like this gives no happiness, now or later
One knows what is right and what is wrong	One is unsure about what is right and wrong	One is convinced right is wrong and vice versa
One is alert and fixed on the present moment	One hankers, and looks to the future	One is debilitated by lamentation and lack of hope
Works smartly and dutifully without excessive effort	Works very hard, desirous of enjoying the fruits	Avoids work; lazy, inactive and prone to sleep

MOKSHA: LIBERATION FROM BIRTH AND DEATH

MOST TRADITIONS AGREE THAT LIBERATION IS THE ULTIMATE GOAL OF HUMAN LIFE. THE MAIN DIFFERENCES FOCUS ON TWO ISSUES: FIRST, THE MEANS OF ACHIEVING MOKSHA; SECOND, ITS PRECISE NATURE.

The Advaita traditions teach that moksha is achieved through knowledge and the realization that the individual soul is identical to an impersonal God. The dualistic traditions claim that the atomic self remains ever distinct from a personal Supreme and that liberation depends on devotion, self-surrender and the grace of both God and guru.

MONISTIC PHILOSOPHY
In Advaita philosophy, the soul is compared to a drop of water, which, with liberation, merges into the vast ocean representing the Supreme. A further analogy is that of the water pot, which has both inside and outside. Once the pot is broken, the two

Below Burning ghats besides the Ganges in the holy city of Varanasi. Hindus believe that dying here hastens liberation for the departed soul.

immediately disappear. Similarly, while the soul is embodied it perceives itself to be limited, but upon liberation realizes its identity as the all-pervading Supreme. Hence, for the Advaita schools, the soul and God are identical in every respect. Liberation entails realization of one's Godhood as the atman merges into Brahman, the all-pervading consciousness, or, some say, realizes that it never was separated.

DUALISTIC PHILOSOPHIES
Other schools have compared liberation to a green bird entering a tree. It appears to have 'merged', but actually the bird (the self) retains its separate identity from the tree (God). Although the soul realizes its identity as Brahman (spirit), different from the perishable mind and body, it remains an individual, distinct from God and other souls.

Above For some Hindus, liberation means merging with the supreme consciousness, as a water drop loses its individuality upon merging with the ocean.

In response to the pot analogy, dualists cite the example of clay, which can be moulded into different forms such as cups, bowls and plates. Similarity, both the individual soul and God, though of the same substance, exhibit different spiritual forms. Union for the personalist refers to a unity of purpose, through loving service. Liberation means returning to a spiritual world to engage in activities of loving exchange.

DEBATES ON LIBERATION
In early Vedic Hinduism, life's main aim was to reach a temporary heaven. Somewhat later, the Upanishads postulated an eternal world. Shankara viewed this as a vibrant impersonal energy called the brahmajyoti (Brahman effulgence). Ramanuja was the first to write of Vaikuntha, a complete paradise in which the liberated self is an eternal associate of Vishnu. Later schools delineated up to five different types of liberation, which include both Shankara's and Ramanuja's conceptions.

There has also been wide debate about the soul attaining liberation before death. Ramanuja and his followers consider it impossible. Most Advaitins and some personalists, like the Bengali Vaishnavas, deem

Above For some Hindus, the soul retains its individuality, despite perceived unity with God, as with this bird in a tree.

dull elephant, and so the unfortunate monarch was reborn as Gajendra, king of the elephants. Naturally, he forgot all about his previous birth.

One hot day, accompanied by female elephants, he went to enjoy bathing in the crystal waters of a nearby lake. The water's inhabitants were disturbed and, in anger, the chief crocodile immediately seized Gajendra's leg with his powerful jaws. A great fight ensued, but within the water the elephant became weak, whereas the crocodile's power increased. Despite his considerable strength, Gajendra realized his helplessness, and in his desperation remembered the mantras he had repeatedly recited in his previous life. Offering these prayers, he sought God's shelter. Vishnu immediately swept down, riding on the back of his giant eagle, Garuda. With his disk, he severed the head of the crocodile, whose soul immediately merged with the Lord's own effulgence. Gajendra was saved and, in a four-armed spiritual form, mounted the back of Garuda, who whisked him back to the spiritual world.

Below A poster of Vishnu flying down on Garuda to liberate the elephant Gajendra.

it possible and call the liberated soul a 'jivanmukta'; here, jiva is another term for soul, and mukti, an alternative for moksha, means liberated.

There are also widely different opinions as to the precise causes of liberation, variously posited as conduct, knowledge, detachment and devotion. Polemics also revolve around contrary stances on the respective roles of grace and personal endeavour. Some devotional schools advertise an aim of life above even liberation, namely prema (love of God). For them, God-infused saints even shun liberation, for they reside always in the spiritual realm even while apparently walking the earth.

GAJENDRA THE ELEPHANT

Though the following story is popular with the devotional schools, the great monist Shankara refers to it in his prayer called 'Eight prayers dedicated to Lord Krishna'. It indicates popular belief in the primacy of grace in achieving liberation.

A powerful king in South India retired from active life to meditate in the jungle. One day, the famous sage Agastya entered the hermitage, but the king, deep in meditation, failed to welcome him properly. The angry Agastya cursed the king to become a

THREE ASPECTS OF GOD

HINDU TEXTS DESCRIBE THE ABSOLUTE REALITY AS SAT-CHIT-ANANDA: 'ETERNAL, CONSCIOUS AND BLISSFUL'. FOR MANY SCHOOLS, THESE QUALITIES CORRESPOND TO THREE PERSPECTIVES ON GOD.

Texts describe three aspects of the divine: first, Brahman, God existing everywhere; second, antaryami, God situated within the heart; and third, Bhagavan or Ishvara, God residing outside, beyond this world.

These three features are compared to the sun, the sunshine and the sun's reflection in pots of liquid. As heat and light, the all-pervading sunshine is qualitatively like the sun, yet the fiery and luminescent orb retains its separate form and identity. Furthermore, as that one sun is

Below According to Hindu thought, the air exists outside solid earth, but also within it. Similarly, the impersonal Supreme (Brahman) pervades everything.

reflected in numerous pots of water, the same God is reflected in the hearts of all living beings. Hindu denominations often favour one of these three aspects and dispute the relationships between them. The sun analogy is favoured by monotheists, who claim that the personal aspect of God, Bhagavan, is the source of both the impersonal Brahman and the Lord within.

GOD EVERYWHERE

Brahman refers to the all-pervading aspect of the absolute. Since everything comes from the absolute, it is identical with it. The Upanishads state, 'Everything is Brahman'. The same texts relate the story of Svetaketu, whose teacher instructs

Above A painting showing a yogi meditating on the antaryami, God's form within his heart.

him to dissolve salt in a tumbler of water. Asked if he sees the salt, the boy replies 'no'. However, when his teacher asks him to sip the water repeatedly, after each sip pouring some away, Svatakeu affirms that each time he can taste the salt. The lesson is that Brahman, despite being invisible, pervades the entire universe.

This sat or eternal aspect of God is initially perceived by apprehending the eternal nature of the self. This insight is the foundation for much Hindu thought and forms Krishna's first instruction in the Bhagavad-gita. According to the impersonal school, this realization is complete when one apprehends oneself as the all-pervading Supreme. For monotheistic schools, Brahman realization is but a preliminary phase of knowledge.

GOD WITHIN THE HEART

Antaryami, means 'the controller within' and refers to God within the hearts of all living beings, and within each atom. By this means, the Supreme is omniscient and it represents his chit (knowing) aspect. According to the Puranas, the Antaryami is initially perceived in three ways. In matter, he is reflected in the awesome features of nature; in the lower species, he is revealed as instinct; and in humans, he is perceived as memory, intelligence, inspiration, conscience and exceptional ability. He is the object of meditation for many mystic yogis. The Katha Upanishad likens the atman and the Antaryami to two birds sitting within the tree of the heart.

GOD AS A PERSON

Ishvara means 'lord', and indicates God, or a particular god or goddess, situated outside oneself or beyond the world. The alternative term, Bhagavan, means 'one who possesses unlimited opulence'. Parashara Muni, father of the author Vyasa,

Right God or 'Bhagavan', here represented as Krishna, lives in his own world, way beyond the material creation.

has listed six categories of opulence: fame, wealth, strength, beauty, knowledge and renunciation. This feature of the absolute embodies both omnipotence and ananda (happiness).

Bhagavan refers to a person with whom the soul can have a direct relationship as a source of spiritual pleasure. For some scholars, and

many bhakti traditions, all pleasure is essentially derived from relationships. The words Bhagavan and Ishvara quite closely resemble the English term 'God'. The word Brahman is a more philosophical term, better translated as 'spirit' or 'Absolute Reality'.

DIFFERENT SCHOOLS

Most traditions accommodate the three aspects of the divine, but understand them and their respective statuses differently. For the pure monist, the personified deity (Ishvara or Bhagavan) falls within the world of illusion, and deity worship is a means toward the higher realization of the impersonal Brahman. For many bhakti schools, with elements of dualism, the personal form of God as Bhagavan or Ishvara is the highest, and the impersonal Brahman is but God's effulgence. The mystic yogis, who initially perform hatha-yoga exercises, often meditate on the Antaryami, the lord within. The various religious orders also differ as to their precise understanding of the many gods and goddesses.

GOD WITH AND WITHOUT FORM

HINDUS ACCEPT GOD WITH AND WITHOUT FORM. DEBATE FOCUSES ON THE RELATIONSHIP BETWEEN THESE TWO FEATURES, THEIR RESPECTIVE STATUSES AND EXPLAINING THE MANY DEITIES.

Hinduism accommodates many concepts of God, including pantheism and polytheism. However, the high scholarly traditions emphasize the singularity of the Supreme, an idea that often underpins even village practices and the veneration of many gods and goddesses. Within

Below Some scholars consider the universe a form of God, as seen in this carving of Krishna at a temple in Guwahati.

modern Vedanta, there are two main doctrines: Advaita (monism) and Dvaita (dualism). Monism propounds an impersonal absolute. Dualism, sometimes also called monotheism, conversely teaches that God is intrinsically personal. The two corresponding features of God are called nirguna Brahman (the absolute without attributes) and saguna Brahman (the absolute with attributes). Generally speaking, the

Above A representation of God as the formless, all-pervading consciousness.

nirguna feature has no form and the saguna feature has form. The two main doctrines argue about which feature, if either, is higher.

ADVAITA (MONISM)

Advaita means 'non-dual' and refers to the doctrine of monism, by which the soul, God and matter constitute a homogenous whole. As Brahman, the soul and God are identical in all respects. This doctrine was most effectively propagated by Shankara (788–820CE), who taught that Brahman is ultimately nirguna, without form, activity and personality. The unperceivable and inconceivable Brahman is represented through personalized deities for the understanding and veneration of common people, who project their mundane experience of form on to the impersonal divine. These forms are therefore called 'anthropomorphic'. For Advaitins, God is ultimately nirguna. The saguna feature may be helpful but is ultimately imaginary and illusory.

DVAITA (DUALISM)

The dualistic schools teach that the soul and God are eternally distinct. Furthermore, God is saguna, exhibiting eternal form, activity and personhood. The view is theomorphic, holding that human form is shaped on God, and that this world reflects the prototypical spiritual realm.

Above The Indian monsoon refracts white light into seven colours. For many Hindus, the many deities represent the diverse attributes of the single impersonal Supreme.

For its inclusion of lesser gods and goddesses, this stance has been termed 'inclusive monotheism'.

The theological foundations for monotheism were laid down by Ramanuja, who qualified Shankara's uncompromising 'monism'. Like Ramanuja, most post-Shankara theologians accepted elements of Advaita. Only Madhva taught the antithesis, dualism, thus refuting any similarity between the soul and God. Strictly speaking, the word Dvaita refers to Madhva's teaching of 'pure dualism'. Most schools teaching dualism – in its broader sense – acknowledge nirguna Brahman, while also accepting, or even favouring, the personal, saguna feature.

EXPLAINING MANY DEITIES

The two broad schools differently explain the many devas (gods) and devis (goddesses). Monists consider all deities equal, with each representing a specific attribute of an impersonal God. They liken the

Right This temple mural in Dallas, Texas, depicts belief in a God who enjoys spiritual form and personal relationships.

deities to the colours of the rainbow, revealed as white light refracts though rain drops. When the one impersonal divine is distorted through this world, humans apprehend many deities.

The monotheistic stance likens God to the prime minister, the head of many government officers. Most deities are considered subordinate to the main Deity, and dependent for their power and authority. As citizens approach the government through a representative, similarly veneration of lesser gods is an indirect means of approaching God. The analogy conveys how God and his authority pervade the universe, while he retains his personal form, identity and residence.

THE MURTI

Of several other core notions related to God, two are paramount. First, the idea that God can 'expand' or duplicate himself into unlimited forms, without diminishing his original potency; second, the view that God can descend as an avatara ('one who comes down'). A key type of avatara is the murti, the sacred image, whose worship has historically met with much opposition and violence. However, sophisticated Hindu theologies imply that it is hasty to dismiss image worship as mere superstition or 'idol worship'.

Advaitins teach that the omniscient and omnipresent Brahman is unarguably present in the murti, which makes the inconceivable and

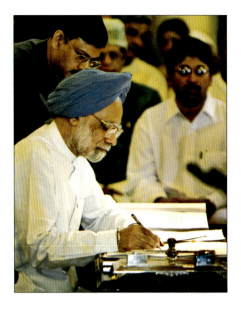

Above Former Indian prime minister Manmohan, surrounded by other ministers, reflects the idea of one Supreme Person assisted by many subservient deities.

unperceivable visible to human eyes. They often describe the murti as a meditational aid, and its worship may be discarded upon adopting the higher, difficult path of impersonal, nirguna worship.

For the personalist, and in much common practice, the murti is more that a 'container for the spirit'. It actually is the deity, fully conscious of the worshipper. Devotional schools teach that in order to receive and reciprocate the devotee's love, God or a specific deity appears in a form that is visible yet fully spiritual. For devotees, divine relationships are real, and the blueprint of mundane familial affairs. They can be intimate, devoid of fear and inordinate reverence. Out of love, God may even take an apparently inferior role, as a loyal servant, affectionate child or hen-pecked lover. There are many stories of the temple deities talking and reciprocating with their devotees, or even quitting the shrine. In one temple in the sacred town of Vrindavana, the altar curtains are swished open only momentarily in case Krishna again leaves to sport with his devotees.

SOURCES OF AUTHORITY

HINDU TEACHINGS ARE DERIVED FROM TWO MAIN SOURCES; THE FIRST, HINDU HOLY TEXTS, AND, THE SECOND, THE REALIZATIONS OF HOLY PEOPLE. A THIRD SOURCE OF AUTHORITY IS CONSCIENCE.

When a Hindu boy undergoes his sacred thread initiation, to become 'twice-born', he ritually accepts scripture as his spiritual mother and the guru (spiritual teacher) as his new father. A third authoritative voice, the Antaryami or 'guru within', acknowledges the need for reflection and a high degree of self-autonomy.

SCRIPTURE
Hindu groups are legitimized not by allegiance to a particular creed but by broad submission to the Vedic scriptural authority. However, such subscription is not whimsical, and requires an aspiring tradition to write insightful textual commentaries. Many sacred lineages also trace their origins to a particular deity,

Below In the holy town of Udupi is a golden statue of Vyasa dictating the Mahabharata to his scribe, Ganesha.

implying that God remains the fountainhead of all authority.

Hindu scripture is called shabda-brahman (spiritual sound), alluding to its oral transmission. Tradition teaches that texts were only written as human memory began to falter, around 3,000BCE. Shabda-brahman, or simply 'shabda', is often considered the most reliable form of authority for spiritual matters. When using other forms of evidence, such as empirical and rational knowledge, shabda remains the guiding standard. Many groups acknowledge that the flawed mind and senses are unable to extend human knowledge to the spiritual dimension. To re-awaken the self, an external source of knowledge is required. The Vedas are compared to the mother, who first gives knowledge. Theistic schools have explained how the mother most authentically reveals the identity of the father (God).

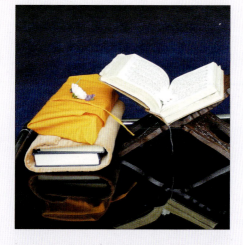

Above Treating sacred texts reverentially acknowledges their authoritative status with regard for spiritual knowledge.

GURU
The guru plays a central role in Hinduism, often serving as an intermediary between the soul and God. Many schools claim that divine guidance and benediction descend through the genuine spiritual teacher, who acts and speaks for God. Also on behalf of the divine, the guru accepts the disciple's service and veneration.

Accepting a true guru is essential for understanding and realising scripture. The Svetashvatara Upanishad (6.38) explains: 'Only unto to great souls who have unflinching faith in both the Lord and the guru, are all the imports of Vedic knowledge automatically revealed'. Realization without mentorship is often considered impossible, as the seeker is inevitably waylaid by *maya* (illusion or ignorance). A guru is required to understand and realize scripture.

There are debates about the guru's exact identity. Some traditions equate the guru with God, whereas others insist that he or she is God's representative. Whatever their opinion, many Hindus still accept initiation from a spiritual teacher, thus becoming formal disciples. Respect is also shown toward other holy figures, such as brahmins and sadhus (monks); even to family elders, and to regular teachers, also called 'guru'.

THE GURU WITHIN

The notion of dharma does not demand blind obedience to duty. Arjuna is praised for displaying foresight and consideration before the battle of Kurukshetra. The entire Mahabharata explores moral dilemmas and the need to take decisions based on unique circumstances. For this, the role of the Antaryami, the 'Lord in the heart', is considered essential. However, acting on conscience is counterbalanced by the need to also reflect on scripture and the guru's instructions, and to assimilate their real meaning.

BLIND FOLLOWING

The following story from southern India illustrates the need to carefully discern the real mood and mission of the guru and, indeed, the actual meaning of scripture:

Guru Paramartha decided to go on pilgrimage. He ordered his five disciples to purchase a horse but, with few funds, they returned with

an old, unsteady nag. Concerned, the guru informed his disciples that they should pick up anything that might fall from the horse.

At an auspicious hour, the sacred journey began. One day, a low branch brushed off Guru Paramartha's turban. An enthusiastic disciple ran back to retrieve it. As he ran forward again, he noted something else coming not off the horse but out of it. In a fit of inspiration, he used the turban to collect it and humbly offered the turban to his guru. Having re-donned his

Above A shrine near London depicts the five most recent members of a lineage of spiritual teachers.

head-piece, Guru Paramartha was somewhat upset, and loudly rebuked and berated his foolish disciple. His student was completely confused. Had he not sincerely followed his guru's orders?

'All right, all right!' conceded the holy man. 'Okay, take your notebook and write down these items. If any of *these* fall off, pick them up and return them to me. Otherwise, please leave them! Okay, here they are; turban, umbrella, water cup, meditation beads ...' And so the list went on. The disciple was happy, and Guru Paramartha anticipated no more dousing with horse manure.

However, on a stretch of treacherous road, the old nag slipped and tumbled. The enthusiastic disciple righted the horse and consulted his list. On to the animal's back he faithfully loaded his guru's turban, beads, water pot, Bhagavad-gita – in fact, everything – and joyfully proceeded, leaving his beloved guru writhing in the mud!

Left In New Zealand, a disciple worships a sacred image of his guru, considered the embodiment of spiritual wisdom.

SANATANA DHARMA

SANTANA DHARMA REFERS TO RELIGION UNBOUNDED BY A SPECIFIC 'FAITH', CREED, COUNTRY, ETHNICITY OR TIME PERIOD. FOLLOWERS CLAIM IT IS A TIMELESS, UNIVERSAL AND INCLUSIVE RELIGION.

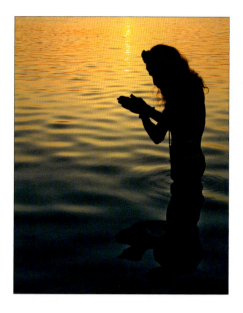

Many Hindus call their own religion 'sanatana dharma'. Some scholars question the idea of 'an eternal religion', perhaps suspecting an attempt to deny change and cling to tradition. Hindu thinkers claim differently, that the term acknowledges the enduring nature of moral and spiritual laws, not dissimilar to physical axioms. The idea of universal, unchanging laws is linked to the Vedic notion of rita, 'the natural order'.

THE MEANING OF DHARMA

Hinduism later adopted the term 'dharma', 'the natural law'. Although popularly translated as 'duty' or 'religion', its more profound meaning is derived from the Sanskrit root 'dhri', which means 'to sustain'. A further connotation is 'that which is integral to an object'. Hence, the dharma of fire is to be hot, of sugar to be sweet. For humans, dharma consists of duties that sustain them according to their innate characteristics.

These human predispositions are twofold, spiritual and material, generating two equivalent sets of duty. The first, sanatana dharma, reflects a person's real identity as the eternal atman. Sanatana dharma nurtures the eternal relationship between the self and God. On the other hand, varnashrama-dharma takes account of the soul's psycho-physical situation, classifying duties according to four ashramas (stages in life) and four varnas (classes). However, since diversity is prevalent in any human society,

Above At the River Ganges, a holy man offers respects to the rising sun. As the sun is the same for all people, sanatana dharma teaches about shared religious truths.

varnashrama is sometimes identified with the eternal order, and considered part of the sanatana dharma.

DHARMA AS INCLUSIVE

A distinctive Hindu view is that 'God' refers to the absolute reality, not merely a human, social or evolutionary construct. Hence, Hindus rarely imply that God is the property of a particular ethnic or religious group. God is one despite variant beliefs. To explain this, gurus cite the analogy of the sun, which remains singular despite variant names in different tongues. The Divine similarly transcends temporary designations such as 'British' or 'Indian', 'Hindu', 'Jewish' or 'Muslim'. The real self (atman) is also beyond such labels. Hence religion, aiming at reunion with God, is above all sectarian designations.

To explain plural religious traditions, Hindu teachings employ another metaphor. They liken

Left Followers of sanatana dharma highlight its inclusive connotations. This statue of Lord Jesus Christ overlooks an ashram in Jeevan Dara, North India.

religion to knowledge, which is common to all, despite students attending different universities. As mathematical theorems are equally valid in Greece, India or Britain, so the topic of study is identical for all religious traditions. Favouring the idea of a shared, inclusive wisdom, Hinduism makes little use of the terms 'creed', 'belief' or 'faith'. Despite this most Hindus value fidelity to a particular religion, denomination or deity, rather than a whimsical, self-selective approach. Many inherit a kula-deva (family deity) and may select a particular ishta-deva (chosen deity) for their individual devotion.

SANATANA DHARMA IN PRACTICE

Many Hindus include members of other authorized religions under the banner of sanatana dharma, whilst retaining a preference for their own 'school'. For this reason, many avoid the word 'conversion', for it wrongly suggests that faith traditions are discrete and mutually exclusive. In practice, most Hindus don't restrict

Below Mumbai University teaches subjects similar to other modern universities. Hindu thought stresses the idea of shared knowledge, despite various institutions or 'faiths'.

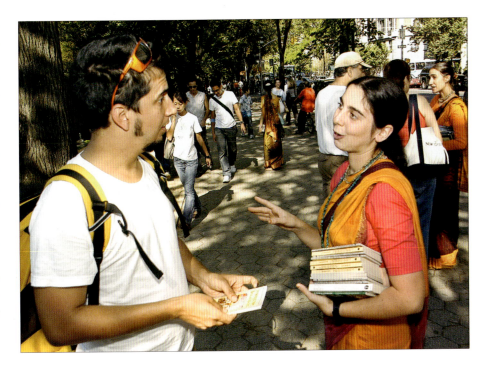

temple attendance to a particular deity or denomination, and are happy to attend churches, gurudwaras and other places of worship.

However, Hinduism doesn't always meet its ideals. Medieval South India witnessed tension and violence between worshippers of Shiva and Vishnu. More recently, conversion attempts by Muslim and Christian communities, and strategies for re-conversion, have fuelled social tensions in Orissa and Kerala. Broader controversies rage about nationalism and the complex relationships between Hinduism and India. Most conspicuously, caste discrimination remains a blot on the inclusive Hindu landscape.

The medieval bhakti saints challenged the hereditary caste system. Some, such as Kabir, drew from other faiths such as Sufism and accepted followers irrespective of their class, gender or religious background. Devotional movements drew on the ideal of sanatana dharama to propagate theories of spiritual egalitarianism, asserting everyone's right to spiritual life and teaching that the inescapable disposition of the living entity (atman) is service (seva). In the 20th century, and especially outside

Above Some Hindus preach, such as this Argentinian member of the Hare Krishna movement selling books in Central Park, New York.

India, many temples called themselves 'sanatanist', indicating preference for an eclectic form of Hinduism without bias toward one specific denomination or lineage.

21st-century scholars have identified two broad ideologies competing for the loyalties of the Hindu community. One of these, Hindu nationalism, largely conflates Hinduism and Indian patriotism. The other, articulated by such figures as Mahatma Gandhi, represents Hinduism as the 'eternal' or 'universal' religion. However, the two ideas are often mixed, perhaps ambivalently, as when nationalists praise India as the sole source of a universal spirituality. On the other hand, for those who favour inclusivity, there are difficult questions as to how far Hinduism should resist aggression. Despite different responses to these issues, the concept of sanatana dharma challenges a narrow understanding of 'religion' and, for Hindus themselves, remains a core ideal.

VARNASHRAMA DHARMA

VARNASHRAMA DHARMA REFERS TO THE ORIGINAL HINDU SOCIAL SYSTEM, WITH DUTIES BASED ON THE CITIZEN'S POSITION IN A PARTICULAR VARNA (SOCIAL CLASS) AND ASHRAMA (STAGE OF LIFE).

According to Hindu texts, varnashrama refers to natural classifications apparent in all societies. The four varnas (classes) take account of different predispositions towards work and the required qualifications. The four ashramas mirror natural phases in life, during which certain duties are conducive to wellbeing. Hindu texts imply that individuals realize their potential by respecting such natural laws, and that society should be organized hierarchically.

Right A diagrammatic representation of the four varnas and their respective relationships with the entire social body.

SPECIFIC DUTIES

The Rig Veda compares the social body to the human form. In that metaphorical body, the priestly and academic *brahmanas* are the head; the kshatriyas (warriors) are the arms; the *vaishyas* (business community) are the thighs and belly; and the *shudra* working class are the legs. The analogy gives insight into the respective

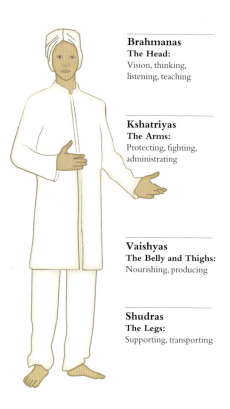

Brahmanas
The Head:
Vision, thinking, listening, teaching

Kshatriyas
The Arms:
Protecting, fighting, administrating

Vaishyas
The Belly and Thighs:
Nourishing, producing

Shudras
The Legs:
Supporting, transporting

WOMEN'S DUTIES

Although women are classified by varna, they have long been considered a section of society in their own right. Women do not pass through the four stages available to men, but through three phases, described in the text called the Manu Smriti:

1 As a child protected by her father
Traditionally, girls did not receive a formal academic education. Women's role was considered essential in preserving social and cultural values, learned mainly at home.

2 As a wife, protected by her husband
Hinduism places great value on pre-marital chastity and this has greatly influenced domestic customs. Girls were betrothed and married at a young age. In married life, the wife's role was centred on the home and she was not concerned with earning family income. Responsibilities as a loving and available parent were considered paramount.

3 As an elder or widow, protected by the eldest son
If the husband died, took sannyasa or became an invalid, the eldest son would maintain her. In respectable families, elders were treated with respect and their opinions sought on key family issues.

In the modern liberal context, the very notion of 'protection' has often been interpreted to suggest exploitation. Although protecting women has remained a core Hindu ideal, reality

Above A family prays at their household shrine. The term 'ashrama' suggests all life stages are 'places of spiritual culture'.

has fallen short. Single women and new brides have been exploited to secure dowries, and widows not only unsupported, but also forced from home to live in ashrams. It remains debatable how much such abuse has been spawned by religious teachings, or conversely by greed, poverty and social anomaly.

Right A modern painting of the four varnas, which represent personal dispositions as well as social classes.

social functions. The brahmanas are responsible for vision, represented by the eyes, and for teaching, symbolized by the mouth. The kshatriya's main duty is to protect society, as the arms do for the body. The main concern of the vaishya (business-community) is material nourishment, and those employed by others, the shudras, support other sections of society. The same metaphor is sometimes used to explain the four ashramas, which are, from the feet up, student life, marriage, retirement and renunciation.

Each varna and ashrama has its own specified dharma. What is desirable for one section of society may be detrimental to another. For example, serenity and contentment are vital to the priestly varna but disastrous to the warrior class. Contact with money and women is essential for householders, but spiritually suicidal for the celibate renunciant. Underlying these social differences are the shared notions of mutual service and incremental spiritual progress.

VARNASHRAMA AND CASTE

The social system called varnashrama is controversial due to its association with modern caste practices. Many Hindus distance themselves from varnashrama, considering it a mere sociological phenomenon or an outdated religious practice. Others accept the four ashramas but reject the four varnas. Most common among Hindu scholars is the view that modern, hereditary caste practice is a perversion of the original varnashrama system. The two are not necessarily synonymous. Mahatma Gandhi, the most famous critic of caste abuse, believed in the original principles of varnashrama dharma. The system of four varnas was apparently based on mutual support and service, allowing for upward and downward mobility. The caste system, as it evolved, became rigid and hereditary, motivated by a desire to artificially maintain privilege and the status quo.

THE FOUR VARNAS
• Brahmins – priests, teachers and intellectuals
• Kshatriyas – armed forces, police and government
• Vaishyas – farmers, business and trades-people
• Shudras – artists, craftsmen and workers

THE FOUR ASHRAMAS
• Brahmachari ashrama – celibate student life
• Grihastha ashrama – householder life
• Vanaprastha ashrama – retired life
• Sannyasa ashrama – renounced life

Right Vaishnava sannyasis, members of the fourth ashrama, at Ujjain.

ONE GOAL, DIFFERENT PATHS

HINDUISM DOES NOT PRESCRIBE ONE PATH FOR ALL. BASED ON INDIVIDUAL DISPOSITION, IT OFFERS DIVERSE INCENTIVES TOWARD LIBERATION AND DIFFERENT PATHS TOWARD ULTIMATE SUCCESS.

Hinduism makes little distinction between sacred and secular, or between religious and worldly duties. Culture and religion have also been closely intertwined. Hence, religious practice accommodates both material and spiritual goals.

FOUR GOALS

Hindu texts list four sequential aims: dharma, artha, kama and moksha. Dharma (righteous living) facilitates artha (the acquisition of wealth). Economic stability enables humans to enjoy regulated kama (sensual pleasure). Finally, the futility of flickering gratification promotes a search for a permanent solution to life's problems, through

Below Jain temple on the holy Mount Girnar, Gujarat. Many Hindus compare the different yogas to equally valid paths up the same mountain.

moksha (salvation). Later lineages, considering the desire for liberation to be self-centred, have advocated a fifth goal called prema (love of God) or nitya-seva (eternal loving service).

Still, most Hindus consider moksha the main aim of human life, toward which the others are incremental steps, adopted according to individual needs. Texts therefore recommend a balanced life with an ultimate spiritual goal. Liberation usually entails union with God, called 'yoga', and the various processes are therefore called yogas or, alternatively, margas ('paths').

DIFFERENT PATHS

There are three main paths: karma-yoga (the yoga of action), jnana-yoga (the yoga of wisdom), and bhakti-yoga (the yoga of devotion). Texts such as the Bhagavad-gita add a fourth called astanga-yoga (the yoga

Above A businessman worships Ganesha and Lakshmi online. Generating wealth is one of four 'aims of human life'.

of meditation). Within these four yogas exist many sub-disciplines, such as hatha-yoga, a stage within the path of meditation. Some traditions, such as the Shri Vaishnavas, consider their chosen path higher than the standard four.

There are different opinions as to the respective merits of each yoga. Some view all equally, like paths up a mountain or rivers merging into the ocean. Choice is determined by personal preference or disposition.

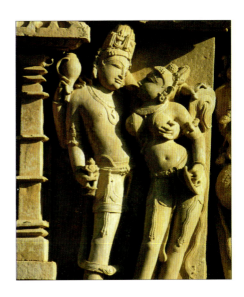

Above The loving exchanges between Vishnu and Lakshmi are esteemed by many following the devotional path.

Other traditions favour one process, citing the example of a ladder and claiming that each rung is a successive step toward the perfection achieved through their particular yoga. Despite the notion of successive stages, the yogas are not entirely separated, and the phases are cumulative, building on previous ones rather than rejecting them. For bhaktas, knowledge is a preliminary stage to the superlative path of devotion; for jnanis, devotion is an elementary process for those ill-equipped for the stringent path of knowledge.

ARE ALL PATHS THE SAME?

Some Hindu teachers, such as Ramakrishna, have recommended that all paths, including other faiths, lead to the same goal. He said, 'A truly religious man should think that other religions also are paths leading to truth'. Others suggest that different paths and processes yield different destinations. In the Bhagavad-gita, Krishna explains, 'Those who worship the demigods take birth among the demigods; those who worship the ancestors go to the ancestors; those who worship ghosts and spirits, take birth among such beings; and those who

worship me will live with me'. Despite differences of opinion, practically all agree on the need for maintaining an attitude of respect towards other religions. A related idea is that of concession, a belief that the individual has to act according to his or her present situation, and specific dharma (duty), even if not ideal. Moving in the right direction is preferable to attempting immediate perfection.

PURITY AND IMPURITY

Hindu teachings imply it is dangerous to be critical of others, even if their specific dharma is less prestigious, as this story illustrates.

Once there lived a very strict brahmin. He was upset that he lived next door to a prostitute, and was irked every time he spied her bringing home a customer. He decided to teach her a lesson. Every time she brought a client home, he lobbed a stone into her garden. As the months and years passed, the pile grew taller and wider. Whenever, the brahmin saw it, he would again be outraged at his neighbour's conduct.

The lady was also upset. Seeing the pile of stones, she would think, 'Due to my past impious activities, I have been engaged in this rotten business. But that brahmin next door is so pure. Oh, I wish I could be like him. Maybe later on, at least in the next life, I will get the opportunity to become saintly'. Although destiny engaged her in a lowly profession, the prostitute was actually a devotee of God.

Life went on. The brahmin thanked fate that he was not like others, particularly his neighbour. And the prostitute contemplated the purity of the brahmin and the trouble she was causing him. The pile of stones continued to grow.

Right Illustration conveying the view that the various yogas are progressive. This version favours bhakti (devotion).

Above Many non-Hindus identify yoga with hatha-yoga, the preliminary stages of the Hindu meditative path.

As fate decreed, both the brahmin and the prostitute passed away. Absorbed in thoughts of his neighbour's sins, the brahmin was born into a wretched and degraded family. The prostitute, aware of her own shortcomings and full of admiration for the brahmin, at once attained the heavenly planets.

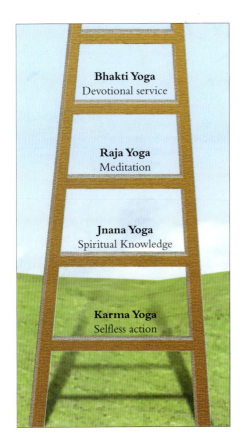

Bhakti Yoga
Devotional service

Raja Yoga
Meditation

Jnana Yoga
Spiritual Knowledge

Karma Yoga
Selfless action

TIME AND SPACE

HINDU IDEAS ON TIME AND SPACE GIVE INSIGHT INTO ITS DISTINCTIVE WORLD VIEW. BELIEF IN CYCLICAL TIME AND INTELLIGENT LIFE ON OTHER PLANETS PROMOTES IDEAS OF RELIGIOUS INCLUSIVITY.

Hindu texts describe expanses of time and space so vast that some consider them fanciful. Traditional historic dates go back tens and hundred of millennia and, even when more recent, usually predate the estimates favoured by scholars. At the heart of this, Hindu versions of history differ from popular views. Traditional myth recalls a glorious heritage, with descent from highly refined rishis (saints), rather than evolutionary emergence from a tribal past.

Such belief is underpinned by Hindu views on time and space, which radically depart from contemporary belief. Time is eternal and cyclical rather than bounded and linear. Space accommodates life not just on earth, but on a multitude of lokas (worlds) occupying various metaphysical dimensions. Hindu cosmology thus suggests that knowledge of time and space is not entirely objective, but is influenced by the perceptive capacity of the transmigrating soul. Enlightenment, or realization of the true self, opens up levels of perception beyond common understanding.

TIME

The concept of eternal and cyclical time is intimately linked to core belief about the self. The atman is neither created nor destroyed. This notion of bi-directional eternity is not confined to the realm of spirit (Brahman) but extends to the material world. Hindu texts do not generally mention an absolute 'year dot' or a final cataclysm. Destruction of the cosmos inevitably heralds its re-creation.

The material cosmos is therefore subject to continuous cycles of creation, sustenance and annihilation, with each function overseen by one of three main deities, the 'Trimurti'. This cyclical idea differs from modern belief in unidirectional progress. On the contrary, Hindu texts describe universal and social devo-

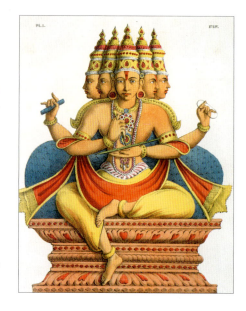

Above Brahma, the creator, with his original five heads, as painted by a Western artist.

lution, with a gradual decline in human morality and wellbeing. This is likened to the shared human experience of physical atrophy, of always aging. However, the Hindu view is that, after steady decline, both the soul and the universe are periodically and rapidly rejuvenated through rebirth. Texts frequently draw such parallels between the universe (the macrocosm) and the physical body (the microcosm).

Left Vishnu emits universes from his pores and breath. Vaishnavas claim he oversees primary creation, with Brahma born in each universe as the 'secondary creator.'

THE FOUR AGES
Hindu notions of time reflect the rhythms of nature. There are four ages that continuously rotate, rather like the four seasons. They are:

Satya-yuga – 1,728,000 years
Dvapara-yuga – 1,296,000 years
Treta-yuga – 864, 000 years
Kali-yuga – 432,000 years

Total cycle – 4,320,000 years

The following Purusha Shukta prayer of the Rig Veda illustrates the Hindu belief that the spiritual realm is larger than the material world.

Oh Lord, the past, present and future universe are creations of your powers. But you are much greater. This material word is only one-quarter of the entire cosmos. The eternal spiritual sky constitutes the remaining three-quarters.

This universe exists for the lifespan of Brahma, the creator. His one day consists of 1,000 maha-yugas (great ages), each comprised of four yugas or ages: the golden, silver, copper and iron ages, each progressively shorter and more depraved. Tradition calculates that we now live 5,000 years into this Kali-yuga, with 427,000 years remaining. Some Hindu writers suggest a far shorter period. At the end of Kali-yuga, the final incarnation of Vishnu is scheduled to appear as Kalki, riding a white horse, slaying the sinful and ushering in yet another golden age.

SPACE
With a cyclical notion of time, Hinduism teaches that the material world is created not once but repeatedly. This universe is often considered to be one of many, which are compared to a cluster of bubbles floating in space. Within this universe are three main regions: the heavenly planets, the earthly realm and the lower worlds. Scripture provides detailed descriptions of these regions and their diversely shaped inhabitants. The idea of Indra's heaven, predominant in Vedic times, has

Right 19th-century diagram of the universe, showing its stratified and hierarchical nature.

more recently been augmented by the idea of an eternal realm, either as the brahman effulgence or as a fully equipped paradise, usually ruled by Vishnu or Shiva. Vaishnavism has developed this latter concept to embrace the notion of lila, or spiritual pastimes replicated within sacred locations on earth when Vishnu appears. Holy places have often been compared to spiritual embassies, or to fords and gateways that provide access to higher dimensions.

There is no one account of creation, but many inter-related stories. The Rig Veda narrates the story of the sacrifice of the primal being (purusha). According to Sankhya philosophy, the universe is created from sound (vach), represented by the Om mantra. Sound corresponds to ether, the subtlest of the five material elements, and the elements are generated successively from subtle to gross. In a manner that mirrors universal creation, the atman, more subtle and powerful than matter,

Above Shiva, Lord of the Dance, is often termed 'the destroyer'. Shaivas also consider Lord Shiva the ultimate re-creator and sustainer.

generates its own successive material bodies. This world facilitates the soul's various, self-centred desires, and ultimately brings him back to his pure spiritual identity as Brahman.

Hindu Values

TEXTS DO NOT DEAL ONLY WITH PHILOSOPHICAL AND THEOLOGICAL KNOWLEDGE. THEY INCLUDE MORAL GUIDELINES AND INJUNCTIONS TO REGULATE SOCIAL, MORAL AND SPIRITUAL CONDUCT.

Texts extensively list human virtues, such as humility, honesty and cleanliness. Hindu thought recognizes the interplay between values and belief, such as in the indestructible atman, and also between values and conduct, as regulated though dharma (duty and etiquette). The greeting of 'namaskara' or 'namaste', uttered with folded palms, is deeply embedded in Indian culture. Hindus use it to greet each other and their sacred images. In celestial social circles, the gods and goddesses use the same salutation, which literally means, 'I bow to you', but more profoundly, 'I bow to you, the eternal self within'. It is based on

Below This painting shows the pitfalls of the Kali age, and how Emperor Parikshit punished the personification of Kali for daring to enter his kingdom.

the foundational belief in both spiritual equality and a hierarchal world. The gesture also embodies specifically Hindu values, such as a humble respect for all. This simple practice reflects both philosophical ideas and spiritual values.

VALUES AND CONCEPTS

Belief in reincarnation has moulded specific attitudes toward issues surrounding the sanctity of life. For example, since the self apparently enters the body upon conception, many texts condemn abortion. More broadly, all life is seen in terms not of its physical symptoms, eating, breathing and reproduction, but its inherent capacity for consciousness, and for pleasure and pain. The Bhagavad-gita defines knowledge as awareness of the self in all life forms; conversely, ignorance as denial of the

Above A warrior pays respect to a brahmin. Members of these two varnas were expected to demonstrate lofty virtues, such as wisdom and nobility.

existence and feelings of others.

According to modern Hindu theology, moral issues are evaluated in terms of the three gunas, or 'material qualities'. Desirable values relate to sattva-guna, the quality of goodness. The quality of passion (rajo-guna), though essential for creative activities, is influenced by greed. The lowest quality of ignorance (tamo-guna) indicates immorality and, according to the Bhagavad-gita, a firm conviction that right is wrong and vice versa.

VALUES AND DHARMA

Values are linked to the execution of dharma (religious duties). Varnashrama is based on the notion that members of the four varnas are determined by their situation within the three gunas and their exhibition of corresponding characteristics. The authentic brahmin is meant to demonstrate goodness and hence serenity, wisdom and detachment. They effectively lead society through real knowledge, a serene and unbiased perception of reality. The other varnas tend to be swayed by political, economic and sensual expediency.

Nevertheless, all varnas are regarded as important, and each is allocated distinctive values as stepping-stones toward ideal character. The values required of a business person are different from those required of a scholar, teacher or doctor, who fulfil brahminical functions. Whereas the business community is closely connected to money, the brahmins were traditionally prohibited from receiving a wage to avoid compromising their integrity and mood of public service. Brahmins were also responsible for education, which focused on character formation as much as earning a livelihood.

The varna system relates to ideas of internal and external purity. The degree of purity of the self or, conversely, of contamination by the three gunas, determines the soul's

Below Vishvamitra, though born a warrior, became a powerful brahmin. Here, the heavenly damsel Menaka tests his detachment.

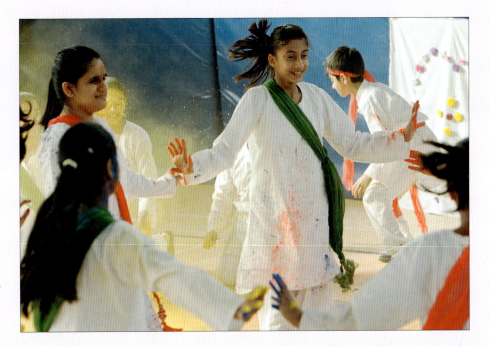

Above Traditional Hindu education, as practised in this Swaminarayan School in London, stresses the importance of character formation.

destination at death. Ideas of ritual purity were exploitatively embedded in the hereditary caste system, by which higher classes avoid intimate contact – through eating, physical contact or marriage – with those of lower status. Such rigid practices have long been contested by reformers and devotional movements who stressed instead the spiritual equality of all people.

The notion of Sanatana Dharma supports the ideal of shared human values. Such virtues are not artificially imposed but nurtured from within through culture and spiritual discipline, including worship, austerity, and meditation. Hindu society emphasises the benefits of sadhu-sanga (or sat-sanga), keeping company with pious, saintly people. Hindus still show them respect by reverentially touching their feet and seeking their good wishes and blessings.

VALUES AND STORY

Story remains an essential means of transmitting values. How heroes and heroines embody key virtues is illustrated through their conduct. Many stories focus on the kshatriyas and brahmins, the two varnas most responsible for maintaining social

and spiritual culture. Hindu stories, such as the Mahabharata, often explore the difficulties in performing dharma and in distinguishing right from wrong under trying or unusual circumstances.

Proverbs and legend are other popular ways of nurturing character and wisdom. Moral instruction is found in Niti Shastra texts, like those written by Chanakya. Also popular are legends that have grown around various key figures such as Birbal, the chief minister of the Mughal Emperor Akbar. More recently, some view Mahatma Gandhi as a champion not only of Hindu values but also of modern egalitarian thought. However, traditional Hinduism also challenges modern liberal and libertarian values by stressing the need for sensual and sexual restraint. In Hindu terms, this indicates the degraded nature of this age, the Kali-yuga, which is typified by hypocrisy and quarrelling, and a lack of four key virtues: honesty, austerity, cleanliness and compassion.

PART II

SPIRITUAL PRACTICES

Hinduism is highly experiential, engaging all five senses. It features the spectacular festival of Divali, with rows of lights, and the enchanting arati ceremony, in which the priest blows the conch shell and offers lamps, incense, flowers, food and a fan to the sacred image. Human awareness is similarly elevated through pilgrimage, festivals and rites of passage.

Attendant modes of worship include song and dance, as well as more formal rites, such as the fire sacrifice and temple worship. Variant focuses of worship acknowledge how the divine resides here on earth, and yet beyond, in the eternal realm. Meditation reveals God's tranquil presence within the human heart. Radiant gods and goddesses confirm that the Supreme is both male and female.

Although Hinduism aims at transcendence, it is intimately linked to the land and its wildlife, to time and its revolving seasons. India is full of sacred places, ranging from towering, hilltop temples to its meandering and sanctifying rivers. Within Hinduism, the divine and the mundane intersect through worship, meditation and celebration of sacred time and space.

Opposite On the riverbank at Ujjain, brahmins and attendees offer lamps as part of the process of puja (ritual worship).

Above A sadhu performs meditation. For many Hindus, worship and meditation are intertwined, aimed at personal perception of the divine.

CHAPTER 4

LINKING TO THE DIVINE

A visitor to a Hindu temple often notices the lack of formality and structure. During the congregational arati ceremony, when lamps are offered to the sacred image, people freely come and go. At any given moment, a family group is taking darshana (audience) of the deity, a man sits in lone meditation, and musicians offers tumultuous praise with cymbals and song. Temples fluctuate between meditative silence and clamorous devotion.

Hindu social life is communal, family-based and interdependent, with little scope for private space. On the other hand, spiritual life is highly individualistic and personalized. Even at home, as the family worships a specific god or goddess, the child may adopt her own 'chosen deity'.

To promote individual spiritual progress, Hinduism has developed four main disciplines. They are often intertwined. Hence, worship has assimilated elements of the other paths: meditation, scriptural study and practical service to others. These paths, called 'yogas', broadly share a common aim, to re-establish the everlasting relationship between self and the Supreme.

Opposite A sadhu, marked with Shaiva tilak, recites prayers and mantras before beginning his daily meditation.

Above At Varanasi, priests perform the evening arati ceremony, also observed in most Hindu homes and temples.

THE PATH OF ACTION

KARMA-YOGA IS THE PATH OF SELFLESS ACTION, ESPECIALLY FAVOURED BY HINDUS WHO ARE ACTIVE IN THE WORLD. IT AIMS TO FREE THE PRACTITIONER FROM KARMIC REACTIONS.

For most Hindus, spiritual activities are executed as part of one of four main *margs* (paths), also called 'yogas' (disciplines). Some consider all yogas equally effective, with choice dependant on personal inclination. Others consider them successive and hierarchical: usually in a way that does not entirely reject the 'lower' processes but assimilates and extends them.

It is clear that the four paths cannot be rigidly defined, and there appear to be higher and lower understandings of each path. Furthermore, each of the four paths includes elements of practice from the other three.

Below Members of Hare Krishna 'Food for Life' distributing free meals in South India after the tsunami disaster in 2004.

Right This old people's home at a temple in Kathmandu, Nepal, demonstrates the Hindu principle of selfless action.

The four main disciplines are:

1 Karma-yoga: the path of selfless action
2 Jnana-yoga: the path of knowledge
3 Astanga-yoga (or Raja-yoga); the path of meditation
4 Bhakti-yoga: the path of devotion.

Most popular today is bhakti-yoga. What most people call 'yoga' is actually hatha-yoga, a preliminary step toward meditation; its actual purpose goes beyond health and physical wellbeing. Traditionally, all the 'yogas' aim at self-realization and union with God. This is implied by the literal meaning of yoga, 'to join', from which is derived the English word 'yoke'.

SELFLESS ACTION

Karma-yoga is based on an understanding that action performed solely for material gain binds the self to the cycle of birth and death. Even good activities entangle the soul – though less severely than bad ones – by awarding a celestial body. By karma-yoga, the soul attains freedom from karmic reaction by relinquishing the fruits of action, not the action itself.

On a preliminary level, karma-yoga includes any action performed for a greater cause. It involves sacrifice

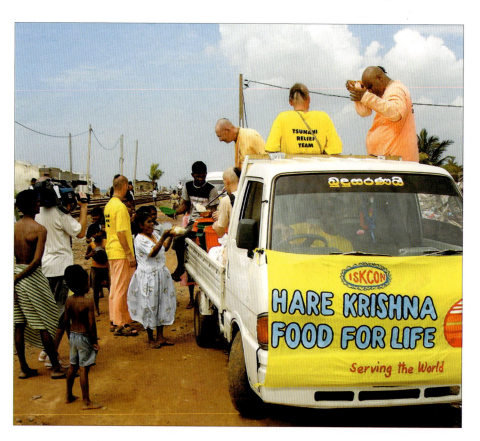

> **KARMA-YOGA**
> The Bhagavad-gita discusses karma-yoga, based on performance of duties according to one's nature, and with detachment.
>
> Therefore, without being attached to the fruits of activities, one should act as a matter of duty, for by working without attachment one attains the Supreme.'
> *Bhagavad-gita 3.9*
>
> The steadily devoted soul attains unadulterated peace because he offers the results of all activities to me, whereas a person who is not in union with the Divine, who is greedy for the fruits of his labour, becomes entangled.
> *Bhagavad-gita 5.12*

and, often, veneration of specific deities to secure material necessities, in this life or the next. On a higher level, karma-yoga is wholehearted dedication to God's service, without desire for reward. Karma-yogis tend to be world-affirming, and they aspire for elevation to higher worlds. Karma-yoga is often favoured by the brahminical (brahmin-led) house-holder traditions, with their stress on social obligations and the performance of private and public ritual.

CHARITY

Customarily, charity has been an essential duty for householders. In the Bhagavad-gita, Krishna recommends discretion in choosing the recipient and discourages donating funds foolishly, to fuel addictive habits, or ostentatiously for fame and profit. Rather, charity should be given selflessly, and to worthy causes related either to spiritual upliftment or to ethical and sustainable solutions to worldly problems.

Traditional Hindu society, built around the extended family, was highly interdependent. Religious obligations included various types of charity, particularly in offering hospitality and feeding others. Most social assistance was offered locally, through the extended family or close community. These days, charity is provided on a broader scale, through global Hindu charities like Sewa International, which collects for victims of floods, earthquakes and other natural disasters. Practically all the transnational religious groups have established charity wings. These include: Food for Life, a vegetarian food relief initiative run by the Hare Krishna Movement; initiatives to help tribal people run by the BAPS

Right A mural of Krishna instructing Arjuna. In the Bhagavad-gita, Krishna recommends selfless action over superficial or premature renunciation.

A STORY ABOUT GIVING

King Rantideva had been fasting for 48 days. As the time to break fast approached, the gods came in disguise, first as a learned brahmin (priest), then a lowly shudra (worker), and finally an outcaste. All were hungry and begged for food. Each time, the king gave portions of his meal, without reservation or consideration of the recipient's status. He finally donated even his water. He prayed, 'I ask not for the eight mystic perfections, nor for liberation from birth and death. I only want to stay among all living beings, suffering discomfort that they become freed from all miseries'. His sentiment illustrates the highest expression of karma-yoga.

Above The fabled King Rantideva gave his food to the needy even after fasting for 48 days.

Swaminarayan Sanstha; and free medical help to the poor from the Ammachi Organization, based in South India. Many organizations contribute toward environmental projects, such as the sacred forests project in Vrindavana and the Bagmati River project in Nepal. In the modern context of climate change, Hindu volunteers draw from ancient ideas about sustainability and compliance with nature's laws.

THE PATH OF KNOWLEDGE

JNANA-YOGA PROMOTES PHILOSOPHICAL REALIZATION OF THE ETERNAL SELF AND FREES THE PRACTITIONER FROM MISCONCEPTION, ESPECIALLY IDENTIFICATION WITH THE PHYSICAL BODY.

Whereas karma-yoga, the path of action, is world-affirming, jnana-yoga, the path of knowledge, relinquishes the world as illusory. The two competing tendencies, toward acquisition and renunciation, are embodied in Lord Shiva. He is portrayed as an affectionate householder, enjoying being with his wife, but also as a lone renunciant, meditating in the icy Himalayas. The moralist Chanakya recognized the human dilemma by writing: 'If you want to enjoy the world, do not develop knowledge; if you desire knowledge, do not try to enjoy this world'. The Bhagavadgita explores this tension whilst examining various types of yoga.

Below In Central India, women of the Murai tribe sell alcohol fermented from tree blossom. Practitioners of jnana-yoga must usually relinquish habits such as intoxication and recreational sex.

JNANA-YOGA

Whereas karma-yogis tend to accept and enjoy the world, jnana-yogis renounce it and embrace austerity for the sake of liberation. An underlying notion is that cessation of action through sensual restraint frees the yogi from karmic reaction and worldly entanglement. This relies on developing wisdom, which is not merely academic but pragmatic, freeing the individual by striking at his or her underlying misconceptions. The core delusion is identification with the temporary mind and body, by which the eternal self thinks, 'I am white and he is black'; 'I am rich and she is poor'; 'I am human and this merely an animal'. Jnanis consider false identification the root of all ignorance, strife and suffering. Adi Shankara, perhaps the greatest exponent of jnana, taught that the self must realize its nature as Brahman

Above The rope–snake illustration depicts a popular metaphor explaining the idea of 'illusion', by which the transmigrating soul accepts the body as the real self.

(eternal spirit). His specific philosophy, called Advaita (non-dualism), entirely equated the individual self with the Supreme Self. Many other schools, though not specifically dedicated to jnana-yoga, recognize the self as Brahman but differentiate it from God, the Supreme Brahman.

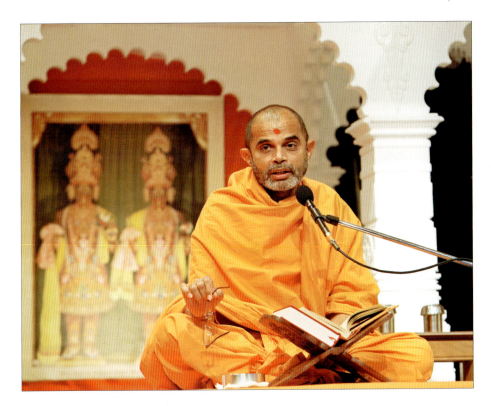

Left A priest gives a lecture. Even in popular Hinduism, enquiry and reflection are encouraged as helpful to spiritual life.

Through illusion, empirical knowledge (gained though the senses) and rational analysis (using mind and intelligence) may simply reinforce error. Hindu texts call these two forms of evidence pratyaksa (direct perception) and anuman (inference). Shankara taught that humans require a third source of evidence, called shabda brahman (sacred sound). It takes the form of revealed scripture, supported by the realizations of the spiritual teacher. Traditionally, the authentic guru didn't just teach scriptural verses, but brought students to self-realization, awareness of their own spiritual identity.

SCRIPTURAL STUDY

The path of jnana gives insight into Hindu epistemology, its approach to acquiring knowledge. Significantly, Hindu texts define dharma not as a 'faith', or a routinely adopted belief system, but as a process of knowledge. Shankara taught that knowledge cannot be merely memorized and repeated, but has to be assimilated, realized and applied.

Since the self is different from the mind and body, intellectual knowledge is insufficient to realize truth. Whatever data humans receive through their mind and senses is prone to incorrect perception and biased evaluation. People cling to erroneous beliefs, and manage to accommodate even contrary evidence within the mistaken view that the self is the body and the world exists simply for individual pleasure. This tendency toward delusion, even in the face of experience and erudition, is termed maya; literally 'that which is not', or illusion. To explain maya, Shankara cited the example of seeing a rope but mistaking it for a snake; an example of not only incorrect apprehension but also of ill-founded emotion, such as fear.

A MEMORABLE LESSON

The following story illustrates how the Hindu teacher tries to invoke insight and realization, not merely theoretical understanding.

A wise and respected guru lived with his disciples in his forest ashrama. One day, a disciple approached the guru and inquired, 'My spiritual preceptor, you are the fountainhead of all knowledge and have realized the import of the Vedas. Please explain what is maya (illusion). When will it release me from her grip?' Gently smiling, the guru replied, 'I will indeed teach you, but not just now'.

Several months passed and the disciple had all but forgotten the incident. As usual, he was chopping firewood for his guru's daily performance of the sacred fire ceremony. Suddenly, he heard a voice – clearly that of his guru – shouting, screaming, 'Help me, let me go. Help! Help! Let go of me!' Seizing his axe, the disciple ran as fast as he could. His mind raced. 'What has happened? Is it a tiger?

Above A Hindu man reads a text to gain insight and personal realization.

Is it a robber? A huge python? What is happening?' The frenzied appeal for help continued. The student ran and ran, blinded to the thorns, unaware of the brambles, mindless of everything but saving his beloved guru. Finally, gasping, he burst into a clearing. There was his guru, tightly embracing a tree and still screaming at the top of his lungs 'Let me go, let me go!'

The disciple never forgot that incident, and realized the Hindu proverb, 'If we cling to our miseries, they will surely cling to us.'

THE PATH OF MEDITATION

ASTANGA-YOGA IS THE PATH OF MEDITATION. THIS TYPE OF YOGA PROMOTES DISCERNMENT OF THE ETERNAL SELF WITHIN, AND AIMS AT COMPLETE DETACHMENT FROM THE MATERIAL WORLD.

Although karma, jnana and bhakti can be listed as 'the three main paths', many books list a fourth called astanga-yoga. More recently, this meditational yoga has been termed raja yoga, 'the king of paths', perhaps attempting to raise its status. Whereas some traditions view all yogas equally, others do indeed argue for the primacy of their own path. Most vociferous are debates between jnanis, philosophers who believe in an impersonal Supreme (Brahman), and bhaktas, devotees of a personal God (Bhagavan). The mystic and meditational yogis tend to concentrate on a third aspect of God, the Antaryami within the heart.

In common with jnana-yoga, the meditational path views the world as suffering, considers all action entangling, and recommends withdrawal and renunciation. However, whereas jnana-yoga stresses knowledge, astanga-yoga values detachment (vairagya).

HISTORY

Yoga may go back to ancient ascetic and forest-dwelling communities composed of rishis (sages) and munis ('silent seers'). The Vedas briefly describe two later sects living on the edge of orthodox Vedic society: first, the Kesins, who had long, matted hair and were associated with Rudra, an early and fierce form of Shiva. They were known for their mystical experiences and supernatural powers, such as their ability to read another's mind. Second, the Vratyas, whom the Atharva Veda describes as warrior-ascetics, somewhat despised by mainstream society. They engaged in strenuous breathing exercises, possibly the prototype of later yogic disciplines. Between 800 and 400BCE, asceticism became more pervasive with the burgeoning of the Shramana traditions. Aligned with the Jains and Buddhists, they stood in contrast to

Above The holy city of Rishikesha, located at the foothills of the Himalayas, is famous for teaching meditative yoga.

the orthodox brahminical traditions, preferring knowledge and detachment to worldly duty and ritual.

However, yogic practices were later embedded within orthodox Hinduism, especially through the assimilation of Patanjali's texts and the subsequent ascendancy of astanga-yoga. Despite this, yoga has always been augmented by the less-orthodox Tantric traditions, which contribute the notion of seven chakras (energy centres) and the practice of kundalini-yoga.

ASTANGA-YOGA AND SANKHYA PHILOSOPHY

'Asta' means 'eight' and 'anga' means 'part.' Astanga-yoga, a practice divided into eight successive stages, is based on the Yoga Sutras of Patanjali and forms the basis for one of the Six Darshanas, namely Yoga. This spiritual discipline is underpinned by another Darshana, Sankhya philosophy, which classifies matter into 25 elements, differentiating the five 'gross' elements from the 'subtle' three: mind, intelligence and false ego. Sankhya comprises a system of discernment, aimed at ultimate perception of the eternal

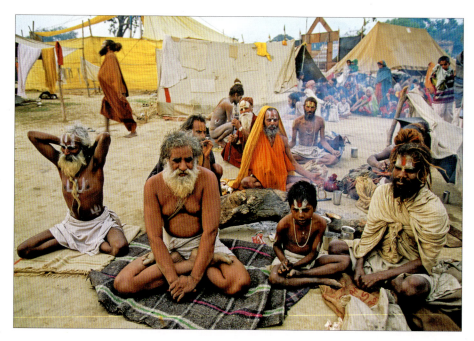

Left Astanga-yoga is favoured by renunciants, shown here in a camp during the Kumbha Mela at Haridvar, 1998.

THE PATH OF MEDITATION

self, later added as 'the 26th element'. Later schools were theistic, adding the 'Super-self', God's form in the heart. Sankhya and Yoga are succinctly explored in the sixth chapter of the Bhagavad-gita, which advocates standards difficult for most contemporary practitioners, requiring celibacy, austerity (tapas) and withdrawal from mainstream society.

MEDITATIONAL YOGA IN MODERN HINDUISM

In the modern age, meditational yoga persists through three main streams. First, the renouncer lineages whose ash-smeared members continue the traditionally austere practice and congregate at the famous Kumbha Mela gathering. Second, through modern organizations, such as Transcendental Meditation and the Shivananda Yoga Centre, which have modified practices to accommodate a wider audience. Third, through popular devotional traditions, which have absorbed many meditational practices, such as mantra meditation.

Below A long-practising yogi, following strict principles, leaves his body to attain the higher moon planet.

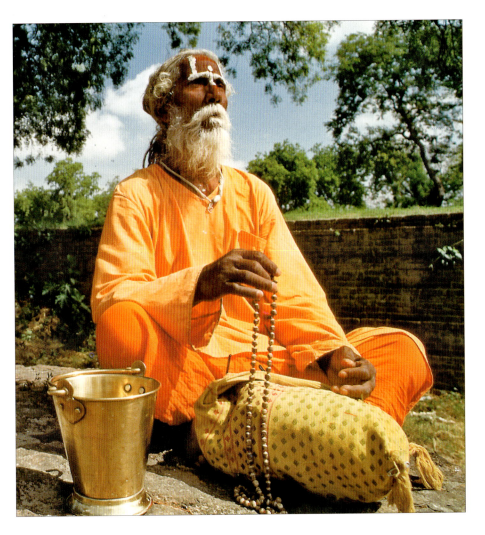

Even worship (puja) is viewed as a means of fixing undivided attention on the object of adoration. Whereas astanga-yoga is largely mechanical, bhakti traditions stress the key role of love and affection in focusing the mind. Despite some differences, the diverse schools share certain beliefs, such as the effect of mental states on the soul's destination, and the social benefits of enhancing human consciousness.

YOGIC POWER

The yoga sutras discuss super states of awareness and the obtainment of eight types of mystic perfection. They include the ability to become 'smaller than the smallest', or 'lighter than the lightest'. India is replete with tales of attendant feats, largely accepted as credible rather than entirely superstitious. None the less, Patanjali warns the yogi not to be

Above Meditational practices are central to 'other' paths. A bhakta (devotee) of Vishnu recites mantras with concentration while fingering prayer beads.

enamoured by such mystic perfections, but to keep the mind fixed on liberation. The highest perfection is to focus without distraction on the divine within, a state called samadhi. Although sometimes translated as 'trance', samadhi literally means 'fixed mind', and refers to a highly alert, absorbed and completely unruffled state of mind. However, Hindu narrative is replete with stories of powerful yogis who fail to control the mind, often falling victim to heavenly nymphs dispatched to break their vows. The famous beauty Shakuntala was begotten by Vishvamitra in the womb of Menaka, who had been sent by Indra, apprehensive of the sage's

THE PATH OF DEVOTION

BHAKTI YOGA IS THE PATH OF DEVOTIONAL SERVICE. IT AIMS TO NURTURE THE APPROPRIATE DESIRE AND ATTITUDE, AND ULTIMATELY PREMA, SPONTANEOUS LOVE OF GOD.

Whereas karma-yoga affirms the world, and jnana-yoga renounces it, bhakti attempts to resolve these conflicting human tendencies. Bhakti theologies teach that everything belongs to God, and thus nothing can be owned or renounced. Some bhakti groups shun even liberation, advocating prema (love of God) as the final and fifth goal of life.

Bhakti traces its history to the latter half of the first millennium and the emotional outpourings of the Tamil poet-saints. Building theological support was left to scholars such as Ramanuja (1017–1137CE), who extended Shankara's non-theistic doctrine into a theology called 'qualified monism'. His teachings strongly influenced both Vaishnavism and, less directly, devotional Shaivism. The Shaivas and Tantrics also fostered their own scholars, such as Abhinavagupta (950–1020CE), who developed an early theory of aesthetics and spiritual sentiment. The first bhakti movement, the 12th-century Lingayats, venerated Lord Shiva.

Above The installation of a Narasimha deity at a temple in Rajkot, Gujarat. Worship of the sacred image is integral to much devotional yoga.

DEVOTIONAL MOVEMENTS

As Islamic rule took hold in India, bhakti swept north. It was popularized by ecstatic saints who threw off the social constraints of both caste and foreign rule. There were two main stands. Through saints such as Kabir, the northern 'sant' tradition preached personal piety, the ever-presence of God, and syncretism with other faiths. Others, like Tulsidas and Chaitanya, focused on building a rapport with a personal God, most often Rama or Krishna.

During British rule, key reformers resisted bhakti, considering puja and the Puranas to be superstitious impositions on the pure, more rational 'Vedic' religion. Other scholars revitalized bhakti, making it accessible to modern thought. Today, it remains the most popular path, extending beyond Vaishnavism and Shaivism to almost every denomination. The widely studied Bhagavad-gita is largely interpreted as a devotional text.

Bhakti has influenced the other paths, but has also assimilated and extended their practices. From karma-yoga it has borrowed practical service to God; from jnana it has developed rigorous theology; from

Left Hindu priests offer more than 700 different vegetarian items at the Swaminarayana Temple on Kolkata during the Annakuta festival.

NINE PROCESSES OF BHAKTI

Texts list nine practices of devotion. The first three are about knowledge, the second three about action, and the third three about sentiment:

Hearing about God
Glorifying the Lord
Remembering the Lord

Serving God's lotus feet
Offering worship (puja)
Offering heartfelt prayer

Feeling oneself God's servant
Nurturing friendship with God
Surrendering everything

the meditative path, it has gleaned musical kirtana, chanting on beads and contemplation on the deity's divine form. From Tantra, bhakti uses Agama texts to regulate puja, and values direct experience and the complementary roles of male and female divinities. A distinctive feature of bhakti is faith in the redeeming power of chanting God's holy names.

Above Women in the Krishna Temple in Udaipur happily sing devotional 'kirtan'. Their joy is conspicuous and contagious.

THE PATH OF THE HEART

Some consider the path of devotion easy, for those of sentimental disposition. Bhakti lineages often lay claim to intellectual rigour. Despite this, they insist that the assimilation of wisdom rests on appropriate attitudes, such as surrender to the divine will. Sophisticated theologies delineate successive stages of bhakti, beginning with regulated service and concluding with spontaneous, unbounded love. The stage of perfection, not easily attained, is typified by spiritual ecstasy, exhibited through horripilation (goosebumps), singing and dancing, and indifference to external surroundings. For bhaktas, such emotions represent the innate, exuberant character of the eternal soul.

Bhakti movements stress not only diligence in devotional sadhana (practice), but the need for God's grace, often received though the guru (spiritual teacher) and other devotees. The precise relationship between grace and personal sadhana is much debated. Theological differences are conspicuous in the Ramanuja sampradaya, which split

Left A Western devotee sews elaborate costumes for temple deities in London.

into two distinct groups, the Vedagalais (who stress God's mercy) and Thenagalais (who equally value endeavour). Many traditions advocate the need for both.

GARUDA AND THE SPARROW

The following story explains how devotional paths acknowledge the role of God's grace as well as determined spiritual endeavour.

Once, a sparrow laid her eggs on the seashore, but the ocean carried them away on its waves. The sparrow was upset and asked the ocean to return her eggs. The mighty ocean ignored her appeal. So the sparrow decided to dry up the ocean. As she began to peck out the water in her small beak, everyone laughed at her impossible determination. The news spread, and at last reached the ears of Garuda, the gigantic bird carrier of Vishnu. Feeling compassion for his small sister bird, he came to see her. Pleased at her determination, he promised to help. He asked the ocean to return her eggs, lest he himself take up the work of the sparrow. At this, the frightened ocean returned the eggs. Thus, the sparrow became happy by the grace of Garuda.

TANTRA

THOUGH CLOSELY LINKED TO RENOUNCER TRADITIONS, TANTRA IS ALSO A PERVASIVE ESOTERIC INFLUENCE. IT ALSO REFERS TO SPECIFIC MYSTICAL DISCIPLINES AND THEIR ASSOCIATED TEXTS.

In popular myth, Tantra is mistakenly associated with esoteric sexual practice, and has been called 'the yoga of sex'. A whole industry has sprung up around this idea. However, Tantra is hard to define, and is best classified in three main ways. First, it can be considered a specific discipline, akin to the four main 'yogas'. It is closely connected to the mystical practices of astanga-yoga. Second, some define it as a particular denomination of Hinduism; in fact, it is closely linked to both Shaktism and Shaivism, and combines elements of both. Third, Tantra refers to a particular branch of Hindu literature, falling largely outside the standard two divisions of Shruti and Smriti. Tantra comprises a third scriptural category, with its own status and field of application.

TANTRA: A DISTINCT PATH

Despite common stereotypes, Tantra is strongly connected to renouncer (Shramana) traditions, with their disposition toward jnana (knowledge) and vairagya (renunciation). However, some Tantrics are strongly inclined to express mystical enlightenment while living in the world, rather than away from it. Tantra is also related to yoga through shamanism and the exercise of mystic powers.

Indeed, modern Tantra shares many concepts with astanga-yoga, including the notion of two nadis (energy channels) and seven chakras (energy centres). In the Tantric practice of kundalini-yoga, the adept raises 'the serpent power' (kundalini) from the base of the

Above A sacred statue of Ardharani, an androgynous deity composed of Shiva and his consort Shakti. The interplay of male and female energies is central to Tantra.

spine up to the 'thousand lotus chakra' at the top of the head. The process is risky, and the novice may lose control of the vibrant energy, only to be marooned on a particular chakra. The chakras correspond to the seven levels of the planetary system, and the centre of attention determines the self's destination at death. For this reason, practitioners are advised to avoid giving inordinate attention to lower chakras, corresponding to lower planets and subhuman species.

Tantra is also identified with the yantra, used as a mystical and meditative diagram, or as a lucky talisman. The most important yantra is the Shri Yantra, a series of hierarchical triangles representing the goddess Lakshmi. The main motif for Tantric traditions is similar: a six-pointed star, with the upright triangle denoting the potent male (Shiva), and the inverted triangle the fertile female (Shakti).

Below The model of seven chakras (energy centres) in the human body is derived from Tantric sources and the practice of Kundalini-yoga.

Sahasrara:
The Crown Chakra

Ajna:
The Brow Chakra

Vishuddha:
The Throat Chakra

Anahata:
The Heart Chakra

Manipura:
The Solar Plexus Chakra

Svadhisthana:
The Sacral Chakra

Muladhara:
The Base Chakra

TANTRA: A DENOMINATION

Based on the male-female dynamic called 'Shiva-Shakti', Tantra is linked to both these deities. Their corresponding communities are intertwined, both through Tantra and because Shaktism has long borrowed doctrine from Shaiva scholarship. Tantra is close to Kashmiri Shaivism. One of its greatest scholars, Abhinavagupta, tried to reconcile the four main sub-groups by writing a text called Tantraloka, 'The Divine Light of Tantra'. The southern Shaiva Siddhanta sect, based on the teachings of St Thirumular, also shares similarities with the Tantric school. Within Shaktism, Tantra is closely connected to the South Indian Shri Vidya community and with Kali worshippers in eastern India.

Elements of Tantra also appear in many Vaishnava bhakti movements, especially those synthesizing male and female principles, as in worshipping Sita-Rama and Radha-Krishna. Tantra

Right An illustration of the Shri (Lakshmi) Yantra.

has connections to Jainism, Buddhism and Tibetan Bon. Although some scholars describe Tantra as a distinct tradition, its pervasive influence is evident in most denominations. A common feature of Tantra is its stress on promoting direct spiritual experience.

Tantra has two main branches. The left-hand path refers to those who deliberately defy social and natural conventions to achieve detachment. They include the Aghoris, who eat from a human skull, live in crematoriums and even eat human excreta. The right-hand path is socially orthodox and uses Tantric texts largely to communally regulate procedures of worship. Tantra further enhances puja by adding meditative and experiential elements, making it a symbolic visualization of Vishnu's Vaikuntha world and other higher realms.

TANTRA: A SET OF TEXTS

As a third definition, Tantra refers to a body of sacred text. Their status is debated, and some brahminical traditions reject the texts as non-orthodox, especially for their joint ownership by Jains and Buddhists. The widely accepted Agamas discuss philosophy, spiritual disciplines and the technicalities of temple worship. For Shaiva and Shakta sects they are core texts. For Vaishnavas, an important sub-division is the 'pancharatra', which complements the main Vedic canon and regulates worship in many South Indian temples, and in specific traditions such as Bengali Vaishnavism. Other Vaishnava groups, such as the Vaikhanasas based in Tirupati, reject the Pancharatrika system and use alternative Agama texts (also called 'Vaikhanasas') derived from the Atharva Veda.

In some ways, the radical elements of Tantric and Shramanic traditions have been held in tension with orthodox, Vedic Brahminism. However, in typical Hindu fashion, the Vedic and Tantric elements have been largely reconciled, symbolizing the interaction of heaven with earth, male with female, and scriptural authority with human experience.

Left Although Tantra is identified with renouncer traditions, more orthodox Hindus use tantric texts to regulate temple worship.

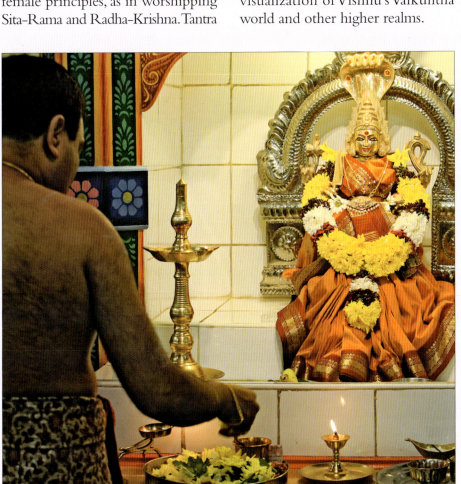

FOCUSES OF WORSHIP

HINDU WORSHIP IS BROAD AND INCLUSIVE. ALTHOUGH IT EMBRACES MANY FOCUSES OF WORSHIP, IT USUALLY AIMS TO REVERE ONE GOD, WHO IS REPRESENTED IN MANY WAYS.

Hindu worship exhibits a number of distinctive and conspicuous features. Although communal worship is central to some groups, much practice is performed individually and with significant emphasis on personal experience of the divine. Public ceremonies are only casually regulated: individuals are free to join, participate as they choose, and leave when they wish. Worship may appear to lack the solemnity often associated with religion. God can be worshipped with awe and reverence but also more affectionately, as if a close friend or relative. The stress on individuality means that much worship occurs outside the public sphere, especially at home.

At home or temple, no specific day of the week is dedicated to worship. In common practice, days are associated with particular deities.

Right A young priest offers arati to the sacred tulasi plant, considered dear to Lord Vishnu.

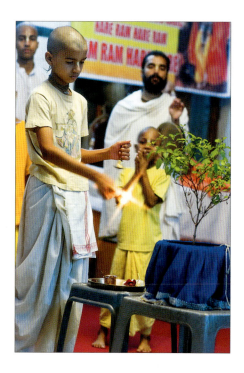

For example, Shiva is propitiated on Monday, and the Goddess on Friday. On the appropriate day of the week, it is customary to perform specific pujas and observe vows such as fasting. In the Western world, rigid and busy work schedules have popularized weekend worship. Festivals falling midweek are often celebrated, additionally or alternatively, at the nearest adjacent weekend.

The time of day is relatively important. Especially beneficial for spiritual practice are the hours

Below An elderly lady dresses and garlands the murtis of Krishna and Radha within the famous Mahalakshmi Temple at Kolhapur, Maharashtra.

SPECIFIC FOCUSES OF WORSHIP

The following list indicates some of the diverse focuses of Hindu worship.

God, as either the impersonal absolute or the Supreme Person

The variety of gods, goddesses and minor deities

The spiritual preceptor, called the *acharya* or guru

The teacher, who is also addressed as 'guru'

The qualified *brahmin*, often including the family priest

The pious monarch, who is a representative of God

Family elders, especially the mother and father

The cow (as mother) and bull (as father)

Sacred plants, such as the Tulasi and Bilva

Sacred rivers, such as the Ganga, Yamuna and Kaveri

The land, especially sites traversed by saints and avataras

All peoples and all living beings, who are parts of God

Above During the Divali festival, Nepalese women garland and offer fruit to a cow, which they consider an incarnation of the goddess Lakshmi.

surrounding dawn, a period considered tranquil and auspicious. In India especially, temples begin their first public ceremony between four and six in the morning. They are closed after lunch, when the weather may be uncomfortably hot, and when temple deities and their caretakers take a siesta. In the early evening, temples again open their doors, and worship finishes around nine o'clock.

UNITY AND DIVERSITY

Perhaps the most conspicuous feature of Hinduism is its inclusivity, and the sheer number of deities and other objects of veneration. Some have described Hinduism as polytheistic, but this is simplistic and misleading.

The worship of so many objects is underpinned by two key concepts. First, all the 'high', scholarly traditions

Right A young pilgrim from Jodhpur offers flowers and incense to the Ganges at the holy town of Haridwar.

recommend worship of a single Supreme. At the same time, they recognize various stages on the path of realization, with a hierarchy of purposes culminating in moksha (liberation). The worship of lesser deities for specific materialistic goals is accepted as conducive to gradual elevation. This hierarchical stance has been termed 'inclusive monotheism', implying acceptance of many deities while considering one to be Supreme: usually Vishnu, Shiva or Devi. Other schools, best described as monists or 'non-dualists', teach that the deities equally represent various attributes of Brahman, the singular impersonal Supreme. However, for both monotheist and monist, the prominent belief is in a single God.

Equally significant is a second idea: God can be worshipped through his or her many representatives. These often take the form of natural, benign authority figures, such as the guru and parents. By venerating them, one shows respect to God; by dishonouring or neglecting them, one disrespects

the Supreme. The tendency for inclusion does not indicate that Hindus can worship absolutely anything, but it does mean that Hindus are generally happy to attend places of worship not directly related to their own chosen deity or denominational background.

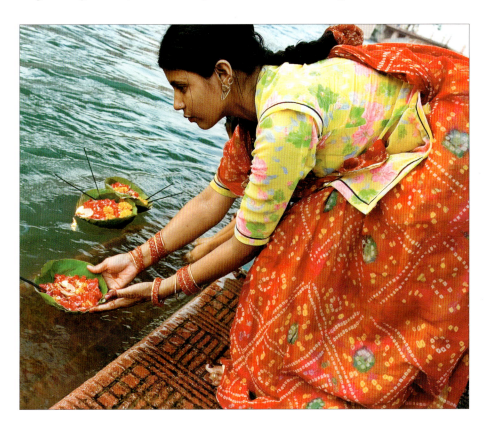

TYPES OF WORSHIP

WORSHIP (UPASANA) ACCOMMODATES DIVERSE PRACTICES, EACH
INTEGRAL TO ONE OF THE FOUR MAIN PATHS. MOST POPULAR IS PUJA,
DEVOTIONAL ADORATION OF THE SACRED IMAGE.

A major historical development within Hindu worship was the transmission from the practice of Vedic yajna (sacrifice) to the subsequent prominence of puja. Puja is most important to the bhakti traditions, and this term, more than others, accurately translates as 'worship'. Yet bhakti assimilated elements of the other three 'yogas'; for example, the notion of seva (service), prominent in karma-yoga; scriptural study, central to jnana-yoga; and the meditational practices at the core of raja-yoga. At the same time, those who follow the other yogas have adopted aspects of bhakti. In dis-

*Below Family members take
darshan (audience) of the deities at
the BAPS Swaminarayana temple in
Neasden, London.*

cussing the path of knowledge, Shankara stressed the need for devotion and humility: for practising astanga-yoga, a prerequisite is *ishvara pranidhana*, 'offering to the Lord'; and karma-yoga remains sectarian without a shared object of service.

Therefore, the practices inherent in all these yogas can be broadly labelled as 'worship'. In the Bhagavad-gita, Krishna suggests that those who study scripture 'worship me with their intelligence'. And, when Shiva saved the universe by drinking an ocean of poison, his service was described as 'the best type of worship'. For these reasons, diverse practices fall under the broad category of 'worship'. It can even accommodate classical forms of dance, first developed for the pleasure of the temple deities.

*Above Playing the harmonium, a young
woman leads the kirtan, congregational
chanting, at a temple near Mathura,
central India.*

MAIN PRACTICES

By identifying practices linked to the Vedic period and, more recently, the 'four main paths', worship can be classified into five main categories:

• The Homa or Havana – the sacred fire ceremony.
• Sewa – active service to the sacred image or holy people.
• Scriptural study, teaching and public recitation.
• Meditational practices, such as chanting mantras.
• Puja, ritualistic worship of the sacred image.

There are five other activities, usually falling under Puja:
• Darshana – 'taking audience'.
• Pradakshina – circumambulation, generally performed clockwise.
• Arati – the main Hindu ceremony.
• Bhajana or kirtana – musical glorification, hymns and chants.
• Prasada – sacred food offered to the deity and then eaten.

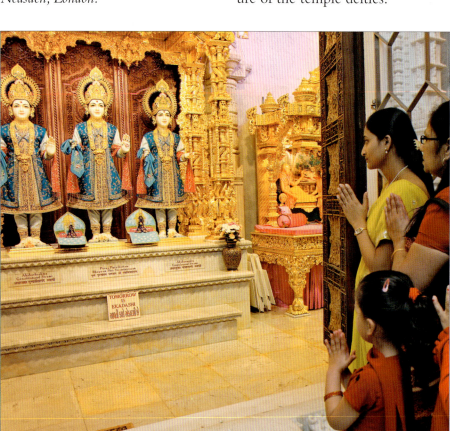

TEN MAJOR ACTS OF WORSHIP

Havana

Havana yajna is translated as 'fire sacrifice'. This Vedic ceremony, also called 'homa' or 'agnihotra' is still performed during rites of passage, such as marriage. Grains and ghee are offered to the Divine through the fire and to the chanting of *mantras*.

Sewa

Active service to the deity is considered a form of worship. Lay members serve the murti by cleaning the temple etc. Many traditions praise the merits of serving sadhus through hospitality, and holy places by sweeping the land and assisting pilgrims.

Scriptural Study

Pravachan refers to a philosophical lecture, based on the holy texts and delivered by a guru, priest or scholar. The speaker often sits on an elevated seat out of respect for the authority of scripture. Scriptural study is likewise an act of worship.

Meditation and Prayer

Traditional meditation includes focusing attention on the self and God within. Mantra meditation includes the quiet recitation of a mantra (japa) and the thrice-daily chanting of the Gayatri mantra.

Above Devotees circumambulate and touch sacred items at a temple in Krishna's holy town, Vrindavana.

Puja

This is the ritualistic worship offered to the deity, in which the images are bathed, dressed and treated as dignitaries. It embraces other practices, often related to welcoming and entertainment.

Darshana

Darshana means 'seeing', though it is better translated as 'audience'. With palms folded in prayer, devotees present themselves before the temple deity or a holy person to request guidance and blessings.

Pradakshina

Circumambulation is a form of offering respect, and is usually performed in a clockwise direction. Within or around many temples are walkways for circumambulation of the deity, and pilgrims often circumambulate holy places and sacred towns.

Arati

This is the most popular Hindu ceremony today and involves the offering of lamps, flowers and other items. It often begins and concludes with blowing a conch shell.

Bhajana and kirtana

Bhajan, meaning 'adoration', usually refers to a devotional hymn. Kirtan, 'glorification', most often indicates the repetition of mantras to musical accompaniment.

Prasada

Temple visitors often conclude their darshana by accepting morsels of prasada (sacred food) offered to the deity. It is believed to purify body, mind and soul, and to bestow considerable spiritual merit.

Left Hindi priests in Varanasi make the sacred fire offering and offer prayers to promote religious unity.

111

PUJA AND ARATI

LINKED WITH DEVOTIONAL TRADITIONS, PUJA EMBRACES MANY
RITUALS, INCLUDING THE ARATI CEREMONY. IT IS REGULATED BY
TANTRIC TEXTS ASSIMILATED INTO THE ORTHODOX CANON.

The word puja literally means 'worship' but specifically refers to ritual adoration of a sacred image. The arati ceremony is the most popular public ceremony

PUJA

The purpose of puja is to nurture reciprocation with God, either directly or through an intermediary, such as the guru. Puja is a means of offering loving service, and acknowledging the supremacy, proprietorship and generosity of God. Having assimilated Tantric principles, and often regulated by such texts, puja is an elaborate visualization of the spiritual realm, a simulation of the loving exchanges between the self and the Divine.

Puja involves bathing and dressing the murti, and presenting pleasing items: water, perfume and flower garlands. It culminates in offering food and the arati ceremony. Texts such as the Agamas list a minimum of 16 acts, beginning with the 'offering of a seat' to welcome the deity. This systematic worship is classified as nitya (continuous), indicating that scheduled temple puja must continue daily, from early morning to late evening. Puja at home is less tightly regulated and often a simplified version of the grand temple services. At the household shrine, the temple murti is often replaced with framed pictures of the family's chosen deity, the family guru and deceased relatives such as parents.

Above The bathing ceremony. Substances considered specially pure, such as milk, yoghurt, honey and water, are poured over miniature deities of Rama and Sita.

ARATI

Temples perform arati up to seven times per day. It is mainly offered to the murti but is also a means of welcoming and honouring sadhus (holy people) and other representations of the divine, such as a holy river. Arati is popularly called 'the ceremony of lights', but employs many other natural items: incense, flowers, water, a lamp with camphor, and red kum-kum (vermilion powder). Holding these auspicious items in the right hand, the worshipper moves them in clockwise circles before the deity, all the time ringing a bell with the left hand. The ceremony lasts 5–30 minutes and is announced and concluded by the blast of a conch shell.

During the temple ritual, the offered lamps are passed around the congregation; in turn, attendees sweep their fingers over the flame and reverentially touch their foreheads. The priest may also distribute the offered flowers and sprinkle holy water over the heads of the assembled devotees. The arati may be embellished with devotional singing or the repeated striking of a gong, creating a distinctive atmosphere and sense of occasion.

Left A pujari (temple priest) sprinkles worshippers with holy water during the arati ceremony at a temple in Vrindavana.

Right A priest offers a lamp to Ganesha during an arti ceremony in Mumbai.

TEMPLE PRIESTS

Each temple has a team of priests, usually recruited from the brahmin community. They perform the nitya (regular) ritual worship, and also the nimitika (occasional) ceremonies, such as rites of passage. Traditionally, only men were allowed to enter the priesthood, though certain movements such as ISKCON and the Lingayats also welcome women. In Western countries, trained priests were originally brought from India, but some sampradayas (lineages) now train them locally. Priests are expected to follow certain rules and regulations, such as adherence to a vegetarian diet, and abstinence from gambling and intoxication. Before entering the inner sanctum, they must bathe and dress in fresh, clean clothes. The technical term for a priest is 'pujari' or 'purohit' and, out of respect for their erudition, they are often formally addressed as 'pandit' or 'panditji'.

THE SACRED IMAGE

Distinctive to Hinduism is widespread worship of the murti. Image worship has met much criticism and violence from religions that consider it a symptom of much-maligned polytheism or 'idol worship'. Possibly influenced by Western thought, some Hindu reform movements, such as the Arya Samaj, also reject the practice as outdated and superstitious. Many contemporary Hindu thinkers, especially jnana-yogis, ultimately reject it while considering it beneficial for less-intelligent, common folk. Possibly shamed by claims of idolatry, some explain the murti as merely 'a meditational aid'. However, for many Hindus, God is actually present in the murti, fully conscious of their thoughts, feelings and attitudes, and sensing even the touch of their hand on the stone or brass.

Scholars have written extensively on the theology of deity worship. Madhva classified the authentic deity as an avatara (divine descent). Adi Shankara taught that because God is present everywhere, he must also be present in the murti. Ramanuja similarly stated, 'Although the Lord is all pervading, using His omnipotent powers He appears before devotees to accept their devotion through an image.'

However, this does not imply that all image worship is acceptable. Corresponding Hindu texts, usually from the Tantras, enjoin adherents to worship only authorized forms of the murti. They set out strict rules for its manufacture, installation and subsequent worship. Image worship is considered both an aesthetic art form and a profound spiritual science, helping Hindu people develop and express their personal relationship with God.

Below The central shrine houses images of Krishna and his consort, Radha. As part of puja, decoration of the shrine is a distinctive, sophisticated art form.

MEDITATIVE PRACTICES

MEDITATION IS EXPLICITLY PRACTISED IN THE YOGIC AND TANTRIC TRADITIONS. ORTHODOX AND POPULAR STRANDS HAVE ASSIMILATED KEY ELEMENTS, SUCH AS THE REPETITIOUS CHANTING OF MANTRAS.

The traditional, orthodox astanga-yoga consists of eight stages, beginning with two sets of prerequisites, called yama and niyama. The five yama (restraints) are non-violence, non-lying, freedom from greed, celibacy and non-possessiveness. The five niyama (observances) are cleanliness of body and mind, contentment, austerity, scriptural study and worship of the Supreme. Stage three, 'asana', entails the adoption of physical postures to promote health and suppleness of body. The fourth step, pranayama, consists of breathing exercises that steady the mind. After this, the yogi sits firmly

Below Pilgrims chant mantras on their sacred meditation beads, which are respectfully used and carried in embroidered bags.

and pulls the mind and senses inward to avoid distraction from the external world. This concludes the first five stages, called external sadhana (external spiritual discipline).

The last three stages comprise real meditation, or internal sadhana. During dharana, concentration, the yogi remains conscious of his or her attempts to meditate, and the object of meditation is sometimes obscured. The seventh stage is called steadfast meditation (dhyana), typified by an unimpeded flow of thought around the object of meditation. The eighth and final stage is complete absorption, samadhi, in which no external event can distract the practitioner. In that state, the yogi is free of all misery arising from contact with the mind and body, and experiences unbounded spiritual bliss.

Above A brahmin engages in morning meditation. Although yogic and meditational practices are central to the Shramanic (renouncer) traditions, which favour Tantric texts, they are also integral to much orthodox, brahminical ritual.

MANTRA YOGA

Since astanga-yoga requires staunch discipline and retirement from everyday life, it appears largely impractical today, except for a dedicated few. However, many elements of meditation have been assimilated into contemporary practice, especially in the devotional schools; for example, mantra meditation, which involves the quiet or silent repetition of a series of sacred syllables.

As the basis for yoga practice, Sankhya philosophy teaches that by controlling sound, the most subtle of the five elements, the practitioner gains mastery over the other elements. This is the theory behind casting charms and spells. The material creation was generated from the first ever sound, the sacred syllable Om. It consists of three sounds: A-U-M, and its visual representation, like an elaborate figure three, is often used as the symbol of Hinduism. Many mantras begin with the sacred Om.

Mantra meditation takes three important forms. The first, chanting of the Gayatri, is observed thrice daily by brahmins and other members of the three higher varnas. Second is japa, the quiet or silent repetition of others mantras, such as 'Om namo Shivaya' or the well-known Hare Krishna mantra. Japa is generally performed on a mala, a string of 108 beads, usually made of tulasi wood (for Vaishnavas) or rudraksha beads (for Shaivas). The chanting should be performed with attention, to discipline the mind and senses and fix attention on the divine. A third form of mantra yoga is kirtana, responsive and melodious chanting to the accompaniment of drums and hand-cymbals. It largely derives from the medieval bhakti traditions, which also use dance as a means of religious expression.

MANTRAS AND PRAYERS

The following are two important prayers:

'Let us meditate upon the worshipable divine effulgence of the sun which illuminates the universe and inspires our meditation.' (Gayatri Mantra, from the *Rig Veda*)

From the temporary lead me to the eternal!
From darkness lead me to light!
From death lead me to ever-lasting life! (*Brihadaranyaka Upanishad 1.3.28*)

Below A man offers prayers at the Menakshi Temple in Madurai.

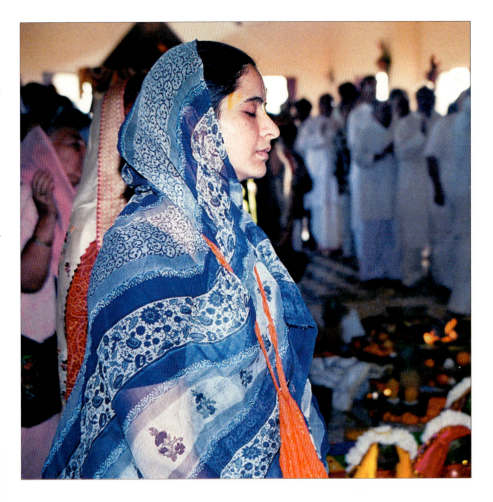

Kirtana meditation is increasingly popular even with non-Hindus, outside of its overtly religious context.

Above This woman appears absorbed in meditation during musical kirtan (chanting of mantras).

PRAYER

Some texts list vandana, the offering of prayer and supplication, as one of nine processes of devotion. However, there is no clear boundary between a prayer (prarthana), a hymn (bhajana) and a devotional poem (kavya). The earliest text, the Rig Veda, contains a prayer called the Purusha Shukta, which is also called 'a creation hymn'. The Vedas also include many prayers to recite during sacrifice, such as the havana. However, they tend be mechanical and functional, with emphasis on precise pronunciation for desired results.

One story tells of how a giant demon, Vritya, was created from the sacrificial fire to kill Lord Indra. However, because the officiating priest mispronounced the mantra, the contrary result was achieved: using his fabled thunderbolt, Indra beheaded his aspiring assassin.

Prayers in the later Epics and Puranas give more attention to appropriate attitude, and are directed toward devotional deities, such as Rama, Shiva and Devi. Later, the Alvars and Nayanmars composed many beautiful poems, and the subsequent northern saints expressed similar spiritual sentiment. Hindus today still recite many of these standard prayers, which often follow set forms. For example, it is a matter of etiquette to request a benediction only after offering glorification. Hindus also compose their own heartfelt prayers, as when coming before the deity for darshana. Prayer is essential in establishing a rapport between the individual self and the divine.

PLACES OF WORSHIP

HINDU WORSHIP IS PERFORMED IN THREE MAIN PLACES: THE HOME,
THE TEMPLE AND OUTDOORS. THESE ENVIRONMENTS SHOULD BE PURE
AND UPLIFTING, AS DEFINED BY THE SCIENCE OF SACRED SPACE.

Places of worship are often connected to sacred sites, which are considered gateways to higher worlds. Favourite spots include rivers, mountains and legendary places associated with a particular saint or deity. There is a reverse notion, by which the presence of a shrine sanctifies a previously mundane spot, making it holy. A relatively obscure deity may acquire a reputation for performing miracles or fulfilling prayers, transforming his residence into a pilgrimage site, with thousands flocking for darshana.

VILLAGE AND ROADSIDE SHRINES
Due to the favourable Indian climate, many shrines there are outdoors, with no external structure, or simply a makeshift covering designating their presence. Deities are

Below Inside a temple in Dhaka, Bengal, a priest hands out holy water to worshippers during Durga Puja.

also worshipped through natural landmarks, such as rocks, trees, rivers or mountains. The streets of most communities are punctuated with many such shrines: roughly shod images at the base of a banyan tree; black stones daubed with vermillion; a tree decorated with strips of coloured cloth.

Some villages feature large unsheltered deities, such as those of Ayyanar, a warrior riding a white horse. In many villages of Tamil Nadu, he is the central deity, surrounded by numerous village guardians. These minor deities, called grama-devata, are usually located at the village periphery. Frequently, the most honoured deity is a local goddess, the mother of the community and its affairs. Also popular, particularly in Nepal, is a fierce form of Shiva called Bhairava. In many rural communities, Nagas (snake deities) are considered nature spirits and the protectors of springs, wells and rivers. They bring rain and fertility,

Above A devotee rings the bell as she enters the Bhairav Nath temple in New Delhi during the nine-day Navaratri festival in honour of the goddess Devi.

but also floods, drought and others natural disasters. Rural shrines often include their grey stone images, with several heads and bedecked with flower offerings.

The village shrine often lacks a full-time priest or caretaker. Instead, community members take turns cleaning, caring for images, and replacing flowers and offerings. Some deities are gradually elevated, and eventually housed in a village temple.

TEMPLES
The Hindu temple is considered the home of God or a particular deity. As embassies of higher realms, temple structures are sacred spaces, ideologically exempt from mundane laws and concerns. Here, the deities receive offerings and, apparently, respond to worshippers taking their darshana (sacred sight). Many temples incorporate palace architecture, reflecting how the deities are treated as kings and queens.

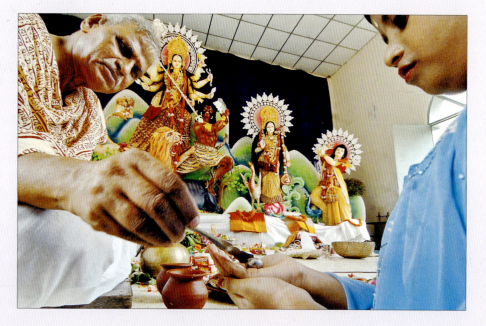

Temples vary considerably in size, beginning with humble village mandirs. The larger temples are elaborate and often the centre of an entire complex with a large number of brahmin priests living within or nearby. The temple of Balaji in Tirupati (South India) is considered the most popular, with a total staff of around 7,000. The geographically largest, at Srirangam, occupies 156 acres, is surrounded by seven concentric walls, and boasts a main gateway 72 metres (78.7 yards) high.

HOME SHRINES

Almost all Hindu families tend a home shrine, at least a few pictures propped on a shelf in the kitchen or living room. Those with sufficient space may dedicate a whole room to worship and meditation. The shrine itself contains pictures of the family's chosen deity, the family guru and elders such as deceased parents. Some families install small murtis of brass, stone or marble, often requiring more strict and regulated puja. This is generally performed by the women of the household early in the morning. Children are often involved, as a way of teaching traditional values and practices. Although children grow up worshipping the

kula-deva (family deity), as young adults they may decide on their own ishta-deva (chosen deity). For this reason, there may be several individual shrines in one household. Some families offer regular arati and sanctify all food before eating themselves.

PORTABLE SHRINES

Shrines can be portable. Visitors to India cannot avoid noticing the miniature iconography propped on the taxi dashboard to bring the driver good luck. Respectable families and

Above A couple worship at their home shrine during the festival of Divali.

sadhus (mendicants) travel with their domestic or personal deities, safely stowed in padded boxes. These they unfold into miniature shrines, allowing them to perform daily puja wherever they travel. Whilst on walking pilgrimage (padayatra), deities ride on ox-driven carts and arati is offered as they stand on a decorated, moveable shrine.

Significantly, the heart of the worshipper is also considered a place of worship. Some Vaishnava traditions have developed sophisticated systems of manasa-seva, 'worship in the mind'. In the sacred town of Vrindavana, the babajis (renunciates) meditate on the daily actives of Radha and Krishna, divided into eight daily periods. Such practice reflects belief in a close relationship between inner and outer space, and the need for acts of worship to be internalized. The body is a temple, and God resides there, within the shrine of the heart.

Left This local outdoor shrine at Maheshwar, Madhya Pradesh, is dedicated to Hanuman and Shiva.

CHAPTER 5

HINDU DEITIES

One of the first things noticed by any visitor to India is the vast number of gods and goddesses. Posters of blue-, black- and golden-complexioned figures smile radiantly from the walls of shops, offices and roadside stalls. They sport flower garlands, and their many hands bear conch shells and lotus flowers, or wield an array of weapons. One palm is raised to bestow bountiful blessings on both the intentional visitor and the casual passer by.

In relation to God, Hinduism displays a number of salient features. Three are most notable. First, notions of God extend beyond the popular Western idea of 'the Creator'; rather, there are three main deities, corresponding to creation, sustenance and destruction. They are Brahma, Vishnu and Shiva, collectively called 'the Trimurti'. Second, goddesses are given equal importance as the various male deities; most gods, beginning with the Trimurti, have their respective consorts or wives. Third, Hinduism tends to be inclusive. Despite an almost bewildering array of deities, most Hindus believe in one God, viewed as the ultimate reality, and common to all people.

Opposite Figurines of Lord Krishna, Queen Rukmini and other Hindu
deities adorn the Shri Krishna Temple, Singapore.

Above A painting of the Trimurti: Brahma, Vishnu and Shiva. Most Hindu gods
and goddesses are linked to the Trimurti and their wives.

THE TRIMURTI AND THEIR CONSORTS

HINDUISM IS FAMOUS FOR ITS MANY GODS AND GODDESSES. MOST DEITIES, ESPECIALLY THOSE POPULAR TODAY, ARE CLOSELY RELATED TO THE TRIMURTI AND THEIR RESPECTIVE WIVES.

The three main Hindu deities are collectively called the Trimurti ('three forms'). They are often dubbed 'the Hindu Trinity', but the Hindu notion of a tripartite Godhead little resembles its Christian counterpart. The three Hindu deities take joint responsibility for this world, and the three phases of matter. According to Hindu thought, all material forms are created, stay for some time, and are ultimately dissolved. Brahma is deemed responsible for creation, Vishnu for sustenance, and Shiva for destruction.

The three deities are sometimes termed guna-avataras or 'incarnations of the three qualities of nature'. Accordingly, Brahma is in charge of rajo-guna, the quality of passion, which excites and creates. Vishnu presides over sattva-guna, the quality of goodness, which harmonizes and sustains. Shiva controls tamo-guna,

the quality of ignorance, which degrades and destroys, thus making way for a new cycle of creation, maintenance and destruction.

WIVES OF THE TRIMURTI

Hinduism teaches that God is both male and female, as represented by 'divine couples'. Consequently, each member of the Trimurti has a consort. Brahma's consort is Sarasvati, the Goddess of Learning and the Arts; Vishnu's partner is Lakshmi, the Goddess of Fortune; and Shiva's wife is Shakti, who personifies Mother Nature. Shakti goes by many other names, such as 'Parvati', 'Kali', 'Durga' or simply 'Devi' ('goddess'). Although the goddesses are often worshipped with their husbands, they are also venerated in their own right, and sometimes considered more exalted than their male counterparts.

Above The three main goddesses: Parvati or Shakti (left), Lakshmi (centre) and Sarasvati (right), are the wives of the Trimurti.

THREE DENOMINATIONS

The main branches of Hinduism are distinguished by their respective focuses of worship. The principal three focuses include only two of the Trimurti, Vishnu and Shiva. Apparently due to a curse, Brahma is now rarely worshipped. The third main focus of worship is Shakti, which specifically denotes Shiva's wife, Parvati, but also refers to other goddesses, including Lakshmi and Sarasvati.

Worshippers of Vishnu, or one of his many forms, are called Vaishnavas (or Vaishnavites). Those who venerate Shiva are termed Shaivas (or Shaivites); and followers of Shakti are called Shaktas. These traditions have different opinions as to the precise relationships between the members of the Trimurti. Though some sub-groups consider them equal, others cite stories that imply the supremacy of their own particular deity. For example, many Shaivas teach that Shiva is not merely the

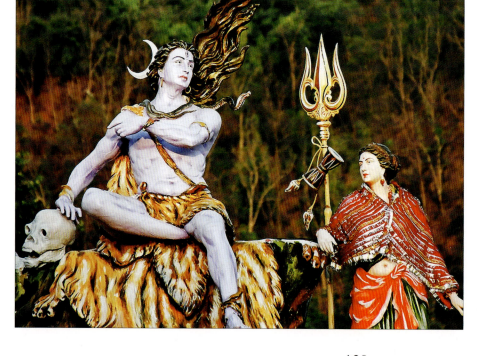

Left At Rishikesha, a diorama shows Shiva with his wife, Parvati.

Above A contemporary painting shows the Trimurti and their respective functions of creation, sustenance and annihilation.

Above Three main denominations, connected to the Trimurti and their wives, are often identified by the tilak they wear. This is one version of a Vaishnava tilak.

destroyer, but is single-handedly responsible for creation, preservation and destruction.

DIVINE RELATIVES
Other key deities are connected to the Trimurti. For the Vaishnavas, Krishna and Rama are two much-loved avataras ('descents', or incarnations). Krishna is often accompanied by his consort, Radha. Rama is similarly worshipped with his wife Sita; also his brother, Lakshmana and his devotee Hanuman. The monkey-warrior Hanuman is frequently worshipped alone and is particularly dear to soldiers and athletes. Shiva and Shakti have two sons, Ganesha (the elephant-headed deity) and Skanda, known in South India as Murugan, Kartikeyan or Subramanian. Worship of the sun god, prevalent in Vedic times, is still somewhat popular, and he is connected to Narayana, an epithet for Vishnu. Many of the nature gods worshipped during the Vedic period are similar to Surya, for they represent various planets, their predominating gods and goddesses, and other forces of nature.

Many groups and sub-groups have specific views on the relative positions of the various deities. For example, members of ISKCON consider Krishna to be the source of Vishnu, rather than vice versa. The BAPS Swaminarayan Mission considers their founder, Bhagwan Swaminarayan, to be the very source of Vishnu. And yet other groups, such as the Arya Samaj, believe in the impersonal Supreme (Brahman) and that all deities are equal, even imaginary. Despite a multitude of deities, and variant views on their respective statuses, most Hindus believe in a single God, common to all.

MAIN HINDU DEITIES

This table shows the main Hindu deities in three main sections:

1–6 The Trimurti and their consorts
7–12 Important deities related to the Trimurti
13–18 The gods who play specific roles in the universe; and most popular during the Vedic period

1 Brahma – the Creator
2 Vishnu – the Preserver
3 Shiva – the Destroyer
4 Sarasvati – Goddess of Learning, wife of Brahma
5 Lakshmi – Goddess of Fortune, wife of Vishnu
6 Shakti (Parvati, Durga, Kali) – Mother Nature, wife of Shiva

7 Rama – form or *avatar* of Lord Vishnu; his wife is Sita
8 Krishna – form or *avatar* of Vishnu; his consort is Radha
9 Hanuman – monkey warrior, servant of Rama and Sita
10 Ganesha – remover of obstacles; son of Shiva and Shakti
11 Skanda (Murugan) – god of war; son of Shiva and Shakti
12 Surya – sun god; a form of Narayana (another name for Vishnu)

13 Indra – rain god
14 Chandra – moon god
15 Agni – fire god
16 Vayu – wind god
17 Varuna – god of the waters
18 Yama – god of death and justice

121

BRAHMA AND SARASVATI

FOR MOST HINDUS, THE CREATOR IS NOT THE HIGHEST DEITY BUT ONE IMPORTANT ASPECT OF THE SUPREME. BRAHMA'S WIFE, SARASVATI, PRESIDES OVER SPEECH, LEARNING AND AESTHETICS.

As one of the Trimurti, Brahma presides over rajo-guna (the quality of passion) and takes charge of universal creation. As the first living being in the universe, he was born atop a lotus flower sprouting from Vishnu's navel. Since he has no mother, he is named 'Svayambhu' or 'self-born'. As the 'architect of the world', he is called Vishvakarma. For creating the world from a golden egg, he is named Hiranyagarbha.

Brahma's main consort is the goddess of learning, Sarasvati, who was manifest from his own self. From their union came all creatures of the world. Brahma is also called Pitamaha, 'the grandfather', and Prajapati, 'the original progenitor'. Among his direct offspring are the seven great Rishis (sages) and the ten Prajapatis (progenitors), headed by Daksha.

HOW BRAHMA IS DEPICTED

Legend recounts that Brahma first had five heads, but that Shiva severed one to punish him for becoming sexually enamoured by his own daughter, Sarasvati. Brahma's remaining heads face the four directions.

Above A traditional painting of the goddess Sarasvati with her musical instrument, the vina, and her carrier, the peacock.

He is shown sitting on a pink lotus flower, or riding a swan, the emblem of discrimination (for it is reputed to separate milk from a mixture of milk and water). In each of Brahma's four hands, he holds the Vedas, prayer beads, a water pot and a spoon to tend the sacrificial fire.

VENERATION OF BRAHMA

In India, Brahma is no longer directly worshipped except once a year at Pushkar, a pilgrimage site in Rajasthan. Some claim there is a second site at Khedabrahma in the southern state of Kerala. Legend holds that Brahma is rarely worshipped due to a curse.

Some attribute this to Shiva, who cursed the creator for being sexually attracted to his own daughter. Others blame Sarasvati, who was late for a sacrificial function. With the Vedic stress on ritual precision, it was essential that Brahma's wife was present and that the ceremony opened at the auspicious time. As the appointed period drew to a close, Sarasvati still had not arrived.

Left The golden deity of Brahma at the famous Erawan Shrine in the centre of Bangkok, Thailand.

Brahma consulted the other gods, who agreed to create a second wife for him, named Gayatri. Sarasvati arrived, well adorned but very late. Seeing her husband next to another woman, she vented her fury by uttering a curse.

Despite this curse, veneration of Brahma remains extremely popular in parts of South-east Asia, especially Thailand and the island of Bali. In India itself, Brahma is renowned as the head of one Vaishnava sampradaya (sacred lineage). By his undertaking severe tapas (austerity), and by the grace of Vishnu, he received divine revelation directly within his heart. Brahma is also represented by the priest officiating at any religious function.

SARASVATI

Brahma's consort is Sarasvati, the goddess associated with all aspects of Hindu culture. Sarasvati has three main forms; first, as the legendary and now dried-up river; second, as Vak, or speech personified; and third, as the goddess of learning and the arts. As the goddess, she goes by other names, such as Bharati (eloquence)

Below Students of Dhaka University pay their respects to Goddess Sarasvati during the festival in her honour.

Above A sculpture depicting the birth of Brahma atop the lotus flower sprouting from reclining Vishnu's navel.

and Shatarupa (goddess of material existence). Through union with Brahma, she gave birth to Manu, the father of mankind and author of the Manu Smriti, a treatise on moral law. The Vedas are also counted among Sarasvati's children, and she is therefore called Vedamata, the 'mother of the Vedas', or the 'mother of knowledge'.

As Sarasvati rules the intellectual and creative realms, worldly possessions interest her little. She does not adorn herself with an abundance of gems and jewellery, as do other goddesses, nor is she a domestic deity. She is shown dressed in a simple but elegant white sari, often with a deep blue border. With two hands she plays

the vina, while the third supports a book and the fourth fingers prayer beads. Sarasvati's colour is white, representing purity, and her vehicles are the swan, goose and peacock.

WORSHIP OF SARASVATI

Sarasvati is greatly praised in the ancient Vedic literature, and some scholars consider her the oldest goddess. Today her main festival is Sarasvati Puja, particularly favoured in Bengal and coinciding with Vasanta Panchami, the first day of spring. Worship of Sarasvati is popular in Kashmir and within some Jain communities. Sarasvati is also worshipped during Navaratri, along with her companions, Lakshmi, Parvati and other goddesses.

Sarasvati is considered the source of prudent speech, creative intelligence and artistic inspiration. Before beginning a concert, Hindu musicians prostrate themselves before her image and pay respects to their musical instruments. Children pray to her before their examinations, and speakers invoke her blessings before presenting a religious discourse.

Sarasvati exemplifies the broad Hindu understanding that religion is a process of learning.

VISHNU AND LAKSHMI

AS ONE OF THE TRIMURTI, VISHNU IS THE SUSTAINER. HE IS ALSO ONE OF THE THREE MAIN FOCUSES OF WORSHIP. HIS WIFE, LAKSHMI, IS THE GODDESS OF FORTUNE, ASSOCIATED WITH THE FESTIVAL OF DIVALI.

The Sanskrit word 'Vishnu' means 'one who enters every-where', and is linked to early Hindu teachings on Brahman, the all-pervading spiritual essence. Some believe that Vishnu is identical to the absolute reality and that devotees who chant his name directly commune with the Supreme. Vishnu has many names, and the Mahabharata includes a popular stotra (prayer) called the 'one thousand names of Vishnu'. Of these, the name 'Narayana' is practically synonymous with 'Vishnu', frequently appearing in Vishnu mantras. In the Tamil language, Vishnu is called Perumal or Thirumal.

THE HISTORY OF VISHNU WORSHIP

During the Vedic period, Vishnu was a relatively minor deity, closely linked to Indra, and to the sun god, who is still called 'Surya Narayana'. Vishnu attained eminence around the time of the compilation of the Epics and Puranas, to become one

Above A 17th-century South Indian murti of Vishnu cast in bronze. Here he holds the discus and conch shell, two of his four symbols.

of the Trimurti. Sentiment toward Vishnu was popularized in South India by the devotional outpourings of the twelve poet-saints, the Alvars. Ramanuja subsequently laid the theological foundations for Vaishnavism. Like Shankara, he accepted the all-pervading nature of Vishnu, but taught of the co-existence of a higher, personal feature, termed the 'Param Brahman' (Supreme Brahman). Many contemporary Vaishnavas believe in a

Left Near the town of Tirupati, pilgrims flock to the famous Tirumala temple, dedicated to the form of Vishnu known as Balaji or Venkateshvara.

Above Vishnu and Lakshmi ride together on the back of Garuda, the giant eagle, c. 1700.

personal God, and the pre-eminence of Vishnu over Brahma and Shiva. In northern India, Vishnu was popularized largely through his incarnations as Rama and Krishna, and especially by devotional saints during the era of Muslim rule.

VISHNU'S ROLE IN CREATION

According to Ramanuja, Vishnu resides in the spiritual realm (Vaikunthaloka), and is known there as Narayana. In relation to the material cosmos, he exhibits three successive duplicate forms. First, as Maha (Great) Vishnu, he is the soul of the entire cosmos. Lying on the waters of causality, he breathes out innumerable universes. His second 'expansion' enters each universe where, as 'the soul of the universe', he creates Lord Brahma. With the third, he enters the heart of every living being, as the Antaryami, 'the lord within'. Vishnu also appears in various types of avatara ('descent'), of which the most popular are the Dashavatara (ten incarnations). When he descends, he has three main functions: to protect his devotees, to destroy the wrongdoer, and to re-establish dharma (righteousness)

Vishnu is depicted in two main form: one standing on a lotus, the other reclining on the coils of the thousand-headed serpent called

Shesha. Vishnu's blue complexion represents the sky and his all-pervading nature. In his four hands, he holds four symbols. The lotus flower and conch shell give pleasure to the pious, whom he protects; in the other two hands, the club and discus are directed against those who defy the laws of nature, precipitating their own destruction. The discus, with a thousand spokes, represents the inexorable wheel of time (*kala-chakra*). Vishnu is occasionally shown in a sitting form, and also riding the giant eagle called Garuda, usually side by side with Lakshmi.

GODDESS LAKSHMI

Lakshmi or Shri is the eternal consort of Lord Vishnu. The couple are often worshipped together as Lakshmi-Narayana. Lakshmi resides on her husband's chest, and he is therefore named Shrinivas, 'the dwelling place of Shri'. Lakshmi is also found massaging her husband's feet and always accompanies him when he descends as an avatara. With Lord Rama, she appeared on earth as Sita, and with Lord Krishna as Queen Rukmini. Although Lakshmi is considered the eternal consort of Vishnu, she made her appearance from the ocean of milk as it was churned by the gods and the demons.

As the Goddess of Fortune, Lakshmi (or Maha-Lakshmi) is also worshipped in her own right, especially during the festival of Divali. She is portrayed standing or sitting on a lotus, and holding a lotus flower and water pot. From a third palm, she showers coins and with the fourth she offers benediction. She is dressed in a deep pink sari and surrounded by lucky symbols, such as decorated elephants bearing flower garlands or showering water from their trunks.

A SOUTH INDIAN STORY

After an argument with her husband, Lakshmi went off in a huff, leaving her heavenly abode for earth. She appeared in the family of King Akasha Raja and was named Padmavati. In search of his wife, Vishnu was born as Shrinivas, to an elderly woman saint called Vakula. With the help of Brahma and Shiva, the couple eventually met and immediately fell in love. Lakshmi, understanding Vishnu's unbreakable commitment, swore to live in his heart forever. The town of Tirupati still commemorates their splendid marriage. Valuable gifts, including opulent saris, are sent from Vishnu's temple on the Tirumala Hill down to Tiruchanur, the abode of Padmavati. Pilgrims rarely visit Tirupati without first paying a visit to Padmavati's shrine, a favourite destination for newly-weds who pray for a blissful married life.

Above A traditional poster of the goddess Lakshmi surrounded by symbols of prosperity.

AVATARAS: INCARNATIONS

AN IMPORTANT HINDU CONCEPT IS THAT OF THE AVATARA, THE 'DESCENT OF GOD' TO EARTH IN A VISIBLE FORM. IT IS MOST CLOSELY CONNECTED TO VISHNU AND HIS 'TEN INCARNATIONS'.

Hindus believe that God possesses multiple forms and potencies, represented directly or indirectly by the various deities. Some traditions consider them equal, each representing a particular attribute of God, who is ultimately nirguna, 'without qualities'. Other traditions consider that God is ultimately saguna, imbued with qualities such as spiritual form, sentiment and personality. For them, the various deities have different roles and positions.

Most deities have several names. Some are simply epithets, alternative names that refer to particular activities or personal qualities. Other names refer to a quite distinct form or 'expansion' (duplicate) of that deity. Some names indicate an

Below A colonial-period, Western depiction of Vishnu's second avatara, Kurma (the turtle), which followed Matsya (the fish).

avatara, or 'descent'. The popular translation of avatar, 'incarnation', is not entirely correct, for Hindu texts claim that God can appear in a form that is fully spiritual.

Shiva and Shakti certainly have forms similar to avataras. However, Vaishnavas have developed the concept most elaborately, listing several distinct categories. Of the innumerable avataras of Vishnu, the ten 'Dashavatara' are most important.

MATSYA, THE FISH
In the first era, the Satya-yuga, a king named Manu caught a small fish, which grew rapidly and even talked. The fish asked Manu to build a colossal boat and load aboard the seven sages, all species of animal and seeds from every variety of plant life. In his form as a giant fish, the lord Matsya later reappeared during a torrential flood and towed the huge boat to safety.

KURMA, THE TURTLE
The gods and demons agreed to a truce and co-operatively churned the milk ocean to extract the nectar of immortality. Mount Meru, which they used as a rod, sank in the mud, and Lord Vishnu took the form of a turtle (kurma) to act as a firm pivot. Once the nectar appeared, the demons stole it. To trick them, and retrieve the nectar for the gods, Vishnu appeared as the enchantress called Mohini.

VARAHA, THE BOAR
A demon called Hiranyaksha was extracting huge amounts of gold and other natural resources from the

Above A 10th-century sculpture of Vishnu surrounded by his avataras.

earth, which consequently fell from its orbit into the depths of the universe. Lord Vishnu assumed the form of a giant boar, rescued the earth with his giant tusks, and killed the demon.

NARASHIMHA, THE HALF-MAN, HALF-LION
Hiranyakashipu was enraged at the death of Hiranyaksha, his younger brother. Aspiring to immortality, he performed severe austerities. Brahma appeared and, unable to bestow eternal life, consented to several boons. Hiranyakashipu thought he had covered all eventualities. When he tried to murder his own son, Prahlada, Vishnu appeared from a pillar as Narashimha and killed the tyrant, without breaking Brahma's word.

VAMANA, THE DWARF
Although born into a family of demons, King Bali was pious and thus offered charity to Vishnu, disguised as a small brahmin boy.

Right An 18th-century painting from
Jaipur, Rajasthan. Reflecting regional
belief, Krishna, rather than Vishnu
himself, stands at the centre of the ten
avatars, as their ultimate source.

Bali agreed to Vamana's request for
just three steps of land. Vamana grew
very tall, crossed the universe in two
steps and demanded somewhere to
plant his third. Bowing low, Bali
offered his own head, showing his
total submission to Vishnu.

PARASHURAMA, THE AVENGER

Lord Vishnu incarnated as a brahmin
and avenged the murder of his father
by a haughty warrior called Kartavirya
Arjuna. With an axe given by Lord
Shiva, Vishnu killed 21 generations of
kshatriyas (warriors). His example
taught that leaders should be humble,
seeking the advice of wise men personally disinterested in power.

RAMA, THE MONARCH

Vishnu descended as Lord Rama to
show the ideal of piously executing
one's dharma (duty), as a family
member and political leader. He killed
the wicked king Ravana, and regained
his kidnapped wife, Sita. While he
ruled the kingdom of Koshala
responsibly, the citizens experienced
not even the slightest unhappiness.

KRISHNA, THE COWHERD

Krishna appeared at the end of the
last age. As a child and youth he lived

in the village of Vrindavana, where
he and his brother, Balarama,
endeared themselves to everyone
with their playful mischief. He later
became the King in Dvaraka and
hero of the Mahabharata, speaking
the Bhagavad-gita to prince Arjuna.

BUDDHA, THE TEACHER

The departure of Krishna marked
the onset of Kali-yuga. True piety
was replaced by empty ritual, and the

Left A reclining Buddha, Burmese style.
Hindus consider Buddha the ninth
incarnation of Vishnu, while the tenth,
Kalki, is yet to come.

brahmins misinterpreted the Vedas in
favour of eating meat and slaughter-
ing animals. To enlighten the world
and promote non-violence, Lord
Vishnu descended to earth as
Buddha, the enlightened one.

KALKI, THE SLAYER

Kalki is predicted to appear at the
end of the Kali-yuga, riding a white
steed and wielding a sword. He will
exterminate practically the entire
human race, which will have
become so sinful that they kill and
eat their own children. Kalki will re-
establish dharma and usher in a new
Satya-yuga (golden age).

RAMA, SITA AND HANUMAN

AS THE SEVENTH OF VISHNU'S TEN AVATARAS, LORD RAMA APPEARED AS THE IDEAL KING. HE IS WORSHIPPED WITH HIS WIFE, SITA, AND HIS LOYAL DEVOTEE, HANUMAN, WHO IS THE MONKEY WARRIOR.

Rama specifically represents the grand, monarchical aspect of the Supreme, and embodies many of the ideals of the warrior varna, such as heroism, chivalry, protection of the innocent and castigation of the wicked. Renowned for his dedication to dharma (duty), Rama is considered the perfect son, brother and husband.

According to tradition, Rama appeared in the second age, the Treta-yuga. Historians tend to date him much later, at around 400BCE. Rama was born as the eldest son of King Dasharatha and Queen Kaushalya, in Ayodhya, capital city of the Koshala kingdom. He had three brothers: Bharata, and the twins Lakshmana and Shatrughna. Rama's story, narrated by sage Valmiki in the Ramayana, is known and loved not only in India but throughout Southeast Asia and, more recently, in other parts of the world. Rama's devotees include the largest Vaishnava monastic order, the Ramanandis, who are renowned for their severe asceticism.

Rama is usually depicted with a dark green or dark blue complexion. He wears a yellow robe and carries a bow and a quiver of arrows. Rama is often worshipped with his consort, Sita, his brother, Lakshmana, and his faithful servant, Hanuman (the monkey warrior). Collectively, they are often called 'Rama Parivara' (Rama's family).

Below The seventh avatara of Vishnu, Lord Rama, stands on the shrine of a British temple with his Parivar ('family').

Above Hanuman massages Rama's feet, while his brother, Lakshmana, fans Rama and Sita looks on.

SITA

Born the daughter of Janaka, King of Mithila in present Bihar, Sita is also known as Janaki. Rama won her in a groom-selection contest by breaking the celebrated bow of Shiva. When Rama was exiled, Sita chose to accompany him to the austere forest rather than remain alone in the palatial city of Ayodhya. While in the forest, she was abducted by Ravana, but never gave in to his lustful advances. Sita is considered the emblem of womanhood, and celebrated for her chastity and faithfulness toward her husband. Despite this, she was again tragically separated from Rama but somewhat placated when she gave birth to powerful twin sons, Lav and Kush. This later episode is not included in some versions of the Ramayana, some say because the author was unable to bear the pathos.

HANUMAN

According to some, Hanuman was born of Shiva and Parvati but adopted by the wind-god, Vayu.

HANUMAN EATS PEARLS

One day, some sadhus presented Hanuman with a costly pearl necklace. On receiving it, Hanuman cracked each pearl with his sharp teeth, looked inside, and disappointedly threw it away. The intrigued saints asked him what he was doing. Hanuman retorted: 'These are no good. I do not see my Rama and Sita in any one of them. What use to me is this necklace?' The saints were confused, if not a little vexed. Hanuman clarified: 'My dear saintly persons, do not be upset. Rama and Sita exist not only in their abode, called Ayodhya, but everywhere. They are also within the heart of all living creatures.' To make his point, Hanuman tore open his own

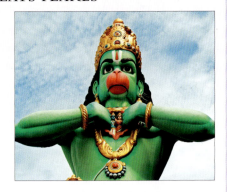

Above At the Batu Caves, Malaysia, a statue recounts the tale of Hanuman tearing open his heart.

chest to reveal Rama and Sita seated there. To this day, devotees try to enshrine Rama and Sita in the core of their hearts.

air, as depicted in many traditional paintings. He is also shown kneeling in prayerful submission before Sita, Rama and Lakshmana, both in picture and murti form.

Hanuman is also worshipped alone. His murti, usually a bright orange colour, shows him standing with folded hands or leaping through the air wielding his symbol, the mace. As the patron of wrestlers, sportsmen and soldiers, Hanuman combines courage and physical strength with humility and devotion to duty. He is often identified with the athletic planet Mars, and is especially worshipped on Tuesdays.

Below The giant statue of Hanuman in Trinidad. During the installation ceremony, flower petals were showered from a helicopter.

He is therefore called Pavanasuta (son of air). As his foster parents were King Keshari and Queen Anjana, he was named Anjaneya (Son of Anjana). Hanuman is usually considered a lifelong brahmachari (celibate), though one temple in Chennai depicts a consort called Suvarchala Devi. His main festival, Hanumat Jayanti, is celebrated in the month of Chaitra and falls some time in April. Worshippers offer sweets and fruit, especially bananas, to his murti and listen to recitations of the Hanuman Chalisa, a Hindi prayer of adoration written by Tulasidas. Games such as wrestling are popular.

Blessed in his youth by the other gods, Hanuman can leap colossal distances and assume any form at will. These exceptional skills helped him find Sita on the Isle of Lanka. During the decisive battle with Ravana's troops, he was dispatched to pick medicinal herbs to cure the critically injured Lakshmana. Forgetting what the prescribed herb looked like, he plucked the entire mountain and carried it through the

KRISHNA AND RADHA

LORD KRISHNA IS THE EIGHTH AVATARA OF VISHNU AND, ALONG WITH RAMA, RANKS AMONGST THE TWO MOST POPULAR INCARNATIONS. HIS CHIEF CONSORTS ARE RADHA AND QUEEN RUKMINI.

Although Krishna is considered the eighth incarnation of Vishnu, some consider him God himself, the source of Vishnu. Historians suggest that his worship started around the 5th century BCE as part of the Bhagavata sect, which gradually amalgamated with the worshippers of Narayana (Vishnu). Devotion to Krishna remains closely linked to the four main Vaishnava sampradayas (lineages). In modern times, Krishna is adored by Bengali Vaishnavas, who worship Radha-Krishna, and by the largely Gujarati 'Pushti Marg' who venerate baby Krishna. In Maharashtra, he is adulated as Vithoba (or Vitthala) by the Vakari tradition. In south India, his worship is most predominant in Udupi, in the state of Karnataka, and in Guruvayor, in Kerala.

Below A 10th-century sculpture showing the birth of Krishna to his imprisoned mother, Devaki, as various gods and goddesses observe them.

Krishna is portrayed with two hands, playing a flute, and wearing a yellow-orange robe. His complexion is blue-black, like a rain cloud, and his long jet-black hair sports a peacock feather. He is often shown surrounded by affectionate cows and with his main consort, Radha.

THE COWHERD BOY

Krishna was born in the city of Mathura to Prince Vasudeva and Devaki. They had been imprisoned by Kamsa, Devaki's brother, who feared a prophetic voice predicting his death at the hands of Devaki's eighth child. Kamsa had already murdered seven of his sister's children, and was intent on killing the newborn Krishna.

However, Vasudeva smuggled the baby out of the cell to the remote cowherd village of Vrindavana, to be raised by foster parents, Nanda and Yashoda. With his brother, Balarama, Krishna displayed uncommon activities. At a tender age, he killed the demons sent by Kamsa and subdued

Above Krishna, shown here with his foster mother, Yashoda, spent his early life in the idyllic cowherd village of Vrindavan.

the Kaliya Serpent, which had polluted the Yamuna river. He lifted Govardhana Hill, proving his supremacy over Indra. As he grew up, he developed affection for the gopis (female cowherds), and enacted the nocturnal rasa-lila dance. In the prime of his youth, Krishna left Vrindavan forever, breaking the hearts of all its residents.

RADHA

Krishna's principal consort is Radha, one of the gopis. Born in the village of Varshana, 10 kilometres (6 miles) from Vrindavana, she became Krishna's ardent lover. Some claim that they were married, perhaps in secret. Radha and Krishna's spontaneous love represents the ideal exchange between the soul and the Supreme. Sophisticated theologies explore their amorous dealings and differentiate them from mundane sexuality, which is considered a poor reflection of the spiritual prototype.

Radha and Krishna are almost always worshipped together. Although Radha's name is not explicitly mentioned in core Vaishnava scriptures, such as the Bhagavata Purana, she has attained an exalted status, especially in the Chaitanya tradition. The residents of Braj – the area around Vrindavan – consider Radha more powerful than Krishna himself. Radha's worship was first revealed by Nimbarka, a scholar in one of the four Vaishnava lineages, and was later popularized by the Orissan poet Jayadeva, in his Gita-Govinda (Song of Govinda). Radha also has a place in the Vallabha sampradaya, which considers her married to Krishna. Despite Radha's affiliation with specific traditions, she features prominently in popular Hindu worship.

KRISHNA AS KING

After leaving Vrindavana, Krishna killed Kamsa and established himself in Mathura as a warrior-king. Years later, apparently harassed by his long-term adversary, Jarasandha, Krishna

Above A modern painting of Krishna, king of the fabled city of Dvaraka, 'the City of Gates', built in the ocean.

retired westward to construct his own magnificent off-shore city called Dvaraka (the City of Gates). Krishna supported many wives (some say 16,108) headed by Rukmini, an expansion of Lakshmi. Temples still worship Rukmini and Dwarakadisha, the Lord of Dwaraka.

In the dispute over the Indian throne, Krishna sided with the five Pandava against their avaricious cousins, the Kauravas. The Mahabharata describes how Krishna tried, unsuccessfully, to broker a peace settlement. Prior to the inevitable battle at Kurukshetra, Krishna spoke the Bhagavad-gita to his dear friend Arjuna. After their victory, the Pandavas ruled India for 36 years, until shortly after Krishna departed this world. This cataclysmic event marked the onset of the present, materialistic age, the Kali-yuga.

RADHA AGAIN MEETS KRISHNA

Once, long after Krishna had left Vrindavana, the residents of the village travelled by bullock cart to Kurukshetra to mark an important eclipse. Krishna, by now a powerful king, also attended, riding a splendid chariot, bedecked with helmet, armour and weapons, and surrounded by ministers, cavalry and elephants. His meeting, after many years, with parents and friends was full of pathos. Radha again set eyes on her childhood sweetheart, but could hardly relate to him in that formal, ceremonious setting. In her heart, she longed to take him home to the simple pastoral village of their youth. The story illustrates the Hindu ideal of intimate, spontaneous love, unimpeded by awe and reverence. Each year, the great chariot festival in Puri symbolizes Radha's imaginary journey, and her taking Krishna back to Vrindavana.

Above A traditional painting of Radha with her beloved. When Krishna left Vrindavana, Radha and the other village residents were heartbroken.

SHIVA AND SHAKTI

SHIVA IS ONE OF THE TRIMURTI. HE AND HIS CONSORT, SHAKTI, ARE TWO OF THE THREE MAIN HINDU FOCUSES OF WORSHIP. SHAKTI IS OFTEN CALLED PARVATI, DURGA OR KALI.

Images found on seals excavated at Mehenjo-Daro resemble Shiva, suggesting that he may date back to the Indus-Sarasvati civilization. During the Vedic period, he was certainly venerated in his form of Rudra, who was associated with the storm, hunting, and the ferocity found in carnivorous beasts. By the time of the compilation of the Epics and Puranas, the names Shiva and Rudra had become synonymous and he was exalted to the Trimurti, with responsibility for universal destruction. However, Shaivas hold

Below In Bangalore, a 20-metre (65-foot) high sculpture of Shiva, the greatest yogi, shows him sitting in meditation in the icy Himalayas.

Right Shiva the householder with his wife, Shakti, in her benign form as Parvati.

him in far greater esteem, as the Supreme deity. The word 'Shiva' means auspicious, indicating that he has assumed a more benign nature. He also goes by the names Mahadeva (great god) and Maheshvara (great controller).

Writers often cite six main Shaiva traditions, though some classify them differently. They include both theistic and non-theistic lineages, and have developed a range of philosophies, connected to Vedanta philosophy as well as Tantric traditions. Shaiva traditions greatly honour the Svetashvatara Upanishad, which raises Rudra to the supreme status.

HOW SHIVA IS PORTRAYED

Shiva is an ambiguous deity, depicted in two seemingly contrary ways: first, he is the husband of Parvati, enjoying life as a householder in sexual embrace; secondly, he is depicted as a yogi, a renunciant, seated in meditation in the Himalayas. In this latter form, he wears a tiger skin, is smeared in ashes and carries a trishula (trident) and a small drum, called a damaru. In both forms, he is shown with a third eye and snakes coiled round his neck and arms. In his matted locks he bears the crescent moon and catches the Ganges as it plunges from heaven. Texts describe his physique as having a whitish complexion with a blue throat, for which he is called Nilakantha (blue-throated), alluding to the time he saved the universe by ingesting a vast dose of poison. Pictures often show him with a blue-black complexion, perhaps accompanied by his bull carrier, Nandi. His two other popular forms are as Nataraja, 'king of dancers', and the cylindrical, symbolic 'lingam'.

PARVATI

Shakti literally means 'energy', and can refer to any female deity, similar to the generic term, devi, meaning 'goddess'. More specifically,

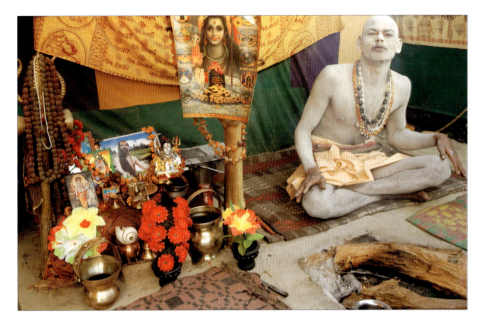

Right *A naga baba, an ascetic follower of Shiva, practises yoga in his tent during the Kumbha Mela (bathing festival).*

Shakti refers to Shiva's wife, who has numerous forms and goes by many names. It is not clear which form, if any, is the original. For example, in Bengal, Shiva's wife is primarily identified with Durga. Others identify her primarily as Kali. However, in popular Hinduism it seems that Shiva's wife is most often identified as Parvati, a benign goddess. Forms of address include 'Devi' (goddess), 'Ma' (mother) and 'Mataji' (respected mother).

Parvati is considered a reincarnation of Shiva's former wife, Sati. Some communities believe her to be the sister of Lord Vishnu. Shaktas have elevated her to the ultimate Divine Shakti, the Great Goddess who embodies the total energy in the universe. Some thinkers have described Shakti as the personification of Mother Nature. Whereas her forms as Durga and Kali epitomize the fierce and cruel aspects of nature, Parvati herself represents her primary propensity for nurture,

Below *Shiva and Parvati with their two children, Ganesha and Kartikeya, as shown in an early 20th-century painting.*

sustenance and compassionate motherhood. Indeed, Parvati is the mother of two key deities, Ganesha and Skanda (Kartikeyan).

SHIVA MARRIES PARVATI

Sati was also known as Dakshayani, the daughter of Daksha, one of Brahma's sons who had helped him populate the universe. Daksha showed great disdain for Shiva and didn't approve of his daughter marrying him. One day, Sati attended a great sacrifice performed by her father. Before the entire assembly, Daksha verbally abused Sati and her exalted husband. Unable to

bear the insult, Sati donned saffron cloth, meditated on the fire element, and burned her body to ashes. Naturally, Shiva was enraged. After taking revenge, he retired to the Himalayan mountains as a widower.

Sati subsequently took birth as Parvati, daughter of the Himalayan mountains. She performed severe penance to win Shiva's attention. In desperation, and colluding with the gods, she coaxed Kamadeva, god of love, to use his fabled bow and arrows to break Shiva's meditation. This infuriated Shiva who, opening his third eye, reduced Kamadeva to ashes. Petitioned by Kamadeva's wife, Rati, Shiva consented to bring her husband back to life, but with an invisible body.

Parvati continued her penance and, through her devotion, finally convinced Shiva to abandon his asceticism. Their marriage was solemnized a day before the new moon in the month of Phalguna, and the anniversary is celebrated every year at the festival of Maha Shiva Ratri. The tale of Daksha's sacrifice illustrates perennial tensions between ascetic traditions, which scorn householders for being attached, and brahminical traditions, which consider poorly dressed renunciants to be socially irresponsible.

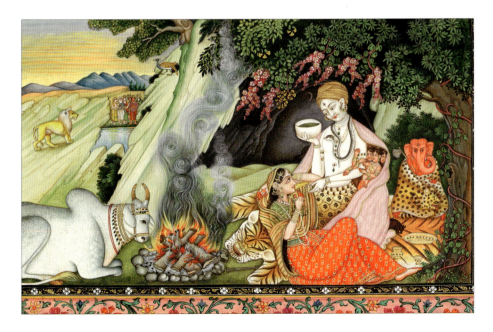

FORMS OF SHIVA AND SHAKTI

SHIVA HAS MANY NAMES AND DISPLAYS DISTINCT FORMS, OR 'AVIBHAVAS'. HIS WIFE, SHAKTI, HAS MANY FORMS, SOME COOL AND DOMESTICATED, OTHERS FIERY AND INDEPENDENT.

Shiva has been awarded a host of names, including Mahesh (great lord), Mahadeva (great god) and Shambhu (giver of prosperity). He is also 'Shankara' (bestower of happiness), and the philosopher Adi Shankara is considered his incarnation. Other names, such as Mahakala, Bhairava and Rudra suggest Shiva's fierce nature. He is also called Dakshinamurti, 'the giver of liberation'. Of the names recited in 'the thousand names of Shiva', some are merely epithets, whereas others refer to distinct forms of Shiva.

THE SHIVA LINGAM
The lingam, meaning 'mark' or 'sign', is a symbol extending back to the early Indus–Sarasvati civilizations. Although some scholars suggest it is

Below In Varanasi, women pour milk on a large Shiva lingam, as the priest reads from scripture.

a naïve phallic symbol, it represents Shiva as the male principle in this world. At the time of creation, he injects the eternal souls into 'the womb of mother nature', as they begin – or, more precisely, continue – their journey through the material world.

The lingam is a rounded, cylindrical image, usually made of stone. They are either carved or are formed naturally, as by a swift-flowing river. They are also made of wood, earth, metal, crystal or precious gems; or of transitory materials such as ice as found in the famous cave at Amaranatha. Most important are the 12 jyotirlinga (linga of light) shrines, scattered across India.

According to the Linga Purana, Brahma and Vishnu once argued over who was the Supreme. When a huge column of fire suddenly appeared before them, they decided to find one end each. Whoever returned first would be acknowledged as supreme.

Above Shiva in his 11 fierce 'Rudra' forms. The central figure poses in Shiva's form as Nataraja, 'the lord of dance'.

Vishnu assumed the form of a boar, and plunged downward. Brahma flew skyward as a swan. After searching for days, they saw Shiva appear in the fiery column. Realizing their mistake, they acknowledged Shiva as the Supreme Deity. The 12 jyotirlingas represent the endless pillar of fire.

THE KING OF DANCERS
Nataraja is the dancing posture of Shiva, specifically as he performs the tandava, the dance of universal destruction. Nataraja is most often depicted in bronze. He dances in a ring of flames, raising his left leg and stepping over a dwarf demon symbolizing ignorance. The upper right hand holds a small drum, shaped like an hourglass and called a damaru. This form of Nataraja was favoured by the Chola dynasty, which installed it at the famous temple at Chidambaram. Nataraja murtis are still found throughout South India, and the form has become a popular motif for Indian culture and aesthetics.

DURGA
For many Hindus, Shakti's primary form is as Shiva's consort, the benign Parvati. Durga and Kali are considered

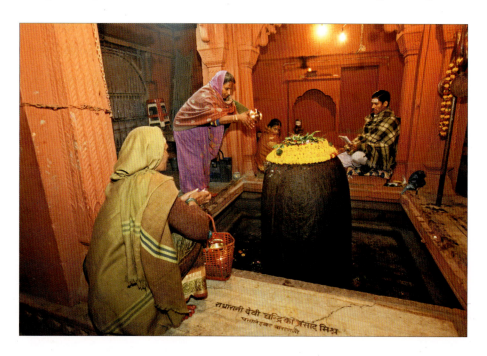

Right Durga, accompanied by Lakshmi and Sarasvati and surrounded by many of her forms.

her militant and cruel aspects. However, in Bengal, the Goddess is primarily identified as Durga, with other forms as her extensions or expansions. Durga has nine primary forms, each venerated over one day during the Navaratri festival.

Durga is shown riding a lion or tiger and wielding in her ten arms an arsenal of weapons. Each god gave her his most powerful weapon, and hence she is equipped with Rudra's trident, Vishnu's discus, Indra's thunderbolt, and so on. Durga is exquisitely beautiful, dressed in a red sari and bearing a quarter moon on her forehead. She is often portrayed fatally spearing the demon Mahisha, as he emerges from his assumed form as a buffalo.

KALI

Broadly defined, Shakti can refer to any of the wives of the Trimurti, who are sometimes listed as Maha Sarasvati, Maha Lakshmi and Maha Kali. However, she is primarily Shiva's wife, who in this particular list is called Kali.

Below A bronze statue of Nataraja.

This form is favoured by Tantric traditions, and she is associated with death and destruction or, some say, with time and change. Some traditions have raised her status by identifying her with the Supreme. In more recent times, Kali has become popular with contemporary feminist and new-age writers, who have adopted her as a symbol of their own ideals.

Kali's most common image is four-armed, carrying a trishula (trident), a recently wielded sword, a severed head and a bowl catching its spouting blood. She is often depicted naked, with black skin, a protruding tongue and a garland of human skulls. The story goes that the gods could not kill the demon Raktabija. Each drop of his blood that touched the earth immediately transformed into another demon. Kali surmounted this problem by catching the blood with her tongue and finally killing the demon.

Shakti has innumerable other forms. Particularly popular in South India is Lalita Tripurasundari, a benign tantric image who embodies not only Parvati, but also Lakshmi

and Sarasvati. Many of the obscure village goddesses, perhaps to promote their status and legitimacy, have been linked, through legend or presumed heritage, to the major Goddess. However, her most important forms remain Parvati, Durga and Kali.

Below Kali standing over her husband Shiva. She holds a trident, sword, recently severed head and a bowl to catch the blood.

GANESHA AND SKANDA

GANESHA AND SKANDA ARE SONS OF SHIVA AND PARVATI. THE ELEPHANT-HEADED GANESHA IS BROADLY POPULAR, WHEREAS SKANDA IS WORSHIPPED MAINLY BY TAMILS, WHO CALL HIM MURUGAN.

As two sons of Shiva and Parvatii, Ganesha and Skanda are venerated by both Shaivas and Shaktas. They are also worshipped by their distinct communities. The followers of Ganesha (or Ganapati) are known as Ganapatyas. Skanda's devotees address him as Kumara ('young prince') and therefore they are called Kaumaras.

ELEPHANT-HEADED GOD

Ganesha is the most universally worshipped of the Hindu pantheon, though rarely as an exclusive object of devotion or as the Supreme God. He is often supplicated before worship of other deities, and his shrine in the temple is usually one

Below A temporary murti (form) of Ganesha is submerged at the end of his main, ten-day festival in Chennai.

of many. It is invariably located near the entrance, as Ganesha is 'the keeper of the threshold'. Being in charge of boundaries, he is also the 'lord of categories' and associated with the academic propensity for discernment and classification. He is therefore called Vinayak (knowledgeable). Primarily, though, he is Vighneshvara the 'destroyer of all obstacles', and thus venerated at the beginning of any ritual, special event or crucial endeavour.

Ganesha is shown with an elephant's head and a rotund body. He is dressed gorgeously and in three hands holds an axe, an elephant noose and a round cake called a modaka. With his fourth hand he awards benediction. One of Ganesha's tusks is missing. One account relates how he used his severed tusk to write down the Mahabharata as

Above An opulent painting of Lord Ganesha with his traditional symbols.

sage Vyasa dictated it. Ganesha is depicted in seated, standing and dancing poses. He is particularly fond of sweets, and shows a tendency to over eat. Despite his size, Ganesha's carrier is the rather small bandicoot, a species of rat. Some consider Ganesha to be a brahmacharin (celibate), whereas others claim he has two wives, called Siddhi (perfection) and Buddhi (intelligence).

Devotion to Ganesha is widely diffused and extends to Jains and Buddhists, and well beyond India, into China, Japan, Tibet, Indochina and Indonesia. In India, he is most popular is the south and in Maharashtra, where eight key shrines are situated within a hundred kilometres of the city of Puna. Ganesha Chaturthi, his birthday celebration, occurs in August or September, and is extremely popular in Mumbai.

SKANDA, GOD OF WAR

In South India, Skanda is considered the second son of Shiva and Parvati. He was born to kill Taraka and other demons. To fulfil this purpose, the gods prompted the unmarried Parvati to ask Kamadeva, the god

Left Lord Murugan, holding his vel (spear), watches over pilgrims at the Batu Caves in Malaysia.

peacock, and his military emblem the cockerel. He is the military commander of the Devas (gods). Skanda has two consorts, who confer upon his devotees the boons of earthly happiness and heavenly bliss. They are usually called Valli and Devayani. However, in Bengal and Orissa, devotees consider Skanda a lifelong brahmacharin (celibate bachelor).

A further symbol is the six-pointed star. The number is significant. There are six principal holy abodes, or 'battle camps', dedicated to Murugan, including Palani, where annually his golden image circumnavigates the hilltop shrine on a golden chariot. About half a million pilgrims flock there on the main festival day. However, the main Murugan festival, shortly after Divali, is called Skanda Shashthi and lasts for six days. It celebrates Skanda's killing the demon called Surapadma, for which purpose he was born.

of love, to fire his fabled arrows at the meditating Shiva. The ensuing child was named Kartikeyan because he was first brought up by the Krittikas, the wives of six of the seven great Rishis (sages). These six sisters later became the six stars of the Pleiades constellation.

Skanda is most popular in areas of Tamil influence, especially Sri Lanka, Malaysia and southern India, where he is called Murugan. He is less widely acclaimed in other parts of India. In Sri Lanka, Buddhists and Hindus worship him together in the highly revered Katharagama temple. Like most Hindu deities, he is known by many other names, including Subramanian and Shanmukha, 'one who has six faces'.

Skanda is depicted with six heads and two or twelve arms. His symbol is the vel (spear), his carrier the

RACE ROUND THE COSMOS

One day Parvati explained to Ganesha and Skanda how she represented the entire cosmos. When she had finished, the two brothers challenged each other to a race around the universe. Skanda, proud rider of the peacock, thought he would beat his brother, who was riding a paltry rat. He flew off at breakneck speed. Ganesha got up, bowed to his mother Parvati, circumambulated her three times and quietly sat down. In this way he defeated his brother, who was so mortified that he renounced the world and retired to the Palini Hill, taking his form as a lifelong celibate.

Right A 6th-century sandstone figure from the Punjab Hills, depicts Skanda riding his peacock.

WORSHIP IN THE VEDIC PERIOD

WORSHIP IN THE VEDIC AGE WAS TYPIFIED BY THE PERFORMANCE OF SACRIFICE, CALLED YAJNA. MANY OF THE VENERATED DEITIES WERE ASSOCIATED WITH THE MANAGEMENT OF THE UNIVERSE.

Above A painting of Indra, c. 1700, one of the two main deities during the Vedic period.

The Vedic Age corresponds to the period of compilation of the Vedas, the oldest texts of Hinduism. Scholars locate it approximately between 1,500 and 500BCE, and the culture prevalent during that thousand-year period is called the Vedic civilization. The mode of worship was performance of yajna, or sacrifice, which included the chanting of Rig Vedic verses, singing of hymns and recitation of mantras. The priests executed rituals for the three upper social classes (varnas), strictly excluding members of the fourth, shudra, class. Members of these upper varnas offered sacrifice for an abundance of rain, crops, cattle, and sons, and for gaining access to heaven. Stay in the celestial realm could be prolonged indefinitely by descendants who regularly performed the appropriate yajna. Such practices were underpinned by the notion of rita, 'the natural order', presided over by numerous deities in charge of nature's functions. They were collectively called the Vishve-devas (universal gods).

INDRA AND AGNI

The Vedic deities were placated mainly though the sacred fire ceremony, in which offerings of ghee (clarified butter) were first received by Agni, the fire god. Of similar stature was Indra, god of rain, king of heaven, and much celebrated for slaying with his thunderbolt a huge demon called Vritra. Other deities were intimately connected to the elements, including Vayu, lord of air, and Varuna, lord of the waters. Many of these deities have entered the contemporary pantheon, usually as minor gods. Cosmological accounts suggest that the Vedic deities resided in the heavenly material worlds, and their positions were not entirely stable. Later there emerged the notion of an eternal transcendent realm, reserved for major deities such as Vishnu and Shiva.

PLANETARY DEITIES

Soma was a ritual drink important among the early Indo-Iranians, and the later Vedic and Persian cultures. The hymns of the Rig Veda frequently eulogize its energizing qualities. It was prepared by pressing juice from the stalks of a certain mountain plant, which has not been conclusively identified but has hypothetically been linked to mead, honey, alcohol, cannabis, blue lotus, pomegranate or psychedelic mushrooms. Soma was also personified as a deity, associated with the moon, and 'Soma' remains an alternative name for the moon deity, popularly called Chandra. Some scholars suggest that soma juice,

Left Replicating the ancient Vedic sacrifice, two Hindu priests kindle the sacred fire, representing Agni, before a wedding ceremony in New Jersey, USA.

Above A contemporary poster of the goddess Gayatri, with the corresponding mantra written above her five heads.

with its metaphorical link to the celestial moon, was not an inebriating intoxicant but a life-giving nectar similar to the Greek 'ambrosia'.

The Vedic peoples venerated other planets and their respective deities. Worship of Surya, the sun god, was popular largely through a group of solar deities called the Adityas. Surya was later closely identified with Narayana (Vishnu) and is still venerated indirectly through the chanting of the Gayatri mantra. The famous 13th-century Konorak temple in Orissa testifies to the popularity of sun worship in medieval times. In South India, Surya is still widely adored during the festival of Pongal. Members of the Smarta tradition include Surya as one of their five or six worshipful deities, and his followers, called Sauryas, are sometimes counted among the seven great Hindu traditions.

The worship of planetary deities has endured to the present day. In modern South India, many temples feature an auxiliary shrine, housing nine images set out on a three-by-three grid and called the nava-graha (nine planets). They include the seven planets linked to the weekdays, starting with the sun and moon, plus the two 'shadowy' spheres causing eclipses, namely Rahu and Ketu. It is believed that propitiation of planetary deities can mitigate their channelling of negative karma.

FEMALE DEITIES

Figurines unearthed at Mehrgarh, a key Neolithic archaeological site in modern Pakistan, suggest that goddess worship may be extremely ancient. Such worship was certainly prevalent in the Vedic period. At that time, Prithvi represented the earth, Vak presided over speech, and Usha excelled as the effulgent dawn goddess. These and other female deities generally held subordinate roles, and the Great Goddess – associated with the Supreme – did not emerge until the medieval period. However, like their male counterparts Vishnu and Rudra, many Vedic goddesses survived through assimilation into the later Hindu pantheon. Thus, Pritivi may have evolved into Bhu, one of Vishnu's two consorts; Nirriti, a goddess linked to destruction, may have transformed into the deity now called Kali: and Vak is associated with the modern Sarasvati, perhaps the oldest Hindu goddess.

From about 500BCE onwards, the fire sacrifice was gradually superseded by ritual worship of the sacred image. Attention shifted from the attainment of a temporary heaven to liberation in an eternal world ruled by Vishnu, Shiva or the Goddess. For many Hindus, the continuing presence of many gods and goddesses remains an important sign of the tradition's inclusivity.

Below South Indian women boil sweet rice for the Pongal festival, which primarily honours the sun-god.

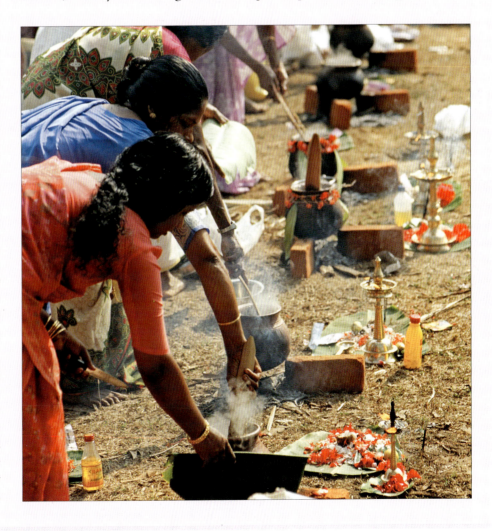

OTHER DEITIES

THE HINDU PANTHEON INCLUDES MANY MINOR GODS AND GOD-
DESSES. MYTH DESCRIBES OTHER SUPERNATURAL BEINGS, INCLUDING
SUBTERRANEAN MAN-EATERS AND CELESTIALS IN GARDEN PARADISES.

Above Guardian deities protect the boundary of a south Indian village.

In contrast to the pan-Hindu denominations, many local and popular traditions are confined to a small geographical area, often a single village. Rather than focusing on major deities, local communities usually venerate devatas, minor deities with jurisdiction over a particular river, forest or village, and guardian deities, who stand as sentries at the village boundary. Worshippers are less concerned with renunciation and moksha, and more intent on meeting immediate needs, such as harvesting crops and avoiding epidemics. The languages of transmission are often vernacular rather than the Sanskrit of the 'high', brahminical traditions, and many rural customs are sustained by lower castes.

HIGH AND LOW TRADITIONS

Despite different religious priorities, the so-called high and low traditions are closely related. Through a process called 'Sanskritization', the great traditions significantly impact local practices, including those of some tribal peoples. Through Sanskritization, those lower in the caste hierarchy seek upward mobility by emulating the rituals and practices of the upper, dominant and intellectual classes. One clear example is the adoption of vegetarianism.

There are many instances of the opposite situation, in which 'grass-roots' practices have influenced the high traditions, often through the assimilation of local gods and goddesses into the Hindu pantheon. One example is the local smallpox goddess, Sitala (Mariyamman in South India) who is now associated with Durga. More dramatically, the minor goddess Santoshi Ma achieved international fame overnight through a blockbuster Indian film, called *Jai Santoshi Ma*. As the putative daughter of Ganesha, some claim she is a new goddess; other evidence suggests that the film merely popularized an existing but relatively obscure deity. More gradually, the deity of Ayyappan,

popular in one district of Kerala and possibly connected to the Tamil deity called Ayyanar, has recently gained pan-Indian appeal.

POLITICAL TRENDS

A significant factor in the exaltation of deities is their appropriation for social and political ends. In Mumbai the annual Ganesha festival was popularized by nationalist reformer B.G. Tilak, but remained popular after independence and divested of political incentive. Around the same period, the deity of Mother India emerged, draped in the colours of the Indian flag and carrying Gandhi in her protective arms. More recently, goddesses such as Kali and Draupadi have been transformed into emblems of modern feminism, challenging the stereotypical notion of the submissive female.

For the scheduled castes, deities such as Ellaiyamman have become iconic symbols of collective resistance and a motif of social liberation theology. As a guardian deity, Ellaiyamman guards the boundaries of lands belonging to the low Paraiyar caste. In her emerging role, she protects their social, cultural and geographical space from the colonizing ambitions of high-caste Hindus.

Left A father and son perform pilgrimage to the celebrated shrine of Ayyappan at Sabarimala. Each carries the traditional kadavi (holy bundle) on his head.

140

Above Former Indian prime minister Atal Behari Vajpayee prays to a picture of Bharat Mata (Mother India).

CELESTIAL AND SUBTERRANEAN BEINGS

Besides the array of venerated deities, aligned to both scholarly tradition and local folk practices, there are numerous other beings, largely the heroes and villains of narrative. They are related to Hindu cosmology, and inhabit various worlds within three planetary systems: the lower, middle and higher realms. The Epics and Puranas tell of the continuous and gruesome struggle between forces of the Devas (gods, or demigods), commanded by Skanda, and the demonic Asuras and their hordes of grotesque and malign beings. In tales not dissimilar to Milton's 'Paradise Lost', the Asuras continuously strive to conquer the heavenly kingdoms and for short intervals successfully depose Indra. They normally reside in the shadowy underworld called Patala.

Within these higher and lower realms live a whole range of fantastic beings, including angels, celestial dancers and musicians, snakes, and man-eating demons. Ravana, the anti-hero of the Ramayana, was born to a family of Rakshasas. They are the living nightmares of Hindu mythology, inhabiting caves, jungles and cemeteries, partial to human flesh, and increasingly powerful as the sun's rays decline. Other demonic forms include the Daityas and

Danavas, far more uncouth than the sophisticated Asuras. Their favourite pastime is to defile sacrificial arenas by flying over them and dropping blood, flesh and human waste.

More pious and amiable beings inhabit the higher worlds. The Gandharvas are heavenly musicians, and the Kinnaras are akin to angels. The most famous are the Apsaras, the celestial courtesans who make Indra's heaven an alluring and extravagant delight. They have other uses. Whenever a yogi performs severe and prolonged austerity, Indra suspects an attempt to depose him. He therefore dispatches an Apsara to earth, to charm and seduce his possible competitor, and to exhaust his accumulated merit through sexual pleasure. Such ideas reflect Hindu belief in many worlds, their diverse inhabitants, and the multitude of deities representing the Supreme.

Below This 16th-century painting shows the gods and demons churning the milk ocean to yield the nectar of immortality.

CHAPTER 6

SACRED PLACES

At Prayaga in Uttar Pradesh, in northern India, during the largest human gathering in recorded history, 66 million pilgrims flocked to the 2001 Kumbha-Mela (bathing fair). On the main day, which had been determined by planetary configurations, a ritual plunge into the water was taken by five million visitors, ranging from aristocratic, silk-clad ladies to naked, ash-smeared ascetics. Here the milky-white waters of the Ganga merge with the bluish waters of the Yamuna and the invisible waters of the mythical Sarasvati.

A common term for holy place is 'tirtha', meaning 'ford'. As a gateway between earth and heaven, it is where prayers readily rise upward and blessings descend. Although Hinduism focuses on the other world, 'the far shore', holy places are intimately linked to its rural heritage; to the earth, nature and its sacred rivers, forests and mountains.

As home to the presiding deity, the temple is also a holy site. The fabulously opulent temple of Venkateshvara in Tirupati, South India, receives 30,000 visitors daily. Many magnificent temples and places of pilgrimage are now found well beyond the Indian sub-continent.

Opposite The River Ganges at Varanasi, city of Lord Shiva. Further upstream at Prayaga, 'Mother Ganga' is joined by the Yamuna and the mythical Sarasvati.

Above The BAPS Swaminarayana Temple in Neasden, London, symbolizes the burgeoning of Hindu holy sites outside India.

PILGRIMAGE AND HOLY SITES

IN INDIA, THOUSANDS OF HOLY PLACES ANNUALLY ATTRACT MILLIONS OF PILGRIMS. EACH SITE, SANCTIFIED BY ASSOCIATION WITH A SPECIFIC SAINT OR DEITY, OFFERS A UNIQUE BOON OR BLESSING.

The word tirtha means 'ford', a shallow stretch of water through which one can cross 'to the other side'. The term alludes to a popular poetic metaphor of crossing a treacherous river or the ocean of samsara: the cycle of birth and death. In poems and prayer, the spiritual preceptor is compared to the expert pilot and the human body to favourable winds that can help the soul toward ultimate emancipation. The tirtha, a threshold between heaven and earth, is not only a place for the upward crossings of prayers and offerings, but for the downward 'descent' of deities and their respec-tive benedictions. A holy site may also be termed a kshetra (field), pitha (seat), or dhama (replica of the spiritual realm).

HOLY TOWNS

There are four great dhamas, corresponding to the cardinal directions in which four monasteries were established by the great Hindu philosopher, Adi Shankara. The four dhamas are Dvaraka to the west, Kedarnath in the cooler north, Puri on the east coast, and Rameshvaram, overlooking the straits between India and Sri Lanka. Another key site is the ancient city of Prayaga, one of

Above In Tirupati, tens of thousands of pilgrims daily take darshan of the fabulously rich deity called 'Balaji'.

four sites dedicated to the 12-yearly Kumbha Mela (bathing festival); the other sites are Hardwar, Ujjain and Nasik. However, the most famous tirtha, counted among the 'seven ancient holy towns', is the city of Varanasi.

Also known as Benares or Kashi, Varanasi is situated on the west bank of the Ganges, 450 miles down-stream from New Delhi. It is one of the oldest continually inhabited cities in the world, and is similarly revered by Jains, Hindus, and Buddhists. Its principal mandir, the Golden Temple, is dedicated to Lord Shiva, known here as Vishvanatha. The city is famous for its riverside cremation ghats, and corpses are transported hundreds of miles for burning there. With the aim of liberation, many Hindus retire there, and others bring the ashes of departed kinsmen to scatter in the Ganges.

Left In the ancient city of Dvaraka, one of the four great 'dhamas', Hindu families gather at the main Temple dedicated to Lord Krishna.

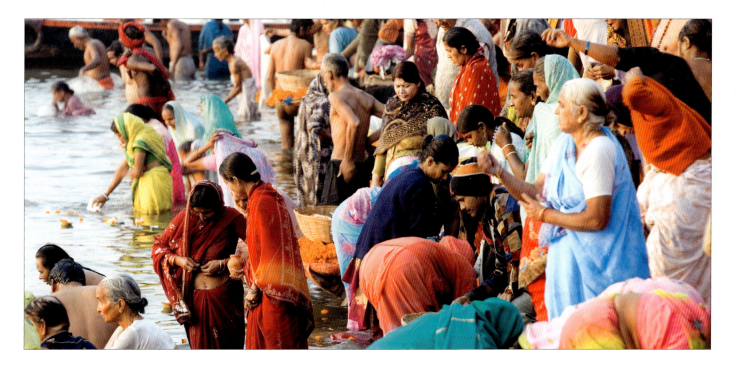

Above Pilgrims bathing in the Ganges at Varanasi. Bathing, one of several popular practices performed on pilgrimage, is thought to wash away karma.

PILGRIMAGE

With its emphasis on austerity, simplicity and detachment, yatra (pilgrimage) is most important to members of the third ashrama, as they gradually withdraw from worldly life. Pilgrims observe vows, such as celibacy, fasting from certain foods, and walking barefoot to respect sacred ground. Besides regular puja (worship), yatra also involves circumambulation, giving in charity and hearing myths and legends associated with the site. A primary purpose is to accrue spiritual merit, especially by taking darshana (audience) of the deity residing at the local shrine or temple.

Below Map of India and the surrounding area, showing the principal rivers, mountains and holy towns.

Below These pilgrims trek barefoot to Muzaffarpur, in Bihar state, to pay respects to Lord Shiva.

145

NORTH INDIAN TEMPLES

TEMPLES ARE CONSIDERED THE HOME OF THE PRESIDING DEITY.
THEY ARE USUALLY SITUATED ON HOLY SITES AND ASSOCIATED WITH
SPECIFIC LEGENDS ABOUT THAT DEITY.

Temple construction dates back about two millennia, marking the broad transition from Vedic yajna (sacrifice) to puja, ritualistic image worship, and the simultaneous emergence of three main traditions focused on Vishnu, Shiva and Shakti. The period from about 700CE onward saw the proliferation of thousands of temples but was curtailed, especially in the north, by Muslim occupation and wide desecration of the murti and its home. During British rule, migration spawned the establishment of temples abroad. In the 20th century, many in the West were first housed in disused schools or church halls; these have often been replaced by

Below Pilgrims enter the Badrinath Temple in northern India with its distinctive, Himalayan architecture.

costly, magnificent complexes, incorporating both ancient and modern architecture. In India, the rise of the middle class contributed to a similar spate of temple construction.

THE TEMPLE'S FUNCTION
The mandir (temple) is primarily the home of God, or a particular deity, represented by the image installed on the shrine. The mandir is traditionally dedicated to one 'presiding' deity, optionally with a number of subordinate gods and goddesses. Some temples, especially outside of India, are more eclectic and are equally dedicated to several deities. The worship of the sacred image is normally performed by a resident priest or an entire team. To maintain the temple's sanctity, there are rules governing the moral conduct of

Above This temple floor plan typifies the northern style, which broadly encompasses the western and eastern regions.

priests and visitors, and non-Hindus are sometimes excluded: a practice increasingly less prevalent. One of the main functions of the temple is to maintain an atmosphere charged with spirituality. Hence, they are often built on holy sites, near rivers, or in other places of natural beauty.

Above The Swaminarayan Temple at Illinois in the USA was constructed from Italian marble in the traditional northern style and has 1521 pillars.

Temples provide opportunity for reflection and meditation, but are sometimes extremely lively and noisy.

TYPES OF TEMPLE

Hindu scriptures, such as the Shilpa-shastra, lay down standards for temple construction. Acknowledging a correspondence between microcosm and macrocosm, temples are designed geometrically to mirror the physical structure of the universe. They are built with reference to vastu, the Indian science of sacred space, which deals with geomancy, astrology and propitious times for starting various phases of construction. Existing structures display a number of architectural styles, such as those peculiar to the Himalayan region in the far north, to the eastern state of Orissa, and to Kerala, running along the south-west coast. Architectural styles can be broadly classified as North Indian (Nagara) and South Indian (Dravidian).

NORTH INDIA STYLES

The Nagara style, developed from the 5th century, is characterized by a tower (shikhara) shaped like a bee-hive and made up of horizontal layers of stone. The plan is basically square but the walls are so multi-layered that the tower appears circular. The basic temple consists of an inner sanctum, the garbha-griha ('womb-chamber'), directly beneath the tower and housing the sacred image. There is often a space or corridor around all four sides to enable circumambulation of the deity. In front stands a pillared congregation hall, and possibly an antechamber and porch. In some temples, a statue of the deity's servant or carrier stands facing the shrine; for example, before Shiva often stands Nandi the bull, and before Vishnu, a statue of Garuda, the giant eagle.

INSIDE THE TEMPLE

At the temple threshold is an area, and sometimes racks, for removing and storing shoes. Inside the main hall, there usually hangs a bell, rung to announce one's arrival before the deity. This hall itself is often brightly coloured, hung with pictures, and open, without chairs. There may be a special seat reserved for a speaker and, in modern temples, seating for the elderly along the side and back walls.

Before the shrine itself, a donation box for cash also serves as a place to leave offerings of flowers or uncooked food, such as rice, dhal and vegetables. There is a table for sipping holy water, or a raised area where a priest spoons it out to visitors, and distributes morsels of prasada (sacred food). The shrine itself is only accessible to priests, as are some auxiliary areas such as a kitchen and preparation room.

Larger temples feature a host of public facilities, including shops, auditoriums, administrative offices, and residential quarters for the pujaris (priests).

THE JAGANNATHA TEMPLE

The broad northern style of temple architecture incorporates diverse and distinctive styles, especially in the west, east and far north. The temple in Puri, also called Jagannatha Puri after the town's main deity, dates back to the 12th century and is typical of the eastern state of Orissa. The 65-metre (213-foot) tower is adorned with Vishnu's chakra (discus) and a long flag that is changed daily. Each summer, pilgrims flock to Puri for the annual Rathayatra or 'cart pilgrimage'. Puri is one of four dhamas, situated at the four corners of India.

Right The Jagannatha Temple in Puri exemplifies architecture in the north-eastern state of Orissa.

SOUTH INDIAN TEMPLES

TEMPLE BUILDING PARTICULARLY FLOURISHED IN SOUTH INDIA FROM 900CE ONWARD. THE ARCHITECTURAL STYLE FEATURES CONCENTRIC COMPOUND WALLS AND ORNATE TOWERING GATEWAYS.

Temple building in South India was patronized by powerful royal dynasties, such as the Cholas, Pandyas, and Pallavas, and the rulers of the short-lived but magnificent Vidyanagar (City of Victory). The Cholas, particularly under King Rajaraja, extended Hindu territories into Indonesia and the Indo-China peninsula, where there remain important examples of Dravidian architecture, most notably at Angkor Wat. These achievements were part of a broad cultural expansion, perhaps as significant to human civilization as ancient Greece.

SOUTHERN ARCHITECTURE

The distinctive characteristics of the Southern or Dravidian style are the vimana and the gopuram. The vimana is a tall pyramidal tower

Below In Madurai, priests perform complex rituals within the famous Minakshi temple, dedicated to Shiva's wife, Parvati.

standing on a square base and consisting of several progressively smaller storeys. As part of the main temple, and housing the shrine, it usually stands at the centre of a vast ecclesiastical complex, surrounded by several concentric walls. Access is gained through successive gopurams, tall gateways adorned with hundreds of sculptures of deities. Other features include a number of smaller shrines, and tanks of water for bathing before entering the shrine. One of the most striking examples of Chola craftsmanship is at the Brihadishvara Temple in Thanjavur, where the temple headstone alone weighs over eighty tons.

TEMPLES IN TAMIL NADU

There are many other important temples, especially in Tamil Nadu. Kanchipuram, situated on the Palar river, is one of the oldest cities in South India. It was a centre of learning for both Tamil and Sanskrit scholars and rose to prominence

Above The distinctive southern-style gopuram (gateway) at the Adi Kumbhakonam Temple in Tamil Nadu.

during the reign of the Pallava dynasty between the 4th and 9th centuries CE. It was later governed by the Cholas and the Vijayanagara dynasty. Dubbed 'the religious capital of the South', Kanchi is equally important to Shaivas and Vaishnavas. It is headquarters to one branch of the Shri Vaishnava sampradaya, and the philosopher Ramanuja lived there for several years. Shankara's Smarta lineage also has a branch there called the Kanchi matha (monastery).

Kanchipuram was once known as 'the city of a thousand temples'. Only 126 now survive, with at least two built by the Vijayanagara dynasty. The Ekamabaranadhar temple, with its 58.5-metre (192-foot) tower, is one of five major Shaiva temples, each uniquely associated with one of the 'five elements' of Sankhya philosophy. This temple represents earth, and the complex covers 40 acres. Vaishnavas largely worship at the Varadaraja Perumal temple. Legend states that Robert Clive, who helped establish British rule in India, presented the Vishnu deity with an emerald necklace.

Kanchi remains popular to this day, especially with Hindu women who admire its exquisite, hand-woven silk saris.

South-west of Kanchi, in the town of Trichy, the Srirangam Temple stands next to the River Kaveri and is dedicated to Vishnu. Covering 156 acres, it is the largest temple complex in India, and the largest functioning mandir in the world (Angkor Wat is the largest non-functioning temple). The seven concentric walls, with a total length of over 9.6km (6 miles), enclose a marvellous 'thousand-pillared hall'.

130km (80 miles) south-west of Trichy, in the town of Madurai stands the Minakshi temple, dedicated to the goddess Parvati. Minakshi, meaning 'one with fish-shaped eyes', is considered both Shiva's wife and Vishnu's sister. This temple, patronized by the Pandhya dynasty, features a hall of 1,000 pillars and 12 gopurams between 45 and 50 metres (147–164 ft) high. Shrines are also dedicated to Minakshi's husband, Shiva – here called Subdareshvar – and to their son, Ganesha.

Below In Tamil Nadu, Brahmin priests bathe in the ponds at the Kolivur temple complex dedicated to Shiva.

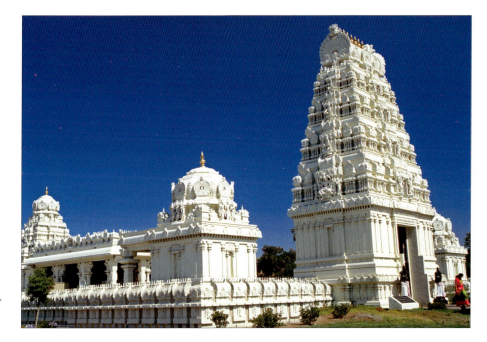

Above There are many South Indian style temples outside India, like this one in Malibu, California.

SABARIMALA

Further west in Kerala state and amidst the rich forest wilderness of the Western Ghats, lies one of India's major pilgrimage centres. Here at Sabarimala, the temple houses the image of Lord Ayyappa, reputedly born from the union of Shiva and Mohini. As the only feminine incarnation of Vishnu, Mohini appeared to delude the demons and retrieve the nectar of immortality. Her bewitching beauty enticed even the greatest of yogis, Lord Shiva, and thus Ayyappa was born, though some orthodox traditions dispute the story.

Although the shrine is remote, it draws between three to four million pilgrims each year. Before beginning the arduous walk through the mountain jungles, pilgrims prepare themselves with 41 days of fasting, celibacy and meditation. Pilgrims carry a double-pouched 'sacred-bundle' on their head. The rear pouch carries articles for the pilgrim's sustenance, such as rice and cooking paraphernalia. The front section, marked with the sacred syllable 'om', contains sacred items, such as camphor,

incense, vermilion, sandalwood paste and, most importantly, ghee (clarified butter) as an offering to the deity. Women between the ages of 10 and 50 are not allowed to visit for fear of testing the deity's vow of celibacy. The temple building, like others in Kerala, is largely made of wood. Sabarimala is one of India's many sacred mountains.

Below The gopuram at the Varadaraja Perumal temple in Kanchipura. Legend claims Robert Clive donated an emerald necklace to the presiding Vishnu deity.

SACRED HILLS AND MOUNTAINS

HINDUISM CONSIDERS HILLS AND MOUNTAINS TO BE SACRED. LEGEND AND FOLKLORE SAYS THAT THEY EMBRACE MYTHICAL KINGDOMS, THE ABODES OF DEITIES AND GATEWAYS TO HIGHER REALMS.

In Jain, Hindu, and Buddhist cosmology, Mount Meru (or Sumeru) is the central axis of the universe, on whose peak rests Brahma's celestial city of gold. When the gods and demons agreed to extract the nectar of immortality, they used Mount Meru to churn the milk ocean. Many Hindu temples, including the impressive structures at Angkor Wat in Cambodia, have been built as symbolic representations of this sacred mountain.

THE HIMALAYAS

One earthly representation of Mount Meru is Mount Kailash, Lord Shiva's home in the Himalayas. The Sanskrit word himalaya means 'the abode of

Below The Vaishno Devi Temple, dedicated to three goddesses, nestles in the Trikuta mountains in the north of India.

snow', and for Hindus this colossal mountain range is the abode of the gods and the favourite haunt of ascetics. Located here are some of the most popular pilgrimage sites in India, including Amarnath, Kedarnath and Badrinath, and the glacial sources of two holy rivers, the Ganga and Yamuna. Further down the Ganges, nestled in the Himalayan foothills, is the town of Rishikesh, called 'the gateway to the Himalayas' and more recently 'the world capital of yoga'. Another popular site, north of Amritsar, requires pilgrims to trek 13km (8 miles) and climb hundreds of steps to reach the cave of Vaishno Devi. The cave is dedicated to three goddesses, Lakshmi, Kali and Sarasvati, and is the only temple in India where all three are worshipped simultaneously.

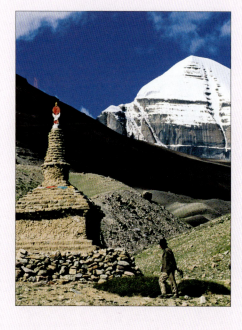

Above In the Himalayas, Mount Kailash, the sacred abode of Lord Shiva, forms a backdrop to a simple Buddhist stupa.

GOVARDHANA HILL

Further south, scorched by the fierce Indian summer, rests the famous hill called Govardhana. According to legend, the child Krishna convinced his father, the head of Vrindavana village, to replace the customary Indra-yajna (rain-sacrifice) with veneration of the hill. Insulted and enraged, Indra poured pillars of rain on to the village, causing widespread flooding. To protect his cows and kinsfolk, Krishna plucked up the hill and with the little finger of his left hand, held it aloft for an entire week, just like a 'frog's umbrella' (toadstool). Falling within the five days of Divali, Govardhana Puja remains a popular festival, and the hill a powerful motif for the Hindu ideal of taking shelter of the all-powerful divine.

Situated in the region of Vraj, ('land of the cows'), Govardhana is 25 km (15.5 miles) from both the holy city of Mathura and the adjacent Vrindavana, now a bustling, congested pilgrimage town. A popular practice for local and visiting Vaishnavas is to worship stones taken from the hill, as a form of

Above During the autumn festivities in Vrindavana, this exhibit celebrates Krishna's lifting of the Govardhana Hill.

Lord Krishna. The main pilgrimage season falls in the autumnal month of Karttika, during which thousands of visitors complete the 11-km (6.8 mile) circumambulation of the renowned hill.

SOUTH INDIA

Far south of Mathura, the Vindhya Mountains separate northern India from the Deccan (southern peninsula). Bounded by the western and eastern 'Ghats' (coastal ranges), South India is more undulating than the North, and features many sacred peaks. Within the state of Andhra Pradesh, the seven hills of Tirumali are dear to Vaishnavas, and the 853m (2,800-foot) peak of Vyenkata Hill is crowned with the famous Tirupati temple. Some claim this to be the richest pilgrimage city in the world. Daily, around 30,000 pilgrims take darshana (audience) of the reclining form of Vishnu, called Balaji or Vyenkateshvara (Lord of Vyenkata Hill). Before entering the main temple, visitors abstain from smoking, drinking spirits and eating non-vegetarian food, and must bathe and

don clean clothes. As a means of atonement and giving thanks, many pilgrims – both men and women – shave their heads.

Also in the state of Tamil Nadu, the Palani Hills are an eastward extension of the Western Ghats, the range running down the west coast. It is home to a famous shrine, sacred to Murugan worshippers, who climb 670 steps to reach the main temple. The deity of Murugan is a lifelong celibate, and the story goes that he came here to renounce the world after being outwitted in a racing competition by his elephant-headed brother, Ganesha. During festivities lasting up to ten days, devotees circumambulate the hill and carry a kavadi, a canopy-like structures made of cloth, string and bamboo. As a form of severe austerity, each structure is supported by wires hooked into the body of the penitent who carries it up steps to the hilltop temple.

Another famous hill is the Arunachal Parvat, on which the 20th-century saint Ramana Maharshi established his hermitage near Pondicherry in the state of Andhra Pradesh. Ramana claimed that the mountain's herbs and flowers had tremendous healing properties, and compared it to the famous peak carried by Hanuman. The location of shrines and ashrams on mountains, or near other geographical features, suggests that Hinduism, whilst 'other-worldly', is closely connected to the earth and Mother Nature.

Below The ornate Murugan Temple atop the Palani Hills in South India.

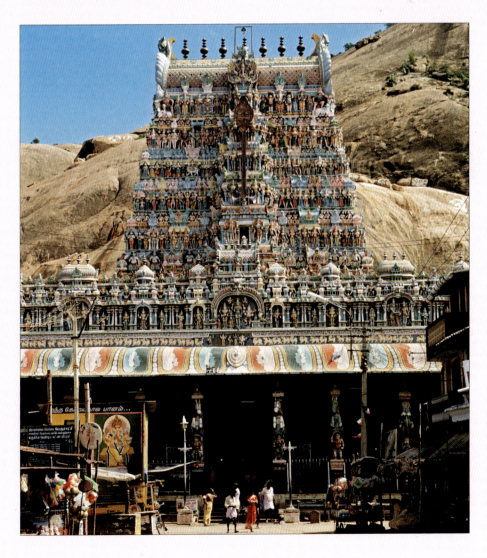

HOLY RIVERS, LAKES AND OCEANS

INDIA'S SACRED RIVERS ARE LEGENDARY. THEIR SANCTIFYING WATERS ARE NOW POLLUTED, BUT HINDUS STILL FLOCK TO THEIR BATHING GHATS. MANY LAKES AND OCEANS ARE SIMILARLY REVERED.

Water is of special significance within Hinduism, not only for its life-sustaining properties but also for its additional use in ritual, and personal hygiene. For centuries, and for physical and mental cleanliness, practically all Hindus have taken a bath in the morning. Bathing also has religious significance, especially in waters considered sacred.

MOTHER GANGA
Traditionally, of the seven principal rivers, the Ganga, Yamuna and Sarasvati are most sacred. According to different opinions, the ancient Sarasvati is now invisible, flows underground, or has long dried up. Some say that, unseen to the human eye, she still meets the Ganga and Yamuna at Prayaga, and hence the

Below Among the fishermen's boats, pilgrims bathe at Kanyakumari (Cape Comorin), the confluence of three seas.

spot is called trisandi, 'confluence of three rivers'. Taking a dip here, especially during the 12-yearly Kumbha Mela ('bathing fair'), is considered most auspicious.

India's longest river is the Ganges. From its glacial source in the central Himalayas, it flows south and eastward, 2,500km (1553 miles) to the Bay of Bengal, where it forms the world's largest delta. More than half of India's population lives within 500km (310 miles) of its live-giving waters. The river is personified as a heavenly goddess called Ganga, who wears a white saree and rides a crocodile. In the Mahabharata, the goddess Ganga plays a decisive role in the opening storyline, becoming the proud mother of Bhishma, a central character until his glorious death in the Kurukshetra war. The Mahabharata also recounts the story of the descent of Goddess Ganga's descent, which is linked to

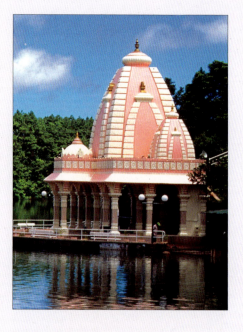

Above A temple on the sacred lake of Ganga Talao in Mauritius.

both Vishnu and Shiva. Ganga's water, sanctified by contact with Vishnu's lotus feet, is collected and transported for use in ritual and puja.

SACRED LAKES AND OCEANS
Some lakes are also considered sacred. In the holy region of Vraj, around Krishna's birth town of Mathura, Vaishnavas venerate Radhakunda and Shyamakunda, twin ponds dedicated to Radha and Krishna. Devotees have built replicas outside India, illustrating how pilgrimage has evolved beyond the subcontinent. A Shaiva tradition recounts how Shiva and Parvati were circling the earth, with the sacred river Ganges still balanced on Shiva's head. Noticing an exquisite tropical island, he touched down there, but inadvertently spilled a few drops of water, thus creating a lake. Shiva informed Mother Ganga that the people scattered along her banks would one day emigrate, settle on the island and congregate to worship her. That sacred lake in Mauritius hosts one of the largest Hindu pilgrimages outside India, especially popular with Shaiva sects.

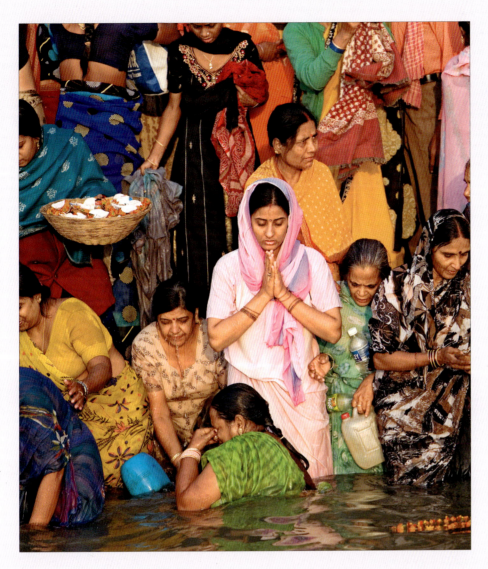

Above At Varanasi, pilgrims pray and bathe in the River Ganges. Its purifying waters are thought to wash away karma and dissolve worldly bondage.

Certain shorelines are also holy. Kanyakumari is a town located at Cape Comorin, on the southernmost tip of the Indian Peninsula. It is a Shakta pitha (holy site), dedicated to the virgin goddess Parvati, who performed penance here to obtain Lord Shiva's hand. Some say that they wedded here, and the seven colours of rice thrown as confetti transformed into the seven-hued sands. The site features memorials to Gandhi and Vivekananda, and a gigantic 40.5m (133 foot) statue of the Tamil poet-saint Thiruvalluvar. Pilgrims bathe here, in the confluence of three bodies of water, the Arabian Sea, the Indian Ocean and the Bay of Bengal.

MOTHER GANGA'S DESCENT
Bhagiratha, the Emperor of India, was saddened to hear that 60,000 of his ancestors had met premature deaths, burned to ashes by the mystic glance of the sage Kapila. Troubled at heart that they had failed to reach heaven, he visited the sage, who informed him that only the waters of the river Ganga could liberate his ancestors. Kapila further explained that long ago, Lord Vishnu, in his incarnation as a dwarf brahmin, had crossed the entire universe in only two steps. Whilst taking the second step, his big toe touched and cracked the wall of the universe. Water trickled in, and became the Ganges, which flowed through the celestial worlds as the River Mandakini.

Following Kapila's advice, Bhagiratha offered prayer and performed severe austerities. Lord Vishnu was pleased and ordered the goddess Ganga to descend to earth. However, Bhagiratha feared that her turbulent waters might destroy the earth. Lord Shiva offered to catch the falling river. In paintings, Shiva is still shown with the river cascading into his coiled hair. King Bhagiratha then led the river across India, and she eventually divided herself into a hundred streams. Reaching the ashram of Kapila, she washed the ashes of the long-dead princes, purifying their souls and making them eligible to enter heaven. Millions of Hindus still bathe in the Ganga. She is purified of the accumulated sin only by the touch of the many saints who also bathe in her famous waters.

Below A Kolkata man carries Ganges water home for use in ritual and worship.

CHAPTER 7

SPECIAL OCCASIONS

Hinduism as a joyous, colourful tradition is most evident during festival time. Divali features fireworks and rows of flickering lamps. During Holi everyone is doused with dyed water and brightly hued powders. In the public sphere, fairs and festivals bring together friends, families and communities. Within the family, rites of passage celebrate life's milestones and achievements.

Hindu festivals are opportunities for linking with the divine. They often reflect an aspiration for liberation, yet are intimately related to this world: the land, nature and the ever-turning cycles of life. Through festivals, Hindus adore the lives of liberating gods and goddesses, and of liberated saints. Festivities mark the blossoming of spring, the fulfilment of the harvest and the joys of love and friendship.

The rites of passage recognize similar cycles: the anticipation accompanying a new birth; the promise of adulthood; the fruitfulness of married life; and the wisdom that precedes the gradual closing of life. Hindu teachings acknowledge the inevitable suffering that accompanies embodied life. However, vibrant holy days celebrate life itself, and the relationship of the real self with the eternal divine.

Opposite Many Hindu festivals celebrate the importance of family relationships.
Women and girls of all ages seize the opportunity to dress up and wear their finest clothes.

Above A Chinese groom and Malaysian bride offer oblations into the sacred fire at their
Hindu wedding ceremony near Auckland, New Zealand.

HINDU FESTIVALS

HINDUISM BOASTS SO MANY FESTIVALS THAT THE LARGEST TEMPLE, AT SHRIRANGAM, ANNUALLY OBSERVES NEARLY 400. MOST HINDU HOLY DAYS ARE CONNECTED TO SPECIFIC SAINTS OR DEITIES.

Festivals are times of celebration, characterized by ritual, colour and gaiety. They uplift the atmosphere and turn the mind toward spiritual matters. Often highly communal, they bring together friends, families and villages. Some of the most popular are celebrated throughout India, often as national holidays; in other parts of the world, a few are recognized as public holidays, when Hindus themselves can take time off from work or school. Nowadays, those festivals falling midweek are often celebrated at the weekend, so that more family members can attend.

MAIN PRACTICES

Hinduism has been dubbed 'the kitchen religion', and no festival goes without fasting, feasting and the wide distribution of food. Celebrants often travel to meet relatives, attend worship and donate alms to shrines. Some events require the manufacture of a temporary murti, worshipped with flower garlands, smouldering incense and flaming camphor. In public processions, images are held aloft on carts or palanquins, to the blare of horns and the clashing of cymbals. Festivals are also visually aesthetic, with attendees drawing rangoli patterns, wearing new clothes, and decorating temples with flags, fruits and flowers; mango leaves dangle from festoons and banana plants provide ornamental shade. Increasingly popular are musical and theatrical performances, depicting stories linked to the festival and the corresponding gods and goddesses.

DIVALI

The most widely celebrated festival in India is Divali. It is also commemorated by Jains, Sikhs and Buddhists. This 'festival of lights' spans a five-day period at the juncture of the months of Ashwin and Karttik. It falls in autumn, during October or November. In India, as the mild winter sets in, it is a time for feasting,

Above During Divali celebrations in Bangalore, South India, a young woman completes an elaborate rangoli pattern.

visiting relatives, exchanging gifts, decorating houses, and wearing new clothes. One conspicuous feature is the incessant thumping of firecrackers.

There are various origins associated with Divali. South Indians commemorate the marriage of Lakshmi and Vishnu, whereas most Bengalis dedicate it to the goddess Kali. Vaishnavas fondly recall the story of Rama and Sita.

On the first day, dedicated to Lakshmi, business people invoke a prosperous new year by offering puja to their recently balanced account books. The second day celebrates Krishna's killing of a demon called Narakasura and his freeing thousands of captive princesses.

The main festivities fall on the third day. At dusk, houses are decorated with rows of deepas, small

Left Pilgrims pull the three chariots at the annual Ratha-yatra celebrations in Puri. This festival is now observed worldwide.

TYPES OF FESTIVAL

There are four main types of holy day. They commemorate:

1 A key event in the life of a deity, such as the jayanti ('appearance day', or birthday).
2 The birth, life and achievements of a Hindu saint, often the founder of a specific lineage.
3 Seasonal festivities and customs, as related to nature and the harvest.
4 Family relationships, and loyalty and affection between relatives.

Festivals in the first category are often celebrated internationally and as Indian public holidays. Special days within the second category are often only relevant to a particular group (sampradaya) for which the saint in question has significant relevance. Festivals in the third category are often regional affairs, or regional variations of broader festivals: Pongal, for example, is the Tamil version of the widely observed Makara Sankranti. Some spring festivals, such as Holi, are now celebrated internationally. Within the fourth category, festivals such as Raksha Bandhana have also won global recognition.

Above In Ahmedabad, the main city in Gujarat, a girl lights a ghee lamp on the eve of the Divali festival.

earthenware lamps filled with oil. These flickering lamps are also dotted along the parapets of temples, and set adrift on rivers and streams. On this day, Lord Rama returned to his capital. Accompanied by Sita, and leading a vast army commanded by Hanuman, Rama triumphantly entered Ayodhya. It was the dark night of the new moon. Rama's joyous subjects bedecked the entire city with lamps, illuminating the

route and welcoming the entire entourage with pomp and gaiety. Also on this third day, the rows of lamps are thought to beckon the goddess Lakshmi into the family home, and the goddess of learning, Sarasvati, is also revered.

The fourth day marks Govardhana puja, worship of the sacred hill lifted by Lord Krishna. Worshippers retell the story, construct replicas of the hill, and offer a huge feast. Some traditions mark this festival as annakuta, the offering of food, and others perform go-puja, veneration of the cow.

On the fifth and final day, sisters grant blessings to their brothers, and wish them a successful new year.

Right During the harvest festival called Annakuta, priests in Texas, USA, offer food to the temple deities.

THE HINDU CALENDAR

THE HINDU CALENDAR IS BASED ON THE ORBITS OF BOTH SUN AND MOON. MEASURED AGAINST THE WESTERN CALENDAR, DATES VARY EACH YEAR, BUT FALL WITHIN THE SAME 30-DAY SPAN.

The Hindu calendar (panchang) lists important festivals and astrological data, such as auspicious periods, planetary transits and phases of the moon. Some versions list fast days, including the regular ekadashi falling on the 11th day of each fortnight. For calculating dates, the most widely used text is the Surya Siddhanta, written in its current form around the 10th century. Texts reveal remarkably precise calculations, with one unit of time spanning less than a fifth of a millisecond.

THE YEAR

The Hindu calendar is based on real months, corresponding to the cycles of the moon. There are 12 months of about 29½ days, totalling approximately 355 days per year. The shortfall explains why each festival

Below Five stages of the waxing moon. This 'bright fortnight' starts on the day after the new moon (day 1) and finishes on the full moon itself (day 15). The dark fortnight also consists of 15 such 'lunar days'.

moves back about 10 days from one year to the next. To rectify this, a leap month is added every three years. The calendar is therefore lunisolar, based on both sun and moon. By the Gregorian calendar, dates vary each year, with up to 30 days between the earliest and latest possible dates.

The year, beginning with the sun's entrance into Capricorn (Makara), is divided into two halves, and six seasons reflecting the natural phases of the Indian climate. There are various ways of reckoning the New Year. The most common identify the day after the dark moon in the month of Chaitra (March or April) or the day after the Divali new moon. For numbering the years, several eras are used. The most popular are the Shaka Era, counted from 78CE, and the Vikrama Era, beginning with King Vikram in 57BCE. In rituals, the priest often announces the dates according to the onset of the present age, the Kali-yuga. According to these three systems, the year 2000 corresponded to 1922, 2057 and 5102 respectively.

Above Built in 1725, the Jantar Mantar observatory, or 'The Yantra Mandir', features many large astronomical instruments.

THE MONTH

Within each month, there are two 'fortnights', each consisting of 15 'lunar days'. Technically, the solar day and the lunar day begin at different times, so each solar day is ascribed a particular lunar day, numbered from 1 to 15. There are 15 days in both 'the bright fortnight' (waxing moon) and 'the dark fortnight' (waning moon). As months average out to 29½ days, occasionally a day will be dropped. For example, in one month, the first day of the waxing moon may be followed by the third.

Right The Hindu 'lunisolar' calendar, showing northern and southern months (outer rings) and their relationship to the Gregorian and solar calendars (inner rings). The year has six seasons.

Less frequently, two consecutive days will be the same lunar day; for example, both Monday and Tuesday may be the fifth day of the moon.

There are two main calendars. In the north, the month begins with the full moon, and in the south with the new moon. Festival dates still fall on the same day, but the name of the month may be different. For example, although Krishna's birthday falls on the 8th day of the dark moon, in the north it is in the month of Bhadra, and in the south it is in Shravana.

THE WEEK AND THE DAY

As in the West, the week is divided into seven days corresponding to the seven planets. No day is particularly special, but each is associated with a specific deity. For example, Monday is connected to Shiva, and Tuesday to Hanuman. Hindus often propitiate a deity, perhaps by fasting and prayer, on the corresponding day. The day usually begins at dawn, or just before, depending on the adopted astronomical and astrological systems. The daytime is divided into 15 muhurtas of 48 minutes, and similarly the night. For worship and spiritual practices, the morning hours before dawn are considered most propitious.

Right This key (to the diagram above) explains in detail the Hindu calendar. Festival dates are approximate as the precise dates change relative to the Gregorian calendar, with a month between the earliest and latest possible dates. A few Hindu festivals, such as Makara Sankranti, are determined by the sun alone, and the Gregorian dates are the same each year, or within one day.

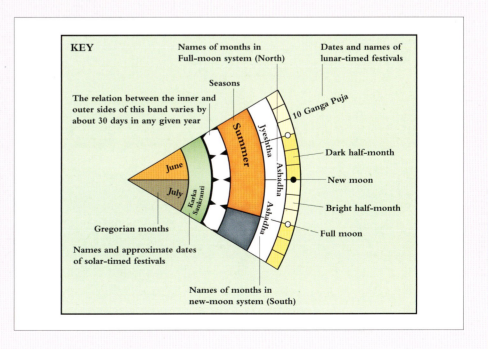

159

SPRING AND NATURE FESTIVALS

MANY FESTIVALS MARK THE CHANGING SEASONS. THREE ARE MOST IMPORTANT: THE SOLAR FESTIVAL CALLED PONGAL, THE WELCOMING OF SPRING, AND THE ROWDY BUT COLOURFUL HOLI.

Pongal is observed by Tamils worldwide to celebrate the end of the main harvest period. In the Tamil language, Pongal means 'it has boiled', referring to the sweet rice offered to the sun god, Surya. In Punjab it is called Lohri, and, more widely, Makara Sankranti, the auspicious time when the sun enters the astrological sign of Makara (Capricorn). The festival is associated with the principle of rebirth.

The first day, called Bhogi, honours Lord Indra. In preparation for the main festivities, old clothes

Below A Bangladeshi student offers prayers during the festival of Sarasvati Puja, which also welcomes the spring.

and materials are burned or thrown away, marking the end of the old. On the main day of Pongal – the second – celebrants put on new clothes to symbolize the start of a new cycle. As an offering to Surya, women boil rice in fresh milk, using new clay pots. The preparation, topped with raisins, cashew nuts and jaggery (palm sugar), is allowed to boil over the sides of the vessel, symbolizing prosperity. On the third day, farmers wash and garland their cattle, paint their hooves and horns, and lead them in procession. On the fourth and final day, festivities conclude with visits to friends, relatives and nearby towns and cities.

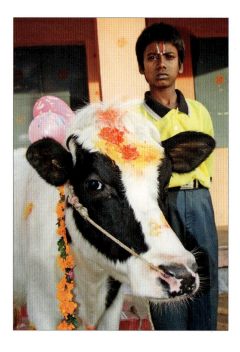

Above A South Indian boy with his cow, specially decorated for the harvest festival of Pongal.

VASANTA PANCHAMI AND SARASVATI PUJA

The festival of Vasanta Panchami is celebrated annually on the fifth day of the month of Magh and marks the first day of spring. Poets have designated spring 'rituraja', the king of seasons, and the Bhagavad-gita identifies it with God's splendour and opulence. According to Hindu texts, the deity of love, Kamadeva, is always accompanied by the god in charge of spring. Therefore, wherever Cupid travels, trees burst into blossom, the cuckoo begins his long-awaited song, and lovers become intoxicated by the scent-laden air.

The spring festival coincides with Sarasvati Puja, adoration of the goddess of learning. On this day, ancestors are worshipped, brahmins sumptuously fed and children taught to write their first words. Colleges offer special prayers to Sarasvati, and schoolchildren reverentially place pens and notebooks at the goddess's feet, seeking her benediction for passing their exams. Artists and musicians ask the goddess to bless their tools and instruments.

On this day, everyone wears yellow. The goddess is draped in yellow silk, celebrants eat sweets dyed with saffron and, especially in Punjab, the fields blaze with blossoming mustard. Spiritually, the colour yellow is associated with the planet Jupiter and with growth, wisdom and prosperity. Children express their joy by flying kites, and women adorn their houses with auspicious rangoli patterns.

HOLI

Falling on the full moon day of the month of Phalguna (February–March), Holi is perhaps the most rowdy and colourful of all Hindu festivals. Celebrants smother each other with fluorescent powder, and children, armed with buckets and large syringes, douse the passer-by with coloured liquid. It is a time for breaking with custom and transgressing standard codes of etiquette. In some

Below In Nandagram, where Krishna lived as a child, Holi revellers bombard each other with coloured powders.

THE STORY OF HOLI

Long ago there lived a wicked and atheistic king called Hiranyakashipu. His name means 'gold and soft beds', implying that he was highly materialistic. His son, Prahlada, was just the opposite. Indeed, 5-year-old Prahlada was a great devotee of Vishnu. This enraged his demonic father who tried at first to rectify his son by educating him in the arts of diplomacy and deceit. When this proved useless, the king resolved to murder Prahlad, in various inventive ways: hurling him from a cliff top; casting him into a snake pit; and dashing him under the feet of charging elephants. Throughout the ordeal, the boy's ardent prayers invoked Vishnu's protection, and he remained unharmed. Hiranyakashipu seethed with fury. Breathing heavily, he summoned his evil sister, Holika. He knew she had received a boon from Agni that she could not be harmed by fire. Agreeing to her brother's proposal,

Above Near the symbolic Holi bonfire, a priest daubs sacred ash on the forehead of a celebrant.

she carried her faultless nephew into the midst of a blazing fire. However, Prahlad remained unscathed as Holika burnt to ashes.

villages, wives ritually beat their husbands and, on this day, superiors can be mocked and taunted without fear of retribution. More passively, mothers carry their babies clockwise around bonfires to invoke the protection and benediction of Agni, the fire-god.

Different stories are retold. In South India, people remember how Shiva burnt to ashes the god of love, Kamadeva, who tried to interrupt the ascetic god's meditation with his fabled arrows. Around Krishna's birthplace in Mathura, elders relate stories of how Krishna and the milkmaids used to pelt each other with dyed water and fluorescent powder. This day is also connected with the appearance of the half-man, half-lion incarnation of Vishnu, who finally killed the tyrant called Hiranyakashipu. During Holi, Hindus remember how Vishnu protects his devotees and destroys evil.

CELEBRATING FAMILY RELATIONSHIPS

SOME HINDU FESTIVALS CELEBRATE FAMILY RELATIONSHIPS. THE MOST POPULAR IS RAKSHA BANDHANA, WHICH APPLAUDS THE POWERFUL BOND OF AFFECTION BETWEEN BROTHER AND SISTER.

The festival of Raksha Bandhana coincides with the full moon in the month of Shravana. 'Raksha' means 'protection', and 'Bandhana' 'to tie'. This ritual may date back to the initiation rite, when the guru knotted a red thread about his disciple's wrist: a procedure still prevalent in religious rituals to symbolize a vow or commitment. During the modern festival, the sister affectionately ties her 'rakhi', a decorative silk amulet, around her

Below In Bopal, central India, a woman inspects rakhis on the eve of the full moon festival of Raksha Bandana.

brother's right wrist. He reciprocates by giving his sister a gift and making a solemn pledge of protection. Before Raksha Bandhana, stalls and shops sell hundreds of rakhis, silk bracelets bearing baubles of brightly coloured thread, cloth or tinsel.

A similar event, observed on the fifth day of Divali, is called 'sister's day'. Many aeons ago, Yama, the god of death, visited his sister, Yamuna. She decorated her brother's forehead with the auspicious tilak mark. Yama subsequently declared that one who received tilak from his sister on that same day would be liberated from all miseries.

Above At Raksha Bandana, a young Hindu woman ties a sacred bracelet on her brother's right wrist before offering him sweets.

BROTHERLY LOVE

The rakhi is not reserved just for brothers, or even Hindus. Many stories indicate how tying a rakhi to any man's wrist makes him an adopted brother. When threatened by the military might of the Gujarati sultan, Queen Karnavati of Chittor appealed to the Mughal emperor Humayun by sending him a rakhi. The chivalrous emperor abandoned a prolonged military campaign to ride to her rescue, though unsuccessfully. In Kerala, devotees hear how Lakshmi tied an amulet on King Bali to win his favour. Lord Indra, rendered invincible by a rakhi charged with sacred mantras, ousted the demons from his heavenly realm.

The festival also relates to Lord Krishna who, after using his disk weapon, was left clutching a cut finger. Draupadi, wife of the Pandavas, tore a strip of silk from her sari and tied it around his wrist as a tourniquet. Krishna declared himself bound by Draupadi's affection, and promised to repay her good deed a thousand times over. Years later, when the ruthless Kauravas tried to disrobe Draupadi, Krishna protected her honour by supplying an endless length of sari.

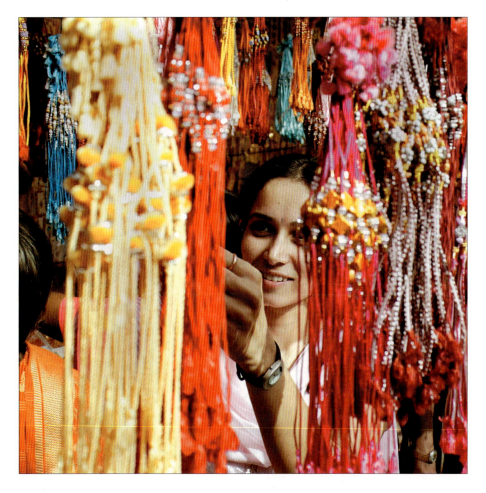

KARVA CHAUTH

A traditional festival for married women, Karva Chauth is observed mainly in North India. On the fourth day of the waning moon, eleven days before Divali, married women fast for a whole day to enhance the longevity of their husbands. The ritual signifies the wife's love and devotion to the husband, on whose behalf she performs austerities. Although some modern women have objected to this as sign of male domination and female servility, it remains a popular festival. The southern equivalent celebrates the story of Savitri, whose devotion saved her husband Satyavan from the clutches of death.

A few days prior to the Karva Chauth festival, married women buy new spherical earthen pots, called 'karvas'. On the outside they paint ornate designs, and they place bangles, ribbons, cosmetics and home-made sweets inside. On the evening before the main day, they start a 24-hour fast. The following evening they don their best clothing and adorn themselves with henna and jewellery.

Below A traditional depiction of Shiva and Parvati, whose marriage anniversary is celebrated on Mahashivaratri.

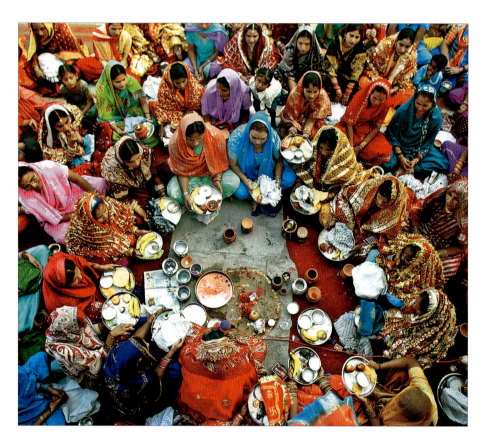

Above During the festivities of Karva Chauth, married women from the northern city of Chandigarh pray for their husbands' welfare.

They first spot the rising moon indirectly, reflected in a platter of water or through a sieve. They subsequently worship the lunar deity, Chandra, praying for the wellbeing and longevity of their husbands. In turn, each husband offers his wives the first sip of water and the first bite of food. Later on, a sumptuous dinner is served. On that evening, or sometime afterwards, ladies exchange their decorated karvas. One who observes this vow is respected as 'Shaubhagyavati', a joyous and fortunate wife.

MAHA SHIVA RATRI

Hindu festivals also celebrate the dealings between the gods and goddesses, who are variously related to each other. Most academics describe such family connections as anthropomorphic, a projection of human experience on to the unfathomable divine. However, some Hindu traditions suggest the reverse: worldly relationships indicate the existence of original, eternal and archetypal exchanges. Consequently, devotional movements such as Bengali Vaishnavism have developed theologies based on rasa, the ontological pleasure derived from affectionate dealings. Many festivals and attendant stories, such as the Ramayana, glorify loyal and loving family relationships, and Hindus still relish repeatedly hearing of them.

In late February or March, the festival of Mahashivarati honours Lord Shiva, and more specifically his marriage to the goddess Parvati. The divine couple are considered the ideal husband and wife. On this day, the 14th day of the waning moon, devotees fast throughout the night and carry pots of sacred water to shrines and temples. Traditionally, young girls pray for a husband who, though not necessarily wealthy, will be as virtuous as Lord Shiva. A man with a wife like Parvati also considers himself divinely blessed.

GOD'S APPEARANCE

MANY OBSERVED FESTIVALS ARE LINKED TO THE VARIOUS HINDU
DEITIES. THEY COMMEMORATE KEY EVENTS, SUCH AS APPEARANCE DAY
(BIRTHDAY), A WEDDING, OR VICTORY OVER DEMONIC FORCES.

Above To celebrate Ganesha's birthday, devotees carry his murti through the streets of Mumbai.

Maha Shiva Ratri ('the great night of Shiva') commemorates the marriage of Shiva and Shakti. Some five or six weeks later, in April, Hindus mark the birthday of Rama with readings from the Ramayana, theatrical presentations and the chanting of Rama mantras. A week later, Hanumat Jayanti celebrates the birthday of Rama's dedicated servant, Hanuman, particularly with recitation of the prayer called Hanuman Chalisa. In late summer, Janmashtami celebrates the birth of Lord Krishna, one of the most loved of all deities.

Below One of the largest gatherings of Hindus outside India occurs near London over the Janmashtami festival period.

KRISHNA JANMASHTAMI

'Janma' means 'birth', and 'ashatami' refers to 'the eighth day'. Krishna was born on the eighth day of the dark fortnight of Shravana, and the anniversary falls between mid-August and early September. Krishna was born at midnight, and many Hindus fast for the preceding 24 hours. Late that evening, devotees offer milk sweets to baby Krishna and greet him with a midnight arati. Other festivities include singing bhajanas, retelling the story of Krishna's birth and swinging a cradle before the temple shrine.

Popular in the Mumbai area is a competition in which young men build human pyramids in order to reach a pot (handi) full of prize money. This game mimics the activities of Govinda (Krishna), who with his playmates stole butter from pots suspended from the rafters.

KRISHNA'S BIRTH

Lord Krishna was born in prison, to Queen Devaki and King Vasudeva. Devaki's brother, Kamsa, had previously heard a prophetic voice announcing that the eighth son of Devaki would kill him. He had therefore imprisoned Vasudeva and Devaki, and ruthlessly murdered their first seven children. On the occasion of Krishna's birth, Vasudeva miraculously escaped the prison, and carried his newborn son over the turbulent river Yamuna. There, in the rural village of Vrindavana, he left Krishna to be brought up by his foster parents, Nanda and Yashoda. When Krishna was an adolescent, he returned to Mathura, killed his wicked uncle and later became the powerful King of Dvaraka.

Krishna is also famous for his amorous pastimes with the gopis (cowherd girls), headed by Radha. Her birthday, Radhastami, falls a fortnight after Krishna's and is celebrated by dressing her sacred murti entirely in flowers.

Another Krishna-related festival is the ratha-yatra (cart pilgrimage). Though centuries old, it still takes place each summer at the seaside town of Puri. The black-complexioned and wide-eyed deity Lord Jagannatha ('Lord of the Universe') is carried on a huge chariot, while his brother, Balarama, and sister, Subhadra, ride on similar vehicles. The carts stand over 15 metres (49 ft) high, and ride on 12, 14 and 16 wheels respectively. Thousands of pilgrims take turns at pulling the chariots by rope. The word juggernaut, indicating a huge lorry, is derived from the name Jagannatha. Since the late 1960s, this festival has been celebrated annually in cities throughout the world.

GANESHA CHATURTHI
Some 12 days after Janmastami, Ganesha Chaturthi celebrates the birthday of the elephant-headed son of Shiva and Parvati. Observed in the Hindu month of Bhadrapada, it starts on the fourth day (chaturthi) of the waxing moon. A clay image of Ganesha is installed in a temporary pavilion for 10 days, during which arati is performed and prasada distributed. After the final arati on the 11th day, the deity is ceremoniously submerged in the river or sea.

This modern version goes back to 1893, when B.G. Tilak, nationalist and freedom fighter, transformed the annual festival from a private, family affair into a grand public event. The festival promoted community participation in the form of dance, theatre, poetry recital, musical concerts and philosophical debate. He chose Ganesha because of the deity's wide appeal as 'the god for everyone'. Indeed, Ganesha remains Hinduism's most popular deity, though – unlike his father – he is rarely considered the Supreme deity.

NAVARATRI
Almost a month after Ganesha's birthday, on the first day of Ashwin, the 'Festival of Nine Nights' centres on the adoration of Parvati and other goddesses. It is one of the relatively few pan-Indian festivals. In the household, a brass image of Parvati is installed, puja performed twice daily, and a ghee lamp left to burn continuously for the entire nine days. A single-strand garland is offered daily and special food offered at midday. Each night, Hindu families congregate in halls and temples to enjoy rasa-garbha, traditional folk dances, in which decorative sticks are struck together in time to devotional music. Celebrants dance around a six-sided shrine. According to local custom or regional preference, goddesses other than Parvati may also be worshipped, including Lakshmi, Sarasvati, and nine different forms of Durga. The tenth day is celebrated as Dussehra, and is linked to both the Goddess and Rama, specifically his victory over the ten-headed Ravana. Featuring the burning of a huge effigy of Ravana, it remains the most popular festival in modern Nepal.

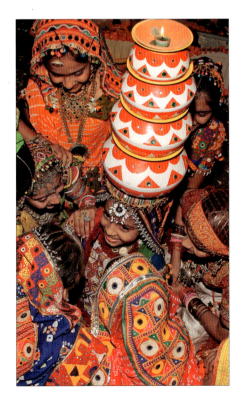

Below In Ahmedabad, young Indian dancers chat between performances. The 'nine-night' Navaratri festival honours Devi (Shakti) and other goddesses.

REMEMBERING SAINTS

FESTIVALS ALSO COMMEMORATE THE LIVES AND ACHIEVEMENTS OF HINDU SAINTS. MOST IMPORTANT ARE THEIR APPEARANCE DAYS (BIRTHDAYS) AND DISAPPEARANCE DAYS (DEATH ANNIVERSARIES).

Within Hinduism there is often a vague and contested boundary between saint and deity. In south India, the female poet-saint Andal was later identified as the incarnation of Vishnu's consort called Bhu. After the passing of the Bengali saint Chaitanya, his devotees identified him as the dual incarnation of Radha and Krishna. Similarly, Sahajananda Swami was later considered God by some followers of the Gujarati Swaminarayan mission.

Debate about succession and the divinity of saints and founder has long caused sacred lineages to branch into several distinct groups. For this reason, festivities associated with saints tend to be confined to certain geographical regions, or to particular traditions or their sub-branches. Such events share the pervasive ideal of respecting holy people and keeping their precious company.

GURU PURNIMA

One widely celebrated event falls in late summer on the full moon in the Hindu month of Ashadha. Observed as Guru Purnima, it is sacred to the memory of Vyasa, considered the original guru and compiler of many texts. On this day, spiritual aspirants worship him, and disciples perform

Above Ramakrishna (1836–86), whose birthday is celebrated annually, especially in parts of Bengal.

a 'puja' to their own respective spiritual preceptors. Many hold a similar event on the actual birthday of their guru, whether living or deceased. Other birthdays honour the exalted founders of particular movements. Many Bengalis honour the birthdays of Ramakrishna and Vivekananda, and Vaishnavas celebrate the birthdays of great acharyas (founders of sampradayas) such as Ramanuja and Madhva. Many Smartas similarly commemorate the birth and life of Adi Shankara by ritually bathing his murti in milk and reciting the Vedas.

REMEMBERING GANDHI

Gandhi's birthday is a national Indian holiday called Gandhi Jayanti. It is celebrated worldwide by many Hindu groups, including youth organizations, which recount Gandhi's life story and sing his favourite bhajanas. Although Gandhi's legend has been adopted by nationalist movements, he is also associated with a broad-minded, inclusive approach, underpinned by the values and teachings of medieval devotional traditions. In 2007, the United Nations General Assembly declared 2 October, Gandhi's birthday, to be 'The International Day of Non-violence.'

BIRTHDAY HYMN

The following lyrics, from one of Gandhi's two favourite bhajanas, are frequently sung on his birthday:

He is the true Vaishnava who feels another's woes as his own. Always serving those who are unhappy, he never entertains vanity. Bowing in humility to everyone, he criticizes none, and keeps pure his thoughts, speech and deeds. Blessed indeed is the mother who begets such a saint!

He looks upon all with an equal eye. Devoid of lust, he reveres every woman as his very own mother. If he even attempted to utter an untruth, his tongue would fail him. He does not covet another's wealth and the worldly attachments do not bind him, for his mind is immersed in renunciation.

Right *During Gandhi's birthday celebrations in 2007, an Indian student dressed as the Mahatma mimics his weaving cotton on his spinning wheel.*

At every moment, he is eager to recite the holy name of Lord Rama. All the holy places are ever-present in his body. He has conquered lust, greed, deceit and anger. Narsinh declares that the very sight of such a Vaishnava liberates 71 generations of one's family.

SONGS OF SEPARATION.

The following select verses are from a bhajana (hymn) sung on the death anniversaries of Bengali saints. They express the sentiment of separation from holy people.

He who brought the treasure of divine love, and who was filled with mercy and compassion: where has such a saintly personality as Shrinivasa Acharya gone?

Where are my Svarupa Damodara and Rupa Gosvami? Where is Sanatana? Where is Raghunatha Dasa, the saviour of the fallen?

Where are my Raghunatha Bhatta and Gopala Bhatta, and where is Krishnadasa Kaviraja? Where did Lord Gauranga, the great dancer, suddenly go?

I will smash my head against the rock and enter into fire. Where will I find Lord Gauranga, the reservoir of all wonderful qualities?

Being unable to obtain the association of Lord Gauranga, accompanied by all of these devotees in whose association he performed his pastimes, Narottama Dasa simply weeps.

ENTERING SAMADHI

The passing of a saint is termed 'entering samadhi', implying their attainment of liberation by fixing the mind on God. Samadhi also refers to the tomb honouring a saint. Interred within is an embalmed body or other holy relics, such as flowers from garlands once worn by the saint. The samadhi serves as a shrine, at which disciples and pilgrims pray, offer respects and recall the saint's example and achievement. A saint's passing is an occasion for simultaneous joy and sadness: joy that the saint has achieved a glorious destiny, and lamentation for feeling bereft of such company. Such conflicting emotions are revisited on the anniversary of the saint's passing.

Above Bhaktisiddhanta Sarasvati (1874–1914), a prominent guru in the Bengali Vaishnava tradition. To mark his birthday, his picture has been adorned with flowers.

Below A statue of the Vaishnava theologian Madhva (1238–1317). Like other great theologians, his birthday is marked annually.

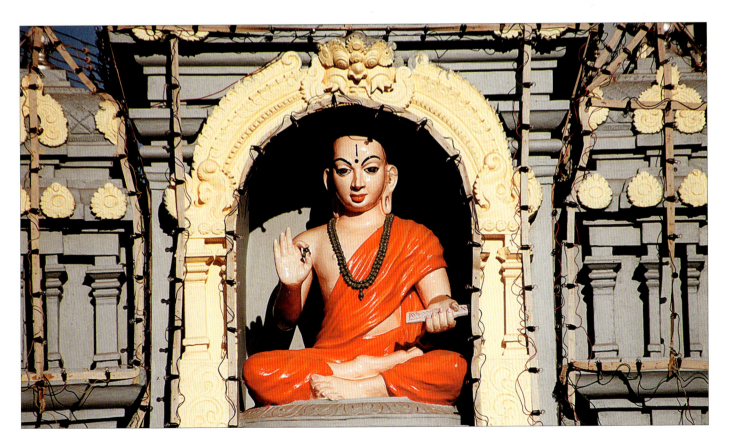

THE JOURNEY OF LIFE: RITES OF PASSAGE

HINDU SACRAMENTS (SAMSKARAS) HAVE BOTH SOCIAL AND SPIRITUAL SIGNIFICANCE. THE STANDARD NUMBER IS 16, STARTING BEFORE BIRTH AND CONCLUDING AT DEATH.

Samskara means 'mental impression', indicating that the rites were intended to create a favourable mentality for moving positively from one phase of life to the next. They served to purify the soul, especially at critical junctures in life.

The first samskara, prior to conception, is closely connected to belief in pre-existence and rebirth. Called 'purification of the womb', it was intended to sanctify the consciousness of husband and wife before attempting conception. This reflects the belief that the mental states of the couple determine the disposition of the soul entering the womb. If members of the upper three, 'twice-born', varnas neglected this ceremony, impelled only by lust, the baby might lack the spiritual merit expected of their social class. The rites of passage were intended to preserve the purity of the individual and the various stratifications of society.

After conception, two further pre-natal ceremonies are intended to enhance the wellbeing of mother and unborn child. The total number of samskaras, often cited as 16, varies according to region, denominational affiliation and historical modification. Still widely popular are four clusters of ceremonies, related to birth, adulthood, marriage and death.

BIRTH AND CHILDHOOD

The Jatakarma ceremony welcomes the baby back into the world, and into a new family. This rite includes the ceremonial cutting of the umbilical cord, purifying the newborn with herbal infusions to assist recovery from birth trauma, and reciting prayers for the baby's health, intelligence and longevity. The father

Below In the southern city of Madurai, a father shaves his son's head as part of the 'mundan' samskara.

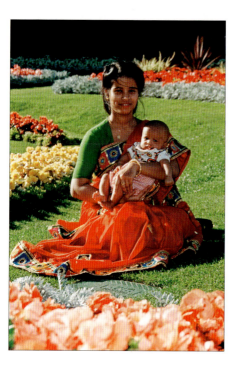

Above A Hindu woman cradles her son. The name-giving ceremony is the fourth samskara, yet the first performed after birth.

THE INITIATION CEREMONY

The ceremony starts with shaving the boy's head, and his bathing and donning new clothes. Sometimes, he takes a meal from the same plate as his mother, after which he will eat strictly from his own plate. During a havana (fire ceremony), he is invested with the sacred thread, which is draped over his left shoulder, around his torso and under the right arm. The boy then hears the Gayatri mantra, whispered in his right ear by his priest or guru. Thereafter, with the sacred thread wrapped around the thumb of his right hand, he will meditatively chant this prayer thrice daily, at dawn, noon and dusk. The boy takes vows to study the Vedas, serve his teachers and observe celibacy. He concludes the ceremony by offering his teacher the mandatory dakshina (donation).

anoints the baby's tongue with
honey or jaggery (palm sugar), often
mixed with ghee (clarified butter).
Around the 11th day after birth,
parents celebrate the name-giving

*Below Thrice daily, this Hindu man
quietly recites the Gayatri mantra.
Around his right thumb is strung the
sacred thread, first received during
the upanayana ceremony.*

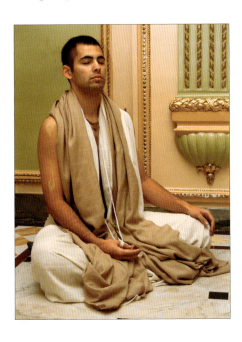

*Above A boy receives the sacred thread
from his father and family priest during
the upanayana ceremony.*

ceremony (namakarana) by dressing
the infant in new clothes. The family astrologer may announce the
child's horoscope, predict its future
and suggest its name, chosen with
reference to the moon's position in
the birth chart. The rites are accompanied by songs, refreshments and a
sacred fire sacrifice.

Various other ceremonies follow,
including 'the first outing', during
which the child takes darshana (audience) of the sun, the temple deity
and the evening moon. This is followed by three other ceremonies: the
first grains (around the time teething
begins); the first haircut, called mundan (between one and three years);
and piercing of the ear lobes (normally between three and five years)

INITIATION (UPANAYANA)
The sacred-thread samskara is essential to the members of the three
higher classes and marks a boy's

official acceptance into adulthood
and his specific varna. Symbolically,
he becomes 'twice-born', accepting
a guru as his father and the Vedic
canon as his mother. Along with
the sacred-thread (yajnopavita) he
sometimes receives a new, spiritual
name. There is also a distinct samskara to mark the beginning of
education, but today the two ceremonies are often combined.

Upanayana literally means 'sitting
close by', referring to the boy's
taking shelter with the spiritual
mentor. Traditionally, after initiation,
the boy moved away from home to
live in the teacher's hermitage, called
gurukula (house of the guru).
Even members of royal families were
trained to live simple lives, free from
luxury and sense-gratification.
The understanding was that when a
young man later married, he would
remain attached to the spiritual
values nurtured in his youth.
The educational emphasis was on
strict celibacy, study of the Vedas,
character formation and the gradual
assimilation of knowledge.

THE HINDU WEDDING

VIVAHA (MARRIAGE) IS PERHAPS THE MOST IMPORTANT SAMSKARA.
TRADITIONALLY IT WAS THE ONLY RITE COMPULSORY FOR ALL, EXCEPT
THE FEW MEN WHO TOOK LIFELONG VOWS OF CELIBACY.

Originally, marriage was a commitment for life or, in higher varnas, until the husband took sannyasa. Divorce was not allowed, and in some communities the very term was unknown until recently. Those who abandoned partners were often shunned or ostracized.

ARRANGED MARRIAGES

Matches were usually arranged by parents and elders, based on astrological principles and with consideration of personal and social compatibility. Despite modern derision of this practice, some claim that these marriages worked relatively well. Until recent times, women were often married very young, to protect their chastity and because women mature earlier than men. Many now object to 'child marriage', though some say that this was usually a system of betrothal.

Marriage was usually between members of the same varna (broad social class) and jati (occupational sub-caste). Scripture approved of a woman accepting a partner from a higher varna, but not the opposite. Men in some varnas were allowed to accept more than one wife, provided they could maintain them adequately, and there are rare instances in which polyandry occurred; in the Mahabharata, princess Draupadi married all five sons of Pandu. Almost all contemporary marriages are monogamous. By ancient custom, a dowry was seen as an expression of affection by the bride's father, and the gift belonged to her. It has increasingly been viewed as payment to the husband's family to enhance their financial and social standing. Widespread misuse of the dowry system in India led to its criminalization in 1961.

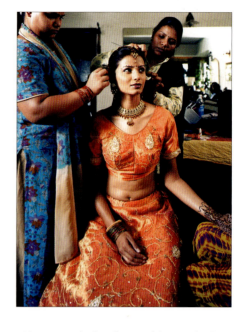

Above Just before her wedding, a bride has her hair done and her hands painted with henna.

TYPES OF MARRIAGE

The Manu Smriti, 'the codes of mankind', lists eight types of marriage, in order of preference. Not all were considered meritorious, and they represented various sections of society and their prevalent values. One form is the warrior practice of kidnapping a princess, and fending off other nobles for her hand. A regional monarch might arrange a svayamvara ('self-selection') ceremony, in which his daughter would garland the groom of her choice. This might depend on fulfilment of a specified condition, to test the prowess and martial skill of the suitors. For example, in the svayamvara of princess Sita, the candidates had to break the ancient bow of Lord Shiva. Rama, the young prince of Ayodhya, snapped the colossal bow as if a mere twig and thus won Sita. Similarly, Arjuna gained Draupadi by exhibiting extraordinary skill in archery. As was retold in the Mahabharata, he successfully pierced the eye of a fish suspended above the spokes of a revolving wheel, while looking at the target reflected in a pot of trembling water.

THE WEDDING CEREMONY

The Hindu wedding is elaborate, often lasting more than a day. There is much regional and denominational variation, but certain features are common. These include:

Welcoming the bridegroom
Exchanging flower garlands
Giving the daughter to the groom
Performing the fire ceremony
Anointing the clasped hands
Circumambulating the sacred fire
Marking the bride's hair-parting red
Taking seven steps together
Knotting the couple's clothes
Viewing the Pole Star (if at night)
Reciting vows and prayers
Receiving the elders' blessings

Above During a wedding ceremony, the groom applies the traditional red mark to his bride's forehead.

Most contemporary Hindus follow the 'Brahma' system. Once the boy completes his studies, his parents approach the parents of a girl from a suitable family to request their daughter's hand. The girl's parents approve a bridegroom with suitable prospects and character. Often, the prospective couple meets and subsequently decides whether to continue or break the relationship. In the ritual of kanyadan, the father freely bestows his daughter, without the commercial transaction prevalent with modern dowries. On an auspicious day, brahmin priests conduct the elaborate ceremony, which might span several days.

Below A Hindu wedding in Trinidad. The bride's relatives welcome the groom by offering him the sacred flame.

Above The bride and groom join hands, which the priest then anoints with water to sanctify the union.

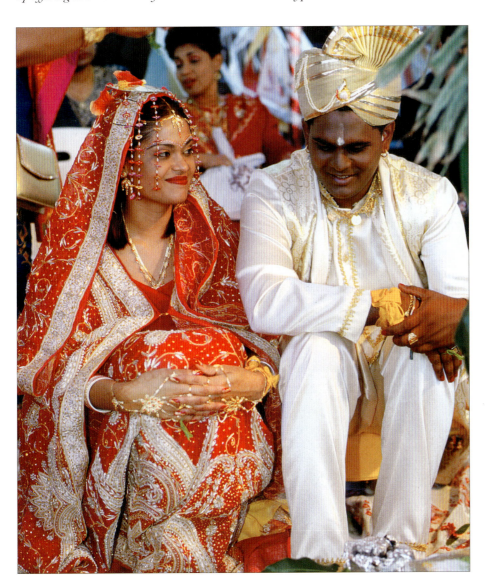

WEDDING PRAYERS
These prayers are usually recited.

Prayer by the groom, addressed to the bride:
I am the sky, you are the earth.
I am the seed,
  and you are the ground,
I am the mind, you are speech,
I am the lyrics,
  and you are the melody.

Prayer by the bride:
I adore the Supreme Lord,
  the unifier of hearts.
As I leave my parents' home
  for my husband's,
I pray that He may keep us
  perpetually united.
With this offering, I pray for
  my husband's long life
And for the prosperity
  of all our relations!

Prayers recited together:
Let us be devoted to each other.
sharing each other's joys and sorrows.

Let us wish each other well,
And look upon each other with love.

Let us live together
  for a hundred autumns.

DEATH AND FUNERAL RITES

THE FINAL SACRAMENT OCCURS AFTER DEATH, AND REFLECTS HINDU NOTIONS OF REINCARNATION. THE FUNERAL AND SUBSEQUENT RITES LARGELY AIM TO ASSIST THE SELF IN ITS JOURNEY TOWARD MOKSHA.

Above A simple funeral procession winds through the narrow streets of Varanasi.

After marriage, most Hindus spend the rest of their lives as householders. Once the children have left home, there is generally a period of gradual retirement and increased dedication to spiritual life. This corresponds to the third stage of life, called varnaprastha (forest-dweller), which few couples now adopt formerly. A few men still take sannyasa, leaving home to become mendicants. Hindu texts suggest that human life, with its various samskaras, should prepare the individual for the next chapter of life.

PRE-FUNERAL RITUALS

At a deathbed, relatives and priests may perform certain rituals such as the recitation of mantras and the administration of drops of Ganges water into the relative's mouth. For an auspicious departure, some lay the person on the ground with an oil lamp burning near their head. Such rites are not always practical in the West, though medical and palliative care professionals have published books to help colleagues meet the spiritual needs of terminally ill Hindu patients.

After death, the rites follow similar patterns, as described in holy books, such as the Garuda Purana. Variations occur according to the family's status, ethnic region and specific religious affiliation. Most Hindus cremate their dead, though not the bodies of saints and small children, who are considered pure and undefiled. The rationale behind burning is that it enables the departed soul to abandon any attachment to its previous habitat and move unimpeded to the next life.

Funeral ceremonies should be performed as soon as possible after death: by dusk or dawn, whichever comes first. In India, this occurs within hours. Elsewhere, regulations extend this period, sometimes to the distress of family members. Traditionally, the body is washed by relatives, dressed in fresh cloth, and profusely bedecked with flowers, such as roses, jasmine, and marigolds. A few drops of Ganges water are placed in the mouth, and the corpse is decorated with sandalwood paste. The corpse is then carried on procession to the cremation grounds accompanied by kirtana, the chanting of mantras such as 'Ram nam satya hai' ('the name of Rama is truth').

THE FUNERAL CEREMONY

A cremation ground is traditionally located near a river, if not directly on the bank itself. There, a wooden pyre is prepared and the corpse laid on top, with the feet facing southward, the direction of Yama, who presides over death. Thereafter the chief mourner, generally the eldest son, walks anti-clockwise around the pyre three times. While walking, he sprinkles water and ghee on to the pyre. He then ignites it with the flame of a torch. Later, the skull is cracked, to urge the departed soul to move

Left The funeral pyre, here of Indian Prime Minister Rajiv Gandhi, assassinated in 1991, is a reminder that all bow to ultimate death.

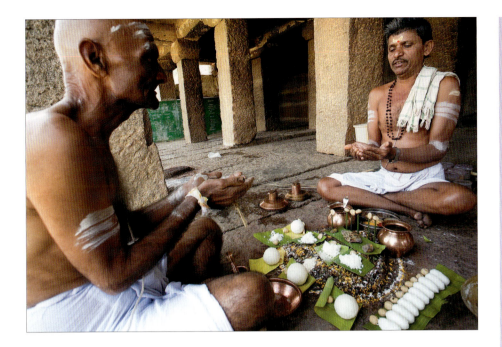

Above A priest performs the shraddha ceremony, in which rice balls are offered periodically for the benefit of the departed.

on, just in case it is still hovering around. During the ceremony, a priest or relative recites appropriate scriptural verses. Outside India, Hindus may be obliged to use modern gas-fuelled crematoria, which some claim are inadequate in meeting Hindu ritualistic needs. Some Hindu scholars have campaigned for traditional open-air pyres.

POST-FUNERAL RITES
Usually three days after the funeral, the eldest son collects the ashes and scatters them in the Ganges, or another sacred river. Relatives living abroad often fly to India for this purpose, though some use local rivers, such as the Thames in England. There follows a period of mourning, lasting about ten days, depending on the family's varna and other considerations. During that period, relatives are considered ritually impure and neither attend religious functions nor eat certain foods, such as sweets. It is a time for grieving, and the Hindu system of medicine notes how repressed or unreleased emotions foster disease.

These rites are mainly for the benefit of the deceased, to ensure their unhindered passage to a higher level of existence. If funeral rites are performed incorrectly, the departed soul might not reincarnate, but remain in its subtle form, as a bhuta (ghost). The most essential ceremony is the shraddha performed on the first anniversary of the death. Pinda, balls of cooked rice, are offered to God and then the departed soul. To perform these rituals, some Hindus travel to the holy city of Gaya in Bihar state.

Below In Mumbai, Nilamben Parikh, the great-granddaughter of Mahatma Gandhi, pours the leader's ashes into the Arabian Sea to mark the 60th anniversary of his death.

PART III

LIVING IN THIS WORLD

Religion seems to pervade every aspect of Indian life. The taxi driver stops unannounced to take audience at a shrine, lorries display religious symbols, and shrines and temples punctuate the many roads and walkways. Almost every shop, house or hotel features sacred iconography.

Worship and meditation help individuals commune with the divine. Hindu texts also stipulate social obligations, more clearly related to this world, which acknowledge human diversity and individual propensity. Personalized duties, called sva-dharma, largely revolve around the varnashrama system, which divides humanity into four broad classes (varnas) and life into four main stages (ashramas).

Hinduism perpetuates its ancient wisdom through cultural and artistic expression, largely within the arena of dutiful family life and through religious organizations and their spiritual teachers. As Hindus continue to migrate, and their tradition expands beyond its original Indian context, many movements and thinkers are actively re-assessing their identity, and the specific contribution of Hinduism to the opportunities and challenges of the 21st century.

Opposite In the sacred town of Vrindavana, north of Agra, modern Hindu children celebrate the ancient festival of Govardhana Puja.

Above Famed Hindu surgeon Susrutha, here about to fit an artificial earlobe, is known as 'the father of surgery'.

CHAPTER 8

HINDU SOCIETY

Atourist often experiences India as one of the most densely populated countries in the world. There is little sense of private space, except perhaps in terms of spirituality, which is highly personalized. This stands in contrast to much of the modern world, where faith is valued as a community builder to complement self-driven, individualistic lifestyles.

Hinduism has long acknowledged human dependence on other people, nature and the divine. It also recognizes life as a long journey, as the eternal self passes through innumerable lives. These ideas have been embodied on the ancient social system called varnashrama dharma, whereby society is divided into four classes (varnas) and human life into four stages (ashramas).

Although few modern Hindus adopt all four ashramas, the idea of a spiritually oriented student life, followed by responsible marriage and then gradual social withdrawal remains a powerful ideal. On the other hand, the idea of four varnas remains controversial for its identification with modern caste practices. Many religious leaders now oppose caste for its inconsistency with the Hindu ideals of spiritual equality and 'the world as one family'.

Opposite Hindu society revolves around the extended family. Simultaneously, it has integrated the ideals of austerity and renunciation.

Above *Indian women labour on a Rajasthani building site. Issues surrounding women's roles raise broader questions about Hindu teachings on social equality.*

VARNASHRAMA AND CASTE

WITHIN THE HINDU WAY OF LIFE, SOCIAL ORGANIZATION IS LINKED TO ANCIENT RELIGIOUS TEACHINGS. HOWEVER, MODERN CASTE PRACTICE HAS BEEN WIDELY CRITICIZED BY BOTH INSIDERS AND OUTSIDERS.

Hinduism has long considered itself broad-minded and tolerant. However, its reputation for inclusivity has been tarnished by the caste system, which allocates members to a particular social class (varna) and occupational sub-class (jati). Caste practice has fostered social and economic exploitation, particularly of the lower varnas, and of the 'untouchables' who technically fall below the fourth, shudra varna. More recently called the 'scheduled castes' or 'dalits' (the oppressed), untouchables customarily held jobs deemed most contaminating, such as sweepers, leather workers and crematorium attendants. They were allowed neither to live within the confines of regular village life, nor to share public facilities, such as wells and temples.

The caste system is not peculiar to Hinduism in India, but is found in other faith communities, including Islam, Sikhism and Christianity (though they rarely endorse them). This has prompted some Hindus to attempt to discount caste as a sociological phenomenon, distinct from the religion itself. Others reject this argument on two accounts. First, as 'a way of life', Hinduism doesn't isolate religion from its social expression;

Above Taken in the 1890s, this photo of Maharaja Nripenora of Kuch-Behar reflects the power and nobility customarily associated with the kshatriya varna.

second, the system of four varnas is explicitly mentioned in the oldest religious text, the Rig Veda.

ANCIENT AND MODERN PRACTICES

To account for this, many Hindu thinkers describe caste as an aberration of the older system. The earlier framework, called varnashrama, allocated civic and religious duties according to its four varnas (classes) and four ashramas (stages in life). It allowed social mobility, and scripture recounts tales of people elevating their status: Vishvamitra,

Below In Shri Rangam, learned brahmins chat in the courtyard of the great Shri Ranganathaswami temple.

FEATURES OF THE SOCIAL SYSTEM

Caste has five main elements, though similar principles may have applied to the original varnashrama society. These practices have significantly influenced Hindu lifestyles.

Division of labour: The original varna system was based not just on four divisions of labour but their expected code of conduct. The varnas thus represented different psychological dispositions. However, some Hindus still refuse to do certain jobs, even clearing away rubbish from before their front door.

Social/Economic Interdependence: In the original system, each varna, as a part of the social body, served the others. However, the rigid caste system became exploitative rather than mutually supportive.

Purity: Texts stress the need to develop finer human qualities, with varnas representing a hierarchy of spiritual purity. Members would avoid intimate dealings with those less spiritually mature. This degenerated into condescension, as when brahmins thought themselves polluted by the touch of another's shadow.

Regulation of Diet: Caste prohibited Hindus from eating with those of lower status. This was especially relevant when classes ate foods forbidden to others, such as meat and fish. At large social gatherings, vegetarian food cooked by brahmins was acceptable to all.

Inter-caste Marriage: Endogamy, marriage between members of the same varna, was to ensure compatibility and produce cultured offspring. Texts endorse inter-marriage when the groom comes from the higher varna. Some parents still insist that their children's partners belong to the same varna and jati.

Right In California, a Western bride marries a groom from the vaishya varna, responsible for generating prosperity.

though born a warrior, qualified himself as a powerful brahmin; others disqualified themselves through inappropriate conduct. In the Bhagavadgita, Krishna endorses the ideal of social mobility, teaching that varna is determined by guna (personal virtue) and karma (inclination for work). He makes no mention of birth.

At some undetermined stage, so it seems, the system became hereditary, reserving prestigious jobs for men born in higher varnas and marginalizing the lower classes. Particularly disadvantaged were the untouchables, whom Gandhi renamed the Harijans (children of God). Proposing to absorb them into the shudra varna, Gandhi recognized differences between caste and varnashrama.

Below Dependent employees, here at a dyeing factory in Tamil Nadi, were traditionally considered shudras.

More explicitly, he stated: 'Varna is generally determined by birth, but can be retained only by observing its obligations. One born of the [brahmin] parent will be called a brahmin, but if he fails to reveal the attributes of a brahmin when he comes of age, he cannot be called a brahmin.

He would have fallen from brahminhood. On the other hand, one who is born not a brahmin but reveals the attributes of a brahmin will be regarded as a brahmin.' This idea is shared by some contemporary Hindus, whereas others dismiss varnashrama as well as hereditary caste.

GAUTAMA'S DISCIPLE

A young boy approached Gautama Muni and requested to become his student. It was customary that only respectable brahmins would be enrolled for such spiritual training. Gautama therefore inquired, 'Who is your father?' 'That I do not know', the boy replied. 'So, please ask your mother', the guru instructed.

The boy's mother subsequently admitted, 'My son, I have entertained many men. I have no idea who is your father'. The boy returned to Gautama Muni, and relayed the embarrassing message. 'Sir, my mother has no idea who my father is.' Gautama concluded, 'Yes, you are a brahmin! I accept you because you are thoroughly honest.'

SOCIAL TENSIONS

CASTE HIGHLIGHTS HOW FAITH PRACTICES CHANGE AND HOW SOCIAL
REALITY DIFFERS FROM THE RELIGIOUS IDEAL. INDIA FACES MANY
OTHER SOCIAL PROBLEMS, OFTEN LINKED TO ITS RELIGIOUS LIFE.

The Bhagavat Purana teaches that spirituality should inform all areas of human endeavour to promote the welfare and liberation of all. Religious truth and sentiment should not be harnessed merely for sensual, economic and political ends. In modern Hindu communities, many anomalies revolve around social and economic status, especially with regard to women.

WOMEN'S ISSUES
Puranic texts evaluate the moral status of a society by its treatment of five types of citizens, including women. To safeguard women, the Manu Smriti suggests that a woman passes through three stages of life, supported in turn by her father, husband and eldest son. Some commentators

Below A form of child marriage is practised in Jodhpur, Rajasthan. A boy enjoys his own wedding ceremony. More precisely, it is a form of betrothal.

condemn the restrictions this places on women. Others claim it is hasty to dismiss Hinduism as sexist, as it should not be judged solely in terms of modern standards, which inordinately value a self-centred life.

Despite Hinduism's lofty ideals on women's protection, there are well-documented cases of abuse. Reform goes back to at least to the 12th century CE and the female saint and reformer, Akka Mahadevi. Subsequently, Muslim rule and its austere morality moulded attitudes, perhaps reinforcing the practice of women's domestic confinement. British rule certainly precipitated change. The colonialists were alarmed by the practice of sati, in which wives mounted their husband's funeral pyre. It was voluntary and largely confined to royal orders, though some accounts suggest forced compliance. However, the British may have exaggerated sati's frequency and barbarity to justify

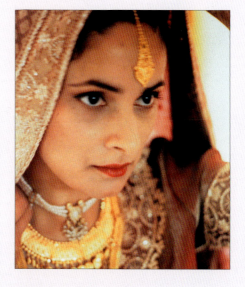

Above A dowry of valuables from the bride's father was originally a sign of affection. The practice was often abused, and in India became illegal in 1961.

their rule, which largely rested on sati's legal abolition in 1829. The British also expressed concern about polygamy, though it was only outlawed after independence, in 1951. Hindu teachers claim it was useful to redress the gender imbalance in earlier societies where practically all women married and significant numbers of men remained celibate.

More recently publicized is the practice of child-marriage. Since sexual transgression is considered injurious to spiritual life, Hindu scripture recommends marriage at an early age, particularly to maintain the chastity of girls. Many so-called child marriages were actually a form of betrothal, and the marriage was not consummated until the wife came of age. It is unclear how severe related problems are today, and how much they are linked to religious life.

One undeniable blight on modern Indian society is the phenomenon called 'dowry death'. Originally, in respectable Hindu families, the dowry was an affectionate gift from the bride's father, and it remained the wife's personal property. Today, unscrupulous in-laws

Above Azharuddhin Ismail, known *worldwide for his role in the film* Slumdog Millionaire, *sits with his father outside his home, a makeshift tent in Mumbai.*

think it automatically belongs to the husband's family and terrorize brides who provide insufficiently. Most dowry deaths occur when the young woman, unable to bear the pressure, commits suicide. Sometimes, to open the doors to a further dowry, the wife is murdered by setting her on fire, a practice known as 'bride burning'.

ECONOMICS AND POVERTY

Underlying many social ills is gnawing poverty. Through the media, the affluent world often perceives India in terms of a long-standing economic challenges. However, many authors write that India was once affluent and only later drained of her fabulous wealth and resources, first by Muslim rulers and later by the British. Certainly, travellers such as Marco Polo described India as extremely prosperous. Today, with the rise of the middle class, India is becoming wealthier, though still with a wide gulf between rich and poor.

Hindu approaches to wealth and poverty seem to be contradictory. However, teachings clearly distinguish between forced, debilitating poverty and a simple life purposefully adopted for spiritual growth. In analysing the roots of economic discord, texts identify two causes: greed and poverty. Both distract and

Above Untouchables in Kelwara support *a political party promising to uplift their social status.*

disturb the mind. According to the Hindu perspective, even a seemingly affluent society exhibits a form of poverty if both husband and wife toil long hours merely to pay the mortgage. Mahatma Gandhi was especially concerned about establishing a globalized, industrialized economy, and he recommended local, rural systems as the most sustainable.

TACKLING UNTOUCHABILITY

Gandhi also fought for the case of the outcastes, or untouchables. He called them Harijans, 'the children of God', proposing to accommodate them within the fourth, shudra varna (class). Ranji Ambedkar, born an untouchable but later a lawyer and reformer, disagreed with Gandhi over the future status of untouchables and tribal peoples, advocating instead a classless society and later converting to Buddhism to register his grievances. He was one of the main architects of the new Indian constitution of 1950, which outlawed untouchability and gave equal status to all citizens.

The Indian government has since implemented remedial measures, such as reserving a certain percentage of jobs and scholarships. Higher-class Hindus have challenged this legislation for denying places to more qualified candidates. Although caste practice is slowly being eroded, it remains a source of extensive debate.

Below Poverty is a way of life in India. *An elderly women begs for alms inside the Minakshi temple, Madurai.*

FAMILY LIFE

HINDU ATTITUDES TOWARD FAMILY LIFE MAY APPEAR AMBIVALENT. ASCETICS STRESS HOW IT ENTANGLES THE SOUL. ORTHODOX TRADITIONS VIEW IT AS THE BACKBONE OF A RIGHTEOUS SOCIETY.

Ideologically, worldly pleasure and asceticism are reconciled within the system of four ashramas, which accommodate both tendencies at suitable phases in life. Although the second, householder ashrama, is differentiated from materialistic wedlock, it still encourages the ethical earning of wealth (artha) and regulated sexual pleasure (kama).

GETTING MARRIED

Most Hindu marriages are arranged or supported. Relatives initially suggest prospective partners, with consideration of respective family backgrounds, and personal compatibility as evaluated by the family astrologer. In a rural setting, final decisions are often made by elders, with little consideration for the

Below Three generations stand in front of the Somnath Hindu temple in Gujarat for an extended family portrait.

couple's opinion. Among middle-class families, especially in urban areas or outside India, couples are often allowed to meet a few times before endorsing or declining the liaison. Especially since the late 1900s, and with the increasing influence of alternative cultures, many young Hindus find prospective spouses through socializing and dating, and later inform their parents. Even today, the two families are usually involved in the final decision.

THE EXTENDED FAMILY

The basic building-block of traditional Hindu society is the joint or extended family, which consists of three or four generations living in close proximity. The women of the family collectively cook and share domestic responsibilities, while the men provide the income. Elders make important decisions and draw on their practical experience to

Above Sharing food, with humans and animals, is customarily a core obligation for householders.

guide younger members. Within the family, property usually passes from father to son and, once married, women customarily join their husband's family. Although males make most key decisions, women carry considerable influence within the domestic sphere.

Hindu families usually demonstrate strong ties of affection, and social lore meticulously defines etiquette between family members. For example, a grandchild may tease a grandparent in a familiar way, that is not permissible with the father or mother.

The different relatives are allocated specific terms of address, rather than a generic 'aunt' or 'uncle'. For example, paternal and maternal grandfathers are addressed in Hindi as 'dada' and 'nana' respectively, and the corresponding grandmothers are addressed as 'dadi' and 'nani'. An important ideal is to promote intimacy without familiarity, as by not using first names, even between husband and wife. For example, a husband may address his wife as devi, 'goddess'. These days, many use first names.

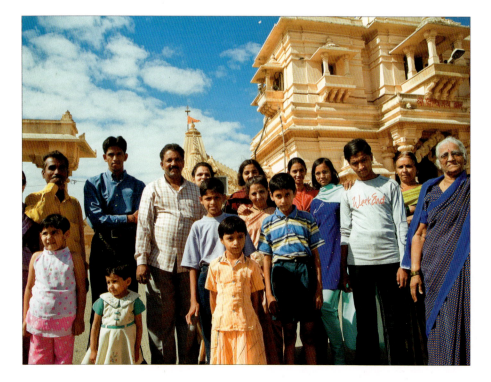

SOCIAL SUPPORT

Marriage itself is a broad social and religious obligation, acknowledging human interdependence. The extended family traditionally provides shelter for the elderly, the disabled and the economically disadvantaged, and also practical and emotional support, especially when children are born. Children are expected to show gratitude toward their parents by supporting them in their retirement, old age and infirmity. A further advantage of the extended family is that marriage stability is not overly reliant on the fluctuating state of the couple's emotional ties. Divorce was traditionally prohibited and the equivalent Indian words are quite recent.

Despite the perceived benefits of family stability, individuals had relatively little identity separate from the family. Possibly for this reason, much religious practice is highly individualized, even when outwardly congregational. Furthermore, social trends indicate that the extended

Below Many modern Hindus, especially outside India, now prefer the freedom afforded by the smaller, 'nuclear' family.

family is increasingly less popular, as young couples value the freedom afforded by the nuclear family. They have also adopted many other aspects of the modern lifestyle. Television is more popular than worship, and strongly influences family values.

SCRIPTURAL REFERENCES

There are many scriptural references to the advantages and disadvantages of married life. The Bhagavat Purana states that: 'Persons without self-knowledge do not inquire into the problems of life, being too attached to fallible soldiers like the body, spouse and children. Although sufficiently experienced, they do not see their inevitable destruction'. However, this verse appears to condemn not family life itself, but mundane attachment.

Texts also narrate how many saints and esteemed authorities were married. The Bhagavad-gita condemns both over-attachment in family life and renunciation that is considered premature, irresponsible or pretentious.

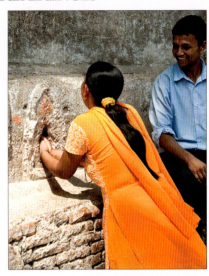

Above A Hindu couple play a game in the Kathmandu Valley, Nepal. Extra-marital mixing between men and women is traditionally discouraged.

FAMILY DUTIES

When a man marries, he is expected to complete paying the three debts owed to the rishis (sages), the pitris (forefathers) and the devas (gods). Through celibacy and scriptural study, a young man repays the rishis. In married life, he repays his ancestors by begetting children, especially sons to continue the family lineage and perform his own funeral rites. Indebtedness to the gods is expressed through the performance of sacrifice and the 16 rites of passage (samskaras).

The householder has further obligations, to human society, the animals (bhuta) and mother earth. Gratitude for material gifts is expressed by donating alms to the poor, hosting religious mendicants and freely distributing food, even to birds and beasts. Many family duties were originally laid out in auxiliary Vedic texts called the Grihya Sutras, the 'codes of household life'. The current popularity of domestic puja exemplifies the idea of the home as an ashram, a place of spiritual shelter.

CHILDREN AND EDUCATION

FROM EARLY TIMES, THE MAIN PURPOSE OF HINDU MARRIAGE WAS TO RAISE CHILDREN. THEIR WELFARE WAS PARAMOUNT, ESPECIALLY THROUGH EDUCATION THAT PROMOTES SELF- AND GOD-REALIZATION.

Above *For hundreds of generations, Hindu truths and values have been passed down largely through story. Here, a mother reads to her daughter.*

During the Vedic period, sons were especially valued for continuing the family lineage and performing last rites for parents' attainment of heaven. Later texts eulogize mothers and fathers for nurturing good citizens, promoting social values and enriching children with spiritual merit. These ideals are not always matched by practice, and Indian society today is beset by child labour and other forms of exploitation. There is extensive debate on the likely causes, whether religious or mundane.

CHILDREN

Hindu texts emphasize that children should be loved and never neglected. In the Bhagavad-gita, Krishna alludes to the social problems arising from

Below Children often learn to worship by participating before the household shrine with their parents.

'unwanted children'; those born solely to satisfy lust. Hindu texts discourage purely recreational sex and strongly condemn abortion. Some members of the higher, cultured varnas still perform a rite of passage before attempting to conceive. Children are generally treated with affectionate indulgence, especially before schooling.

Traditionally, only members of the three higher varnas received a formal education as brahmacharin students. Shudra boys stayed at home, trained by the father. Girls were also educated at home, largely in domestic skills, and were then married at a relatively young age. Unmarried girls were not allowed to stay away from home for fear of extra-marital relations.

In today's societies, practices have changed considerably. None the less, pious families still encourage the transmission of cultural values,

as children participate in daily worship and the reception of guests. Hindu temples and specific groups have organized more formal means, such as Sunday schools to nurture children in their faith. The internet and other forms of global communications help youngsters research their roots and better understand their religious heritage.

EDUCATION

Through the manoeuvres of 19th-century British politician Thomas Macaulay, the traditional Indian education was largely ousted by an Anglicized system founded on the utilitarian ideals of Scottish philosopher James Mill. The ancient gurukula, 'the house of the guru', was a type of boarding school, attended by boys of the upper three varnas. Emphasis was on acquiring character and spiritual merit, over and beyond the knowledge and skills needed for a livelihood. For memorization, the Hindu approach preferred rote learning to cramming, but was also highly experiential, valuing wisdom, critical thinking and assimilation of knowledge. Study of the Vedas required mind and sense restraint, and a simple, uncluttered routine in which students carried out menial service, such as collecting firewood for the guru's daily fire ceremony. The Bhagavad-gita lists

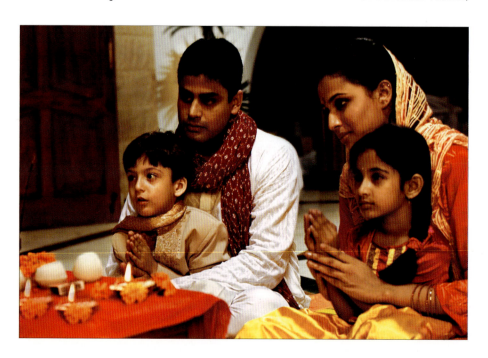

SVETAKETU'S LESSON

Hindu education aimed to promote insight beyond the mere acquisition of information and technical skills. The Upanishads relates how one teacher, called Uddalaka, asked his disciple Svetaketu to dissolve salt in a cup of water. The next day, Uddalaka asked Svetaketu to look for the salt, to which the boy replied 'I can't see it anywhere'. The guru asked his disciple to sip the water. 'It is salty', came the boy's reply. 'Now', Uddalaka continued, 'tip away half the liquid, and sip it again'. 'Again, it is salty', responded Svetaketu. 'Finally', the guru instructed, 'pour it all away but for a few drops and taste it again. 'It is still salty', said the student. 'Yes', concluded the teacher, 'you cannot see the salt but it's there. In the same way, humans may not see Brahman, the absolute reality, but it pervades everything throughout the upper, middle and lower worlds.'

This story indicates not only Hindu belief in a metaphysical reality (Brahman), beyond normal sense perception, but also the need for realized knowledge beyond mere theory.

Above Students recite the Vedas. This traditional 'gurukula' in Gujarat specializes in nurturing character and self-realization.

how education was originally free to avoid compromising the guru's integrity or promoting market-driven education. Drawing on such theories of knowledge and learning, some modern organizations are trying to rejuvenate the ancient system: they include ISKCON, the Swaminarayan Movement and the Ramakrishna Mission. In Gujarat in 1992, with governmental support, the renowned public speaker Rameshbai Oza founded a priest-training school called the Sandipani Vidyaniketan. In 2008, the first state-funded Hindu school opened in the UK, based on the idea that God, Krishna, is the friend of everyone, irrespective of race, gender and religion. As in most Hindu schools, pupils are taught to see the eternal self (atman) in all living beings.

Below Pupils perform morning worship at the modern Krishna Avanti primary school, the first state-sponsored Hindu school in the UK.

three entry requirements: ardent enquiry, practical service and a humble disposition. Even royalty underwent arduous scriptural and military training, and Lord Krishna himself attended the hermitage school of Sandipani Muni, still situated in the holy town of Ujjain.

The guru-student relationship was a hallowed tradition. In medieval times, it became a central tenet for theological lineages, and many Hindus still take sacred vows to accept diksha (initiation) from a guru. They also offer the traditional guru-dakshina (donation), reflecting

RENOUNCED LIFE

POPULAR IMAGES OF HINDUISM INCLUDE SHAVEN-HEADED, SAFFRON-CLAD MONKS AND NAKED ASCETICS WITH MATTED LOCKS. DESPITE THIS STEREOTYPE, SENSE-RESTRAINT INDEED PLAYS A KEY ROLE.

From ancient times, ascetic anti-social lineages have competed with brahminical orthodoxy. An ancient tale recounts a violent fracas between a wealthy and proud brahmin called Daksha, and the scantily clad followers of Shiva. Despite this, the competing tendencies for enjoyment and renunciation have also been viewed as complementary.

HISTORY OF ASCETICISM

Some Hindus believe that asceticism goes back to Daksha's time, shortly after universal creation. Other Epic and Puranic tales feature sages living secluded lives, tucked away in the forest for penance and meditation. Some were married, and Rama and Sita adopted a comparable role, dressing in tree bark and subsisting on roots and fruits. Another abstinent was the single, celibate mendicant, acting as a spiritual mentor. These

Below Wielding symbolic weapons, Naga Babas return from their sacred bath at the Kumbha Mela festival.

two types of ascetic, the anchorite and the renouncer, resemble the third and fourth ashramas in the later varnashrama system.

Academics suggest that organized ascetic communities first arose in Jain and Buddhist monasteries reacting against the world-affirming brahminical tradition. Indeed, these non-orthodox, Shramana traditions favoured alternative texts called Tantra. However, the Vedas themselves mention renouncer groups. Earliest references describe the long-haired Keshins, and the Vratyas, warrior ascetics similar to the 'Naga Babas' who still frequent the Kumbha Mela (bathing fair). Among the earliest Shaiva ascetics, the Lakulas carried a skull-topped staff and smeared themselves with ashes to imitate Rudra. In medieval Kashmir, the Kapalikas frequented cremation grounds and one sub-branch, the Aghoris, are still renowned for eating out of skulls, ingesting uncooked flesh and otherwise contravening moral norms to

Above Naga Babas, members of a specific group of renunciants, enjoy their ritual bath in the Ganges at Prayag.

foster detachment. Also still visible are the yogis of the Nath tradition, established by Gorakshanatha around the 11th century.

Amongst Vaishnavas, who are generally quite orthodox, the Ramanandi tradition is the largest purely monastic tradition. Predominant among the Smartas are the ten orders of sannyasin established by Shankara. The formal renunciant, the

Below A woman sadhu with her traditional trident, water pot, meditation beads, and matted locks.

RAMANUJA'S LESSON

The scholar Ramanuja detected that his celibate, brahmin disciples were proud. One night, after entering their quarters, he tore strips off their dhotis (robes), draped from the communal washing line. The next morning, the disciples quarrelled and insulted each other so vociferously that Ramanuja was forced to intervene.

Shortly afterward, the scholar pronounced, 'One of my married disciples is Dhanurdasa, a lowly wrestler. He poses as a great devotee, but, like other householders, remains attached to his possessions. This evening, he will come here. As I detain him, go to his house to retrieve the jewellery with which he decorates his wife. Then we will see the extent of his attachment!'

The disciples joyfully complied and, reaching Dhanurdasa's house, saw his wife lying within. Stealthily, they removed her golden bangles. However, only pretending to be asleep, she turned over so that the students might remove bangles from her other arm. Startled, they fled.

Back in the ashram, Dhanurdasa was about to leave. Ramanuja ordered the returning celibates to follow the wrestler home and observe what happened. They were astounded to hear Dhanurdasa rebuke his wife for scaring the thieves away, and for thinking that the bangles were hers to give away. The couple agreed that everything belonged to God, and they were honoured by the students' visit. Astonished, the brahmin disciples later relayed to Ramanuja all they had observed. Their guru then reminded them of their conduct over the torn cloth. They hung their heads in remorse as Ramanuja instructed them that personal character was the criterion of spiritual success, not one's varna or any external show of renunciation.

THE DOCTRINE OF RENUNCIATION

Renunciation is closely tied to the belief that the pursuit of sensory pleasure propels the atman through various species of life. Abandonment of selfish desire is essential for liberation. Some paths, such as jnana and yoga, teach that austerity and relinquishment of all desire free the self from worldly bondage.

Later bhakti schools, believing that the self has nothing to renounce, stress the redeeming power of love and spiritual desire. The varnashrama system grants a place to both enjoyment and renunciation. However, Hinduism rejects hedonism and tends to value inner detachment, demonstrated as external renunciation in old age, before death steals everything.

Below These formal Smarta sannyasis are from the orthodox, Brahminical tradition, rather than the socially-peripheral Shramana communities. They may have been previously married.

sannyasin, has an ambivalent role. He is both a part of varnashrama society and yet civically dead, preparing to leave the world unknown to others. Renouncing contact with fire, wealth and women, he stays in one place for no more than three nights, save during the four-month rainy season. Unlike the Shramana followers, who go around almost naked, the sannyasin dresses in saffron and carries a staff and water pot.

Besides the orthodox Vedic sannyasins and the socially peripheral ascetics, there are other types of sadhu (holy man). Many have become tourist attractions, notoriously wearing saffron simply to eat or to pass off magical stunts as mystical power. A well-documented trick is to construct a metal seat, so that the sadhu appears to levitate himself, albeit suspiciously close to a vertical pole touching his robes.

ANCIENT AND MODERN LIFESTYLES

MODERN HINDUISM IS VISIBLY LINKED TO ITS ANCIENT HERITAGE. AT THE SAME TIME, SOCIAL AND HISTORICAL CHANGES, SUCH AS MIGRATION AND INDUSTRIALIZATION, HAVE ALTERED LIFESTYLES.

Above A Rajasthani woman looks in control cooking vegetables in relatively simple conditions.

Hindu society has long evolved in response to outside cultural influences and its own spiritual impetus. Especially since independence, India has emulated the West and rapidly modernized, seeking social, economic and material progress. During the same era, many Hindus have emigrated, bolstering overseas communities. As Hindu communities have evolved, so have individual lifestyles.

THE RURAL LIFESTYLE

Unavoidably, ancient Hinduism was nurtured in a rural setting. Nevertheless, its teachings explicitly promote a simple, spiritually focused life, free from extraneous endeavour.

Below In the southern town of Hampi, a girl pours water for her calf. In parts of India, the cow and bull still provide much renewable energy.

The social structure of varnashrama is closely associated with an agrarian culture, which recognized cosmic hierarchy, human interdependence and reliance upon God and nature. According to modern theology, the simple village is sustained by goodness (sattva), the town compelled by passion (rajas) and sinful places steeped in ignorance (tamas).

Goodness rules the tranquil morning hours. In India, people tend to rise early, between four and six. Almost without exception, everyone bathes, often in a river or pond. The visitor still sees Hindus standing on the roadside, patiently brushing their teeth with a twig from the medicinal neem tree. Outside the city, life is relatively unhurried. Morning hours are most propitious for worship, with temple services starting around 5 a.m. Breakfast follows at around

8 a.m., and shops, stalls and offices open quite late, around ten. The main meal is around midday when, according to the Ayur Veda, the power of digestion is at its zenith. After lunch, life subsides as both mortals and temple deities take a siesta in the sultry afternoon. Shops and shrines are open from late afternoon well into the cooler evening, when people throng again to the streets and temples.

Outside urban areas, life is intimately linked to nature's elements. Water is drawn from wells or rivers. Cooking is conducted over open fires, often while squatting on the floor. Village homes have a frequently replaced earthen floor, mixed with cow-dung, which is considered antiseptic. Animals are an integral part of life. Dogs are generally not domesticated. On the other hand, cows are highly respected, and given leeway to roam freely. Wild pigs are valued for their function of waste disposal. Monkeys are notorious for stealing, especially spectacles, which they apparently exchange for bananas at the local opticians. Camels, ponies and buffalo are seen pulling carts. In the south, elephants are used extensively in temple rituals. Folklore tells of the cobra's mystical powers and of physicians who cure snake bites by mantra rather than serum. Mysticism is an acceptable part of the rich fabric of

Above Sari shopping on the well-known Ealing Road in Wembley, England.

everyday life, illustrating how the physical and metaphysical worlds collide. On the one hand, Hinduism is mystical and world-transcending; on the other, it is intimately related to this world: to the land, its wildlife and the endlessly revolving seasons.

SOCIAL CHANGE IN INDIA

Today, India is an incongruous blend of ancient and modern. The wiry renunciant sports a mobile phone; loud-speakers, as if to explain their name, relentlessly blare religious songs; driving relies more on faith than a highway code; gods and gurus beam from billboards, teaching the passer-by that even religion has become a consumer product.

More people are moving to towns and cities, and in rural areas, the ancient varnashrama has long given way to hereditary caste, with different communities assigned their own regions within the village. The revered bull has given way to

Right Blending tradition with modernity, a Hindu family ride their motorbike bearing the name of Lord Krishna, said to have lived up to 5,000 years ago.

the chugging tractor. Indeed, industrialization is taking its toll. Holy sites are strewn with litter, especially water bottles and plastic bags. For India's sacred rivers, deforestation and massive hydroelectric dams have disrupted the water-flow, creating parched beds in spring and torrential spates during the summer monsoon. Some Hindu organizations are addressing these issues and raising ecological awareness as India travels the path of modernization. Television and the film industry are

having their impact, evident even in small hamlets. Influenced by the media, the younger generation often looks to the West for inspiration.

HINDU LIFESTYLE ABROAD

Many Hindus living outside India have different lifestyles than their ancestors. They tend to get up somewhat later in the day. The extended family is diminishing. Some Hindus remain strict about a vegetarian diet, others adopt local eating habits. Unlike India, the temple has become a centre of social activities and an emblem of Hindu identity. Although Hindu communities outside India appear most vulnerable to incongruous influences, they are often most concerned about preserving tradition. Young Hindus are reluctant to blindly inherit rites and rituals without sound articulation of their significance. To promote their own values, Hindus maintain schools, clubs and internet sites, address social issues and reflect on their own values in voting for political leaders. One of the key challenges is understanding how traditional notions of Hindu society, such as varnashrama and a rural economy, are relevant to contemporary debates and lifestyles.

CHAPTER 9

HINDU CULTURE AND THE ARTS

A visitor to any Hindu home or community soon becomes familiar with the 'namaste' greeting. Uttered with folded palms and a slight bow of the head, this embodies two complementary ideals: first, of a hierarchical world view, in which all living beings hold different stations in life; second, the accompanying notion that all people are spiritually equal – as indeed are all creatures – as tiny sparks of the divine. Respect, appreciation and love are especially exhibited through Hindu hospitality.

Until recently, Hindu culture was largely inseparable from the religion itself. Although Hinduism clearly has roots in ancient India, it has also developed the notion of a spiritual, inclusive and universal culture. For the high scholarly strands, culture entails rigorous spiritual discipline, including the study of ancient Sanskrit texts. Popular Hinduism has been disseminated more though song, music, dance and other forms of cultural and artistic expression. Culture is viewed as a means of refining the self, so that it may be gradually elevated toward self-fulfilment and liberation.

Opposite A Kolkata dancer and her students rehearse a sequence depicting the goddess Durga. In Hinduism, religion and culture are still significantly connected.

Above *This gouache and watercolour painting of Radha and Krishna implies that even the deities are aesthetically inclined.*

SANSKRIT AND SCHOLARSHIP

HINDU SCHOLARSHIP REVOLVES AROUND SANSKRIT AND OTHER SACRED LANGUAGES. SANSKRIT REMAINS THE MAIN LANGUAGE OF WORSHIP, BUT IS SPOKEN IN ONLY A FEW COMMUNITIES.

'Sanskrit' means 'the most refined language' and refers to the ancient tongue intimately connected to Hinduism. The Indian word for culture is 'Sanskriti', which literally means 'refinement'. The similarity of the two terms indicates a close relationship between religious scholarship (mainly the preserve of the brahmins), and Hindu culture (as a popular vehicle for spiritual upliftment).

SANSKRIT

Hindus praise Sanskrit as 'deva-bhasa', the language of the gods. William Jones (1746–94), the pioneering Sanskrit translator, described it as 'more perfect than Greek, more copious than Latin, and more exquisitely refined than either'.

Below In modern Pakistan, these ruins stand at Taxila, site of an ancient centre of Indian learning.

He also observed that Sanskrit bore a resemblance to classical Greek and Latin and suggested that the three languages shared a common Indo-European root. Subsequent experts in philology, the science of language, conjectured that Sanskrit was imported by the invading or migrating Aryans. Hindus themselves often assert its Indian heritage. Whatever Sanskrit's precise roots, its linguistic status in South and South-east Asia is akin to that of Latin and Greek in Europe, for it has significantly enhanced Hindu thought and culture.

The earliest known form of Sanskrit goes back to the four Vedas, recorded as far back as 1500BCE. Many texts were subsequently written in a later, classical style, as codified by the Indian grammarian Panini (5th century BCE). However, Sanskrit was largely the preserve of priests and pandits, and so

Above A 12th-century marble deity of the goddess Sarasvati, who still presides over language, learning and the arts.

non-brahmins spoke simpler varieties called Prakrits, 'natural languages', which developed into a myriad of local tongues and their corresponding dialects. Today, Sanskrit is one of India's 23 official languages.

OTHER LANGUAGES

The ancient rivalry between North and South India extends to language. The north insists on the primacy of Sanskrit texts, and advertises Sanskrit as the genuine 'sacred language'. The south, particularly Tamil Nadu, claims that Tamil predates Sanskrit and that certain Tamil texts are equivalent to the Sanskrit canon. Ramanuja and other scholars synthesized the two traditions, and today the Shri Vaishnava community uses a Tamilized Sanskrit called 'Manipravala'. In the Shrirangam temple, the Tamil poems of the Alvars are recited alongside Vedic hymns.

From 1200CE onward, the emerging bhakti traditions augmented much brahmin-led religion and gave rise to a huge body of vernacular literature, which was often written for ordinary people by non-brahmin authors. Important Sanskrit-related languages include Avadhi, Punjabi, Bengali, Gujarati and Hindi, the Indian national tongue. In the south of India, the Dravidian languages form a different 'family', which, in addition to Tamil, includes Kannada, Telugu and Malayalam.

Hindus differ on the religious significance of their native languages. Some feel that without fluency in Sanskrit or Tamil their tradition cannot be properly studied or assimilated. Others teach that its universal truths, often associated with Sanatana Dharma, can be expressed in any language. Clearly, there are indisputable difficulties in translation. For example, English has no concise equivalent for some terms and related concepts, such as 'dharma', 'atman' and 'brahman'. Sanskrit therefore retains its importance as a language of scholarship and liturgy, and there are attempts to revitalize its use less formally, as a spoken language.

Below The Oxford Centre for Hindu Studies today continues the City of Oxford's long-standing tradition of teaching Sanskrit, especially important in studying primary Hindu texts.

Above The Sanskrit script, shown here, is called 'Devanagari', implying that it is spoken by the gods and hence capable of elevating human consciousness.

LITERARY TRADITIONS

Hindu literature forms the basis for most Hindu arts and sciences. This vast body of religious text encompasses a wide range of literary genres: song, story, drama, prayer, poetry, proverb and history. It is often hard to distinguish the genres. The two epic tales, the Ramayana and the Mahabharata, take the form of long poems: some consider them not only mythological, describing various worlds and dimensions, but also historically accurate. Key philosophers were often talented poets; poetry, often integrating prayer, has been set to music by devotional traditions. Tying together these diverse literary genres are spiritual themes derived from the common source of Hindu narrative.

Narrative, perhaps always integral to the Hindu tradition, rose to prominence in the Epic and Puranic periods. Since that time, story has been central in transmitting Hindu views and values, and, in disseminating popular Hinduism, is more important than philosophical or theological exposition. Stories were customarily passed down domestically, particularly by elders to children and grandchildren. Publicly, they have been popularized by dancers and musicians, by itinerant troupes of actors and storytellers and, more recently, through printed media, television and Bollywood film.

At the core of the story are the hero and heroine, who epitomize human virtues. Their exploits explore the nuances of dharma (duty) and the challenges of its practical application. Although many stories are ancient, Hindu people speak of their hero figures with a sense of intimacy and immediacy, as if they were alive today. They serve not as tribal ancestors, nor advocates of a specific 'faith', but as powerful archetypes, the inhabitants of a more glorious age whose example remains relevant to the modern world.

DANCE, DRAMA AND MUSIC

INDIAN'S PERFORMING ARTS RANGE FROM LOCAL FOLK TRADITIONS TO WORLD-RENOWNED CLASSICAL DISCIPLINES. DESPITE FOREIGN AND MODERN INFLUENCE, MOST STYLES STILL FEATURE RELIGIOUS THEMES.

The earliest known treatise on the performing arts is the Sanskrit classic, Natya Shastra, compiled by Bharata Muni around 300BCE. He described nine different 'rasas' (sentiments), their attendant bhavas (emotions) and various techniques of dramatic expression. The earliest artistes, called devadasis (maidservants of God), performed in temple courtyards before the presiding deities. During Mughal and British rule, dance and music moved to the royal courts as forms of entertainment. However, the performing arts today still explore spiritual themes derived from the Epics, Puranas and other texts.

DANCE AND DRAMA
These art forms are intimately linked to Hindu deities. In his form as Nataraja, 'the Lord of Dance', Shiva

Below A Balinese dancer poses as Lord Krishna.

performs the rigorously male tandava to initiate the cosmic annihilation. Krishna, called Natavara, 'the best of dancers', is celebrated for his intricate footwork in subduing the many-headed serpent called Kaliya, and for his romantic rasa-lila, enacted with his cowherd girlfriends. The word 'lila' refers to the sporting activities of deities, performed in loving exchange with devotees. Bhakti traditions have developed intricate theologies on the spiritual sentiment nurtured and expressed though music, poetry, dance and drama.

Most popular are the Krishna-lila dramas performed in Braj, the region of Krishna's birth, and through highly stylized dance in the eastern state of Manipur. The northern festival of Rama-lila features huge open-air productions of the Ramayana. Best known to Europeans

Below Along a North Indian street, women perform a traditional stick dance.

Above This South-Indian Kathakali actor is ornately dressed as Lord Rama.

is the drama by Kalidasa called 'Shakuntala'. Its English translation, published by Sir William Jones in 1789, made a profound impression upon such Western scholars as Goethe. Today, traditional theatrical styles have been augmented with contemporary forms.

MUSIC
Indian music, or 'sangita', is associated with the heavenly singers, the Gandharvas. The first recipient of

TYPES OF DANCE

Dance is divided into two main categories: folk and classical. The most popular folk styles are Garbha and Dandiya, both originally from Gujarat but now globally popular during the nine-day festival of Navaratri. Garba, a clap-dance using circular movements, is popular with women. Dandiya is traditionally performed in late autumn by mixed groups using decorated wooden sticks to maintain the rhythm. Punjab is well-known for its Bhangra, an energetic and colourful harvest dance favoured by men and boys, and for the more graceful Giddha dance for women.

Classical forms of dance, frequently with religious themes, are usually performed in concert halls. Kathak is the major northern style. It relates stories (katha) and employs chunky ankle bells and intricate, stamping footwork. Bharata Natyam, the major southern dance style, is grace-

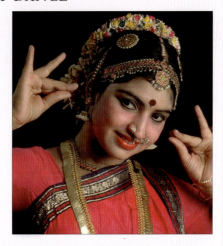

Above A classical dancer exhibits hand-gestures (mudras) and facial expressions to tell a story and convey thought and feeling.

ful, relying on facial expressions and hand gestures (mudras). Dance and drama are often intertwined, as in Kathakali, a southern discipline distinguished by its elaborate and colourful face masks.

this celestial art was the ancient rishi called Narada, often depicted carrying his vina (lute). The oldest teachings, found in the Sama Veda, consist of melodies for the recitation of hymns during ritual sacrifice. From these remote beginnings, music was not merely entertainment but a moral and spiritual redeemer with the potency to raise consciousness and award liberation. Indeed, learning music still resembles spiritual discipline. According to Ravi Shankar, the famous sitar-player, accomplishment has three prerequisites: first, an accomplished guru coming in disciplic succession; second, humility on behalf of the student; and, third, diligent and disciplined practice (sadhana).

Right To evoke spiritual sentiment, Vaishnava musicians from Manipur perform kirtan with drums and cymbals.

Bharata Muni describes two core principles of Indian music, namely tala (rhythm) and raga (melodic scale). Both were meticulously chosen to invoke the appropriate sentiment (rasa). In discussing the aesthetics of music, Bharata Muni delineates nava-rasa, nine principal 'sentiments' or 'relationships'. Later theologians, especially from the Chaitanya and Vallabha schools, further developed the science of rasa to encompass spiritual sentiment. These bhakti movements integrated meditational music and dance into their worship. Perhaps the most famous musician, one of the 'nine jewels' in Akbar's court, was Tansen (1480–1575). Influenced by Sufism, and devotional Hinduism through a saint-musician called Haridas, he apparently performed miracles simply by singing in the famous Dhrupad style.

Today, bhajana (hymns) and kirtana (musical chants) feature in many temple services. Instruments include small hand-cymbals, two-headed drums, such as the dolak and mridanga, and the harmonium, a keyboard instrument adapted from the church organ. South India has its unique musical traditions. Processions holding aloft the temple deities are accompanied by ensembles of nadasvaram, similar to an oboe, and tavil, a stout, two-headed barrel drum. The prevalence of music in worship shows the importance Hinduism places on sound, as the source of creation and as a means of unravelling the soul's entanglement in matter.

ART AND SYMBOLS

HINDUISM IS A RICHLY VISUAL TRADITION, ILLUSTRATED BY A HISTORY OF ICONOGRAPHY IN SCULPTURE AND PAINTING. IT USES RECURRENT MOTIFS AND SYMBOLS, SUCH AS THE COW, LOTUS AND TRIDENT.

Indian drawing and painting dates back to the prehistoric cave-shelter drawings at Bhimjabetika, near modern-day Bhopal. They include few, if any, explicitly religious themes. The cave paintings of the first millennium CE, as at Ajanta and Ellora, were dominated by Jain and Buddhist themes. The Gupta period furnished fine examples of Hindu workmanship. In modern-day Madhya Pradesh, they include, at Udayagiri, the 4th–5th-century rock relief depicting Vishnu rescuing the earth goddess. The 6th-century

Below This Mughal-era painting depicts Shiva destroying the demon Andhakari.

Dashavatara Temple in Deogarh, has sculptured panels depicting Rama and Krishna. Almost all early representations were through sculpture.

DRAWING AND PAINTING

The oldest surviving paintings include the 11th- or 12th-century Chola frescoes uncovered in 1931 within the circumambulatory corridor of the Brihadisvara Temple in Thanjavur (Tanjore), Tamil Nadu. The first fine-art paintings came later, and during Muslim rule there emerged several distinct schools of classical art, known as the Mughal, Kangra, Pahari, Kalighat and Rajasthani styles. Manuscript painting

Above This fresco painting, on rock-cut architecture at Ellora, Maharashtra, shows Shiva's abode on Mount Kailash.

became a delicate art as passages from the Ramayana and the Mahabharata were colourfully illustrated in a style mirroring folk tradition. Although secular and courtly art was increasingly popular, the subjects often maintained religious themes. Brightly hued Pahari miniatures from the Himalayan foothills depicted the sensuous pastimes of Krishna and his consort, Radha. Other paintings recorded the lives of everyday people, including sadhus (holy men) and brahmins (priests).

During British rule, Victorian and European styles predominated through artists such as Raja Ravi Varma (1848–1906), whose portrayals of epic characters won him first prize in the 1873 Vienna Exhibition. In modern times, B.G. Sharma has popularized both classical Indian art and the devotional Nathadwara style from Rajasthan. Now, with the ready availability of printed posters, colourful depictions of Hindu gods and goddesses abound in Hindu shops, homes and temples.

FOLK AND RELIGIOUS ART

Even with the rise of classical art, folk influences played a key role in regional courts, most notably in the design of royal furniture and architectural decor. Today, village homes are still adorned with rangoli patterns, using natural motifs such as swans, peacocks, mangoes, flowers and creepers. Using rice flour, women and girls construct these lace-like patterns early each morning on walls and thresholds. For their ability to ward off ill-luck and invoke good fortune, they are associated with the goddess Lakshmi. Using coloured powders, especially complex designs are drawn on major festival days. Festivals and temple puja have generated their own unique art forms, such as the construction of temporary images, the weaving of flower garlands and the embroidery of backdrops and costumes.

HINDU SYMBOLS

Hinduism is rich in symbolism. Drawing on Tantric principles, ritual worship (puja) is a form of visualization in which the worshipper simulates activities performed in higher worlds. The scope of symbolism is broad, including dress and tilak, forms of the murti such as the lingam, and sacred geometrical designs called yantras. It also includes physical gestures, such as offering obeisance with folded hands, which helps induce the right mood and awareness within the practitioner.

Below The Victorian artist Raja Ravi Varma specialized in scenes from the Epics and Puranas. This oil painting shows a Hindu woman plucking her vina.

Above Like much Hindu art, the rangoli pattern, which employs sacred symbols and nature motifs, is used to invoke auspiciousness, as in these flower patterns for the Karaga Festival, Bangalore.

Religious motifs, often drawn from flora and fauna, are considered auspicious and embody the ideal of sanctity. For example, the lotus symbolizes purity and transcendence as it emerges from the mud of human struggle and ignorance. Such sacred emblems are displayed in the home or temple to invoke good fortune. As Hindus have tried to define their religion as a single, unified tradition, the sacred syllable Om, resembling an elaborate figure three, has been adopted as its defining symbol, rather like the Christian cross or the crescent moon of Islam.

TEN IMPORTANT SYMBOLS

These symbols are popular:

1 **Om**: the most important Hindu mantra and symbol, used as the emblem of Hinduism.
2 **Hands in prayer** (anjali): a sign of reverence towards the sacred, and a respectful form of salutation.
3 **Lotus** (padma): a symbol of purity and transcendence; though resting on water, it does not touch it.
4 **Conch shell** (shankha): one of Vishnu's four symbols, and widely used in the arati ceremony.
5 **Swastika**: though misappropriated by the Nazis, it is an ancient solar sign to invoke auspiciousness.
6 **Trident** (trishula): a weapon symbolic of Shiva, often carried by Shaivite ascetics.
7 **Pot and coconut** (kalasha): the coconut, resting on mango leaves, is used in many rituals.
8 **Cow** (Go-mata): a symbol of the earth, motherhood and *ahimsa* (non-violence).
9 **Lotus feet** (Charana-ambuja): touching the feet of superiors illustrates service and submission.
10 **Lamp** (dipa): the symbol of light and wisdom intimately connected to the festival of Divali.

HINDU SCIENCES

INDIA'S ART FORMS ARE SUPPLEMENTED BY VARIOUS SCIENCES, SOME
VERY ANCIENT. THEY INCLUDE MATHEMATICS, MEDICINE, METALLURGY,
ASTRONOMY, ASTROLOGY AND THE SCIENCE OF SACRED SPACE.

Early Hindu sciences, far from being just mechanistic, integrated spiritual knowledge and technique to promote self-realization. Today, the potential contribution of Hindu arts and sciences to human wellbeing is increasingly recognized in the West.

MATHEMATICS

India is credited with contributing our current numerals and the crucial concept of 'zero'. Hindu mathematicians formulated an ingenious system of mental arithmetic used in astronomical and astrological calculations. This science of 'Vedic mathematics' was recently revived by a prominent sannyasin, Shri Bharata Krishna Tirthaji

(1884–1960). From only 16 Sanskrit sutras (aphorisms), he expounded an entire mathematical discipline, expediting the performance of difficult calculations. His writings include a concise proof of Pythagoras's theorem and a Sanskrit verse, of uncertain age, that codifies the value of pi to 31 decimal places. Vedic mathematics is now taught in some Western schools, though some dispute its actual age and authenticity. Related disciplines include numerology, with its notion of sacred and mystical numbers, such as the lucky '108'.

Below The northern-style astrological chart for Mahatma Gandhi, showing the twelve signs (and 'houses') and the nine planets.

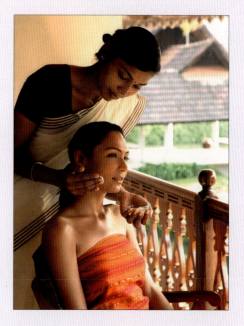

Above Health clinics based on the ancient Ayur-veda, such as this clinic in Kerala, are increasingly popular with non-Hindus.

ASTROLOGY AND ASTRONOMY

Astrology is a widely used Vedic science. Largely derived from the Jyotisha Shastra, one of the six Vedangas, it is underpinned by notions of karma and reincarnation. Whereas most people in the West treat astrology with some scepticism, Hindus consider it to be a respectable science, and texts eulogize authentic astrologers as highly learned brahmins. The West tends to label belief in subtle phenomena as 'superstition', whereas the East frames it within the context of 'subtle science', dealing with real phenomena beyond regular sensual perception.

There are different schools of astrology, and of all authorities the father of Vyasa, called Rishi Parashara, is considered the foremost. Indians often claim that astrology originated in their country and came westward via the Greeks. Most families still request a local brahmin to cast a chart for the new baby. Not all astrologers are accurate or reputable, and practice of the science requires considerable knowledge, insight and character.

In many South Indian temples, the nava-graha (nine planets) are represented as sacred images. The nine planets are the Sun, Moon, Mars, Mercury, Jupiter, Venus, Saturn, Rahu (north node of the Moon) and Ketu (south node of the Moon). Some are considered auspicious (Jupiter, Venus, Mercury and the full Moon) and others inauspicious (Saturn, Rahu, Ketu, Mars, the Sun and the new Moon), though these influences are modified by their specific positions. Some Hindus seek to placate the ruling deities of poorly placed planets through remedial measures such as sacrifice, chanting mantras and wearing gemstones. In some temples, the nine planets are worshipped to invoke good fortune, especially on those days when dreaded Saturn enters a new sign.

USES OF ASTROLOGY

Hindu astrology has several distinct purposes, including:
• predicting important periods and trends in a person's life
• identifying areas of personal potential, as in career, or hurdles, such as health problems
• choosing auspicious times to start a ceremony or new venture
• assessing compatibility between prospective marriage partners
• answering specific queries, often by constructing a chart for the exact time of the query

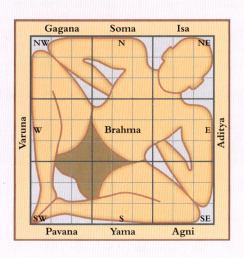

Left This diagram of the 'Primal Person' is much used in vastu, the Indian science of sacred space. Vastu aims to raise human awareness and cultivate an auspicious lifestyle.

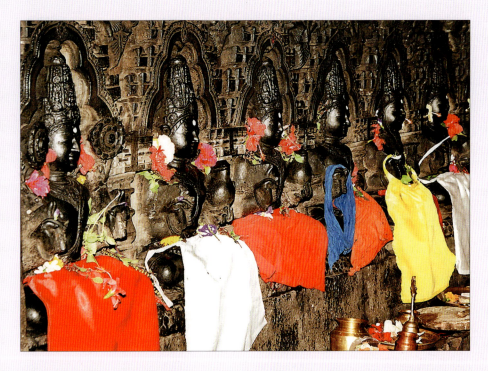

Above The nine planetary deities worshipped at Konark, Orissa. Each cloth matches the colour linked to the specific planet, such as red for Mars.

AYUR-VEDIC MEDICINE

Ayur-veda refers to a system of indigenous Indian medicine, mainly derived from texts called the Sushruta and Charaka Samhitas. The science is attributed to Dhanvantari, an incarnation of Vishnu who appeared from the milk-ocean churned by the gods and the demons. He taught that sickness is rooted in an imbalance in three bodily humours: wind, bile and phlegm. Harmony is achieved by balancing these 'doshas', and through balanced diet, regulated lifestyle, positive mental attitude and prescribed natural remedies. The system is preventative rather than reactive, and treats individuals according to their unique constitutions. It is still practised throughout India, and is increasingly popular in the West.

Related to Ayur-vedic medicine and the preparation of mineral remedies is the science of alchemy, based on two key elements, sulphur and mercury. They correlate to the Tantric, male-female symbolism of Shiva and Shakti, and to the sun and moon. Some claim that yogis can transform base metals into gold. One method, fatal to most people, was to drink mercury and then urinate on red-hot copper!

VASTU

Experts in Vastu claim that it goes back five millennia, pre-dating its Chinese cousin Feng-shui. It is closely related to other Vedic sciences, such as geometry, astrology and architecture. It deals with the science of sacred space and with harnessing natural and beneficial energies in the design, construction and decoration of buildings. It is connected to the microcosm–macrocosm relationship illustrated in the story of the primal man found in the Rig Veda. Much information on Vastu is derived from the architectural texts called Shilpa Shastra, and new books regularly appear on the market.

SCULPTURE AND ARCHITECTURE

THE HINDU TEMPLE HAS INSPIRED INDIA'S GREATEST ARTISTIC AND ARCHITECTURAL ACHIEVEMENTS. SCULPTURE HELPED TO DEPICT MYTH, EMBELLISH SHRINES AND FASHION SACRED ICONS.

Archaeological finds in the Indus Valley reveal evidence of early Indian architecture and include sculptures, such as a bronze dancing girl. The subsequent Vedic period (1500–500BCE) has yielded few artefacts, but contributed the sacred text called the Shilpa Shastra. Expounding on one of the 64 branches of Hindu art, the Shilpa Shastra includes guidelines on sacred architecture and sets iconographic standards by prescribing precise proportions for sculptured figures.

Above A sculptor in Tamil Nadu puts the finishing touches to a murti.

THE SACRED IMAGE

Panini, the great grammarian of the 5th century BCE, mentions sacred images venerated in temple shrines. From at least that time, the carving of sacred figures became a unique, sophisticated art form requiring years of disciplined training. The shilpa (stonemason) and the shapati (murti-maker) fashion each image according to scripturally specified dimensions. Some murtis are cast in brass or an alloy of five metals. Specialized artisans are also expert in constructing temporary images out of clay, wicker and other natural materials for the festivals of Durga Puja and Ganesha Chaturthi. Modern organizations constructing temples outside of India often bring over such master craftsmen.

Below Hinduism has developed the carving and casting of figurines into a fine art, as illustrated by this shrine depicting Ganesha and his worshippers, at the Batu Caves, Malaysia.

SCULPTURE

Indian sculpture dates back to the Indus Valley civilization, from which period stone, bronze and terracotta figures have been unearthed. As Hinduism developed alongside Jainism and Buddhism, India produced extremely intricate temple carvings. The huge shrines at Ellora, Maharashtra, were carved not from assembled stone blocks but out of solid rock. Similar sites include Mahabalipuram, where a bas-relief recounts the descent of the celestial River Ganges, and the Elephanta caves in Mumbai harbour, which house forms of Shiva and the Trimurti.

During the Gupta period (4th to 6th century CE), sculpture attained more delicacy, especially by using sandstone from around Mathura. The end of the first millennium saw a proliferation of free-standing figures, both cast and carved. The southern Chola dynasty produced exquisitely wrought forms of Lord Shiva, and the Hoysala dynasty (1026–1343CE) of present-day Karnataka depicted feminine grace using soapstone, and the Hindu epics using horizontal friezes (decorative mouldings). The royal temple at Halebidu has been described as 'a milestone in Indian architecture'. Further north, 400km (248.5 miles) south-east of present-day New Delhi, the erotically carved figures at Khajuraho have aroused much debate about their meaning. Some Hindu traditions say that they

Above The colossal complex at Angkor Wat, Cambodia, was built during a spate of magnificent temple construction.

symbolize the abandonment of mundane desires before entering the sanctity of the temple. Today, South India's temples and towering gateways remain famous for their multicoloured figurines of gods, goddesses and other celestial beings.

ARCHITECTURE

One of the most enduring achievements of Indian civilization is undoubtedly its architecture. Vishvakarma, the son of Brahma, is considered the draftsman of the universe, the builder of the gods' palaces, and the patron deity of architects and stonemasons. Temples themselves are representations of Mount Meru, the home of the gods. Some traditions view them as embassies of the spiritual realm, unaccountable to worldly law.

Temples were few during the Vedic period and proliferated later on, as ritual worship superseded public sacrifice. Some claim that the oldest still-functional temple was established in 108CE in Bihar. The famous Shiva temple of Shrisailam, in present-day Andhra Pradesh, may have been founded in the 2nd century CE. However, most large structures date back to the period 900–1300CE, when building enterprise flourished throughout India.

One of India's most prized architectural sites is the Brihadishwara Temple at Thanjavur in Tamil Nadu. As outstanding examples of Chola architecture, the temple tower (vimana) stands almost 70m (230ft) high and the shikhara, the bulbous top structure, weighs over 80 tons. Another sublime monument is the 13th-century sun temple standing at Konark in the eastern province of Orissa. Conceived as the gigantic chariot of the sun god, it boasts seven teams of horses and 12 pairs of exquisitely ornamented wheels. Fifty-six kilometres (35 miles) down the coast stands the 12th-century Jagannatha temple, famed for its annual chariot festival.

The Mughal Emperors (1526–1857) added their own distinctive style, spending lavishly on forts, mosques and palaces. However, during Muslim rule, temple building was curbed, and the iconoclastic Aurangzeb razed many temples.

Today's temple structures still display a number of architectural styles, such as those peculiar to the Himalayan region, in the far north, and to the southern state of Kerala, with its wooden structures and pointed roofs clad in copper. However, archaeological styles are broadly classified as North Indian (Nagara) and South Indian (Dravidian). Today, many Hindu temples, including those constructed outside India, use one of these styles, often incorporating modern design and the latest building techniques.

Below The octagonal 'Temple of Understanding' in Durban, South Africa, combines traditional and contemporary architecture.

DRESS AND COSMETICS

HINDU DRESS HAS RELIGIOUS, AS WELL AS AESTHETIC AND PRACTICAL, SIGNIFICANCE. OUTFITS DIFFER ACCORDING TO REGION, CLIMATE, SOCIAL STATUS AND DEGREES OF FOREIGN AND CONTEMPORARY INFLUENCE.

Hindu dress embodies both simplicity and sophistication. Many clothes, such as the woman's sari, can be produced in village workshops without tailoring. For women, the emphasis was traditionally on modesty rather than sexual allurement, and elegance rather than fashion. However, wedding clothes can be elaborate and costly, often now incorporating many elements

Below Modern Hindu women wear popular two-piece garments, which look similar to the traditional one-piece sari.

of modern fashion. It has long been customary to wear only new clothes on festival days.

DRESS
Women's saris, woven from silk, cotton or nylon, come in a range of regional patterns, with various and distinctive ways of wearing them. Punjabi Hindu women usually wear the salwar-kameez, consisting of a tunic (kameez), loose-fitting trousers (salwar) and a chunni (shawl) to cover the head and shoulders. Hindu women, especially outside of India,

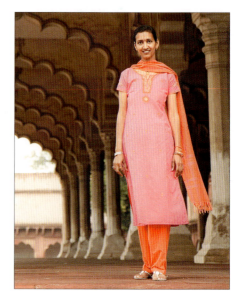

Above A Hindu woman wears a 'Punjabi suit' (shalwar-kameeze), also worn by many Sikh and Muslim women.

often wear Western dress, except when visiting the mandir and on special occasions such as weddings. They are developing modern fashion trends based on traditional attire. Particularly popular is the ghagra-choli outfit, consisting of a ghangra (dress) and a choli, the tight blouse normally worn with a sari. Despite these broad norms, it is difficult to conclusively identify a Hindu woman by her attire alone. Many Bangladeshi Muslims wear the sari and most Sikhs the shalwar-kameez. It is relatively easy to identify a Hindu widow by her entirely white sari and lack of ornamentation.

Earlier than womenfolk, Hindu men started to adopt Western dress, even in India, where it is common to see both ethnic styles mixed incongruously. The traditional outfit, more common in rural areas, consists of a generously cut shirt called a kurta and a white, pleated robe, called a dhoti. In the south, the dhoti may be replaced with a simple wrap-around lunghi, often of coloured material. The shirt may be replaced or supplemented with a waistcoat, or a chaddar (shawl) conveniently wrapped around the torso

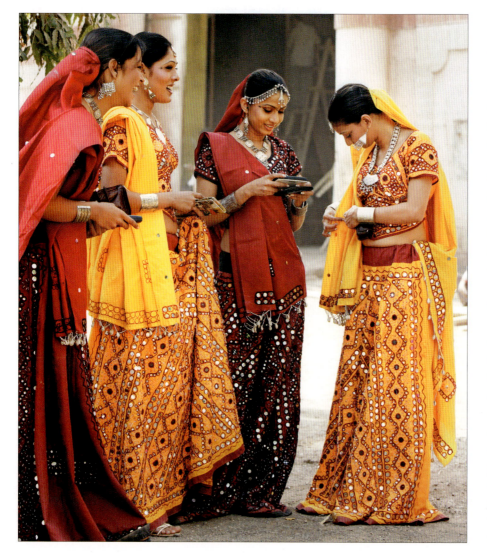

in cooler weather. In many regions, such as Rajasthan, the turban affords protection from the blazing sun.

Of particular religious significance is the saffron dress of sannyasins, members of the fourth, renounced ashrama. Sannyasins are expected to shun all sewn cloth and carry little more than a staff and water pot. Even if not formal sannyasins, most sadhus (holy men) wear the much-respected saffron. To develop detachment, some ascetics roam completely naked or with little more than scanty underwear.

FASHION ACCESSORIES

The Sanskrit term for ornamentation is alankara. Although the word encompasses drama, music, poetry and other aesthetic pursuits, in common parlance it means jewellery. It stems not from mere fashion awareness, but a long-established sensibility to mark all features of life with auspicious symbols and designs.

Ancient Sanskrit texts have laid down the concept of sola sringar, 16 items of feminine adornment.

Below Girls in the USA learn how to apply henna patterns to their palms and wrists.

They are the bindi (red spot), sandalwood paste, earrings, perfume, flowers for the hair, kohl or kajal (mascara), necklaces, armlets (for the upper arm), bangles, henna (for the palms and soles), rings, waistbands, the upper garment, the lower garment, ankle-bells and toe rings. Though the demands of contemporary life makes wearing all 16 items impractical, many women adopt them for weddings and other special events.

Dress and ornamentation indicates marital status. The mangal-sutra ('auspicious thread'), or 'thali' in the south, is a necklace of small black beads worn by married women whose husbands are still living. During the marriage ceremony itself, the groom applies sindur (red powder) to the parting of his bride's hair, and the wife subsequently applies it daily. Once widowed, a woman relinquishes the sindhur. Married women have customarily applied the red 'bindi' dot on their foreheads but, as a contemporary fashion accessory of various hues and designs, it is now also worn by single women and girls. Sometimes during a religious ceremony a red or ashen bindi is reverently applied to the foreheads of both sexes.

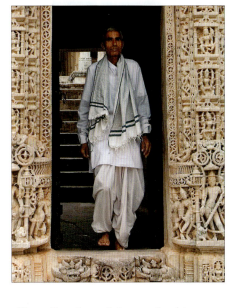

Above Leaving a Jain temple, this man wears traditional Indian dress: kurta (loose-fitting shirt), dhoti (robe) and chaddar (shawl).

PERFUME AND FRAGRANCES

The distillation of Indian fragrances goes back to ancient times, when the two main preparations were pastes (or ointments) and liquids. Sandalwood paste is still made by the painstaking process of rubbing the aromatic wood on a flat stone lubricated with rose-water. In temple ceremonies, the paste is mixed with saffron, daubed on the deity's forehead, and later offered to worshippers. It cools the forehead and soothes the mind. Other Indian perfumes are pure essential oils, made from flower and herbal extracts without added alcohol. They are offered to the temple deity during puja. Also used during the arati ceremony is camphor, a powder of whitish translucent crystals, which creates a distinctive aroma when burned in lamps. Indian incense is familiar to most non-Hindus. It is traditionally used for worship, scenting the home and repelling mosquitoes. As with other sensual stimuli, aromatics are used in Hinduism to create a pure, auspicious and meditative atmosphere.

FOOD AND HOSPITALITY

FOOD GOES BEYOND PHYSICAL NOURISHMENT OR SOCIAL EXCHANGE. BY INFLUENCING MENTAL, MORAL AND SPIRITUAL DEVELOPMENT, IT HAS GREAT RELIGIOUS SIGNIFICANCE.

For medical and religious reasons, there are many meticulous rules for the preparation, serving and consumption of food.

DIETARY REGULATIONS

Drawing from Sankhya philosophy, the Bhagavad-gita has classified edibles according to the three gunas. For Vaishnavas, food should be in the quality of goodness, promoting harmony and longevity. They restrict food influenced by passion, such as hotly spiced foods, and totally avoid edibles influenced by tamas (darkness), such as animal flesh. Shaivites observe fewer dietary restrictions, and Shaktas are perhaps the most inclined toward meat, customarily through animal sacrifice. Although many Hindus now eat meat, almost all avoid beef out of reverence for the cow. Some still hold vegetarianism as the ideal by fasting from meat on festive days. Apart from meat, fish and eggs, many orthodox Hindus avoid other ingredients, such as garlic, onions, mushrooms, root vegetables and non-indigenous foods.

There are also strict rules for eating, which should always be in a clean environment. When food is served, some chant prayers or mantras, and may sprinkle water around the meal. Meals are taken seated, preferably on the floor, in a peaceful atmosphere without undue or disturbing conversation. Some Hindus consider that once one has risen, one should not eat until the next meal. Hence, it is customary that the women of the household serve before taking their own meal. In some spiritual communities, the leaders take this important role. Such service should always be performed with respectful attention and in an uplifting mood.

HINDU CUISINE

Hinduism has developed an incredibly diverse, balanced and nutritious vegetarian cuisine. Milk products

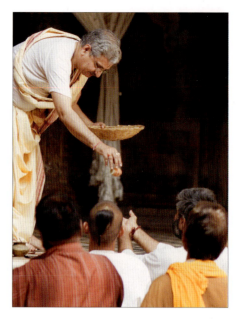

Above A temple priest drops prasada (sanctified food) into the outstretched hands of worshippers.

are often thought essential and ghee (butter-oil) is a widely used frying medium. Spices enhance taste, aid digestion and promote good health. A typical meal consists of rice, dhal (lentil soup), subji (a vegetable preparation) and roti (a round, flat bread). Certain parts of India, such as Bengal, are renowned for their excellent milk sweets. In the very south, the style is quite different, with much use of coconut, and of rice-flour snacks such as dosa, vadam and idli. In non-vegetarian traditions, the diet is supplemented by fish and meat dishes, and has been heavily influenced by foreign cultures.

SANCTIFIED FOOD

Food has great religious significance as an integral part of festivals and puja (worship). According to the Bhagavad-gita, a person eating solely for sensual gratification, without offering the food to God, incurs bad karma. On the other hand, prasada, or the 'remnants'

Left For festivals, food is cooked in large pots, as in this temple on the Andaman and Nicobar Islands.

Right Krishna set an example for hospitality. Here, despite being fabulously wealthy, he washes the feet of Sudama, an impoverished brahmin.

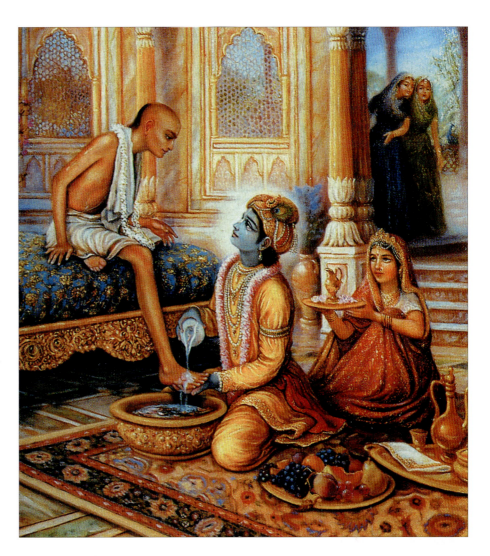

of food offered to deities or holy people, is thought to bestow considerable merit. Temple cooks follow strict standards of personal cleanliness, and there is a widespread belief that the consciousness of the cook pervades the food, influencing the mind of the eater. Ingesting meals prepared with devotion inclines the mind toward spirituality.

Concerns for purity have been rigidly institutionalized through hereditary caste practices, so that members of one caste may shun eating with those of a lower ranking. While features of this system have become exploitative, many Hindus consider purity a legitimate and essential constituent of spiritual life. Meat-eating, if transgressing scriptural regulation, incurs significant bad karma. On the other hand, voluntary fasting is deemed to bestow merit. While self-mortification is generally not recommended, ageing

Below This Indian vegetarian meal is served on banana-leaf plates and in sun-baked clay pots, both easily recyclable.

Hindus often reduce their dependence upon food to attain release from mental and physical cravings.

HOSPITALITY

A fundamental part of Hindu culture is hospitality, and sharing food is a prime duty of the householder. Texts specify that the unexpected or uninvited guest, the atithi ('without a set time'), should be treated as God. There are many stories regarding the benefits of offering a suitable reception to brahmins, sannyasins and other holy people and the bad karma that accrues from neglect. Tradition teaches that a civilized human, no matter how poor, should always offer a guest three items: a sitting place, sweet words and refreshment, at least some water. Scripture also enjoins that one should treat visiting enemies so well

that they forget their animosity. A graphic example is of the warrior class, who would fight during the day and in the evening banquet with their adversaries. In popular practice today, Hindu hospitality is often extremely liberal and lavish.

Free food distribution also constitutes a main branch of charity. Hindus believe that serving food to the poor and needy, the pious and saintly, and to birds, insects and animals, is meritorious. In ancient India, and in some parts today, special kitchens called chatras would cater solely to pilgrims and mendicants (sannyasins). The householder would also give alms to the begging brahmacharins (celibate students). Today, meals are offered to God during religious ceremonies, to departed souls on specific days, and daily to temple visitors.

MODERN EXPRESSIONS OF HINDU CULTURE

HINDU CULTURE IS EXTREMELY OLD. THE TENSIONS BETWEEN ANCIENT TRADITION AND MODERN LIFE ARE REFLECTED IN CONTEMPORARY INDIAN FILM, ESPECIALLY IN EXPLORING HUMAN RELATIONSHIPS.

As a way of life and a spiritual path, Hinduism has both resisted and welcomed the inevitable change brought by contact with diverse peoples, faiths and philosophies. Its culture, though retaining core concepts and values, has been forced to respond to changing circumstances. From the turn of the first millennium CE, Hindu culture has wrestled with centuries of foreign domination and attempts to promote Islamic, Christian and other values. More recently, it has faced the impact of globalization, especially though film, television and media-driven consumerism.

CINEMA AND TELEVISION

Bollywood popularly refers to the Indian film industry based largely in Mumbai (previously Bombay). It boasts the world's largest output in terms of numbers of films and ticket sales. Starting in 1913, early films focused almost exclusively on religious themes from the Epics and Puranas. Some, such as the low-budget 'Jai Santoshi Maa' (1975) had significant religious impact. Overnight, a relatively obscure goddess rocketed to national and international acclaim. Recent films still explore religious themes, often exploring the generational tensions between traditional Hindu customs and contemporary lifestyles. Others aspire to highlight social anomalies in Indian and Hindu society. Some productions are explicitly based on key Hindu concepts, such as karma and reincarnation, with dashing heroes reborn with a mission to avenge the injustices witnessed during a previous incarnation.

Indian television, launched in 1959 in New Delhi, has also had a huge impact. When aired, small-screen versions of the Ramayana and Mahabharata have practically brought

Above Poster of the famous film Om Shanti Om, *in which the hero reincarnates to avenge a murder.*

the country to a standstill. None the less, some Hindu thinkers are concerned about TV's promotion of non-Hindu values and for diminishing other recreational habits such as worship or temple attendance. On the other hand, worldwide communications have helped export Hindu ideals out of India, as with Sir Richard Attenborough's *Gandhi* (1982) and the romantic thriller *Ghost* (1990), which shows shadowy beings transporting a sinful self to its next life. Other blockbusters, such as *Star Wars* and *Xena: Warrior Princess*, draw heavily from Hindu themes and motifs.

HINDU ETIQUETTE

Indian films, especially when incorporating traditional storylines, illustrate perhaps the heart of Hindu culture, namely etiquette. Codes of conduct and decorum reflect at once a hierarchical view of life, and simultaneously one that broadly respects all aspects of divinity, including human relationships. Acknowledgment of seniority is demonstrated through

Left During his sacred thread ceremony, a boy makes obeisance to his mother. In return, she blesses him by touching her palm to his head.

endearing customs, such as touching elders' feet, speaking politely and seeking advice and blessings. Before a musical performance, the artiste offers respect to his or her teacher and a dancer supplicates the supporting earth. Children prostrate and touch the feet of their parents at festivals and other special events, such as birthdays or departure on a journey. To set an example to others, even deities such as Lord Krishna followed such rules.

Numerous practices relate to purity and cleanliness. Although some scholars are dismissive of 'ritual purity', many habits are merely hygienic, such as showering each morning, bathing after using the toilet and removing outside shoes. Generally, the left hand is reserved for dirty actions, such as washing after evacuating, and the right hand for eating, transferring gifts, and counting on meditation beads. It is considered a grave insult to touch anyone, or an article worthy of respect, with the feet or shoes. Additionally, one should not sit with the feet outstretched, particularly toward the shrine. Broadly speaking, a cultured Hindu is expected to be dignified in body language, and to avoid pointing with the finger (used for bestowing a curse) or excessive laughter. One should also

avoid intimate mixing with the opposite sex and, even between married couples, public displays of affection. In India, it is common to see men holding hands, as a sign of friendship rather than a sexual gesture. In public places such as temples, men and women often sit separately.

There are many rules with regard to eating, such as not eating leftovers (juttha), even one's own. A notable exception is 'respecting the remnants' left by the deity or a holy person. Such prasada (sanctified food) has

Above Most Hindus take a morning bath, even if they are living in relatively austere conditions.

the opposite effect, of physical, mental and spiritual purification. It may be thought disrespectful to refuse such prasada. Cooking utensils are kept separate from those for serving and eating, especially where food is sanctified before the temple or household deity. As in other areas of life, while cooking, Hindus traditionally avoid unclean clothes, placing fingers in the mouth or chewing nails. They are sometimes critical of contrary standards of personal hygiene.

Hindu etiquette is not so strictly followed today, and is often challenged by contemporary values, as frequently conveyed by film, television and other media. Still many Indian and Hindu films portray the endearing ideals of humility, courtesy and respect, considered integral not only to social intercourse but to individual spiritual growth.

Left Students eat in a traditional, contemplative style after having first sprinkled water around the meal.

CHAPTER 10

HINDU MOVEMENTS AND LEADERS

Most people are familiar with Hindu groups, such as the Hare Krishna Movement, or with spiritual teachers catering to popular interest in yoga and meditation, such as the late Maharishi Mahesh Yogi. Hinduism has long been transmitted through such institutions and leaders. Many Hindus still take formal initiation to join an ancient lineage of gurus and disciples.

Traditionally, Hindus revere elders, such as the ancient rishis, medieval saints and learned theologians; also brahmins, temple priests and sadhus (holy people). Modern sadhus include naked ascetics, formally clad sannyasins, a scattering of magicians and tricksters, and several notable women gurus. Hinduism has also seen many social reformers and political activists.

With no centralized, ecclesiastical body, Hinduism's authority structures remain diffuse. Recent leaders have tried to unify Hinduism, often by rousing nationalist sentiment. Others and their organizations, often favouring a universal Hinduism, have achieved significant global influence. They testify to the far-reaching impact of the ancient Hindu wisdom.

Opposite Disciples acknowledge their guru as the embodiment of spiritual wisdom, as in this photo of Shankaracharya with his disciples in Kanchipuram, India.

Above Mahatma Gandhi, one of Hinduism's most renowned leaders, enjoys a humorous exchange with his granddaughters.

THE MAIN TRADITIONS

HINDUISM IS LIKE A FAMILY OF RELIGIONS, WITH SHARED FEATURES
SUCH AS FAITH IN THE VEDAS AND BELIEF IN REINCARNATION. THERE
ARE FOUR MAIN TRADITIONS, SOMETIMES EXTENDED TO SEVEN.

Hindu denominations are primarily discerned by their favoured focus of worship. There are three secondary criteria for classification: first, their approach to scriptural and ecclesiastical authority; second, their specific philosophy; and third, their favoured path or spiritual discipline. Other differences, especially within main groups, relate to region, ethnicity, language, polemics over succession and the genuine guru, and approaches toward socio-political reform.

THREE, FOUR OR SEVEN TRADITIONS

The three main Hindu communities relate to the Trimurti and their wives. Since Brahma is rarely worshipped, the two main male deities are Vishnu (worshipped by Vaishnavas) and Shiva (worshipped by Shaivas). The third community, the Shaktas,

Below This man's tilak indicates that he belongs to the Vaishnava denomination.

worships the three goddesses, though primarily Shiva's wife, known as Parvati, Durga or Kali. These three communities are extended by adding a fourth, the Smartas, who worship either five or six deities.

Some writers list seven communities. They extend the four by considering the extra deities the Smartas worship. In addition to Vishnu, Shiva and Shakti, the Smartas worship the sun (Surya), Ganesha (Ganapati) and, sometimes, Skanda (Murugan or Kumara). The three corresponding groups are called Sauryas, Ganapatyas and Kaumaras.

Members of traditions may be identified by their tilak marks. On their foreheads, Vaishnavas sport a V- or U-shaped motif, whereas the followers of Shiva, and some Smartas, wear three horizontal lines. There is no universally accepted mark for Shaktas and other groups, though many sport a simple red dot.

DIFFERENT SOURCES OF AUTHORITY

Some writers identify three historical strands, which differ in the attitude toward textual and priestly authority. The first is Brahminism, the world-affirming and scholarly orthodoxy; the second, are the complementary, but also competing, Shramana traditions, which favour anti-social renunciation and alternative texts called the Tantras. The third is popular, village Hinduism, which rarely engages directly with scholarship. However, the boundaries between these divisions are porous,

Right This sadhu is a Shaiva. Smartas often wear the same symbol. Shaktas apply no tilak but often wear the red bindi.

Above Here adorning a house, Ganapati is widely worshipped, mainly as a functional deity.

as illustrated by orthodoxy's assimilation of renunciant ideals, Tantric texts and local gods and goddesses.

DIFFERENT DOCTRINES

There are six orthodox Darshanas ('ways of seeing'), to which the various groups subscribe. Of these, Vedanta represents much contemporary doctrine. The other Darshanas have faded into degrees of obscurity, though the two 'sister schools' of Yoga and Sankhya are still actively connected to Shaiva and Vaishnava ascetic traditions.

Vedanta has not entirely rejected the other five schools, but has accommodated and assimilated them. Within Vedanta there are numerous schools of thought, but broadly two. The first school is Dvaita, dualism, which teaches that the individual self is eternally distinct from a personal God, and that liberation entails entering an eternal paradise.

DIFFERENT PATHS
The diverse practices of Hinduism largely fall within four main paths or margas, aimed at union with God, and thus also termed 'yogas'. The paths are: karma-yoga (path of action); jnana-yoga, (path of knowledge); astanga-yoga (path of meditation); and bhakti-yoga (path of devotion). Each denomination usually favours one path, attempting to establish its supremacy, though some teach that all paths are equally valid.

Above Hindu women pay homage to the sun-god. His exclusive followers, called Sauryas, are rare.

is Advaita (non-dualism), largely associated with Shankara and his predominant branch of the Smarta tradition. Liberation means realization that the self and an impersonal God are identical. The other main

Below Queen Elizabeth II visits a London temple dedicated to Murugan, whose followers are called 'Kaumaras'.

SEVEN MAIN TRADITIONS AN ALTERNATI

The seven main traditions are listed below.

1 Vaishnavas worship Vishnu, or one of his forms such as Rama or Krishna. They are largely orthodox and personalists, favouring the path of bhakti-yoga (although the Shri Vaishnavas postulate an even higher yoga, called prapatti-yoga, the path of surrender).

2 Shaivas are often associated with ascetic strands drawing from Tantra and Sankhya philosophy, with tendencies toward jnana and astanga-yoga. There are also brahminical strands. Shaivas are often impersonalists, though some bhakti strands view God as ultimately personal.

3 Shaktas tend to be impersonalists, and worship often focuses on the material benefit associated with karma-yoga and meeting villagers' immediate needs. Their theology tends to be less developed, drawing largely from Shaivism and Tantric traditions.

4 Smartas today largely follow the impersonal doctrine of Shankara and favour the path of jnana:

philosophical inquiry and renunciation. More broadly, the Smartas represent a world-affirming brahminical orthodoxy closely associated with Mimamsa philosophy and the ritualistic, karma-kanda section of the Vedas.

5 Ganapatyas worship Ganapati, another name for Ganesh, revered as the remover of obstacles. Despite his affinity to Shiva, many worshippers consider themselves a distinct community. Some elevate his status to that of the Supreme. They are predominant in Maharashtra and South India.

6 Kaumaras venerate Kumara, more often called Murugan, Skanda or Kartikeyan. They are predominant in South India and Bengal. Worship is based on the ancient Tamil Sangam literature and some Puranas, especially the Skanda Purana.

7 Sauryas are worshippers of Surya, the sun. Sun worship is very old, and popular among the warrior class. Lord Rama was born in the dynasty of the sun god. Today few Sauryas remain, mainly in the north-western region of Sind.

VAISHNAVISM

THE LARGEST COMMUNITY WITHIN HINDUISM WORSHIPS GOD AS VISHNU. VAISHNAVAS ARE DIVIDED INTO SMALLER COMMUNITIES, EACH VENERATING A FORM OF VISHNU, SUCH AS RAMA OR KRISHNA.

Vishnu, 'the all pervading', is mentioned in the Vedas but was only later identified as the main object of sacrifice, superseding Indra and Agni.

Traditionally, Krishna dates back five millennia, though many scholars think him more recent. Ancient Krishna-worshippers included the Gopala and Vasudeva sects, and the Bhagavatas patronized by the Gupta emperors. It is not clear how distinct these groups were, but today they are amalgamated under the umbrella of Vaishnavism.

The roots of modern Vaishnavism lie in the poems of the 12 Tamil-speaking Alvars. Subsequently, from the 2nd millennium CE, a number of prominent theologians established their own sampradayas to contest and extend the monistic doctrine of Shankara. The various communities still claim legitimacy through links to one of four sampradayas. Two of these are associated with key theologians, Ramanuja and Madhva; a third to the acharya (spiritual leader) named Vallabha; and the fourth to Nimbarka. Each of the traditions is also headed by a particular deity: Lakshmi, Brahma, Shiva and four child-saints called 'the Kumaras'.

More than other groups, Vaishnavas believe in a personal God, and they follow the path of devotion. Many modern Vaishnava movements, descended from medieval saints opposed to social inequality, now represent a redefined, more inclusive orthodoxy.

Above Women wait outside the Shri Nathaji temple in Nathdwar, Rajasthan. Vallabha, founder of this 'Pushti Marg' lineage, met Chaitanya who similarly founded Bengali Vaishnavism.

SOUTH INDIA

The ancient Bhagavata sect penetrated south India and, by the 3rd century CE, the sensuous Sangam culture had readily assimilated the pastoral and romantic tales of Krishna, known in Tamil as Mayon. Between the 6th and 9th centuries, the outpourings of the 12 Alvars (poet-mystics) laid foundations for the Shri Vaishnava lineage and a later northbound surge of devotion. The Shri Vaishnava sampradaya was actually started by Nathamuni, who compiled the hymns of the Alvars into the Divya Prabhanham. However, its greatest theologian was Ramanuja, who expounded the notion of a personal God living in an eternal paradise above both the temporary Vedic heavens and Shankara's impersonal absolute.

Within a century of Ramanuja's demise, a theological polemic divided his lineage. The northern camp, or 'the monkey school', taught that human beings should strive for God's mercy, as an infant

Left These South-Indian priests in Tamil Nadu belong to the Shri Sampradaya consolidated by Ramanuja.

Right The Akshadharm Temple, New Delhi, was created and is managed by BAPS Swaminarayan Sanstha.

monkey clings desperately to its mother. Vedanta Desika (1269–1370) developed this theology. On the other hand, Manavala Mamuni developed an alternative theology for the southern branch, founded by Pillai Lokacharya (1205–1311). This 'kitten school' taught that Vishnu bestows his grace unconditionally, as the mother cat carries her kittens. By 1400CE, the schism turned into a permanent division between the northern (Vadagalai) and southern schools (Tenkalai). Members are still differentiated by the respective tilaka marks.

BENGAL AND EAST INDIA

One of the most influential Vaishnava sects started with the Bengali saint Chaitanya. Drawing on the poems of Jayadeva, Chandidas and Vidyapati, he epitomized the divine love between Radha and Krishna. Immersed in ecstatic contemplation, Chaitanya wrote only one poem of eight stanzas. The theology for

Below Vaishnavas worship Vishnu, or one of his many forms such as Rama or Krishna (shown here as 'Shri Nathaji').

Gaudiya (Bengali) Vaishnavism was compiled by the Six Goswamis, who blended the teachings of Ramanuja with those of other Vaishnava lineages. The most notable is Rupa Goswami, whose rasa-theology intricately describes the various relationships between the devotee and God, as servant, friend, parent or lover. Around 1718CE, Baladeva wrote a commentary establishing a formal but contested link with the Madhva sampradaya. Bengali Vaishnavism was popularized by the world-famous Hare Krishna Movement but remains most prevalent in Orissa, West Bengal, Bangladesh (previously East Bengal) and the far-eastern state of Manipur.

WEST INDIA

Vallabha, a contemporary of Chaitanya, founded a parallel tradition called the Pushti Marg, the 'path of nourishment'. The name acknowledges the sustaining power of divine grace. Vallabha favoured the devotee treating the Lord as an infant, with a mood of service and protection. The main Krishna deity, Shri Nathji, originally installed in the sacred town of Vrindavan, was

moved to Nathadwara in Rajasthan for fear of Muslim atrocity. The Pushti Marg is particularly popular among Gujaratis, who worship Krishna as 'the butter thief'.

Also popular with Gujaratis is the more recent Swaminarayan movement founded by Sahajananda Swami (1781–1830). Known as the Uddhava sampradaya, it traces its heritage to Ramanuja, and teaches a version of his 'qualified monism'. Of its several distinct branches, the largest is the globally popular BAP Swaminarayan Sanstha, known for its humanitarian projects.

South of Gujarat, in Maharashtra, Vaishnavism was particularly influenced by the northern sant tradition, to which Kabir, Mirabai and Nanak belonged and which spawned the largest Vaishnava monastic community, the Ramanandis. One early northern sant, Namdeva, helped found the Varkari tradition based in Pandhapur in Maharashtra. Its most famous saint is Tukarama (1598–1650CE). This tradition is famous for its mass pilgrimages (vari) in which the pilgrims (vakaris) walk for hundred of miles while singing and chanting.

SHAIVISM

THE SECOND LARGEST HINDU COMMUNITY IS SHAIVISM, WHOSE MEMBERS VENERATE LORD SHIVA. THERE ARE SEVERAL IMPORTANT BRANCHES, SOMETIMES NUMBERED AT SIX.

Shaivism is related to Shaktism through shared links with the Agamas and other Tantric texts. More than Vaishnavism, Shaivism is associated with value-reversing Shramana traditions, and Shiva himself is depicted as a renounced yogi. However, he is also shown as a satisfied householder, sitting with his wife and family.

Particularly through this latter, benign form, Shiva worship has been integrated into orthodox, brahminical Hinduism. In the less scholarly 'village Hinduism', many guardian deities are forms of Bhairava, a fierce manifestation of Shiva. Shaiva texts mention various forms of Shiva (avirbhavas), but there is little reference to avataras as in Vaishnavism. Important forms include Rudra (in angry mood), Nataraja (the King of Dance) and the cylindrical lingam, symbolizing Shiva as the supreme male, generative principle.

Below The Pashupati Temple, Kathmandu. The 'Pashupatis' may be the oldest Shaiva community.

EARLY HISTORY

The roots of Shaivism are anchored in prehistoric India. Archaeological sites at Harappa and Mohenjo-daro revealed seals possibly depicting Lord Shiva. In the Rig Veda, he is mentioned indirectly as Rudra. The oldest Puranic story recounts Shiva's destruction of the sacrificial arena of Daksha, Brahma's son. Shiva was infuriated when his wife, Sati, gave up her life after being slighted by her father, Daksha. This gruesome tale concludes with Shiva's reconciliation with his father-in-law, symbolizing not only conflict between householders and renouncers but also their complementary roles.

Around the time of the Gupta Empire (320–500CE), renouncer ideals were incorporated into the orthodox ashrama system through the sannyasin. At the same time, temples installed the lingam, and brahmins inducted Shiva into householder rites. As Shiva was consolidated within the Vedic religion, renouncer traditions based

Above A painting of four grandmasters of the Shaiva Siddhanta tradition, prevalent in South India.

their practices mainly on Tantra, which they considered divinely inspired and superior to the Vedas. Tantric Shaivism evolved through two main paths; the higher ati-marga, exclusively for renouncers, and the mantra marg, open also to householders.

ASCETIC TRADITIONS

Pashupati Shaivism is perhaps the oldest school to venerate Shiva. Following the path of ati-marga, it aims at liberation through complete detachment. Important sub-sects included the Lakulas, who smeared themselves in ashes from funeral pyres and wielded a staff capped with a human skull. Well-known today are the naked Naga Babas, frequently photographed bathing at the Kumbha Mela fair. Though sadhus are characterized as peace-loving, the Nagas were unabashedly militant, fighting with the Muslims, British and rival sects. The Nagas are still sub-divided into Akharas, 'regiments', though their tridents and swords are now largely symbolic.

Also important are the Tantric yogis of the Natha tradition of Gorakshanatha, who lived sometime

Above In Karnataka, devotees worship a sand lingam on the beach at Gokarna, home to many Shaiva groups, including 'Shaiva Advaita' and the 'Lingayats'.

between the 8th and 11th centuries CE. He stressed the discipline of hatha-yoga, and his teachings influenced early bhakti saints such as Kabir. Another sect, the Aghoris, deliberately transgress social taboos, convinced that by 'reversing all values' they hasten enlightenment. Aghoris eat meat and drink alcohol, whereas most sadhus are vegetarian and teetotal. However, many Shaiva ascetics smoke marijuana, considering it a meditational aid.

SOUTHERN SHAIVISM

Subscribing to the 'path of mantras', Shaiva Siddhanta is the standard form of Shaivism in South India. It originated in Kashmir, where it espoused a personal doctrine stressing the plurality of souls. However, as monistic doctrines predominated in Kashmir, Shaiva Siddhanta migrated southward. Merging with the Tamil teachings of the 63 Nayanars (poet-saints), it absorbed

Right Sadhus carry Lord Shiva's mace towards the holy Amarnath cave. This region nurtured the scholarly lineage called Kashmiri Shaivism.

both devotional sentiment and the southern fondness for poetry. Though the system was revolutionary, stressing the equality of all before God, it was institutionalized by the Chola kings, who patronized temple worship. Shaiva Siddhanta remains strong in Tamil Nadu and Sri Lanka, where priests are drawn from select families called 'the original followers of Shiva'. The main texts are the Vedas, select Agamas (Tantras) and the Nayanmar hymns of the Thirumai.

In the southern state of Karnataka, two specific Shaiva sects are prevalent. They are Shaiva Advaita, which follows a form of Vedanta resembling Ramanuja's doctrine (Vishishtadvaita) and the Lingayats, who propound a similar doctrine of a personal God.

KASHMIRI SHAIVISM

Kashmiri Shaivism was started by Vasugupta, a 9th-century scholar divinely inspired to track down core texts called the Shiva Sutras. Its most prolific writer was Abhinavagupta (960–1020CE), who preached monism (Advaita), forcing the dualistic doctrine to shift south, carried by the Shaiva Siddhanta school. Kashmiri Shaivism is divided into four main schools, and its followers aim to 'become Shiva', regaining their universal nature. This non-dual philosophy is based on the 92 Tantras of Lord Shiva.

This highly philosophical tradition is also known as Trika, meaning 'triad', or three parts. It divides reality into Shiva, his Shakti (energy) and the Jiva (individual soul), and uses the same three-fold model to classify other concepts and its holy books. Despite many renowned gurus, geographic isolation in the Kashmir Valley and Muslim subjugation kept the tradition relatively small. Recent leaders such as Swami Lakshman Joo (1907–95) have attempted to revive it.

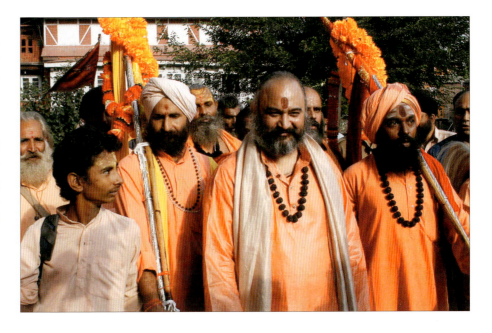

SHAKTISM

SHAKTISM IS THE THIRD LARGEST HINDU DENOMINATION. MEMBERS VENERATE 'SHAKTI' OR 'DEVI', GENERIC TERMS MEANING 'ENERGY' AND 'GODDESS'. SHE IS OFTEN ADDRESSED AS 'RESPECTED MOTHER'.

Although Shaktism embraces the three major goddesses, the respective 'shaktis' of the Trimurti, its members most often worship Shiva's consort, known as Parvati, Durga, or Kali. The worship of Sita with Rama, or Radha with Krishna, does not strictly belong to Shaktism but demonstrates the pervasive influence of the feminine deity.

Shakti ideology is closely aligned to Shaiva teachings. The two communities share Tantric sources, considering that Shiva and Shakti embody complementary male and female principles. Shakti doctrine emphasizes the unity between spirit (Shiva) and matter (Shakti), and accentuates the creative impetus of matter rather than its

Below During Durga Puja, a Bengali woman respectfully touches the forehead of the goddess.

ability to delude and degrade. For this reason, Shaktas worship for material benefit as well as liberation, and are prevalent among many village practitioners. Notable features are animal sacrifice and documented accounts of human immolation. In some communities, such as the Nambudhiri brahmins of Kerala, the sacrificial blood has been substituted with a symbolic red powder.

HISTORY
Archaeological findings suggest that Shaktism dates to prehistoric times. The Goddess features in the Vedas themselves, especially as Prithivi, the earth, and Sarasvati, the sacred river. In the later Epics and Puranas she appears as Durga, and in the non-Vedic Tantras, she is elevated to the role of the Supreme. Shaktism, placing less value on high, theological lineages, has been

Above In India's north-eastern state of Tripura, priests from the Ramakrishna Mission revere a five-year-old kumari ('virgin princess'), thought to embody the goddess Durga.

passed down in a broader fashion, through Tantra, Shaivism, and local, village custom. None the less, Shaktism has been brought within the orthodox fold, particularly by Shankara, and by modern thinkers like Ramakrishna and Aurobindo. More recently, women's liberation movements have adopted fiercer forms of Devi as their patron deity, and wherever Hindus have settled worldwide, there are a number of prominent Devi temples.

Shaktism is less clearly defined than other Hindu traditions. The forms of the Goddess can be roughly divided into three categories: the benign consorts of the Trimurti, especially Parvati; the warlike form of Durga; and the ghastly Kali, and similar forms such as Chamundi. To these three may be added a fourth category encompassing local goddesses, anionic symbols such as stones, tridents and yantras, and female mediums who possess their followers.

REPRESENTATIONS OF THE GODDESS

The goddess, representing Nature, is a contradictory figure: on the one hand she is kind, motherly, and bountiful; on the other, she appears cruel, scornful and malevolent. While the high-ranking, benign and submissive forms have been assimilated into the orthodox framework, the hot-blooded remain radical and fiercely independent, often dominating their partners, if they indeed have one.

In popular, devotional Hinduism, even Kali is relatively mild, and the goddess is worshipped in a manner similar to Vaishnavism and orthodox traditions: through puja, arati, and festivals such as Navaratri. The main pilgrimage sites (pithas) are linked to the legend of Sati, and the places where her bodily parts fell as Shiva carried her body, dancing in wild lamentation. Principal texts include the Devi Purana, the Kalika Purana and the Markandeya Purana. Famous tales

Below A gruesome painting of the goddess Kali during the ritual 'offering to the jackal'.

include the death of Sati, her subsequent marriage as Parvati, and Durga slaying the buffalo demon.

TANTRIC TRADITIONS

Within Tantric traditions, there are two main groups. The first 'family' (kula) is the Kali-kula, focusing on 13 forms of the black goddess. Tantric texts describe macabre rites such as the 'offering to the jackal'. The western branch venerates Kubjika, 'the crooked one', associated with the Tantric practice of kundalini-yoga and its six chakras, or energy centres. The prevalent worship of Durga in eastern regions such as Bihar, Bengal and Assam, is highly influenced by the Tantrics, though Ramakrishna and Vivekananda tried to assimilate Shakti worship into a more respectable mainstream.

The second family, prevalent in South India, is called Shrikula and worships Lalita Tripasundari, a Tantric form of the goddess Lakshmi. She is worshipped through the sacred diagram, the Shri Yantra, and by chanting a 15-syllable mantra. An important sub-group, called Shri Vidya ('knowledge of Lakshmi'), considers the

Above An 11th-century, South Indian murti of the benign goddess Lalita, a tantric form of Lakshmi.

goddess to be Supreme. This Tantric tradition, severed from its Kashmiri roots, was adapted by the Smarta lineage of Shankara, thus aligning it with orthodox brahminical values. It has a complex theology about the precise relationships between the three main deities, whose highest forms are called Maha-Lakshmi, Maha-Sarasvati and Maha-Kali.

VILLAGE HINDUISM

In much village Hinduism, the worship of Shakti, along with forms of Shiva such as Bhairava, often predominates. Village deities usually fall in the category of 'hot' deities, associated with fever, disease and premature death. They need to be cooled, or appeased, through sacrifice. Many of these minor goddesses are connected to the greater goddesses, and some – such as Draupadi – span both the high and low spheres of Hinduism. In its many forms, veneration of the goddess pervades Hinduism, attesting to a broad view that the Supreme embraces both male and female.

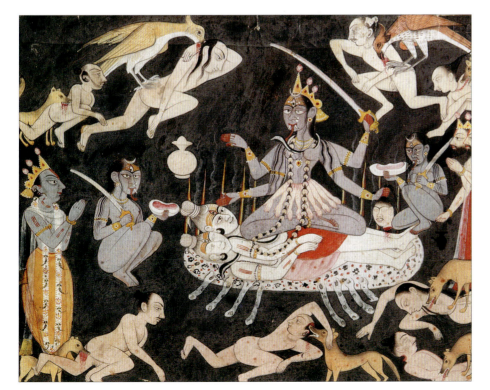

THE SMARTA TRADITION

FOR EMPHASIZING SMRITI TEXTS, MEMBERS OF THE FOURTH MAIN HINDU COMMUNITY ARE KNOWN AS SMARTAS. A SUB-SECT IS SHANKARA'S ADVAITA SAMPRADAYA, WHICH VENERATES FIVE OR SIX DEITIES.

Smartas are traditional, brahminical and strict about scriptural rules and regulations, especially as found in the karma-kanda section of the Vedas. They thus distance themselves from brahmins favouring Jainism, Buddhism or Tantra. Today, the Smarta community is largely associated with the Advaita philosophy of Shankara. However, not all Smartas subscribe to Advaita.

SHANKARA'S TRADITION
Shankara's advaitins claim that by distancing themselves from the exclusive worshippers of Vishnu, Shiva or Devi they represent the truly universal Hinduism. Following the system of panchopasana (five types of worship), they revere five deities: Vishnu, Shiva, Devi, Ganesha and Surya. Especially in the

Below In Kerala, an orthodox Smarta brahmin meticulously performs the arati ritual.

south, they also venerate Skanda through a system called Shanmata, or 'six choices'.

Shankara established the dashanam, ten orders of sannyasins, each identified by the specific suffix after the monk's names: for example, Tirtha, Bharati or Sarasvati. The sannyasins carry an ekadanda, a single rod staff symbolizing the unity of atman and Brahman. Shankara also established four monasteries (maths) corresponding to the cardinal directions: the Jyotir Math (north), Govardhana Math (east), Shringeri Math (south), and Dwaraka Math (west). The successive heads of these and other monasteries are also called Shankaracharya, after the original founder. Shankara himself is often called Adi Shankara ('the first Shankara') to distinguish him from his successors.

The tradition teaches about an impersonal Supreme and exalts jnana-yoga, the path of knowledge.

Above The Sri Adhi Sankarar Temple, Kanyakumari, Tamil Nadu, named after Adi Shankara, who founded what is now the largest sub-group within the Smarta community.

Sannyasa, or external renunciation, is essential for spiritual progress. Many modern leaders and movements claim to follow Shankara's Advaita Vedanta, including the Ramakrishna Math, the Chinmaya Mission and the Divine Life Society. The celebrated saint, Ramana Maharshi, though not a formal Smarta, also taught the Advaita doctrine.

COMPETING TRADITIONS
Differences between Hindu traditions focus on the nature and identity of God. Shankara's monists advocate worship of many deities as a means toward inclusivity. Monotheists among the Vaishnavas, Shaivas and Shaktas argue that their idea of one Supreme Deity is not necessarily divisive or sectarian.

Most competition occurs between the Shaivas and Vaishnavas. Supporters of Vishnu tell the story of Bhrigu, elected by companion sages to ascertain which of the Trimurti was influenced purely by goodness (sattva), and devoid of passion (rajas) or darkness (tamas). When insulted by Bhrigu, Brahma was infuriated, but managed to restrain himself. When similarly insulted, Shiva raised his trident to kill Bhrigu, only to be spared embarrassment by the soothing pleas of Parvati. However, when Bhrigu kicked Vishnu on the chest, the four-handed deity apologized for hurting Bhrigu's tender foot.

Naturally, Shaivas tell another story. For them, Vishnu, plunging downward in his boar incarnation, and Brahma rising high on his celestial swan, both failed to find the

Above A 20th-century painting of Rama, the seventh incarnation of Vishnu, praying to Lord Shiva. Stories like these fuel debates as to who is Supreme.

limits of a vertical pillar of fire. That fiery lingam revealed itself as the transcendent and unfathomable Shiva, who was therefore supreme. Shiva's consort, Devi, has sometimes been similarly elevated, above her husband, to the highest status.

In addition to Vishnu, Shiva and Devi, Smartas worship Surya, Ganesha and Skanda. None the less, these deities also have their own more exclusive traditions. Surya was popular with kings, and Lord Rama's dynasty traced its ancient lineage to the sun-god. Today, Surya is rarely worshipped exclusively. Smartas consider him to be an aspect of Brahman, Vaishnavas a form of Vishnu (Surya-Narayana), and Shaivas as a manifestation of Shiva. He is also worshipped through recitation of the Gayatri mantra and, in the south, observance of the Pongal festival.

The ubiquitous Ganesha is most often a functional deity, widely venerated prior to any ritual or worship. As a son of Shiva and Parvati, he is also dear to their respective followers, the Shaivas and Shaktas. Despite

this, the Ganapatyas consider the elephant-headed deity (Ganapati) their main focus of worship, and sometimes the Supreme. Likewise, his brother Skanda has his own, autonomous traditions, which worship him more exclusively, sometimes as the Supreme and usually by the Tamil name, Murugan.

Below Jayendra Sarasvati, Shankaracharya of the Kanchi monastery: not one of the four cardinal centres, but sacred to many Smartas.

SMARTA SECTS

The term Smarta (or 'Smartha' in the south) is often used to refer to Shankara's lineage. More broadly, it defines any orthodox brahmin, particularly those revering the Shruti, the original Vedas, and following the Shrauta rituals such as the Vedic sacrifice (yajna). Today, the Shrauta tradition is followed by only a few brahmins, such as the Nambudhiri community in Kerala. Many Smartas marry only within their own community.

One important Smarta community is the 'Saraswats'. Originally strict Shaivas, in the last few centuries they became more eclectic, with some adopting the Vaishnava Dvaita philosophy of Madhva. Saraswat Brahmins also form a significant proportion of Hindus in Kashmir. These 'Kashmiri pandits' claim descent from Aryans living near the River Sarasvati and differentiate themselves from other Saraswat Brahmins by primarily worshipping the goddess Sarasvati. The Gaud Saraswat brahmins, residing on the western coast of India, claim decent from these Kashmiri brahmins.

IMPORTANT SCHOLARS

HINDUISM IS NOT A UNIFIED SYSTEM OF BELIEF, NOR DOES IT BOAST ONE FOUNDER. NONE THE LESS, IT POSITIVELY EMBRACES THEORY, EXEMPLIFIED BY MANY FOUNDERS AND THEIR DOCTRINAL LINEAGES.

Much modern Hindu practice rests on theological foundations laid by medieval scholars, who established sampradayas (disciplic successions) to perpetuate their specific teachings. These institutional leaders were often awarded the suffix acharya, or 'one who teaches by example'. The most prominent appeared in three main traditions: the Smartas, Shaivas and Vaishnavas. Shakta doctrine is largely derived from the complementary Shaiva School and their shared Tantric roots.

The first great theologian was Shankara (780–812BCE). Legend holds that he was born of Smarta parents in Kerala and, after taking sannyasa when just eight years old, journeyed widely to defeat contesting scholars. He established ten

Above In Bedford Square, London, this plaque commemorates Ram Mohan Roy, the 19th-century intellectual who contested much traditional Indian thought.

monastic orders and four centres representing the cardinal directions. He is called Adi Shankara to differentiate him from the later pontiffs, also called 'the Shankaracharya'. In founding the Advaita school of Vedanta, Adi Shankara extended the teachings of Gaudapada, his guru's own mentor. Teaching Vedic non-dualism, which some claim resembles the Buddhist doctrine of voidism, he re-established the credibility of the Vedas, thus checking the spread of Jainism and Buddhism. He also reconciled disparate Hindu groups within a reformed Smarta community.

SHAIVISM AND TANTRA

Abhinavagupta (*c.*960–1020CE) was perhaps the most prolific writer within Kashmiri Shaivism. He propounded a form of Advaita philosophy and wrote the multi-volume Tantra-loka, helping transform the marginalized Tantric ideology into a more respectable, brahmin-led religion. He also wrote a highly respected book on rasa (spiritual sentiment) as previously discussed by the dramatist

Left Bhagavan Swaminarayana (left) with his principal disciple Aksharbrahma Gunatitanand Swami. Bhagvan Swaminarayan founded the Swaminarayan sampradaya.

Bharata Muni. Abhinavagupta teachings became central to the Shaiva 'Trika' philosophy and the Tantric 'Kula' sects.

A further key Shaivite theologian was the 13th-century Shrikanta who established a branch of Vedanta philosophy replicating Ramanuja's, but substituting Vishnu with Shiva. Shrikanta firmly located Shaiva philosophy within an orthodox Vedantic framework. In the 16th century, Appaya Dikshita (1520–1593) used these teachings to revive Shaivism in South India, especially in the face of Vaishnava domination.

RAMANUJA AND MADHVA

Born in Tamilnadu, Ramanuja (1017–1137) became the most important acharya for the Shri Vaishnavas. He propounded the branch of Vedanta doctrine called Vishishtadvaita (qualified monism), which addressed seven apparent shortcomings in Shankara's notion of maya (illusion). Ramanuja accepted some unity between the self and God, but also taught devotion to a separate, personal God, Vishnu. He compared the universe to the Lord's body and taught that salvation was attained though God's grace, won exclusively through prapatti, whole-hearted surrender. The emancipated soul enters Vishnu's abode (Vaikunthaloka) and in a spiritual form serves the Lord and his consorts, thus attaining the ultimate goal of human life.

Another Vaishnava scholar, Madhva (1238–1317), was born near Udupi in present-day Karnataka. Considered an incarnation of Hanuman, son of the wind-god Vayu, he is credited with superhuman feats such as eating 4,000 bananas in one sitting and freeing a disciple from a Bengali tiger. A powerful, uncompromising figure, Madhva opposed Shankara's doctrine more vehemently than Ramanuja and founded the branch of Vedanta called Dvaita

(dualism). He is perhaps the only Hindu teacher to propound, for some souls, an eternal hell. Madhva started his own temple in Udupi by installing a beautiful image of Krishna found aboard a distressed ship which he rescued off the nearby coast. Udupi remains an important centre for Krishna worship.

LATER SCHOLARS

Chaitanya (1486–1534) claimed disciplic descent from Madhva's line, and his teachings were written by the six Goswamis. Most important were Rupa Goswami, who wrote a canonical text called 'The Ocean of Devotional Nectar' and his nephew, Jiva, who founded the branch of Vedanta called 'inconceivable simultaneous oneness and difference'. It was Baladeva (1600–1768) who wrote the official bhasya (commentary) to establish the authenticity of Bengali Vaishnavism. His theology draws from all four Vaishnava lineages.

Chaitanya is reputed to have met another great bhakti saint called Vallabha. Although they differed on some points, they both advocated bhakti as the sole means toward

Above Several scholars elaborated on the main theologians. Here, Rupa Goswami writes the devotional texts underpinning Bengali Vaishnavism.

salvation. They agreed that the ultimate goal of life, higher even than moksha, is eternal service to Krishna and participation in his eternal pastimes. Vallabha laid great stress on a life of unmotivated love for God and started the 'Pushti Marg', the 'path of nourishment'. He claimed participation in an ancient lineage going back to Vishnu Swami. Vallabha is most popular among the Gujarati community.

Also in Gujarat, Sahajananda Swami founded the Swami Narayana Mission. He came in the Ramanuja's line and modified his Vishishtadvaita doctrine, thus starting the Uddhava sampradaya. He appeared during an era of social reform, when intellectuals such as Rama Mohan Roy responded to contact with Western thought. Despite their endeavours, the most influential theologies today remain Shankara's monism and a range of monotheistic doctrines derived from Ramanuja.

THE BHAKTI SAINTS

DURING THE ERA OF MUSLIM RULE, THE BHAKTI SAINTS DREW ON
THE SENTIMENT OF THE SOUTHERN POET-SAINTS, VEDANTIC AND
TANTRIC THEOLOGY AND THE TEACHINGS OF OTHER RELIGIONS.

Theistic devotion flourished in South India through Vaishnava saints called the 12 Alvars (6th–9th centuries) and their Shaiva counterparts, the 63 Nayanmars. From 1200CE onward, aided by recent strides in theology, a devotional renaissance swept the entire subcontinent. The bhakti saints rejected the caste system and its prescriptive, brahmin-controlled ritual. Stressing personal piety and selfless devotion, they expressed their sentiment through song, poetry and music. They preferred the spirit of the law to its letter, enabling many of apparently lower status to participate, including several famous women. The exemplary lives of the bhakti saints and their inclusive teachings continue to inspire contemporary Hindus.

Below Many bhakti saints favoured a personal God. Like Surdas, Bilvamangala (shown here) was blind and yet sang of his inner, divine vision of Lord Krishna.

NORTHERN TRADITIONS

The 'Sant Mat' was a loosely knit group of teachers prominent in northern India from about the 13th century onward. The movement was eclectic, ignoring differences in class and religion, and drawing from Sufism, Vaishnava devotion, and the ascetic and Shaiva 'Natha' tradition. Namdev (1270–1350) was one of the first saints, whose influence later extended to western India. Kabir (1440–1518), whose followers are called Kabir Panthis, was born a lowly weaver and his acerbic poems are still revered by Sikhs, Hindus and Muslims. Nanak, founder of the Sikh religion, also appeared in the sant tradition.

In contrast to the sant tradition itself, some bhakti saints favoured a personal God, usually as Rama or Krishna. Surdas (1479–1584), though born blind, is celebrated for his mystic vision and his songs glorify-

Above Kabir was part of the northern sant tradition which favoured an impersonal Supreme.

ing Krishna's playful pranks. Tulsidas (1511–1637) wrote a Hindi version of the Ramayana, known as the 'Rama Carita Manas'. The bhakti saint Mirabai (1547–1614), though born a Rajasthani princess, from childhood considered Krishna to be her real husband and was persecuted by her own family. Her songs and poems are still recited by Krishna devotees.

EASTERN INDIA

One of the most influential bhakti saints was Chaitanya (1486–1534), founder of Bengali Vaishnavism. He drew from the romantic poetry of the celebrated Jayadeva of Orissa, who wrote effusively of the divine love between Krishna and his consort Radha. Though in his youth a brilliant scholar, Chaitanya later considered logic incomplete without devotion. Famous for his spiritual ecstasies, he was later deemed a dual avatara of Radha and Krishna. Despite opposition from orthodox brahmins and local Muslim officials, Chaitanya's multi-caste followers expressed devotion through public singing and dancing.

WESTERN INDIA
One of Chaitanya's contemporaries was Vallabha (1481–1533), a Telugu-speaking brahmin whose parents hailed from modern-day Andhra Pradesh. Vallabha founded the path of nourishment, which affirms the role of Krishna's grace in attaining salvation. Walking barefoot, he completed three pilgrimage tours of India and finally renounced the world. However, his lineage now prohibits adopting sannyasa in the current age. There are many Pushti-marg followers within Rajastan, Gujarat, East Africa and the United Kingdom. They specifically worship Krishna as Nathji, the lifter of Govardhana Hill, and as Bal (baby) Krishna.

Namdev and contemporaries such as Jnanadev became instrumental in establishing an important devotional tradition on Maharashtra, Western India. This Varkari community venerates the deity of Krishna known as Vitthala (or Vitobha) in the town of Pandharpur. Its most important figure is Tukarama (1608–1649), who apparently instructed Shivaji, the famous resistance fighter and scourge of the Mughal dynasty. Tukarama is also famed for his kirtana (congregational music), performed with a roaming entourage of 14 musicians.

Other saints in the West include Narsi Mehta, who wrote many Gujarati songs in praise of Radha and Krishna. Later Gujarati saints include Sahajananda Swami, who started the Swaminarayan mission,

Above A statue of Mirabai, the most renowned woman among the medieval bhakti saints.

and Jalaram Bapu (1799–1881), a devotee of Rama dedicated to feeding the poor. Like bhakti saints before them, they taught of the equality of all and the redeeming power of loving service to God.

Below The bhakti saint Chaitanya is remembered for his public displays of ecstatic singing and dancing.

ATTEMPTS TO REFORM HINDUISM

SOME GROUPS HAVE EXPLICITLY PROMOTED SOCIAL AND THEOLOGICAL REFORM, NOTABLY THE 19TH-CENTURY 'REFORM MOVEMENTS', WHICH COMPLEMENTED THE MAIN TRADITIONAL DENOMINATIONS.

Above Jain nuns on the road in Karnataka. Jainism evolved into a distinct tradition by rejecting orthodox scriptural authority.

Like all religions, Hinduism has struggled to maintain tradition and simultaneously respond to change. Some groups close to Hinduism, such as Jainism and Buddhism, evolved into distinct traditions, particularly though their rejection of Vedic authority. Internally, Hinduism has long seen tensions between its orthodox, ritualistic Brahmanism and its ascetic and antisocial 'Shramana' strands. Through reform, Hinduism has tried to reconcile these polarities and other counter-poised perspectives.

Early reformers included the first millennium devotional poets of South India and the 12th century Lingayats. From 1200CE, the bhakti saints contested the restrictive, brahmin-controlled religion, seeking instead an inclusive egalitarianism.

Ironically, some became theologically sectarian, applauding their own views on the nature and identity of God. However, despite such diversity of belief, Hinduism has little aspiration to rigid uniformity. It was only with the arrival of other, adversarial faiths that it felt prompted to define itself as a single, homogenous religion, distinct from others. The umbrella term 'Hinduism' was first coined during British rule.

THE BRITISH IN INDIA

Early British colonials were often fascinated by Hinduism, to the chagrin of some church leaders. One high-ranking British officer was dubbed 'Hindoo Stuart' for his adoption of Hindu practices, such as bathing daily in the River Ganges. Policy remained liberal until 1813, when the British government conceded to demands that Christian missionaries be allowed to practise and preach in India. As Victorian attitudes stiffened, academics and government officials also aspired to convert and civilize. Under Thomas Babington Macaulay, educational policy was deliberately designed to win over the brahmin, intellectual class. As Hindu thinkers engaged with Western thought, they reflected on their collective identity, a trend exacerbated by social unrest and an upsurge of nationalism. This was particularly prevalent among the 'bhadraloka', the educated class of Calcutta (now Kolkata), the British capital of India until 1912.

THE BRAHMO SAMAJ

Rama Mohan Roy founded the Brahmo Sabha in 1828. He contested the doctrine of reincarnation and fought to abolish traditional but often degraded practices, including sati, caste, polygamy, image worship, and child marriage. His ideas, especially on worship, were drawn largely from Christianity. He was succeeded by Devendranatha Tagore, who renamed the society the Brahmo

Left Rabindranath Tagore, poet, teacher and philosopher, reads to a group of students. His brother, Devendranath, also tried to reform Hinduism.

Above Members of the Arya Samaj, a prominent 'reform movement', protest against a proposed abbatoir in East Delhi.

Samaj, and favoured the secular philosophies of Locke and Hume. Trying to reform the Brahmo Samaj, he worked briefly with another notable figure, Keshab Chandra Sen. Both eventually left to establish their own movements. Today the Brahmo Samaj has a few thousand members and relatively small influence. It only marginally succeeded in its aspirations to blend Hindu metaphysics with Christian morality.

THE ARYA SAMAJ

In 1875, Swami Dayananda Sarasvati founded the Arya Samaj as a radical reform movement. He wished to stem the Christian missionary onslaught and to return to the ancient Vedic tradition. He therefore sought to purge Hinduism of what he considered later additions, such as pilgrimage, image worship and ritual bathing. Although emphasizing the ancient Vedic tradition, Dayananda also sought to modernize Hinduism and to re-absorb Hindus who had converted to Islam or Christianity. His movement, concerned about the influence of 'other religions', paved the way for political activists striving to re-establish Hindu rule in India.

Right A sannyasi of the Ramakrishna movement, founded to present Hinduism in a way relevant to the modern world.

The Arya Samaj is still active worldwide. Members follow 'ten principles' and perform worship by murmuring the Gayatri mantra and conducting the sacred fire ceremony.

THE RAMAKRISHNA MISSION

Ramakrishna was born into a poor but orthodox Bengali Brahmin family and became the priest at the Kali temple near Calcutta (Kolkata). He was later initiated as a sannyasin and experienced mystical visions, especially of Devi, the Goddess. He was profoundly influenced by Islam and Christianity and emphasized the universality of religion. Favouring a monistic doctrine, he preached that 'jiva is Shiva', or 'the soul is God'. He met contemporary reformers, amongst whom Keshab Chandra Sen first made him known to the world.

However, it was Vivekananda (1863–1902) who was to make Ramakrishna world famous. Born into the wealthy Dutt family, and named Narendranath, he joined the Brahmo Samaj but later became Ramakrishna's favourite disciple.

He later received the title Swami Vivekananda. He presented a revised version of Advaita philosophy, called neo-Vedanta, and impressed the Western world in his presentation to the World Parliament of Religions in Chicago in 1893. He travelled extensively, promoting wide reform, and establishing the Ramakrishna Mission, still well known for its social and educational programmes.

NATIONALISM AND MODERN REFORM

The rather secular reform movements were the forerunners of nationalism. Mohandas Gandhi (1869–1947), although a politician, saw himself primarily as a reformer and educator. His ultimate aim was to re-establish on earth 'Rama-rajya', the reign of Lord Rama. He was opposed to British oppression and tried to free his country from urbanization and unhealthy economic dependence. His reform also extended to Hindu society and like many reformers, both before and after him, he challenges the hereditary caste system, untouchability and their attendant social ills.

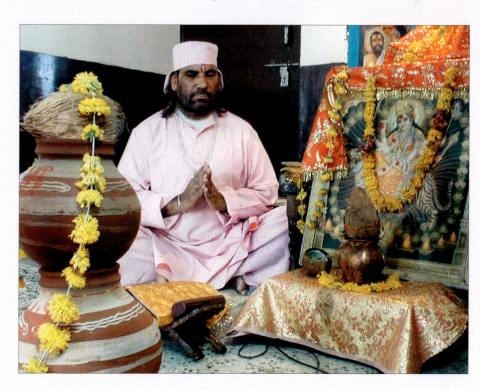

SOCIO-POLITICAL MOVEMENTS

SOME LEADERS AND MOVEMENTS HAVE ADOPTED SOCIO-POLITICAL ROLES. MUCH CURRENT DEBATE CENTRES ON WHETHER HINDU IDEALS POSITIVELY INFORM ISSUES OR ARE BEING MISAPPROPRIATED.

Some reform movements, such as the Brahmo Samaj, assimilated Western ideals. Gandhi, though in many ways traditional, was also amenable to outside ideas. The Arya Samaj opposed Western modernization more robustly, and sought to reclaim 'converts to other faiths'. These diverse initiatives spawned several nationalist movements, many of which are still influential today.

In 1909, to give Hindus a unified political voice, Arya Samaj leaders headed by Mohan Malaviha founded the Hindu Mahasabha, 'The Great Hindu Assembly'. The Mahasabha declared 'Hindustan' the land of the

Above Head of India's Shiva Sena Party, Bal Thackeray, protests against a perceived insult to freedom-fighter Vir Savarkar.

Hindus and demanded governance according to Hindu law. Its greatest advocate, Vir Savarkar (1883–1966), coined the word Hindutva, or 'Hinduness', to differentiate the socio-cultural aspects of Hindu India from the religion itself. Today the word is often associated with Hindu nationalism.

THE BJP AND THE RSS

After partition, the Mahasabha championed reunification, with the slogan Akhand Bharat, 'Undivided India'. When East Pakistan, now Bangladesh, violently evicted Hindus, the Jana Sangha (People's Party of India) was formed to promote a strong pro-Hindu, anti-Muslim agenda. In 1980, several of its splinter groups coalesced to create an umbrella group for political activism, the Bharatiya Janata Party (BJP). Though repeatedly using the religious theme of Rama-rajya, the exemplary reign of Lord Rama – as applauded by Gandhi – critics claim its agenda is political rather than religious. The BJP's youth movement is named Shiva Sen, 'the army of Shiva', after the great Marathi resistance fighter called Shivaji.

Many members of the BJP are also closely connected to the RSS, the Rashtriya Swayamsevak Sangha or 'the National Self Help Association. It was founded in 1925 by K.B. Hedgewar, a long-serving member of the Hindu Mahasabha. He was succeeded by M.S. Golwalkar, who declared that the Hindu nation had a divine mandate to re-spiritualize the world through the agency of the RSS. Today, it has grown into perhaps the most powerful and controversial Hindu organization, with a membership of over five million. It declares its aims as cultural.

THE VISHVA HINDU PARISHAD

In 1964, a prominent sannyasin named Swami Chinmayananda and other religious leaders founded the Vishva Hindu Parishad, 'the Hindu

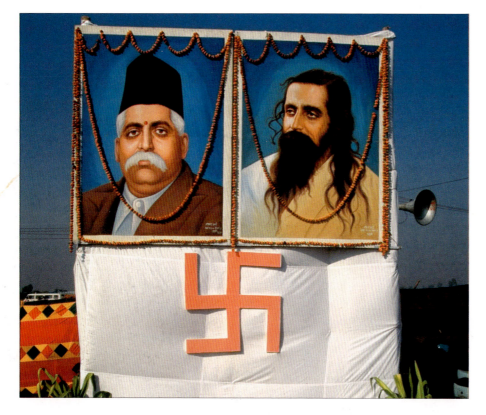

Below Portraits on a banner from 1995 of RSS founder K.B. Hedgewar during the society's annual function in India.

Left Hindu youths climbed the Babri Mosque in 1992 before supporting activists demolished it, claiming it had been built provocatively over Lord Rama's birth-site.

World Association. It aims to reawaken Hindu consciousness and to promote global co-operation between Hindus. Drawing deeply on Vivekananda's doctrine, the VHP propounds a universal Hinduism, whilst stressing – some say paradoxically – the pre-eminence of Indian culture and nationality. To refute the debatable Aryan invasion theory and raise the status of Hinduism, VHP writers favourably compare India's ancient scientific achievements with modern technology feats.

The VHP, through its numerous initiatives worldwide, continues to influence the emerging identity of contemporary Hinduism. It cultivates a common identity by bringing Hindu communities together, sponsoring festivals, and running study camps for youths. Feminist writers in particular have charged it with promoting a narrow, right-wing and aggressive sectarianism. Its youth wing, called the Bajrang Dal, bears the slogan 'Warriors of the Hindutva Revolution'.

COMMUNAL VIOLENCE

Nationalistic tendencies continued throughout and beyond the 20th century. On 6 December 1992, a procession of VHP activists destroyed the Babri Mosque built over Lord Rama's birthplace in Ayodhya.

Hindu nationalism again came to world attention in 1998, after the BJP won national elections in India. In 2002, a train carrying pilgrims from a ceremony to commemorate the rebuilding of the Rama temple was incinerated by a Muslim mob at Godhra in Gujarat. Both the BJP and VHP were blamed for organizing the retaliatory violence directed at Muslims across the state.

Such events highlight the continuing problems of politicizing Hinduism, and of using resentment fermented over seven centuries of foreign domination. A parallel but antithetical approach has been to promote Hinduism as universal, transcending even its Indian roots. The debate raises the question of the ideal relationship between Hinduism's non-sectarian spirituality and its unavoidable social, political and historical dimensions.

GANDHI'S CONTRIBUTION

The contribution of Gandhi, variously considered saint, social reformer and politician, has been the subject of much debate. His early years were dedicated to fighting social ills, such as poverty, untouchability and alcoholism. In 1928, he began earnest opposition to British rule. He drew from traditional Hindu teachings, but also amended them. His civil disobedience movement was based on Satyagraha, 'adherence to truth', and on ahimsa, 'non-violence'. Some of his contemporaries claimed that total non-violence was neither practical, as for Jews in Nazi Germany, nor consistent with the ancient warrior ethic of protecting the innocent. Ironically, Gandhi was heartbroken at the partition of India and the ensuing bloodshed. Though many Hindus still regard him affectionately as the father of the nation, others feel that he made Hinduism inordinately passive. Nevertheless, his ideals on economic reform and social equity are still widely admired, and were emulated by later social reformers such as Martin Luther King.

Right In 1931, Gandhi arrives at 10 Downing Street to meet prime minister Ramsay MacDonald.

RECENT SAINTS AND SPIRITUAL FIGURES

UNLIKE GANDHI AND OTHERS, SOME HINDU LEADERS AVOIDED ALL CONTACT WITH POLITICAL LIFE. FOCUSING ON SPIRITUALITY, THEY HAD A QUITE DIFFERENT BUT EQUALLY POWERFUL IMPACT.

Above A photograph of Shri Aurobindo, who turned away from political activism to embrace spiritual reform.

As a way of life, Hinduism advocates that spiritual values should inform all areas of human endeavour. At the same time, texts stipulate that its spiritual leadership must remain pure and detached, beyond the grip of power, position and sensuality. Hence, many spiritual leaders relinquished social and political aspirations to dedicate themselves solely to self-realization and educating others.

AUROBINDO GHOSH
(1872–1950)

After graduating from the university of Cambridge, England, Aravinda Ghosh returned to India with nationalist sympathies. He founded

Below Shri Ramana Maharshi receives offerings from admirers at his hermitage.

a radical newspaper, and named it Bande Mataram, 'I bow to the Motherland', after the popular, militant slogan directed against British oppression. He was later confined to prison, where he heard God exhorting him to relinquish politics and dedicate his life to spiritual upliftment. After his release, he went into self-imposed exile in the French colony of Pondicherry, to devote his life to yoga and writing on spiritual matters. His ashram attracted many visitors from India and abroad.

Aurobindo, as he became known, attempted to formulate an 'integral yoga', which synthesized Hindu spirituality with modern ideas and social activism. He blended ancient Hindu spirituality with modern belief in biological and social evolution,

stimulating interest among artists and intellectuals. After his death, his disciples were headed by his closest spiritual collaborator, Mirra Alfassa, a Parisian woman of Egyptian and Turkish descent. Known affectionately as 'The Mother', she helped develop Auroville as a model city for the modern world. The work continues today.

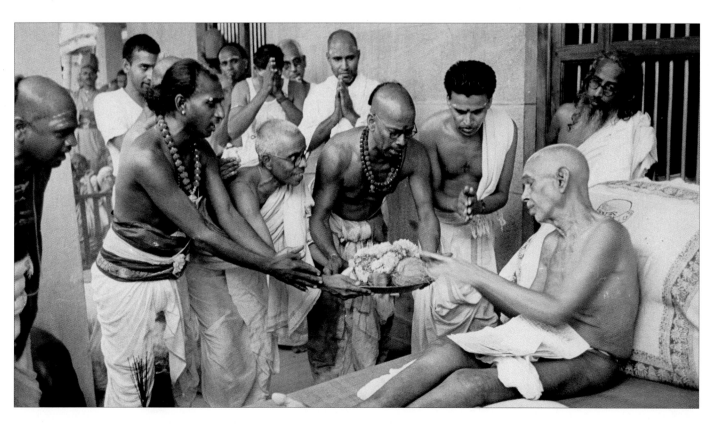

FAMOUS QUOTES

Hindu saints and gurus have diverse different teachings, but a recurrent theme is the primary need for self-realization and personal improvement before seeking to correct the world. Below are some relevant quotes:

'We must return to and seek the sources of life and strength within ourselves. It is the spiritual revolution we foresee and the material is only its shadow.' (*Shri Aurobindo*)

'Wanting to reform the world without discovering one's true self is like trying to cover the world with leather to avoid the pain of walking on stones and thorns. It is much simpler to wear shoes!' (*Ramana Maharshi*)

'Advancement of human civilization depends not on industrial enterprise, but on possession of natural wealth and food, which is all supplied by the Supreme Personality of Godhead so that we may save time for self-realization and success in the human form'. (*Bhaktivedanta Swami*)

RAMANA MAHARSI (1879–1950)
'The sage of Arunachal', Ramana Maharshi, was a widely recognized Hindu mystic who attracted followers from both East and West. After a near-death experience in which he perceived the self distinct from the body, he ran away from home, becoming a renunciant when only 14.

Despite his observing a vow of silence, people flocked to him for guidance. He established a mountain ashram, frequented by influential people, including Somerset Maugham, whose 1944 novel *The Razor's Edge* was influenced by Ramana. The ashram became renowned for a deep sense of peace and tranquillity. Ramana

is credited with establishing the relevance of the Advaita philosophy to the modern world. Though his teaching is associated with jnana-yoga, he highly recommended bhakti, and approved of a variety of paths and practices. He considered humility to be the most esteemed personal quality. Ramana was noted for his love of animals and his assertion that liberation was possible for them too.

A.C. BHAKTIVEDANTA SWAMI PRABHUPADA (1896-1977)
Bhaktivedanta Swami was born into a traditional Bengali Vaishnava family. He was named Abhay, 'one who is fearless', and the family astrologer predicted his future greatness. As a student, he was a follower of Gandhi. Shortly after marriage, his spiritual teacher suggested that spiritual life was too important to wait for a favourable political context, and that Abhay should teach Chaitanya's message in English.

Abhay was committed to family responsibilities, but eventually took sannyasa at the age of 63, receiving the name A.C. Bhaktivedanta Swami.

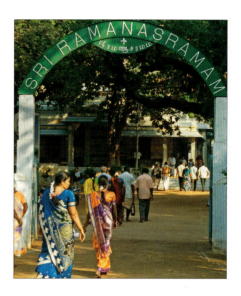

Above To share their specific teachings and insights, gurus often start their own communities. Here pilgrims enter the Shri Ramana Ashram in South India.

In 1965 he secured a free passage to the USA aboard a cargo ship. Despite poverty, obscurity and an unfamiliar New York culture, he attracted followers by chanting the now-famous Hare Krishna mantra. In 1966 he founded the International Society for Krishna Consciousness (ISKCON).

Set amidst the hippie counterculture, his society burgeoned into one of the most authentic of the new Hindu-related movements. Known affectionately as Shrila Prabhupada, he taught devotion to a personal God, established over 100 ashrams worldwide and translated over 70 Hindu texts. He accredited his success to simply having faith in the words of his own spiritual preceptor. He passed away in 1977 and was succeeded by a governing body of leading disciples. His samadhi tomb is situated in Chaitanya's birthplace in Mayapur, Bengal, where his Society has its international headquarters.

Left Sannyasins of the worldwide Hare Krishna Movement pay obeisance to the Society's founder, A.C. Bhaktivedanta Swami Prabhupada.

CHAPTER 11

HINDUISM IN THE MODERN AGE

In modern India, modern technology blends conspicuously with ancient spirituality. Taxis feature miniature dashboard shrines, nuclear-capable missiles bear the name of Agni, the fire-god, and the mobile phone is proudly owned by the saffron-clad ascetic. Ancient notions of an interdependent, hierarchical world clash with modern aspirations for individual autonomy and a classless society. This presents a challenge for modern Hindu thinkers, who attempt to redefine their tradition and its relevance to the world. Prevalent debates revolve around caste, the position of women and the precise identity of Hinduism, especially in relationship to India.

Hindu wisdom is pertinent to many contemporary issues. It contributes the idea of a spirituality that transcends religious borders, and a moral framework that advocates sustainability, non-violence and incorruptible political leadership. Throughout its long history, Hinduism has managed to accommodate new ideas and adapt to changing circumstances. The world's oldest religion, the Sanatana Dharma, looks set to last far into the future.

Opposite The spectacular Swaminarayan Akshardhama Temple in New Delhi. Like several other guru-led movements, the Swaminarayan lineage has been internationally successful.

Above Business people in India greet colleagues in traditional Hindu fashion before starting a video conference.

HINDUISM COMES WEST

ALTHOUGH HINDUISM HAS ONLY RECENTLY BECOME A GLOBAL RELIGION, ITS IMPACT HAS LONG BEEN FELT BEYOND INDIA. IT HAS INFLUENCED PHILOSOPHY, LIFESTYLE AND EVEN THE ENGLISH LANGUAGE.

The English philologist, Sir William Jones, made an elaborate comparison between Greek and Indian philosophy. Plato's famous metaphor of the puppeteer closely resembles the Hindu notion of maya (illusion). In the *Republic*, Plato's class system is similar to the Hindu notion of the four varnas, especially if the Greek 'slaves' practically constituted a working class. Similarly, there are parallels between Hindu and Greek mythology and their pantheons, with Zeus resembling the king of heaven, the lightning-wielding Indra. Although mere similarity does not prove religious and academic interchange, there is much documented evidence of inter-cultural dialogue. Some Hindus suggest that philosophical thought originated in India.

ACADEMIC INTEREST

The German Arthur Schopenhauer (1788–1860) was one of the first Western philosophers to show serious interest in Hindu thought. Of the body of texts called the Upanishads, he wrote, 'It has been the solace of my life, it will be the solace of my death!' Although he leaned toward the pessimism and world-rejection of Buddhism, his views on the suffering within nature, 'red in tooth and claw', resonate with Hindu views on samsara, the cycle of birth and death. Other philosophers, including Nietzsche, flirted with Hinduism, but there was little serious interest until the American transcendentalists. Thoreau, Emerson and their compatriots rejected Locke's empiricism and favoured a more intuitive, experiential approach to knowledge. They showed an affinity for Advaita philosophy and the notion that 'the soul of each individual is identical with the soul of the world'. Akin to Hindu thought, they believed in the innate goodness of the self, rather than an inherently sinful disposition.

It was British contact with India, and the work of European translators, that gave Western thinkers access to Hindu texts. Although early scholars were often favourable to Hindu thought, they later espoused rather biased views. To devout Christians, Hindus appeared idolatrous, polytheistic, and superstitious; and irrational for not eating 'the sacred cow'. On the other hand, many Hindus were horrified by Western standards of diet and personal hygiene. A further feature of contact with India was the English adoption of Indian words – and associated habits – such as cot, chutney, bungalow and pyjamas.

Left Henry David Thoreau (1817–62), American author and naturalist, greatly admired the Bhagavad-gita.

Above The German philosopher Arthur Schopenhauer appreciated Hindu and Buddhist thought.

Western acquaintance with eastern thought was significantly pioneered by the Theosophical Society, co-founded in 1875 by the Russian occultist Madame Blavatski. Theosophy attracted some of the most influential people of its day, including playwright Oscar Wilde, poet W.B. Yeats, and author George Bernard Shaw. Hindus also began to speak out for themselves, and

Below Dr. Radhakrishnan, second president of India, tried to show how Indian and Western philosophy are mutually understandable.

Vivekananda (1863–1902) was hailed as 'the first Hindu missionary to the West', credited with raising Hinduism to the status of 'a world religion'. He is best known for his speech opening with 'sisters and brothers of America', by which he introduced Hindu philosophy at the World Parliament of Religions in Chicago in 1893. Among the 20th-century scholars who attempted to bridge Eastern and Western thought, Oxford lecturer Dr. Radhakrishan (1888–1975) showed how the two were mutually comprehensible.

THE COUNTER-CULTURE

A significant interest in Hindu thought was evident during the 1960s, a decade of social and political upheaval. The emerging hippy counterculture rejected a materialistic lifestyle and post-war optimism in the redeeming power of modern science. Popular hippy habits reflected the marijuana-smoking Hindu ascetics, whereas some religious groups, such as the Hare Krishna movement, took a more orthodox devotional stance. More widely, through groups such as Transcendental Mediation, yoga and meditation became popular,

usually stripped of their religious trappings. Toward the end of that era, especially in the early 1970s, the influx of Hindus from East Africa into Britain, and from India into North America, saw the establishment of authentic Hindu communities, with their own temples and visiting Indian gurus.

ASSIMILATION OF IDEAS

By the start of the 21st century, many Hindu ideas had been assimilated into Western society. Today, commercial advertisements widely exploit the motif of a meditation

Above In 1968 at Rishikesh, the Beatles pose with the Maharishi Mahesh Yogi.

pose to suggest (somewhat ironically) that their products give peace of mind. Further features of Hindu cultural influence include the popularity of Indian cuisine, fashion items such as nose studs, and home products like incense. Even Hindu philosophical concepts have been embedded in Anglicized Sanskrit words, including 'guru', 'mantra' and 'avatar'. The idea of reincarnation has found broad interest, with some scholars attempting rigorous scientific research. At the same time, certain stereotypical images of Hinduism endure. People routinely think 'the notion of karma is cruel'; 'Hinduism is all about caste'; and 'Hindu women, like all others outside modern liberated society, have invariably been exploited'. Some scholars and university faculties are trying to promote a more nuanced understanding of Hinduism, even as Hindus themselves try to understand and mould their identity, and, indeed, their destiny.

Left In 1972, Asian British passport holders in Uganda wait to complete UK entry forms. By 2000, 1 per cent of the UK population was Hindu.

GLOBAL ORGANIZATIONS

MANY HINDU COMMUNITIES CONTINUE TO FLOURISH IN INDIA, OTHERS
HAVE SUCCEEDED AS GLOBAL OR 'TRANS-NATIONAL' MOVEMENTS.
MOST POPULAR ARE THE DEVOTIONAL, TEMPLE-BASED TRADITIONS.

Global organizations have been instrumental in trying to represent and reshape Hinduism, and to promote its relevance to the wider world. Some consist almost entirely of people of Indian descent, whereas others have appealed to a broader, multi-ethnic following.

HARE KRISHNA MOVEMENT

Perhaps most successful in attracting Westerners is the International Society for Krishna Consciousness (ISKCON), widely known as 'the Hare Krishna movement'. Often termed a 'new religious movement, it is actually a prominent branch of Bengali Vaishnavism founded by Chaitanya (1486–1534). Its theology is rooted in much older texts, the Bhagavad-gita and the Bhagavata-Purana.

ISKCON was founded in 1966 by A.C. Bhaktivedanta Swami Prabhupada, a guru in Chaitanya's

Below The cover of Hinduism Today, *published and circulated worldwide by the Shaiva Siddhanta Church.*

lineage. Members are known for their traditional dress, urban book-selling and public chanting of the Hare Krishna mantra. Initiates take vows to chant the mantra a set number of times each day and to avoid gambling, intoxication, meat-eating and extra-marital sex. ISKCON promotes the supremacy of devotion to God, worshipped mainly as Radha and Krishna.

Following Bhaktivedanta Swami's passing in 1977, there have been problems with the ensuing leadership and gurus breaking vows. Consequently, today there are several significant but smaller splinter groups, mainly contesting issues of succession and the precise status of the guru. Despite these challenges, ISKCON has become well established in India and beyond, as a respectable and authentic revitalization of Vaishnavism.

SWAMINARAYAN MISSION

Another Vaishnava group, the Swaminarayan tradition is more ethnically oriented, appealing largely to Gujaratis. The lineage, previously the Uddhava sampradaya, is linked to Ramanuja's Shri Sampradaya and was started by Sahajananda Swami (1781–1830). Like many of his contemporaries, he was a social reformer, and opposed caste discrimination, animal slaughter, and other moral anomalies. Widely considered the Supreme, the origin of Lord Vishnu, he compiled the mission's two core texts: the philosophical Vachanamrita and a code of conduct called the Shikshapatri.

There are now various Swaminarayana sampradayas reflecting varying views on the divinity of

Above The spiritual leader of BAPS Swaminarayana Sanstha, Pramukh Swami, celebrates its centenary in 2007.

the guru, the correct line of succession and the respective statuses of householders and sadhus (renunciants). One of the largest is the BAPS Swaminarayana Sanstha, whose current leader is Pramukh Swami. Devotees begin the day with puja and meditation and take five vows, to refrain from stealing, adultery, alcohol, meat-consumption, and mental or physical impurity. The organization is well known for its magnificent traditional temple in Neasden, London and its Swaminarayan Akshardham (divine abode) Temple in New Delhi. BAPS runs many humanitarian groups, promoting literacy, countering drug and drink addiction, and organizing environmental projects.

'HINDUISM TODAY'

Outside India, Southern Hindu traditions are often less understood than northern schools. One globally prominent southern tradition is the Shaiva Siddhanta Church based in Hawaii. It is a branch of the Shiva Siddhanta tradition, which represents South Indian Shaiva orthodoxy. The Church has strong links to Sri Lanka, and its spiritual heritage derives from the Nandinatha Sampradaya, a branch of the Natha tradition centred in Gorakhpur, just south of Nepal.

Right *Mata Amritanandamayi (Amma) hugs and blesses an admirer at her Manhattan Centre in 2008.*

The Shaiva Siddhanta Church was established in 1949 by an American Hindu, Satguru Shivaya Subramuniyaswami (1927–2001). He founded *Hinduism Today*, now a quarterly magazine published and distributed by the church's head-quarters, the Himalayan Academy based in Hawaii. The magazine is sold throughout the United States and beyond, and by the early 2000s had reached over 60 nations. Its stated aim is 'to promote understanding of the Hindu faith, culture, and traditions'. Unusually, it promotes a 'catechism of Hinduism'. The main monastery in Kauai, Hawaii, is now under the spiritual direction of Satguru Bodhinatha Veylanswami.

WOMEN-LED MOVEMENTS

Throughout history, there have been many famous women saints and gurus. Today, some prominent world-wide groups are led by women. At the beginning of the 21st century, one of the most popular was directed

Below *Members of the devotional Hare Krishna Movement (ISKCON) chant near the British Houses of Parliament.*

by Mata Amritanandamayi, affectionately called Amma or Ammachi (beloved mother) and widely advertized as the 'hugging saint'.

Amma's charitable institutions, founded in 1981, embrace many humanitarian projects. These include educational institutions, health and hospice facilities, the provision of free homes, feeding the poor, and help with large-scale disaster relief. At the heart of the movement are the long-standing Hindu ideals of compassion and unconditional love, exemplified by Amma's hugging thousands of people a day. Amma's movement is not linked to any par-

ticular lineage, but teaches meditation, especially through the singing of bhajanas (devotional songs).

Another prominent movement is 'Sahaja Yoga', founded by Shri Mataji Nirmala Devi, born in 1923 in Chindawara, India. Her movement teaches, free of charge, a form of yoga that purifies specific bodily chakras (energy centres) to counter corresponding psychological and physical conditions. It is a form of kundalini yoga, drawn from Tantric teachings. Sahaja Yoga is one of several globally influential groups leaning away from temple-centred devotion and more towards yoga and meditation.

MODERN YOGA AND MEDITATION GROUPS

SOME GLOBAL ORGANIZATIONS REPRESENT DEVOTIONAL LINEAGES. OTHERS HAVE A BROADER INTEREST IN YOGA AND MEDITATION, BASED ON TANTRIC TRADITION AND PATANJALI'S MORE ORTHODOX YOGA TEACHINGS.

To varying degrees, transnational organizations have adapted yogic and meditational teachings for the modern, global context, often purging them of their religious elements. Additionally, several organizations do not classify themselves as Hindu, even if clearly related.

TRANSCENDENTAL MEDITATION

Transcendental Meditation, or TM for short, is the trademarked name of a meditation technique introduced in 1958 by Maharishi Mahesh Yogi (1918-2008). It rocketed to worldwide popularity in the 1960s, through close association with the Beatles and other pop musicians. The technique, practised twice daily, is a form of mantra-meditation, but excludes concentration. The TM

Below The late Maharishi Mahesh Yogi. Other teachers, such as B. Iyengar and Shivananda, also helped popularize yoga and meditation in the West.

organization has helped conduct scientific research into the health benefits of meditation. Based in the Netherlands, it has also established Vedic Universities and a politically conscious 'Natural Law Party,' asserting that meditational techniques help promote world peace.

SHIVANANDA YOGA

Swami Shivananda of Rishikesh claimed to integrate the four paths or 'yogas' into a well-balanced spiritual discipline. The resultant 'Shivananda Yoga' is a modernized type of hatha yoga, integrating physical exercise and breath control with relaxation, a vegetarian diet and positive thinking. In 1957, Swami Shivananda sent his disciple, Swami Vishnu Devananda, to the West to establish the International Shivananda Yoga Vedanta Centres. In 1959, the first centre opened in Montreal, Canada. In 2008, the organization advertised 80 centres, ashrams and affiliated

Above Shri Shri Ravi Shankar, spiritual guru and founder of the 'Art of Living' movement.

branches worldwide. Over five decades, it has trained more than 10,000 yoga teachers.

ART OF LIVING FOUNDATION

The foundation's stated mission is to uplift society by strengthening the individual through programmes that restore human values and create a sense of belonging. It encourages people from all religious and cultural backgrounds to come together in celebration and service. It boasts programs in over 140 countries and offers courses to unlock the deepest human potential and nurture complete fulfilment. The AOLF, which claims to be non-denominational, was founded by Shri Shri Ravi Shankar from South India. Its international headquarters are in Bangalore.

HINDU-RELATED GROUPS

Several organizations do not classify themselves as Hindu but are obviously related. These include the Satya Sai Baba Organization, headed by Shri Sai Baba. Born in South India

Rajneesh, promoted a liberal form of Tantric sexual practice. The Ananda-Marga, 'the path of Bliss', is another Tantric group, whose male members wear orange outfits complete with turban and promote socio-political activism. Although many such movements emerged in the 1960s, others still appear, representing both orthodox Hinduism and a peripheral multi-faith approach often associated with the New Age movement. Whether orthodox or progressive, contemporary expressions of Hinduism share an understanding of the complementary roles of male and female, either by harmonizing psychic and physical energies or by worshipping various 'divine couples'.

Above The late jazz musician Alice Coltrane in the ashram she founded, with a portrait of her guru, Satya Sai Baba.

Below A map showing the Indian headquarters of the most important Hindu movements worldwide.

in 1926, he was soon considered a reincarnation of two saints, Kabir and Shirdi Sai Baba; and later, an avatar of Shiva and Shakti also. The organization understands itself as spiritual rather than religious, embracing all faiths. It advocates five core human values, namely satya (truth), dharma (right conduct), ahimsa (non-violence), prema (love for God and all) and shanti (peace).

Also at the periphery of Hinduism, the Brahma Kumaris World University teaches meditation through a discipline called Raja Yoga, a modern interpretation of classical astanga-yoga. This global organization was started in 1937 by philanthropist Lekhraj Kripilani, who subsequently became known as Brahma Baba. Today, the movement is largely run by women and is especially active in promoting values education. Unusually, it advocates celibacy even within marriage. Besides the University itself, one splinter group also uses the name Brahma Kumaris and claims to be offering advanced knowledge of Raja Yoga.

The many other quasi-Hindu groups include Osho, whose late and controversial leader, Bhagwan

1 Shivananda Yoga
2 Brahma Kumari World University
3 Swaminarayan Movement
4 ISKCON (Hare Krishna Movement)
5 Ramakrishna Mission
6 Transcendental Meditation
7 Osho Rajneesh
8 Satya Sai Baba
9 Shri Shri Ravi Shankar
10 Mother Amma (Ammachi)

237

WOMEN AND HINDUISM

ANCIENT TEXTS PRAISE THE SOCIAL AND SPIRITUAL CONTRIBUTIONS OF WOMEN. SUCH IDEALS CLASH WITH MODERN STEREOTYPES AND THE WIDELY REPORTED ABUSE OF WOMEN IN CONTEMPORARY INDIA.

Some blame women's exploitation on outdated religious beliefs, others on a decline in religious values and a wider moral and social decay. The issues are undoubtedly complex and controversial, but they are highly relevant to the tradition's future.

Despite changing ideals and doctrinal reinterpretation, famous Hindu women still serve as lasting role models. Typically diverse, they include classical goddesses, female saints, epic heroines, historical figures, political activists, and trendy female gurus. They also display divergent attitudes, embracing everything from passive submission to fiery radicalism.

Below To mark the 60th anniversary of Indian independence, an Indian girl poses as a national heroine, the Queen of Jhansi.

WOMEN IN ANCIENT INDIA

Although heroines often upheld chastity and other classical virtues, they were often assertive and influential. This challenges a modern view that humility belies weakness. A key example is Draupadi, heroine of the Mahabharata. Married to the five Pandava princes, she demonstrated customary fidelity but was a fiery, assertive woman, even knocking down a warrior called Jayadratha when he tried to accost her. Many other heroines are found in the Mahabharata, including Queen Kunti, whose devotion to Lord Krishna never faltered; she even prayed for adversity to promote remembrance of him. Both Kunti and Draupadi are included among the 'the five great women of Hinduism'; the others are Mandodari (wife of Ravana), Tara (wife of Vali) and Ahalya (wife of sage Gautama). The Mahabharata includes the famous story of Savitri whose devotion delivered her husband from the clutches of Yama, lord of death.

MEDIEVAL SAINTS

Among the 12 South Indian Alvars (poet mystics), Andal (725–55CE) was the only woman. Overwhelmed with love for Vishnu, she refused to marry anyone else and, according to legend, merged into the deity of her lord, Shri Ranganatha, after ritually marrying him. In south India, her image stands in many temples, where she is considered an incarnation of Bhu (mother earth), one of Vishnu's two consorts.

Akka Mahadevi, who lived during the 12th century, is today considered an unusually modern

Above Ramakrishna's wife, Sarada Devi, is one of Hinduism's many female gurus.

women saint, and remembered for her 435 Vachanas (poems) in praise of Shiva. The Lingayats venerate her as a symbol of women's equality and an early exponent of female emancipation. Travelling widely in search of liberation, her non-conformist ways caused consternation, especially as she refused to wear any clothes – common practice among male ascetics, but shocking from a woman.

Mirabai (1547–1614), born into a royal family and famous for her songs dedicated to Lord Krishna, is perhaps the most well-known of all female saints. Other women of her period became institutional gurus, including Jahnava Mata, who helped unite and consolidate Chaitanya's tradition after his passing.

MODERN HINDU WOMEN

Hindu women have also made significant political contributions. The Queen of Jhansi (1835–58) boldly fought the British, who seized her kingdom after denying the legitimacy of her adopted son. On the other hand, Kasturaba Gandhi (1869–1944) played a more traditional role, and the Hindu community still honours her as a great support to her famous husband.

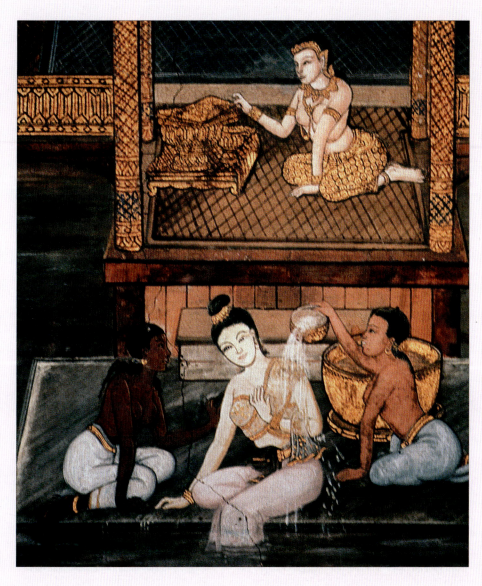

Above Rama's wife, Sita, is one of the classical women who exemplify fidelity. This illustration from a Thai version of the Ramayana shows the pregnant Sita bathing.

However, one of the oldest texts, the Manu Smriti, grants women no independent status, apparently because they are easily exploited. Some authors have equated the ideal of protection with denial of rights, though Hindu scholars contest this, adding that the Manu Smriti has often been misinterpreted. According to Hindu ideals, a woman is considered a powerful energy, a facet of Shakti, the divine Goddess. As a child she is kanya, the young Durga; as a wife she is devi, 'the resplendent one', and an equal partner in her husband's religious duties; and as a parent she deserves more respect than the highly revered guru.

Naturally, there are differences between such ideals and practice. Furthermore, even highly accomplished women expressed their spirituality and individuality in different ways. As modern women object to being stereotyped, it is also misleading to rigidly typecast Hindu women.

Below A modern Hindu woman enjoys the Divali festivities in the centre of Leicester, England.

Not all women of Hinduism are of Indian origin. One of the earliest foreigner enthusiasts was Russian-born Helena Blavatski (1831–91) who co-founded the Theosophical Society in 1875. Annie Besant (1847–1933), an English social reformer and prolific writer, became the society's president in 1907 and co-founded Benares Hindu University.

Modern women have also become gurus. Ramakrishna pushed his self-effacing wife, Sharada Devi, to become a well-renowned saint, and after his death she directed the mission. Also from Bengal, Anandamayi (1896–1982) adopted Tantric teachings and is credited with abilities in healing and precognition. Today, prominent women gurus include Nirmala Devi (founder of Sahaja Yoga), Mother Meera, considered the Goddess herself, and Ammachi, known as 'the hugging saint'.

MODERN DEBATES
The status of women in Hinduism is contentious. Some writers claim that women's position was better in ancient times, before foreign occupation brought more restrictive practices like confinement to the house.

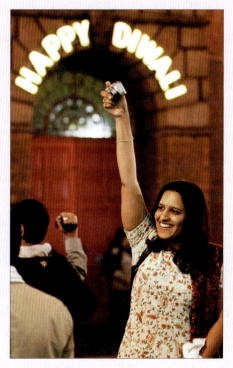

MORAL ISSUES

HINDUISM IS NOW A GLOBAL RELIGION, PROMPTING DEBATE ON
HOW ITS MORALITY EXTENDS BEYOND ITS ANCIENT RURAL, INDIAN
CONTEXT TO ADDRESS GLOBAL AND SCIENTIFIC ISSUES.

Hindu thought explores not only metaphysics, the study of a transcendent reality, but also ethics. These two branches of philosophy are integrated through two complementary concepts: Brahman (absolute reality) and dharma (duty). Hinduism thus recognizes an intimate link between knowledge and action, and their shared link to human virtues.

KNOWLEDGE AND IGNORANCE

Hindu philosophy explores morality in terms of 'knowledge versus ignorance'. This implies that moral judgment relies on clear perception of the world. Conversely, the nurture of knowledge requires moral conduct. The Hindu canon therefore includes practical injunctions to promote wisdom and regulate human conduct.

Below Some groups use Hindu teaching to promote human virtue and well-being, as in this event organized by the Brahma Kumaris World University.

A central text within the dharma shastras (moral codes), the Manu Smriti, prescribes morality in the context of traditional Indian society divided into four varnas. To address moral debates in the contemporary world, modern thinkers favour the transferable principles discussed in other texts, such as the Bhagavad-gita.

In the Bhagavad-gita, Krishna's teachings constitute a pragmatic response to Arjuna's dilemma. Arjuna could win his rightful throne only by slaying his cousins, teachers and grandfather. He also realized that running away was no option. His dilemma symbolizes the perplexity of all humankind: on the one hand, humans desire to enjoy the world; on the other, they perceive a moral conscience prompting them to consider consequences, for themselves and others. Krishna addresses these moral tensions by outlining key Hindu concepts: duty (dharma), spirit (Brahman) and matter's three qualities (gunas).

Above Arjuna fights his half-brother, Karna. Dharma was especially valued by the chivalrous warrior class.

DHARMA

A recurrent theme in the Mahabharata is that of dharma. A pivotal passage relates how the ruthless Kauravas tried to disrobe Princess Draupadi before the royal assembly. The court nobles watched passively, including Bhishma, the grandsire of the dynasty. However, he had his reasons. Many years earlier, to facilitate his father's second marriage, he had vowed to support the Indian emperor. The Kauravas were in power, so as Dushasana tried to disrobe Draupadi, Bhishma remained silent. Some Hindus alternatively suggest he was fearful or affected by bad company

A film version of the Mahabharata depicts Bhishma's dilemma. With one hand he starts to unsheathe his sword, while the other hand, oozing blood, grips the top of the blade, trying to restrain his fury. It was Krishna who protected Draupadi, by mystically supplying an endless sari. For failing to intervene, Bhishma and the other warriors reaped the karmic consequences by dying at Kurukshetra. The story also illustrates how dharma should be performed conscientiously, with foresight and the ability to juggle conflicting needs.

THE THREE GUNAS

Dharma is linked to the three, hierarchical gunas, which represent a continuum between sattva (wisdom)

To help explain the existence of evil, Hindu teachers cite the example of the sun. Although it is the source of everything in the solar system, no darkness resides in the sun. Similarly, there is no evil in God, or the absolute. Rather, when the self turns away from the sun, it sees darkness as its own shadow. The atman's ignoring of the divine, and its subsequent misidentification with the body, is the cause of all strife and suffering.

and tamas (ignorance). Goodness, embodied by the wise brahmin, represents ideal morality. The intermediate quality of passion (rajas) is related to the warrior varna; it stimulates action, but can foster greed and ambition. The lowest quality, tamas, leads to despair. However, texts regulate some potentially degrading activities, such as drinking alcohol, for citizens who cannot avoid them.

This illustrates a distinct feature of Hindu morality. It does not simplistically divide right from wrong, but considers circumstance, including the disposition of the individual soul. There are different 'specific duties' for the four varnas and four ashramas. Although goodness is desirable, there are practical injunctions for those impelled by passion or addicted to ignorance. Goodness itself is typified by specific values, such as sustainability, freedom from compulsion and empathy for others.

THE PROBLEM OF EVIL

Many Hindu thinkers explain 'the problem of evil' by recognizing the role of the individual in creating a unique destiny. The theologian Shankara suggests that social injustice is only apparent for, according to the law of karma, the soul reaps the results of moral actions sown in a past life. More widely, God is widely accepted as all-knowing (omniscient), all-powerful (omnipotent) and all-good. At the same time, the individual self (atman), as a part of God, has a quantum of power and independence. The atman thus creates its own fortune and misfortune. Some critics have labelled the 'law of karma'

Below Bhishma lies on his 'bed of arrows'. This Mahabharata story explores karma, dharma, warfare, good and evil, and protecting the innocent.

Above In Wales in 2007, protests against the mandatory slaughter of Shambo, a bull with Bovine TB, raised questions about the contemporary relevance of Hindu morals.

a philosophy of blame. Hindus themselves suggest otherwise: it is about responsibility and accountability, without necessarily implying judgement, social apathy or idle submission to fate. On the contrary, they claim that a recurrent trait of the embodied soul is to abdicate responsibility by blaming personal mishaps on others, including God.

SCIENCE AND THE ENVIRONMENT

NURTURED IN RURAL INDIA, HINDUISM IS RELEVANT TO CURRENT DEBATES ON ECONOMICS, THE ENVIRONMENT AND GLOBAL WARMING. IN MEETING SUCH CHALLENGES, IT FOCUSES ON SPIRITUAL SOLUTIONS.

Hinduism defines itself as science, a process of knowledge. It resists the polarized view that 'science deals with fact, and religion with faith'. From a Hindu perspective, all science involves faith in authority, and authentic religion promotes direct perception of truth. Since physical and metaphysical realities are ultimately inseparable, restricting study to one sphere creates an incomplete body of knowledge.

Some Hindus suggest that modern technology is intrinsically dangerous, impelled by a materialistic agenda and an inflated sense of human mastery. Others propose that science is entirely compatible with religion. Some writers, as if to promote India's greatness, claim that Hindu metaphysical statements are indistinguishable from the findings of modern science, thus predating and excelling it. Hindu opinions on science are extremely diverse.

THE SANCTITY OF LIFE

The tradition most clearly departs from popular belief in addressing the nature of life, identified as awareness itself rather than its external signs, which are eating, breathing and reproduction. Orthodox teachings attribute this life, the consciousness, to spirit not matter. According to the Bhagavad-gita, a non-changing self (as humans experience) can never emerge from transient combinations of matter. Hence, Hindu thought largely rejects materialism, and some scholars challenge the parallel theory of Darwinian evolution.

Hindu views on the source of consciousness inform attitudes toward sanctity of life and on related topics, such as abortion, animal rights and negative discrimination. Against the backdrop of the soul's transmigration through many mutually devouring species, a key moral principle is

Above For Hindus all human life is sacred. A Hindu woman consults a doctor about the birth of her child.

ahimsa, 'non-violence'. For humans, violence is the greatest transgression of the natural law. It betrays the trust of the soul seeking shelter, as a baby does of its mother, an animal of humans, or citizens of their leader.

MEDICAL ETHICS

Ahimsa is particularly applicable to dietary choices and medical ethics. Many Hindus are vegetarian, and object to the suffering inflicted on animals within medical research. Widespread belief in the soul entering the body at conception means that abortion is similarly condemned as a maha-papa (great sin), at least theoretically. In reality, abortion is quite widely practised and, with the introduction of prenatal gender selection, more often in favour of males to avoid anticipated dowry payments.

Based on belief that karma cannot be circumvented, suicide and euthanasia are generally condemned for exacerbating and prolonging suffering. Texts assert that after suicide,

Left At Barcelona in 2007, Hindu activist Vandana Shiva hugs a tree before the first International Meeting for Friends of Trees.

Above While learning about Hinduism, children watch working oxen at the Bhaktivedanta Manor Temple near London.

the soul is not promptly reborn, but suffers frustration as a ghost. However, it is acceptable to fast in old age or with terminal illness, even if this hastens death. In response to contemporary medical debates, decisions on organ donation, infertility treatment and embryonic research rest not on direct scriptural injunctions – for there are none – but on the application of broad principles and individual conscience. To address these issues, and to improve health and hospice care for Hindu patients, specialized books are now available to medical professionals.

ENVIRONMENTAL PROJECTS
Ancient texts do not explicitly address modern environmental challenges. However, the teachings were nurtured in a largely rural setting and yield many relevant principles, such as interdependence, cyclical time and sustainability. Early Vedic texts stress compliance with rita, the natural order, and include the earth (Prthivi) as a mother goddess. Modern Vedanta teaches about global karma, the equality of all creatures and the omnipresence of the divine. A key tenet of economics is respect for the cow and

bull, which provide humankind with milk products, fertilizer, and sustainable power and transport. Hinduism highlights the moral roots of ecological chaos, including human greed, implying that technological solutions alone will fail.

Hindu movements have long addressed environmental issues. In the 1700s, over 300 members of the Bishnois sect of Rajasthan gave up their lives to protect trees from unscrupulous loggers. They were emulated by the 20th-century Chipko movement, a group of largely female farmers who hugged tress to protect them from the state forest department. A leading Chipko

member, Sundarlal Bahuguna, also campaigned to protect sacred groves in the pilgrimage town of Vrindavana and against the Tehri dam on the sacred river Bagmati. In India's holy rivers, dams and deforestation have produced an erratic water flow, fluctuating between fatal flood and devastating drought. Mahatma Gandhi, perhaps foreseeing such consequences, was an enthusiastic proponent of simple village economics. He doubted the viability of a global market, vast expenditure on unnecessary transport and paradoxical ideas such as 'sustainable economic growth'.

Today, global Hindu organizations actively promote environmental projects. In the UK, the Hare Krishna centre near London features a 'cow protection' programme and trains oxen for milling, ploughing and transport. Likewise, the international BAPS Swaminarayan Sanstha has instigated a massive program of tree planting. Many meditation groups advertize the benefits of finding happiness within, rather than relentlessly seeking external gratification.

Below Hindu women fast in a temple, protesting against the Tehri Dam Project and its social and environmental impact.

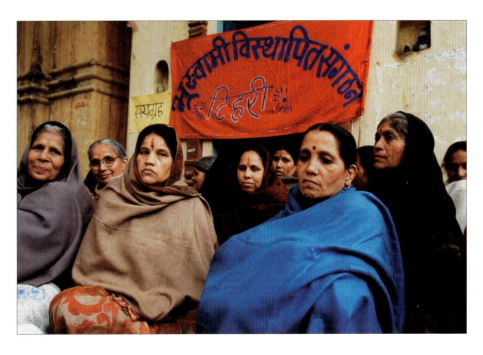

CONFLICT, VIOLENCE AND DISCRIMINATION

HINDUISM IDENTIFIES THE CAUSE OF STRIFE AS IDENTIFICATION WITH THE MATERIAL BODY. HOWEVER, MUCH MODERN SOCIAL PRACTICE, SUCH AS CASTE, SEEMS INCONSISTENT WITH SUCH TEXTUAL IDEALS.

Hindu responses to discrimination certainly seem ambivalent. Doctrine advocates the equality of all, yet views reality as hierarchical, as reflected by stratified Hindu society. Hindu thinkers advocate that this seemingly inconsistent stance accommodates both unity and diversity. Unity refers to a common spiritual identity, and diversity to the various physiological attributes adopted by the transmigrating soul.

CLASS DIFFERENCES
Much brahminical religion, valuing family lineage and social duty, favoured class differences, which became fossilized through the hereditary caste system. Resisting this trend, medieval bhakti traditions

Below At a Hindu ashrama, flower garlands adorn pictures of Lakshmi and of Jesus with his mother, Mary.

championed equality based on the eternal relationship everyone has with God. However, some still accept elements of the more flexible varnashrama system. Western scholars often disparagingly label varnashrama as 'a tool for legitimizing difference'. Some Hindus similarly claim that it is outdated; others that it recognizes inevitable social diversity.

Despite egalitarian ideals, discrimination in Hindu society is prevalent, revolving largely around caste and gender. There is much debate on the degree this exploitation is fostered by religious belief or, alternatively, by socio-political pressures. Certainly the two are interrelated and religious sentiment has been exploited for political ends. Simultaneously, an inclusive, tolerant religious identity has often been eclipsed by one narrowly defined in terms of ethnicity and nationality.

Above Tribal activists in New Delhi protest against what they said were forcible religious conversions by Christian missionaries. Christians now face similar aggression from hard-line Hindus.

VIEWS ON OTHER FAITHS
Hinduism is widely regarded as religiously inclusive. The very idea of conversion is relatively new. Whereas some claim that one is a Hindu only by birth, most prefer a universal approach, accepting the commonality of faiths in worshipping the same God. In practice, groups attracting 'non-Hindus' require no pledge of creedal allegiance, nor official rejection of former beliefs. Overall, the very idea of conversion has, until recently, been incongruous with the holistic Hindu mindset.

Foreign domination and coercive religion spawned the idea of Hinduism as a single, unified 'faith', comparable to its Abrahamic counterparts. Insiders first adopted the term 'Hindu' during Muslim rule, when poorer families converted to avoid the discriminatory jizya tax. The noun 'Hinduism' only emerged in the 1800s, to differentiate largely indigenous traditions from other, imported faiths. The 19th-century reform movements responded to Christian conversion attempts and some, like the Arya Samaj, introduced the idea of re-conversion. By then, however, Hinduism had developed its own exclusivity based on caste, and many 20th-century Dalits sidestepped class exploitation by converting to Buddhism. Today, some initiatives try to return them and other 'converts' to the Hindu fold.

Problems continued into the 21st century. In 2008, after a Hindu monk was murdered in Orissa, Hindus went on a violent rampage forcing Christians to convert to Hinduism. The strife has been blamed on political manoeuvring, especially by the VHP and their

Below Many Hindus contribute to inter-faith meetings like this one in Lahore attended by Charles, Prince of Wales, and his wife Camilla.

militant youth wing, the Bajrang Dal. In turn, some Hindus have blamed other faiths for their initial, provocative attempts to convert, often by offering material incentive. Despite commendable ideals, Hinduism today is not an entirely peaceful religion.

WAR AND TERRORISM

Hindu approaches to war and violence are similarly complex. Capital punishment was used in its ancient judicial system. With regard to warfare, Lord Krishna urged Arjuna to fight at Kurukshetra whilst also instructing him on the virtues of non-violence. The rationale seems to be the regulation of war and violence, rather than their total abolition. Ancient texts set down clear guidelines on warfare: only warriors could fight, never civilians; it was a great sin to kill women, children or the elderly; even a warrior was spared if he had surrendered, turned his back, or dropped his weapon.

However, during the great Battle of Kurukshetra, marking the start of this Kali age, the warriors began bending the rules. Arjuna's own son, the young Abhimanyu, was unfairly surrounded and slain by six great generals. The traditional military values, although idealistic, indicate an approach to leadership based on duty, chivalry and personal example.

Above In Shringar, Kashmir, Indian Border Security Forces pray at a shrine within their barracks.

They imply that terrorism, despite attempts to legitimize it through religion, is far from noble. By ancient Hindu standards, even today's regular warfare loses moral credibility.

THE MAHABHARATA

At Kurukshetra, the five Pandava princes found themselves fighting against their grandfather, Bhishma. Unable to defeat the elderly general, Arjuna solicited the help of Shikandhi. Born a female, he had undergone a change of sex. Knowing this, Bhishma refused to fight Shikandhi and, as he lowered his weapons, was riddled with shafts released by Arjuna. Later in the battle, Arjuna killed his own half-brother Karna, who was straining to raise his chariot wheel from the mud. Although Arjuna did not want to slay Karna unarmed, Krishna ordered it, for Karna had repeatedly transgressed the warrior codes, and helped unfairly kill Arjuna's son. The battle at Kurukshetra heralded the demise of chivalry, and human decline into unethical warfare.

THE FUTURE OF HINDUISM

THE FUTURE PRESENTS OPPORTUNITY AND CHALLENGE. AS THE OLDEST LIVING RELIGIOUS TRADITION, HINDUISM MUST CONTINUE TO ADAPT ITSELF AND DEMONSTRATE ITS RELEVANCE TO THE MODERN WORLD.

Within Hindu communities, key debates revolve around issues of identity related to gender, class discrimination and inter-faith discord. Especially crucial is adequately defining Hinduism, its exact relationship with India, and its role in the contemporary world.

In examining modern Hinduism, scholars have identified two emerging trajectories. On the one hand, there are moves toward exclusive identity formations, which attempt to conflate Hinduism, or 'Hindu dharma', with the Indian nation state. Proponents often attempt to reinforce boundaries, deny internal diversity and establish a single voice representing all Hindus. On the other hand, a parallel trend applauds universality, stressing the commonalty of all, irrespective of race, nationality and religion. Advocates tend to celebrate diversity and recognize the plurality of religious voices, within their tradition and beyond. Between these two broad responses, there are many other opinions on the identity and future of the ancient Sanatana Dharma.

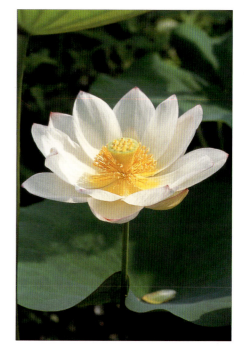

Above The lotus flower symbolizes transcendence, and the ability of spiritual beauty and purity to emerge from the 'mud' of human suffering.

RELATING TO THE DIVINE

Some have criticized Hinduism for its lack of a single ecclesiastical voice. Others suggest that a fluid and tolerant diversity has facilitated its long survival. Behind its complexity, a unifying theme is a hierarchical, interdependent world view, often expressed in the social sphere. This is counter-balanced by valuing individual spirituality. Spiritual groups have often attempted social or political reform. More prominently, personal practice has transcended transient social and political circumstance to focus on the lasting relationship between the self and the divine.

The bhakti traditions in particular have developed sophisticated theologies on the reciprocation between the atman and God. Scholars have meticulously classified the key roles of admirer, servitor, friend, parent and lover, and have described the associated spiritual sentiments. All reality has been explained in terms of relationships and their capacity to bestow fulfilment or frustration. The monists view the relationship between the self and God as illusory, but similarly extol the unity of life and the benefits of humility, service and harmonious personal relationships. Whatever the practitioner's preferred path or emphasis, it usually embraces four key elements: service, philosophical insight, personal detachment and loving devotion.

Below Much Hindu thought holds that the eternal reality can be defined in terms of loving relationships. Here a modern couple present offerings before an ancient shrine.

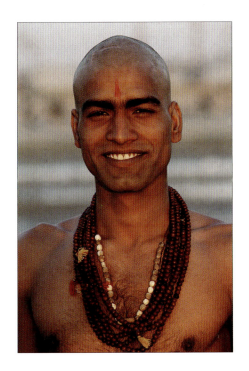

Above A young celibate radiates joy, which Hindu texts claims is found in the realization of the eternal self.

LOVING OTHERS

The traditional view of love is not 'love at first sight', but of affection nurtured through service. In marriage, affinity between couples is actively cultivated rather than passively expected. Although physical love and sexuality are accommodated, doctrine discerns love from lust. According to the Bhagavad-gita, love exalts the self, whereas lust, alongside anger and greed, is one of 'three gates to degradation'. Within marriage, as in religion, a prerequisite for love is fidelity. Traditionally, divorce was unknown and the corresponding Indian words are newcomers to the vocabulary.

Despite Hinduism's disposition toward ultimate renunciation of worldly ties, the Vedanta Sutra affirms the self as innately pleasure-seeking. Ananda, bliss, can never be successfully renounced but the self finds fulfilment on the spiritual platform. Love and pleasure require not abandonment, but purification. Even the fourth stage of life, sannyasa, represents not a cynical relinquishment of love but its expansion to embrace others. The sannyasin is no longer a member of one family, one community, one country, or one religion. He is a citizen of the world. Many texts stress the redeeming potency of sadhu-sanga, keeping company with mahatmas, 'great-minded saints'.

REAL SELF-INTEREST

Despite teaching about the ultimate goal of liberation, Hindu teachings advocate a balanced life.

Maintaining a healthy body and mind helps the transmigrating self take advantage of the rare human faculties. The approach toward human wellbeing is holistic, stressing all aspects of health. The ancient science of Ayur Veda advocates not merely treating symptoms, but addressing the deeper causes of disease prevalent in this Kali-age: anxiety, imbalanced diet, compulsive habits, lack of hygiene and irregular lifestyle.

Theological teachings compare embodied life itself to a disease, and attempts at material happiness to mere symptomatic treatment. Spiritual practice is considered the most effective 'medicine', striking at the root cause of distress: the self's false identification with the temporary body. Through enlightenment, the self becomes situated in its true glory and is never shaken, even in the midst of the greatest turmoil.

TOWARD A PEACEFUL WORLD

Hindu texts note how personal disquiet perpetuates social unrest. Without inner serenity humans can never be happy. Hinduism itself faces tough challenges in trying to adapt its ancient teachings to a rapidly changing world. It shares with contemporary humankind specific types of threat and adversity: terrorism, epidemics, poverty, global warming and economic instability. Despite a long and rugged history, Hinduism remains a relevant, vibrant and uplifting tradition. Many feel that its ancient values, based on service, responsibility and the equality of all, will make a lasting contribution to the 21st century, and well beyond.

Below On the island of Bali, Hindu women offer prayers for peace as the next generation tries to follow their example.

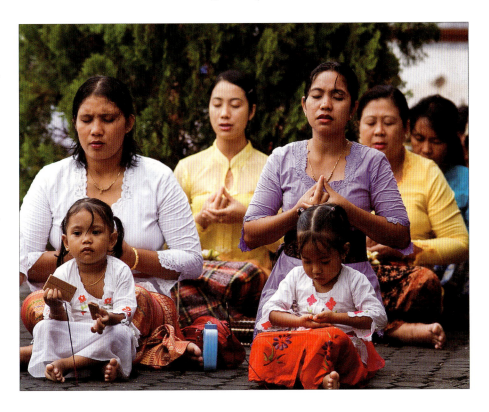

GLOSSARY

ADVAITA non-dualism; the philosophy that the soul and God are identical

AGAMAS Tantric texts, not directly Vedic; many have been assimilated into more orthodox traditions

AHIMSA non-violence, a core Hindu virtue, as taught by Gandhi

ALVARS South Indian, early-medieval poet-saints who worshipped Vishnu and sang in the Tamil language

ANTARYAMI God living within the heart and guiding all living beings

ANUMANA inference, or knowledge based on reasoning

ARATI a popular Hindu ceremony in which auspicious articles, including a camphor lamp, are offered to the murti

ARTHA economic development, one of the four aims of human life

ARYA SAMAJ a principal 19th-century reform movement

ARYAN 'noble people', those with spiritual values; European scholars considered Aryans a specific race

ASHRAMA a place where spirituality is cultivated; one of the four stages in life

ASTANGA-YOGA the eightfold meditational path culminating in samadhi (trance). One of the four main paths

ASURAS the demons, who are powerful but impious beings, constantly fighting with the gods (the Devas)

ATMAN literally 'self', it ultimately refers to the soul

BENGALI VAISHNAVAS (Gaudiya Vaishnavas) the followers of Chaitanya

BHAGAVAD-GITA the 'Song of God', the text spoken by Krishna to Arjuna

BHAGAVAN literally 'possessing all opulence'; a popular word for God; also used for some saints

BHAGAVAT PURANA one of the major Puranas, containing the famous stories of Krishna

BHAJANA adoration with song, chanting, and so on; a hymn

BHAKTI the path of devotional service; one of the four main paths

BRAHMA the four-headed deity in charge of creation

BRAHMACHARIN a celibate student, member of the first stage of life

BRAHMAN the absolute and all-pervading reality

BRAHMANAS one of four main divisions of text in the Vedas

BRAHMIN (or brahmana) a member of the highest varna; a priest, teacher or intellectual

BRAHMINISM (or Brahmanism) the orthodox strand of Hinduism supervised by brahmins

BRAHMO SAMAJ a 19th-century reform movement

CHAKRA Vishnu's disk weapon, also called Sudarshana; an energy centre in Tantric-yoga

DALIT 'the oppressed', or 'schedules classes', outcastes, previously called the untouchables

DARSHANA 'seeing', the act of taking audience of a deity; also, 'perspective', referring to six orthodox Hindu philosophies

DEVI 'goddess', most often referring to the consort of Shiva

DHARMA religious duties that sustain humans and the universe

DIVALI the well-known festival of lights, coinciding for many Hindus with their New Year

DRAVIDIAN 'from the South', in contrast to the north often linked to the Aryans

DVAITA dualism, the theology that the soul and God are different, especially as taught by Madhva

GAYATRI a mantra of 24 syllables chanted thrice daily by Brahmins

GITA song; an abbreviated form of 'Bhagavad-gita'

GOPURAM a lofty South Indian temple gateway, often adorned with figurines

GUNA literally 'rope', one of the three qualities that control matter

GURU a spiritual teacher

HAVANA (or Homa) the sacred fire ceremony of Vedic times

HINDU MAHASABHA political party, a forerunner to many nationalistic movements

HOLI spring festival in which participants douse each other with dyes and coloured water

ISHVARA literally 'ruler' or 'controller', it refers to God or any male deity. The feminine form is Ishvari

ISKCON The International Society for Krishna Consciousness, popularly known as the Hare Krishna Movement

JAPA the meditational practice of reciting mantras silently or quietly on prayer beads

JATI occupational sub-group within each of the four varnas

JNANA knowledge; jnana-yoga is the path of wisdom, one of the four main paths

KALI-YUGA the fourth age, the age of iron or the age of quarrel

KAMA sensual gratification, especially sex; regulated sensory pleasure is one of the four aims of life

KARMA literally 'action'; often used to mean 'reaction', or the accumulated stock of such reactions

KIRTANA 'glorification', usually referring to the musical chanting of mantras

KSHATRIYA 'one who protects', a member of the second varna, the warrior class

KUMBHA MELA 'The pot-fair', a huge triennial bathing festival

LILA the transcendental, sporting activities of some deities

MAHA great, as in Mahatma, meaning 'great soul'

MANDIR temple, the home of the sacred image

MANU SMRITI the 'codebook for mankind', ascribed to Manu; an ancient text dealing with morality

MATAJI 'respected mother', a form of address for any lady or goddess; in the south, 'Amma' or 'Ammachi'

MIMAMSA literally 'reverential enquiry'; one of the Six Darshanas

MOKSHA liberation from samsara, the cycle of repeated birth and death

MUNI a sage, or deep thinker

MURTI literally 'form', it specifically refers to the sacred image

NAVARATRI literally 'nine-nights', a nine-day festival in honour of Devi

NAYANMARS the 63 Shaiva poet-saints of southern India

NYAYA logic, one of the six orthodox schools (Darshanas)

OM (Aum) the most important Hindu mantra, of three syllables

PADMA lotus, a key symbol used to denote beauty e.g. 'lotus eyes'. It is symbolic of beauty and purity

PITHA literally 'seat', a Shakta holy site; a holy seat belonging to the various religious schools

PITRI the forefathers; during Vedic times, Hindus aspired to reach pitriloka, the world of the ancestors

PRAKRITI material energy, in contrast to eternal brahman; it consists of three tendencies or qualities

PRASADA God's 'mercy'; secondarily, it refers to any item sanctified by offering to God, especially food

PRATYAKSHA direct perception, one key source of evidence

PUJA ritualistic worship, most often of the installed murti

PUJARI the temple priest, who performs the puja

PURANA 'very old'; the texts containing many popular and ancient religious stories

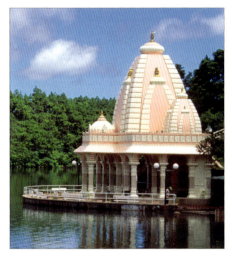

PURI flat bread fried in oil or ghee; also a holy town in East India

PURUSHA person, specifically male; refers to the soul or to God

PUSHTI MARG 'the path of nourishment', a Vaishnava lineage started by the saint called Vallabha

RAJA 'king' or 'kingly'; maharaja literally means 'great king'

RAJO-GUNA (or Rajas) second of the three material qualities; the royal quality of passion or ambition

RAKSHA BANDHANA festival in which sisters tie a rakhi (bracelet) on the wrists of their brothers

RAMAYANA 'the journey of Rama'; the earlier of the two Hindu Epics, composed in Sanskrit by Valmiki

RANGOLI a pattern made by Hindu women and girls; also called 'kolam' in Tamil, Rangavalli in Sanskrit

RASA-LILA the divine dance that Krishna performs with his girlfriends, the gopis (cowherd girls)

RIG VEDA the foremost and possibly earliest of the four Vedas

RISHI sage or seer, usually from ancient times

RITA 'the natural order', an important concept during the Vedic period

RUDRAKSHA berry from which Shaiva prayer beads are made

SADHU a saintly person; often refers to sannyasins, members of fourth ashrama

SAMADHI 'fixed mind', the final perfect stage of meditational yoga; also the tomb of a saint

SAMHITA one of four sections of the Vedas; also the name of some Tantric texts

SAMPRADAYA a disciplic succession, or lineage, of gurus and disciples teaching spiritual knowledge

SAMSARA the perpetual cycle of birth and death; the process of suffering on account of this

SAMSKARA literally 'mental impression', referring to a sacrament or rite of passage

SANATANA DHARMA 'the eternal religion', the eternal function of the soul; often preferred to the more recent term 'Hinduism'

SANGAM 'gathering', specifically ancient South Indian conventions; also refers to the ancient Tamil literature

SANKHYA one of the six darshans, it analyses matter in detail and also identifies the atman

SANSKRIT 'the most refined language', the sacred tongue of Hinduism

SANSKRITIZATION a process by which village gods and practices are elevated to 'high', scholarly Hinduism

SANT saint, especially of the northern, esoteric and eclectic devotional tradition from 1200CE onwards

SATTVA-GUNA the highest of the three material qualities, characterized by serenity

SATYA 'truth'; satyagraha, a term coined by Gandhi, means 'adhering to truth'

SHABDA sound, also referring to scripture as a source of reliable evidence

SHAKTAS the worshippers of Shakti

SHAKTI a generic term to refer to the female deity, especially the consort of Shiva

SHASTRA literally 'that which commands'; scripture, used particularly of some texts e.g. the dharma-shastras

SHRAMANISM the anti-social renouncer traditions, in contrast to orthodox Brahmanism

SHRI VAISHNAVAS one of four main Vaishnava sampradayas, founded by Ramanuja and others and popular in South India

SHRUTI that which has been heard'; one of two main sections of Vedic texts

SHUDRA a member of the fourth varna, an artisan or labourer

SMARTAS one of the four main denominations; members worship five or six deities

SMRITI 'that which is remembered', the second broad category of Hindu texts

SOMA a celestial intoxicant used in Vedic sacrifice; also the moon

SUTRA literally 'thread'; an aphorism that can be spun out indefinitely to reveal ever-fresh insight

SVETASHVATARA UPANISHAD one of the Upanishads, canonical for many Shaivas

SWAMI 'master' or 'controller'; a title used for sannyasis, who must control their senses

SWAMINARAYANA MISSION a Vaishnava sampradaya, popular among Gujarati Hindus

TAMAH-GUNA (or Tamas) lowest of the three material qualities, typified by darkness, laziness and ignorance

TANTRA strand of Hinduism, and texts, stressing esoteric discipline based on complementary male–female energies

TILAK a clay mark applied to the forehead, denoting the wearer's denominational affiliation.

TIRTHA literally 'ford'; a holy place

TRIMURTI the three main deities, Brahma (creator), Vishnu (sustainer) and Mahesh, or Shiva (the destroyer)

TULASI a plant of the basil family, sacred to Vaishnavas who use the leaf for worship and the wood for beads

UPANISHAD philosophical texts identified with Vedanta and one of four sections of the Vedas

UPAVEDAS four texts, supplementary to the Vedas and explaining traditional arts and sciences

VAISHNAVAS worshippers of Vishnu or one of his forms or avatars

VAISHYA a member of the third varna, the farming and mercantile community

VARNA the largest social unit, originally based on disposition but now usually on birth

VARNASHRAMA-DHARMA social system with different duties allocated to four classes and four stages in life

VEDA literally 'knowledge'; the Vedas are the four main Shruti texts at the heart of Hindu literature

VEDANGAS texts supplementary to the four Vedas

VEDANTA 'the conclusion of the Vedas', one of the six darshanas, representing much modern thought in Hinduism

VEDANTA SUTRA an important, philosophical section of the Smriti literature

VEDIC 'connected to, or derived from, the Vedas'. Also, 'linked to the period when the Vedas were compiled'

VISHNU, one of the Trimurti, the sustainer

YAJNA 'ritual sacrifice', as prevalent during the Vedic age but still performed through the havan

YAMA moral restrictions; also the God of Death, 'one who controls'; positive moral observances are called 'niyama'

YANTRA a geometrical diagram connected to meditational Tantra

YOGA union with the Supreme, or any practice aimed at self or God realization

YOGI one who performs yoga; the feminine is 'yogini'

FURTHER READING

A.C. Bhaktivedanta Swami Prabhupada, *Bhagavad-Gita As It Is* (Bhaktivedanta Book Trust, 2002)

William Buck, *Ramayana* (University of California Press, 2000)

Christopher Chapple, *Yoga and the Luminous* (State University of New York Press, 2008)

Rasamandala Das, *Atlas of World Faiths: Hinduism* (Franklin Watts, 2007)

Rasamandala Das, *The Heart of Hinduism* (ISKCON Educational Services, 2002)

Krishna Dharma, *The Mahabharata* (Torchlight, 1999)

Gavin Flood, *An Introduction to Hinduism* (Cambridge University Press, 1996)

Anita Ganeri and Rasamandala Das, *Hindu Prayer and Worship* (Franklin Watts, 2006)

Sue Hamilton, *A Very Short Introduction to Indian Philosophy* (Oxford University Press, 2000)

Linda Johnsen, *The Complete Idiot's Guide to Hinduism* (Alpha, 2002)

Klaus K. Klostermaier, *Hinduism: A Short History* (One World, 2006)

Klaus K. Klostermaier, *A Survey of Hinduism* (State University of New York Press, 2007)

Kim Knott, *A Very Short Introduction to Hinduism* (Oxford University Press, 2000)

Gwyneth Little, *Meeting Hindus* (Christians Aware, 2002)

Ranchor Prime, *Vedic Ecology* (Mandala Publishing, 2002)

Hillary Rodriguez, *Introducing Hinduism* (Routledge, 2006)

INDEX

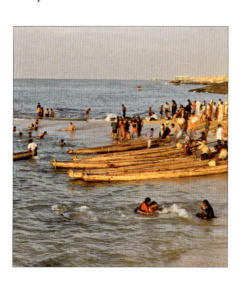

This edition is published by Lorenz Books, an imprint of Anness Publishing Ltd, Blaby Road, Wigston, Leicestershire LE18 4SE; info@anness.com
www.lorenzbooks.com
www.annesspublishing.com

Anness Publishing has a new picture agency outlet for images for publishing, promotions or advertising. For more information please visit our website www.practicalpictures.com

Publisher: Joanna Lorenz
Editor: Joy Wotton
Designer: Nigel Partridge
Illustrations: Anthony Duke
Production Controller: Helen Wang

ETHICAL TRADING POLICY
Because of our ongoing ecological investment programme, you, as our customer, can have the pleasure and reassurance of knowing that a tree is being cultivated on your behalf to naturally replace the materials used to make the book you are holding. For further information about this scheme, go to www.annesspublishing.com/trees

PUBLISHER'S NOTE
Although the advice and information in this book are believed to be accurate and true at the time of going to press, neither the authors nor the publisher can accept any legal responsibility or liability for any errors or omissions that may have been made.

PICTURE ACKNOWLEDGEMENTS
Alamy: /© ephotocorp 2; 31b, 241b; /© Flame 3t, 147t, 255t; /©Tim Gainey 6t; /©ArkReligion.com 6b, 163b, 176; /© Bruce McGowan 12t, 217t; /© Dinodia Images 93b; / © Louise Batalla Duran 99b, 106t, 160t, 161t, 169t, 197t, 206b; /© David Clegg /ArkReligion.com 129t; /© Philip Bigg 144b; /© Philip Game 154; /© Mike Hill 158b; /© Andrew Holt 168t; /© Bjoern Backe 170b; /© Just the

Right Click 175; /© Hornbil Images 179t; /© Pep Roig 183t; /Frans Lemmens 182t; /© Steve Speller 182b; /© Tom Allwood 194t; /© Neil McAllister 204b; © Melvyn Longhurst 218t; World Religions Photo Library 218b; Interfoto 219t; /Steve Atkins Photography 220t; /© David Pearson 229t; /© Angela Hampton Picture Library 242t.
The Ancient Art and Architecture Collection: 22t, 32t, 33b, 46t, 117b, 130b, 196b.
The Art Archive: 25t, 36t; /Harper Collins Publishers 13m, 34b; /British Museum 31t, 222t; /British Library 52t, 91b; /Stephanie Colasanti 57t; /Mireille Vautier 61t; /© Musée Guimet Paris/ Gianni Dagli Orti 124t; /Ashmolean Museum 125b; /Gianni Dagli Orti 147b; /Victoria and Albert Museum/ Eileen Tweedy 217t; /Wat Phra Keo, Royal Palace, Bangkok/Françoise Cazanave 239t.
Vishnu Balgobin: 37b.
BAPS Swaminarayan Sanstha: 5b, 11t, 13r, 53b, 101t, 110b, 143, 213t, 220b, 230, 251t.
Artwork courtesy of The Bhaktivedanta Book Trust International, Inc. www.Krishna.com. Used with permission: 7b, 18, 19t, 28b, 41t, 46b, 48bl, 55b, 58t, 59t, 60b, 61b, 63t, 64t, 64b, 66, 69, 71t, 71b, 77b, 79t, 87t, 90b, 92b, 99t, 103b, 121t, 130t, 131t, 132t, 134t, 205t, 205b, 221, 223b.
Brahma Kumaris World Spiritual University: 240b.
The Bridgeman Art Library: 26t, 33t, 126t, 127t, 127b, 128t, 128t, 133b, 137b, 141b, 192t, 193t, 197b, 228t, 240t; © The Trustees of the Chester Beatty Library, Dublin 12l, 63b; /© National Museum of Karachi, Pakistan 21b; /British Museum 24t; /© World Religions Photo Library 25b, 142; /Dinodia 29t, 131b, 191, 213b; /The National Army Museum 34t; /© Bristol City Museum and Art Gallery 35b.
Christians Aware: 84b; 7.
Corbis: 166t; /© Lindsay Hebberd 1, 195b, 216b; /© Gavin Hellier/Robert Harding World Imagery 3b, 210br, 214b; /© Michele Falzone 4t; /© Ken Seet 8t; /© Bob Krist 9t, 212b; /© Najlah Feanny 9b; /© epa 10t; /© Peter Guttman 11b; /© Ocean 14–15; /© Michele Falzone/JAI 16, 201t; /© Chris Hellier 20t; /© Atlantide Phototravel 26br; /© Roger Ressmeyer 28t; /© Adam Woolfitt 30t; /© Stapleton Collection 32t, 42, 47t, 126t; /© Underwood & Underwood 37t; /© Hulton-Deutsch Collection 38t, 178t; /© Craig Lovell 39nl; /© Kapoor Baldev/ Sygma 41b, 172b; /© Brooklyn Museum 44b; /© Frédéric Soltan /Sygma 45b, 100b, 102t, 102b, 161b, 164t, 224t; /© David Nicholls 47b; /© Luca Tettoni 49, 123t, 196t, 198t; /© Ivan Volvin/JAI 54t; /© Peter Adams 59b; /© Christie's Images 65t, 125t, 138t; /© Reuters 72b, 157t, 211t, 244t; /© Amit Bhargava 73b, 81tr; /© Christophe Boisvieux 78b, 139b, 149bl, 208; /© Piotr Redlinski 85t; /© David H. Wells 86b; /© Brian A. Vikander 89dl; /© Historical Picture Archive 90t; /© Kazuyoshi Nomachi 94–5; /© Kristian Buus/In Pictures 98t; /© Lindsay Hebberd 103t; /© Narendra Shrestha 109t; /©Arvind Garg 117t; /© Steve Allen/Brand X 118; /© Rafiqur Rahman/ Reuters 123b; /© John Van Haselt/Sygma 124b; /© Will & Deni McIntyre 132b; /© Anders Ryman 134b; /© Bettmann 135t, 209; /© Philippe Lissac 107b, 135br; /© Julain Kumar/Godong 136t; /©Tibor Bognar 137t; /© Tony Kurdzuk/ Star Ledger 138b; /© Gideon Mendel 145bl; /© Joseph Sohm/Visions of America 149t; /© Gian Berto Vanni 149br; /© Dinodia Photo Library/ Brand X 150b; /© James Neilsen/ZUMA 157; /© Sybil Sassoon/Robert Harding World Imagery 158t; /© Raj Patidar/Reuters 162b; /© Ajay Verma 163t; /© Bob Krist 171b; /© Sheldan Collins 178b,

195t; /© Cat180t; /© STR/epa 181tl; /© Image Source 183b; /© Peter Adams 186bl; /©Tiziana and Gianni Baldizzone 186r; /© Ken Stratton 189t, /© Jayanta Shaw 190; / © DK Limited 200b; /©Tracy Kahn 202t; /© Karen Kasmauski 203b; /© Fred Derwal 210bl; /© F.O. Hoppé 224b; /© Graham Bell 231; /© Peter Wijnands 236b; /© J. Emilio Flores 237t; /© Liz Barry/Eye Ubiquitous 244b.
Ananta Shakti Das: 65b.
Rasamandala Das: 51t, 62t, 83b, 119, 120, 139t, 144t, 155, 167t, 169b, 222b, 223t.
Shanta Vigraha Das: 129b.
Food for Life Global: 98b.
photo courtesy of Food for Life Vrindavan Charitable Society fllvrindavan.org: 174–5.
Getty Images: 114t, 164b, 232br, 233t; /Karan Kapoor 10b; /Robert Harding World Imagery 57b, 192b; /Grant V. Faint 76b; /Robb Kendrick 81tl; /Keren Su 84t; /AFP 88t, 93t, 105b, 111b, 113t, 116t, 116b, 136b, 141t, 153b, 156t, 160b, 165t, 165b, 166b, 173b, 215b, 216t, 225t, 225b, 227t, 238b, 239b, 242b, 245t; /John Henry Claude Wilson 88b; /Allison Michael Orenstein 89tr; /Martin Harvey 96; /Peter Adams 145t; /Barnabas Kindersley 151b; /Frans Lemmens 153t; /Zubin Shroff 170t; /Andrea Booher 180b; /Dream Pictures 202b; /Raveendran/AFP 219b; /Time & Life Pictures 226b, 228b, 232t; /Sebastian D'Souza/AFP 226t; /FPG 232bl; /Peter Essick/Aurora 243b; /Medioimages 246b; /Art Wolfe 247t.
Goloka Books: 22b, 60t, 78t, 91t, 92t.
Hinduism Today: 56t, 214t, 234b.
Images of Asia: 122t.
ISKCON Educational Services: 40t, 72t, 81b, 82t, 83t, 105b, 128b, 151t, 187, 201b, 235b.
iStock: 8b, 13l, 68t, 74b, 85b, 135bl, 248, 256.
The Krishna Avanti Primary School: 185b.
Mandala Publishing: 125b, 136t.
Bhavit Mehta: 50b, 55t, 73t, 185t, 207b.
M. Narasimhachary: 27t, 29b, 44t.
The Oxford Centre for Hindu Studies: 193b.
Photoshot: 162t, 184t, 194br; /© India Pictures 5t, 184b, 253t; /© UPPA 38b; /© NHPA 75m; /© World Pictures 97, 122b, 148t; /Bill Wassman 150t; /© Authors Images 152t, 249, 255b; /© India Pictures 152b; /© UPPA 227b.
Ramakrishna Mission: 238t.
Claude Renault: 23b, 43, 45t, 48t, 54t, 56b, 67, 68b, 70t, 70b, 95, 101b, 105t, 108t, 109b, 115b, 133t, 140b, 148b, 156b, 168b, 172t, 173t, 177, 179b, 181tr, 181b, 186t, 188t, 188b, 200t, 203t, 207t, 210t.
Rex Features: 206t, 234t, /Dinodia/Stock Connection 171t, 211b; SIPA Press 229b, 233t 235t; /Action Press 236t; /Dimitris Legakis 241t; /Tim Rooke 245b.
Astrid Schultz: 243t.
Lakshmi Sharath: 140t.
Param Tomanec: 4b, 15m, 17m, 27b, 35t, 50t, 52b, 53t, 58b, 62b, 74t, 75l, 75r, 80b, 82b, 87b, 101b, 104t, 108t, 110t, 111t, 112t, 112b, 113b, 114b, 115t, 120b, 146b, 167b, 189b, 194bl, 199t, 204t, 212t, 215t, 247b.
Werner Forman Archive: 30b; /Edgar Knobloch 21t.

p.1 Calcutta woman touching statue of the goddess Durga. p.2 Palakhi pilgrimage. p.3 top Temple in Illinois. p.3 bottom A sadhu or Indian holy man. p.4t A golden statue of Vyasa and Ganesha, Udupi. p.4b Family praying on the festival of Divali. p.5t The temples of Angkor Wat, Cambodia. p.5b Devotees at the BAPS Swaminarayana temple in Neasden, London. Left Devotees and pilgrims climb the steep steps to a popular Shiva temple, in Khajuraho, Central India.